# PREPPER
# GUNS

# PREPPER GUNS

## Firearms, Ammo, Tools, and Techniques You Will Need to Survive the Coming Collapse

## Bryce M. Towsley

SKYHORSE PUBLISHING

Skyhorse Publishing books may be purchased in bulk at special discounts for sales promotion, corporate gifts, fund-raising, or educational purposes. Special editions can also be created to specifications. For details, contact the Special Sales Department, Skyhorse Publishing, 307 West 36th Street, 11th Floor, New York, NY 10018or info@skyhorsepublishing.com.

Skyhorse® and Skyhorse Publishing® are registered trademarks of Skyhorse Publishing, Inc.®, a Delaware corporation.

Visit our website at www.skyhorsepublishing.com.

10 9 8 7 6 5 4 3 2 1

Library of Congress Cataloging-in-Publication Data is available on file.

Cover design by Rain Saukas
Cover photos credit: Bryce Towsley

Print ISBN: 978-1-63450-587-1
Ebook ISBN:978-1-63450-967-1

Printed in China

For my children, Erin and Nathan, and for Brendan who married into this mess. It's their future we are fighting for.

*"Learning is not compulsory. Neither is survival."*
—W. Edwards Deming

*"Apparently there is nothing that cannot happen today."*
—Mark Twain

# CONTENTS

# AUTHOR'S NOTE

There are two terms you will see throughout the book that are in common use with preppers.

**TEOTWAWKI:** The end of the world as we know it.

**TSHTF:** The shit hits the fan.

Both are used here to describe the time following any sort of event that leads to a social or economic meltdown. In short, they describe the situation that you are prepping for.

www.skyhorsepublishing.com

# FOREWORD

*I*n the decades since Mel died in 1980, several writers have asked if they could update *Survival Guns*. After they explained what they wanted to do, I told them "No" for one reason: They did not understand why Mel wrote the book.

When a friend whose judgment I trust asked if I would write a foreword to Bryce Towsley's *Prepper Guns*, I was dubious but said that I would take a look at it, very much aware that time and technology have rendered most of Mel's specific recommendations obsolete, but not the reasoning behind them.

My concerns were put to rest when I came across these remarks of Bryce early in the book: "Simply put, this is a gun book, not a survival book. It won't teach you how to survive, but it does explore the guns you will need to accomplish that goal." These words delighted me, for they sum up the reason Mel wrote *Survival Guns* forty years ago.

Bryce certainly knows his firearms and explains why he recommends specific calibers, makes, and models in an engaging style. Heed his advice and you will make smarter choices as you decide which guns make sense for you and your circumstances.

His personality and strong opinions about the direction this country is heading pervade his book, just as Mel's did. But whether you agree or disagree with Bryce's views, *Prepper Guns* will make you stop and think. As he puts it, "Be mad at me if you want, be offended, be horrified, be whatever; but read the book and be safe."

Mel would agree.

Nancy Tappan

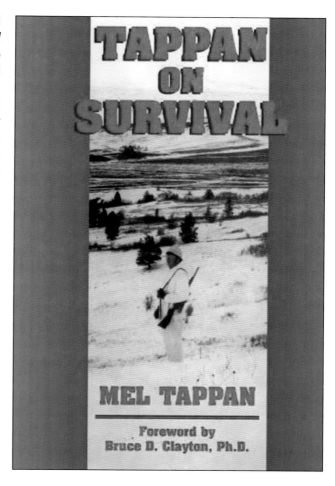

# INTRODUCTION

## The Inspiration for This Book

While researching this book project, I bought both of Mel Tappan's books. For those of you who don't know, he was pretty much the godfather of the prepper movement. They called it survival back then, but Tappan ruled the market in those bleak Jimmy Carter years. Although he died young and unexpectedly, his 1977 book *Survival Guns* is a classic. After his death, his wife put together some of his columns from *Guns and Ammo* and *Soldier of Fortune* and created the book, *Tappan on Survival*.

I read both of these books back when they were first published, and I never missed his *G&A* column. It was interesting, particularly the gun stuff, but I didn't take it very seriously. I was young and had nothing, so I figured I had nothing to lose. Today, I am looking at

it all with a more mature perspective than I had back in the '70s when I was young, dumb, and bulletproof.

I am amazed at not only the high quality of his writing, but also just how right he got most of it. Of course, the gun stuff is very dated today, but at the time he was "right on" (as we liked to say back then). In the '70s the world didn't have Glocks or other high-cap, plastic pistols. The semiauto fighting rifle options were extremely limited, and ammo, particularly for handguns, was just starting to claw its way out of the muck of the round-nose, lead-bullet era.

As might be expected with anybody who wrote predictions about the future, almost forty years later some of it has proven incorrect. He has a skeptical warning about global cooling, which proved to be just hysteria. (For those who don't know, global cooling was all the rage with the "sky is falling" crowd back in the '70s.) I am sure the result is not unlike how today's global warming alarmists will be viewed thirty years from now. Tappan also wrote a lot about the possibility of nuclear war with Russia. It was a big concern then. But the trouble is, we tend to look at things from our current perspective. In recent years most people would have thought that, too, was dated and just past paranoia, until recent events have put such a scenario back on the table. In fact, the Russia–USA thing is probably a more dangerous scenario now than it was in the 1970s.

Tappan was convinced that there was no way to avoid an economic meltdown. He was concerned about the national debt, which was $650 billion at the time and exceeded the amount of money in circulation. In other words, the government owed more money than existed, which is a bad thing. He also pointed out that the way inflation happens is by the government printing more money, which devalues the currency. If a piece of silver is worth one dollar, by printing enough money to double the amount in circulation the silver is now worth fifty cents. For those of us who remember the Carter years, it was happening, and inflation was 12.5 percent when Reagan took office.

Things are moving so fast now that anything I put in this book regarding economics will be horribly dated before the book is even published. But for reference, there were approximately $1.37 trillion in circulation as of June 4, 2015, of which $1.32 trillion was in Federal Reserve Notes. Federal Reserve Notes have no backing with anything of value. They are printing money at a rate of $560 million per day. Five percent of that, or about $28 million per day, is new money added to the kitty. That means that they are adding ten trillion, two hundred twenty million extra dollars into circulation every year!

The national debt as of today, July 27, 2015, is $18,629,694,522,000. It is increasing at a rate of $2.31 billion per day! That means that our national debt today is almost fourteen times the amount of all the US dollars that even exist, which shows just how much worse things have gotten. Tappan was worried that national debt was exceeding the amount of money in circulation. Now, despite printing money at an alarming rate, we have exceeded the amount of money in circulation by almost 1,400 percent!

In fact, on September 4, 2014, the debt took a record jump of more than $300 billion. This apparently was the first day the federal government was able to borrow money under a deal President Obama and Congress sealed that week. Did you know anything about it? Me neither. The press is part of this because they are not doing their job. We have exceeded $18 trillion in debt and they don't think it's worth mentioning?

Not to worry, Obama has it all figured out. His answer to record debt that we cannot possibly ever pay back is to borrow even more money—that, and to print more, under the foolish illusion that printing money has no consequences. The Treasury is printing money as fast as it can, increasing the amount of money in circulation and reducing the value of each and every dollar. The Fed is keeping inflation rates down artificially by manipulating interest rates and other means, such as buying an unprecedented number of bonds; but that can't hold. This has been tried before in other economies, and it always ends in disaster.

All this, while America is distracted by a multitude of meaningless things so that we are not even noticing that our future is being tossed in the dumpster by the children we elected to run our country.

What Tappan failed to see was Ronald Reagan. With his election, we dodged a huge bullet and delayed the economic crash. If we had reelected Carter, America would probably be a much different place.

Sadly, we did reelect Obama, and he is making Carter look like the JV team when it comes to destroying America.

This is not sustainable, and America is headed for very bad times. How and when is anybody's guess, but at this point it appears to be unavoidable.

Tappan warned that the average US household has less than two weeks' worth of food on hand. He said that the average US city only had eight days' worth of food, and the worldwide supply was just eighty-four days' worth of food. I know that today the average American household number has dropped to something like three days' worth, but I can't find any data on the rest. However, I suspect it's lower than it was in 1980.

This is just looking at the economic side of our problems, which go much deeper and are worldwide. When you look at them in total, they will scare you spitless. I am reluctant to even talk about national and world events here, as they are changing so fast that most of them will be old news before this book is in the reader's hands. However, from a prepper standpoint all this can't be ignored.

My paternal grandmother was an amazing woman. She was of French Canadian descent and most likely, judging by her looks, a good deal Algonquin Indian (although her generation kept those things secret). She was a tiny, five-foot ball of energy and could outwork anybody well into her eighties. She had little formal education but ran several successful businesses and raised five children spread out over more than two decades in age. She developed her own system of math that nobody else could understand, but it worked. She talked fast, with an accent and language that was half French Canadian, half Vermont woodchuck, and partly just grandma. She was a woman of many talents, and one of them was reading the cards to tell the future.

Many may scoff, but she was right too many times for me to reject it. She predicted my mother's death and tried to warn her. She knew my first baby's sex. She warned me to stay home the night a friend was killed. It's a very long list.

I believe that I inherited a bit of that from her. My "little voice" has given me advice for most of my life. I can't control or predict it and I don't always listen, but when I do, it's never wrong.

The strongest my little voice has ever spoken to me was during Obama's speech at the 2004 Democratic National Convention. I had never heard of him prior to the announcement that he would give the keynote speech, but this unknown upstart was clearly being groomed for something. As the eighteen-minute-forty-seven-second speech unfolded, my little voice was screaming in my head. It was telling me that this guy represented a huge danger to America and to our way of life.

To be honest, I dismissed it. There was nothing I could do anyway; but he was new, unknown, unproven, and African American. Those were disadvantages in traditional American presidential politics, so I was sure it would be many years before we would have to deal with him.

Then, just four short years later, he was president. How did that happen? He was a nobody with no record, stepping out of nowhere. He gave one good speech and then we made him president? You don't need a little voice to understand that something is going on here. He didn't do that alone.

I was even more shocked when he won reelection. No president has ever defended such a failed administration and won reelection. Nothing in our history suggested he could win. Not only that, but I believe his opponent, while not my first choice, would have been one of the better presidents in history. Yet through sleight of hand, or the ignorance and greed of our citizens, or the combination of the two, BO got another term.

I was in a hunting camp in Texas that night, and I felt physically sick with the realization of what this meant for America. I couldn't sleep and finally just showered and left early for the three-hour drive to the airport. I noted the subdued mood of everybody I met on my journey home. Everybody was quiet and moody, as if the country understood it had made a huge and irreversible mistake.

I lived through the Jimmy Carter years, but this is different. Carter was a buffoon; this time I feel the evil.

I have watched in horror as Obama has attacked America with the brilliance that has allowed him to succeed now for almost seven years. As stated, our economy is a house of cards waiting for a hurricane. The national debt is almost 103 percent of our gross domestic product, and $57,000 of debt per citizen. Or, if you want to consider who is paying the bills, it is $154,394 of debt per US taxpayer. That is not sustainable.

The Treasury is printing money as fast as it can, and never in history has that ended well. Just ask Zimbabwe. True unemployment is at a modern-day record high, with 93,700,000 United States citizens no longer in the work force. Think about that: As of July 2015, almost a third of our population has checked out. Only about a third of our population is actually working full time. The number of people sucking a free government tit is the highest it has ever been; half of all American households are getting government assistance. Those of us who are working are paying record taxes and have not seen a raise in our paychecks for as long as Obama has been in office.

Obamacare is a huge disaster that is destined to get much worse. For example, the death panels are back, as predicted. We are ignoring the threats from China, Russia, and North Korea. We owe China more money than we can ever repay. Europe is melting down, and Obama is ignoring it with impunity. He is ignoring ISIS terrorists as they run rampant over the Middle East and grow stronger by the day. Obama is letting illegal immigrants flood the country, and that threatens to destroy the economy. He is letting violent criminals out of jail by the thousands while trying to remove our right to protect ourselves.

Americans are pitted against Americans as Obama has divided us on a course for civil war. Police are now the enemy and, in many places, can't or won't continue to do their jobs. The military has been decimated and he has fired most of the top military leadership. The Supreme Court has been bought and paid for and many of its recent rulings are bizarre, to say the least. The justices no longer follow the Constitution, and each time they ignore it, the document becomes less relevant. The Republicans in Washington are corrupt and weak, or they are secretly on his side. It's difficult to tell which and it probably doesn't matter.

America has become a joke throughout the world. Our relationships with our traditional allies are in the toilet. Our friends don't trust us, and our enemies don't fear us.

Obama is on a path that ignores or hurts the citizens of this country. Nothing he is doing will advance or improve our lives or the future of America. It's all intended to destroy and tear down our country, but it's carefully crafted under the guise of "fairness." The useful idiots who can't see far enough into the future to recognize the outcome believe he is doing good work and enable him to continue.

The law-abiding taxpayer is being punished, while the lawless and the non-citizens are rewarded. Yet the American people do nothing. Our ancestors went to war over much less, but we just continue to keep our faces in our phones and ignore the world around us. Well, to be fair, we did elect some Republicans and sent them to Washington to fix the problem, but then they abandoned America and sold out the voters who elected them.

Obama's agreement with Iran, perhaps the most dangerous nation state in the world, defies logic. The agreement is that we will give our enemy billions of taxpayer dollars to use for terrorism as we let them continue to build nuclear bombs unfettered. That's what they get. America gets nothing. One hell of a deal, right? Congress can stop this deal, but they won't.

The agreement dooms Israel and ensures we will go to war. It's bizarre and defies logic. By the time we elect a new president, it will be too late to reverse what is happening.

If that's not bad enough, it would seem that natural disasters are on the rise, too. It's as if the world is decaying and headed into chaos.

It's no longer a question of *if* we will be faced with a survival situation, but *when*. If the wheels come off and we are left on our own, are you ready? How much food do you have in your house? What means do you have to protect it from being stolen from you? Do you have a plan?

I sincerely hope none of this happens—that we will put grownups back in charge soon. In fact, I think that is the most likely scenario. It won't stop the inevitable, but it will delay it for a while.

But the odds of going the other way are increasing every single day and at an escalating rate. Wouldn't it be smart to prepare at least a little? What's the worst that could happen, that you have too much food and too much ammo in your house? I'll bet that's a problem you can handle.

On the other hand, what's the worst that can happen if you do nothing? I'll let you figure that one out yourself.

## What Is Prepping?

▲ Prepping is more than just storing food.

While I write about prepping for magazines and websites, and although prepping was an undercurrent in my novel, *The 14th Reinstated*, I have never really considered myself to be a prepper. But I guess in looking at the issue, I am one, of sorts. I don't have a bunker or a small army, but then I don't think that's the best place to put your resources. Prepping comes in many forms, and it's more of a mindset than anything else.

The protagonist in my novel, *The 14th Reinstated*, was not exactly a prepper. He prepared for what he saw coming, but not enough and he paid a high price for his mistakes. Yet he learned from them and continued to change and grow to meet the growing challenges. But more than anything else, he was just one of those jack-of-all-trades kind of guys and he was self-reliant. I guess my approach is a bit like his.

What so many are calling "prepping" today is mostly just "life" if you grew up rural and poor.

I think that "prepping" can be broken down into two simple concepts.

### Part One: Education

The first is to be self-sufficient. That means that you must be able to provide food, clothing, and shelter for yourself and your family. Of course, that will have many sub-topics, but the bottom line is you need food, water, heat, shelter, and perhaps some medical knowledge to remain healthy.

How you get all that is a wide-ranging topic. But the more self-reliant you are now, the easier it will be later.

If you already know how to grow a garden, it will be easier to grow food. If you already have livestock, it will be easier to produce meat, eggs, and milk. If you know how to make jerky, can vegetables, or butcher a deer, you are going to find it easier to survive. If you can build a house, repair a generator, or fix a flat tire, it will be easier than trying to figure it all out on the fly. Can you cut and split firewood? Do you even know which trees make the best firewood?

The first neighbors to my west here in Vermont moved next door to me many years ago from Florida. The new house they bought was designed to be heated with wood, something they knew nothing about. The guy who built the house offered to sell them several cords of wood. He thought it was a big joke to sell them wood from poplar trees. This is poor wood for heating a house. It burns hot, but very quickly, requiring at least twice as much wood for any given winter than the traditional hardwoods. Any native of the north knows that, but that cheating bastard thought it was funny to take advantage of some people who in reality were a lot smarter than him, but were "not from around here." They ran out of wood halfway through the winter.

That was a bad winter and after being snowed in for a few days and getting their trendy but useless vehicle hopelessly stuck, they sold out that spring and moved back south. The point is that something as basic as the wrong wood could mean the difference between survival and not making it through the winter in tough times.

We can't do everything by ourselves, so some of it will have to be bartered. That might mean your wood supply. There will be no Internet for research, so you must know things like this in advance.

The best prepping is education. The best education is hands on.

## Part Two: Defending What Is Yours

The second issue is how to keep what you have, including your life. If this all goes south, there will be millions of people who did not prepare. They will be hungry, scared, desperate, and willing to do things they never thought they would do just to survive.

Couple them with people who were bad to start with, the criminal element that is part of any society, and you will have a lot of people trying to take what you have away from you—including your life.

▲ Without the ability and the tools to protect your property and your life, prepping is pointless.

▲ You can never have too much ammo.

The first thing you need to deal with is the mindset. To survive you will probably have to do some terrible things. You will need to get that straight in your head now, because there will be no time to work out the morality of survival when some guy is trying to cut your head off with a machete. You may decide that you can't deal with it and that's fine, but you probably will not survive. I understand that death is preferable for some, rather than bending their moral principles.

But if you decide that it is moral to survive, you must have that clear in your mind before trouble finds you.

The next thing is being able to defend what you have. It's here that education becomes a bit tricky.

Firearms are the only choice, and then only the right firearms. Hollywood may love the crossbow or the sword, but pick those and you will lose every time to a man with a gun.

I have been a professional gun writer for most of my adult life, and I can tell you that currently there is a lot of bad information out there about guns and defense. The Internet has made thousands of morons into instant "experts." If you trust what some cellar-dwelling, pimple-infested, fat kid in Cheeto-encrusted sweat pants is putting on his blog, it can get you into big trouble.

Find the real experts and listen to them. They are still out there. You will need guns, lots of ammo, and the training to use both. The best training is from a true professional. You can find them at places like Gunsite Academy in Arizona or the Sig Sauer Academy in New Hampshire. Don't think you can't learn from them—anybody can. I am as hard-core a gun guy as you will ever meet, with half a century of shooting experience, and I learn something every time I attend one of these classes.

▲ Professional training is always a good option.

While my personal biases will appear in this book and I don't try to hide them, I am trying to cover each category completely and objectively enough to allow you to make informed decisions. For example, you will easily pick up that I am not a fan of the 9mm (9×19mm Parabellum) handgun cartridge for defense, but you will see that I think every prepper should have at least one 9mm handgun. The reasons for both opinions are contradictory, but sound.

My advice is to read this book cover to cover and use the info to help pick the guns you will need for defending yourself, your family, and your home. Spend some time and get it right. Each person and situation is unique, so find the best firearms for you and yours. Then find some classes that can teach you how to use those firearms for defense.

If you can't spare the time or the money for professional classes, there are a lot of good books and videos on the market. Most gun ranges have one or two people who are experienced and willing to help. You might also look at taking up competition shooting. The military and a lot of law enforcement personnel use 3-gun shooting as a training platform, because they know it's the next best thing to actual combat (except perhaps force-on-force training). There are matches springing up all over the country, so you can likely find a few close to where you live. Shoot the match with your defensive guns and think of it as training. You will not win, but compete against yourself with a goal to do better than the last match.

Most clubs welcome new shooters and will be very helpful in getting you through that intimidating first match.

The point is, start now; don't wait until something happens. A survival situation is not the time to get "on the job" training.

Besides, learning all this stuff is a lot of fun.

The time is now to prepare for what's coming. I don't think there is a single aspect of prepping more

▲ An AR-15 custom M4-style carbine with a BLACKHAWK! bug-out bag.

important than protecting life and property. In good times, some make an argument that property is not worth taking a life. That's easy to say when you live in a functioning society and have an income; you can replace the property. But in a survival situation, food, medical supplies, and other property are critical to staying alive. That changes the rules.

What follows is a guidebook to developing a plan and determining the tools needed for survival.

# WHY GUNS FOR PREPPERS?
## What's It All About?

*Prepping is a lot more than just collecting beans, bullets, and Band-Aids.*
*It's about staying alive now, before The End Of The World As We Know It happens, as well as after.*

This book is not going to teach you how to plant a garden, cut up a cow, or build a bunker. It will not teach you about safe drinking water or heirloom seeds. Those are all important topics, but they are not the subject here. This is a book about the guns you will need to survive.

After all, without those, the rest is pointless. If you can't defend yourself, somebody else will drink your water, pick your garden, and eat your beef.

We will take an in-depth look at the tools needed to stay safe during a survival situation, to protect your property, and to supplement your food sources with fresh protein. Simply put, this is a gun book, not a survival book. It won't teach you how to survive, but it does explore the guns you will need to accomplish that goal. If you can't defend yourself or your loved ones after TSHTF, then none of you will survive.

That's a brutal statement, but it's the truth. If things fall apart, you will be on your own. It doesn't matter where you live; sooner or later bad people will find you. If there are no police, no government, and no rules, there will be people trying to rob and likely kill you. This book explores the tools to prevent that.

▲ If you don't have the tools, ability, and willingness to protect yourself, your family, and your survival gear, you won't last long in a hostile world.

The idea that you can survive a massive natural or manmade disaster or a total social and/or economic collapse unscathed without the means to defend yourself, your family, and your property is naive, foolish, and a self-imposed death sentence.

I know that a lot of people don't believe that. They will read this with a condescending snicker, all the while making remarks about tinfoil hats and crazy people. I sincerely hope they are never proven wrong and that nothing bad happens.

Those people refuse to think about the possibilities because it scares them, while others have such a profound belief in our society that they will not even consider the possibility that it can fail. There are other, naive people who believe in the inherent goodness of man and that it's possible to reason with desperate and/or evil people under any circumstance. If any of this is describing you, this is probably not your book.

But if you believe in personal responsibility and think that protecting yourself and your family are not only moral, but also your primary job in a crisis, read on.

It's not hard to find examples of what happens when the "system" breaks down. Just look at New Orleans after Hurricane Katrina. It was chaotic, and a lot of the cops turned out to be worse than the looters. Speaking

of the looters, a few were shooting at the helicopters that were showing up to rescue people, probably including themselves. How insane is that? You simply cannot assume that anything will remain predictable or that people will remain civil or act with any sort of logic.

The rules won't apply anymore, and when they no longer constrain the population, the worst of the worst will surface. Then, the law of the jungle applies and only the strongest will survive. The difference with man is that we rose above the animals and developed tools. The strongest now is not about muscle, claw, and fang; the strongest today is the smartest and the best prepared.

Like they say, God made man, but Colonel Colt made them equal. It's an old and worn out cliché, but it's true. Only we have much better guns today than when the Colt Army revolver was winning the West and that phrase was born. A tiny old lady with a pocket-sized handgun can defeat a prison-hardened, street-fighting, 200-pound man in a fight to the death. But only if she is smart, well prepared, and of a mindset to fight back.

If we experience the complete economic and social collapse that so many are predicting, you will be on your own. If you have prepared and have some food

▲ If the system breaks down, you are on your own when evil knocks at the door.

filled with people, look to see how many of them have their noses buried in their phones, are wearing ear buds, or are in any other way oblivious to their surroundings. Do you really think that those people have any "situational awareness" or that they would have a clue how to react if there was an attack?

If it's warm, take a look at how many of them are wearing flip-flops. How can they deal with a crisis where they will need to run or perhaps navigate a debris field of broken, shattered materials with such foolish footwear? These people are not thinking about what can happen because they have complete and blind faith in the system. So far, they have been right. The odds are that nothing bad ever will happen and they can go on being sheep without ever understanding that's what they are. But if something tragic and catastrophic were to happen, they would quickly go from sheep to mutton.

How many of them do you think are prepping? How many do you suppose are carrying a gun right now? How many do you think will survive even the early days of a major crisis?

Remember, it can happen at any moment. Prepping means being ready now as well as continuing to plan for the future. Prepping means preparing for any contingency, not just the end of the world. If you find yourself in a terrorist attack at the mall this weekend and are killed because you didn't have a gun or a plan, then the end of the world will no longer be much of a concern. For you, it just happened.

Prepping means being ready now. You can't schedule a problem; it will happen when it happens and you must be ready. It could be a junkie trying to carjack you or it might be the total collapse of society. You can't predict it and you can't plan to be ready "that day" instead of now.

My friend and fellow gun writer Joseph von Benedikt posted this recently on Facebook:

*"Two days ago, a pit bull leaped into my niece-in-law's van and attacked her. Thankfully she had her Ruger LCR handy. The dog bit down on the gun and a portion of her hand—they were literally in its mouth—when she shot it. The shot knocked the pit bull back, where it started chewing on her leg while she emptied the .38 into it. It died*

and supplies set aside, great; that proves you are smart. After all, what's the downside? If nothing happens, the world gets back on track, and the danger abates, you will have too much food. Is that really a problem? If it is, it's a problem that a lot of the world would love to have. I have traveled pretty extensively in the Third World and when you hear about "first-world problems" there is a lot of truth in that worn out platitude. If you find you have too much food, donate it to a worthy cause. Problem solved.

If you have too many guns, donate them to me. Again, problem solved.

The sad truth is that living in the "first world" has made us soft, complacent, and a bit foolish. If you doubt that, the next time you are in any public place *against the gas pedal. Kudos to a courageous, prepared mama—her four little children were in the van with her.*

*Not all potentially deadly self-defense encounters involve humans."*

Joseph makes a very valid point: Danger comes from more than just two-legged predators. Can you imagine the carnage a savage pit bull could have done to a bunch of kids trapped inside a van? Because that woman was prepared to protect her children, they were protected. But stop and think: How many moms today pack a gun while driving their kids to the mall? Most of them have been conditioned to believe that having a gun puts the kids at risk, rather than protects them. They are foolish and naive, but they are in the majority in America today.

I have a liberal neighbor who is a prepper. He likes to shoot guns and he owns a few, but he will not carry a gun for defense. Nor will he keep one ready. Despite the fact that he is retired and lives with his wife in a rural location, he locks the guns up, unloaded, and puts the ammo in a different location. He buys into a lot of liberal misinformation, and he has been convinced that he has a greater chance of having the gun taken away and used against him than he does for protecting himself with it. Nothing I can do will change his mind. No logical argument or physical demonstration will change his belief. He may be a gun owner, but he is in the same category as the fools wearing flip-flops with their noses in their phones if the shit ever hits the fan. He has stored a lot of food and planted a beautiful garden, which will make some predator fat and happy.

I live in Vermont, which was once the safest state in the nation. While that's changed, mostly due to importing a lot of liberal social causes, it's still in the top five pretty consistently. But a few years ago a pit bull belonging to a homeless guy attacked a sixty-four-year-old man in the parking lot of the store where my wife shops for food. As I recall, the man lost his arm as a result. This happened in a "safe" place in a "safe" state, in good light, in the parking lot of a shopping plaza in a good neighborhood.

The point is, it can happen anywhere.

Back when Vermont was still at the top of the list of safest places to live, a woman who used to be our neighbor was abducted and murdered. A scumbag, who I won't name, was enjoying some quality family time, drinking and smoking crack cocaine with his mother. The mom headed for bed and asked him to turn down the music. So of course, he and his buddy, another low-quality POS, killed her and her boyfriend. Then they carjacked our old neighbor, a sweet grandmother, as she showed up early for work at another food market. Her job was to arrive early and get everything ready in the bakery so that fresh bread and rolls were available when the store opened. It was three o'clock in the morning and nobody was around. It's also notable that the carjacking took place in sight of the city police station.

They drove to New York and kicked her out in the snow. When she started praying out loud, they beat her to death, smashing her head with a boulder. The dumbasses were still driving her car when they were arrested in Arkansas. The "buddy" did the taxpayers a favor and hanged himself in jail, while the first guy admitted his guilt and was convicted under federal law and given the death penalty. Surprisingly, or not, the "do-gooders" in Vermont were more appalled that he received a federal death sentence than they were about his crimes.

More than fifteen years later he is still wasting oxygen and, in fact, a liberal, anti–death penalty, activist judge just gave him a new trial due to a technicality concerning a juror. I would not be surprised if they released him back into our community.

It's a fact that the country is deteriorating fast and the threat level from predators of all kinds is rapidly escalating, no matter where you live. The woman with the pit bull hitchhiker lives in Utah, another "safe" place. Bad things can happen to anyone and in any place.

The government is putting you in danger, not protecting you. If you think you are safe, or that you can call a cop when a problem shows up and he will save you, then you probably believe in unicorns and global warming. There is only one person who can protect you and that is you. You can play the odds and hope nothing will happen and perhaps you will be fine, perhaps not. Or you can decide not to be a victim and take steps to protect yourself and your family. Thank God the mother in Utah chose personal responsibility.

If you decide to carry a gun, remember this simple acronym: ABC. *Always Be Carrying.* You can't decide when and where a problem will happen. You can't schedule an attack, and you can't depend on it occurring when it's convenient to carry a gun. It can happen in a cold, deserted parking lot late at night, in a crowded, well-lit residential area, a busy shopping mall, or on a remote country road. No place is exempt, particularly when you consider that there are a lot of threats out there, both two-legged and four-legged, and their numbers are growing every day.

I am sure this nice woman in Utah didn't decide that was the day a pit bull would attack her, and I know our neighbor had no idea that she would be doing anything other than baking bread on that cold Vermont day. But the outcome for these ladies was very different, because one of them decided to take charge of her personal safety. I don't mean to criticize our neighbor; she did nothing wrong, except trust the system we are told from birth will protect us.

Don't let some piece of shit excuse for a human decide your fate. Make a decision to protect yourself, buy the gun(s) that you need, learn the proper way to defend yourself, and ABC.

That's the first step in prepping.

In addition to everyday personal safety, prepping (as we are primarily discussing it here) is getting ready for a huge structural change in our world and society. You should be armed now, but the requirements for your guns will change if predictions come true. You must prepare for that as well.

The gun you carry now may be fine for today's problems. But, you must think ahead and try to envision every scenario. In many possible situations, you will find that your needs will be much different.

If the collapse happens, there are going to be millions of people who did nothing to prepare. Many of these people live off the "system," which means they expect the lights to be on, the water running, the sewers working, and the grocery stores to be stocked. They have no self-reliance skills and have their heads buried so deep in the sand that any crisis will catch them completely unaware and unprepared. They will have no idea of how to cope and panic will be their first reaction.

Most of them are probably good people. People who play by the rules, go to work every day, pay their taxes, and would never think about taking something that does not belong to them. But what happens when the system they depend on, the system they have total faith in, fails? These are people with a strong sense of entitlement. How will they react when all of a sudden they are not getting the goods and services they believe they are due?

What happens when their belief system is shattered? When everything grinds to a halt? Their water is no longer safe to drink, sewage is running in the streets, they have no food and no way to get any more food. Other people are attacking or threatening them, and they have no defenses, no way to fight back, and no governmental protection.

Perhaps they have been forced out of their homes by looters, fires, terrorists, or even organized troops. They are lost, disillusioned, hungry, and scared. They are watching their children starve, or perhaps they are sick and need medical help. These people are desperate.

Now suppose they discover you have food, water, shelter, and medicine?

"So, I'll just share," you say, "I am a giving person."

Very noble—I admire you. But what happens when the next group shows up? Will you also share with them? What about the next group and the one after that?

I know it is harsh and brutal to think about, but how are you serving your loved ones by giving away all the food, equipment, and medicine that you put aside for just such an emergency? It won't take long before you are in the same sinking boat as all those people who didn't prepare. Your efforts saved nobody and your actions will have doomed yourself and your family.

Now, consider that you have decided your family comes first. What happens when these desperate people show up at your front door? You tell them "No," but they won't listen. You order them to go away, but they ignore you. There are no police to call, no one to help you, no 911. The people who refuse to leave know that and will probably decide to take all of your food and equipment. How do you plan to stop them? By "reasoning" with them as several people have suggested to me in past discussions? Good luck with that one. They are hungry and you can't eat "reason." The facade of civilization has crashed, and they are no longer the good people who paid their taxes, worked nine to five, took their kids to ball games, and would never steal. Those people are gone. This is survival, and in survival situations the rules don't always apply.

In a survival situation the world is going to be harsh and brutal. Most people refuse to think about any of this just because it is so awful to contemplate. But if you have the mindset that you are going to survive, you must think about it. This will no longer be the cushy, civilized world we left behind. The soft and the softhearted are going to die. If you want to survive, as horrible as it is to contemplate right now, you will need to harden your heart. You will need to decide that survival for yourself and your family is the number one priority in life and act accordingly.

It will not be easy, but I believe that we can still maintain a moral compass during this time. That at the end we can hold our heads up and defend our actions to those who sit in judgment. But the line of that compass is going to have to change. The way we think about our lives and the world we live in will need to be much different.

Now imagine that it's not one or two people trying to take your food, but a dozen, or fifty, or a hundred. They have left morality behind and are doing anything they can to survive. Mob mentality will be controlling their actions, and that means they will do anything to get your food and supplies. If they succeed, you and your family are dead. Are you not morally bound to repel the aggressors and save your family?

So then, tell me; how will you do that?

If you do not have the ability to defend yourself, your loved ones, and your property, and if you survive the encounter, you and your family will be joining the ranks of hungry, homeless, desperate people. If they take everything you have, you are now in the same boat they are. That means you must now abandon all morality and find weaker people that you can steal from to survive. That also means you will probably need to murder some of those people, because they will fight back. Do you think you can justify that on Judgment Day?

No?

Well then, you have only two options left. One is death. The other is to prepare yourself physically and mentally to defend your food, your property, and your family.

There are over 321 million people in the United States. Most have done nothing to prepare for a crisis. If you are among the few who did prepare, it will have done you no good if you can't defend what you have. This book is about the tools to defend yourselves, your loved ones, and your property. It's not a book about survival strategy, battle tactics, or how to build a remote wilderness compound. This is a gun book. It looks at the diversity of firearms, ammunition, and accessories currently available to United States citizens. It explores the pros and cons of each and makes a few conclusions and recommendations on what might be best for you and why. How can you pick the proper guns and gear if you don't know what's what? If you don't understand the differences between an AR-15 and an AK-47 except to know that one is American and the other Russian in design, how do you pick the one that's best for you? This book looks at practical issues like ballistics, expected ammo supplies in a time of crisis, and the ease of mounting a quality optical sighting system on the gun.

I suppose from now on, I'll leave the moral issues for somebody else to debate. I have already made up my mind. My family comes first.

I will not steal another man's property, but I also will not let him steal mine. Nor will I let him harm my family or me. I think the morality is clear here. I recognize that some do not see it as clearly, but for those of you who have made your choice, this book will help you decide on the tools you will need to survive.

If it gets as bad as some say it will, guns and ammo will be the coin of the land. If we see the social and economic collapse that so many are expecting, the currency will change. If the dollar crashes and is worth only enough to wipe your ass when there is a toilet paper shortage, then you need a means to buy food and supplies. In a survival situation, guns, ammo, and reloading supplies will be worth more than gold. Stockpiling more than you need simply means you will be wealthy after the crash and have more options.

We will explore why the guns you may have now for hunting are inadequate for defensive use and why depending on them could get you killed. If you think you can survive this with your deer rifle, read on to find out why you are wrong.

It's a dangerous world out there and it is becoming more and more dangerous every day. Millions of people have decided to take responsibility for their own safety and the growth in the concealed carry industry is huge. This book is also full of useful information about guns for protection with or without a major meltdown. It will help you choose which guns, ammo, and accessories might work best for you for concealed carry and for home defense even in "normal" times.

Bottom line, this is a book about guns for the defense and protection of ordinary citizens: now, during, and after a major crisis. It's a book for those who have chosen to take personal responsibility seriously, a book for those who understand that they, and they alone, are responsible for their own future. It's an aid in helping to decide how you will prepare for that future.

Although we are exploring some dark topics, it doesn't need to be boring. I hope that you not only learn, but that you will enjoy reading the book and maybe even get a chuckle out of it now and then. I want this book on your coffee table, or the nightstand beside your bed, or in your bathroom—wherever you do your best reading.

If it's the bathroom, just remember that it contains very important information that makes each page valuable and stick to using dollar bills for the cleanup work, not this book.

▲ Prepping is being prepared for any scenario and storing enough of everything to see you through.

# Guns for the Meltdown

*Think you can survive the end of society with your deer rifle? Think again.*

*I* can tell you that no book worth reading in the history of the world was finished on schedule, including this one. Anybody organized and disciplined enough to do that is not creative enough to write anything other than a boring book.

I know writers like that: precise, on schedule, and very organized . . . and their books are snoozefests. Check into all the great writers in history and you will find that they were mostly free spirits. At least that's the excuse I keep using for this landfill I call a desk. (Remember what Einstein said: "If a cluttered desk is a sign of a cluttered mind, of what, then, is an empty desk a sign?")

It's also the excuse I had for being late getting my novel, *The 14th Reinstated,* finished. That book is set after total economic and social collapse. While it's an action-adventure work of fiction, it deals with exactly the same scenarios we are prepping for today. In fact, it was the inspiration for this book. As you might suppose, considering that I am a gun guy, there is a lot of shooting, a lot of fights, and a lot of guns in that book.

I wanted to publish it in advance of the 2012 elections to cash in on the well-placed fear that people had for the future, given the direction Obama had been pushing the country.

(Full disclosure: There is an "Obama-like" character in the book and he is not one of the good guys.)

I thought that once Romney won the White House things would improve and people would be less fearful about the future and perhaps less inclined to buy my novel. Clearly, there was no way Romney could lose, and I believed it would slow sales to have America back on track again (for the record, a price that I would willingly pay).

Obviously, I underestimated the stupidity of American voters. Throughout history, it's always been bank accounts that drive elections, and no sitting president in history had been able to defend against so bad an economic record and keep his job. But America has changed; voters are motivated by different things now. As somebody (according to Google it could have been any one of Alexander Fraser Tytler, or maybe Alexis de Tocqueville, or Elmer T. Peterson) once said:

*"A democracy cannot exist as a permanent form of government. It can only exist until the majority discovers it can vote itself largess out of the public treasury. After that, the majority always votes for the candidate promising the most benefits with the result the democracy collapses because of the loose fiscal policy ensuing, always to be followed by a dictatorship, then a monarchy."*

The voter motivations that are driving elections now are no longer sustainable and I fear America will end badly, which is the main point of this book. This new direction for America has been good for book sales, but bad for our country.

If you are reading this, then I assume you probably have a clue and are worried about the future. The signs are not good. I keep telling myself that we have made it through bad times before and we will make it through this, but then I look at the news and I fear I am wrong. This time it all feels different.

We can't predict the future, but if you are smart, you are making some preparations. I am not suggesting that you build a walled compound in the middle of nowhere—at least not yet. But you should be making plans to feed, shelter, and protect your family if this does indeed all go south.

I believe protection is most important. Storing "beans, bullets, and Band-Aids" is a worthless gesture unless you have a way to hold onto them. If the law no longer applies and there are thousands of desperate, hungry people roaming around with no social restraints or cops to keep them in line, it will all be up to you.

I know it's a horrible thing to think about and most people refuse to consider it, but truth is an ugly bitch sometimes. We all hope that it will never happen and frankly the odds still favor that it will not, but we must consider that we are moving closer every day to a major disaster in America. Certainly the odds are much higher today for social and economic collapse than they were in 2008. If it happens and if you are not preparing, including for your own defense, you will probably die.

I met a woman at a party the other day. She told me how concerned she is about things going bad. Then, because I was trapped at the table with her, she told me her plans. She is going to leave her house in New York State with no real planning or any gear. She is going to meet her daughter and two young grandchildren at a state campground, because to her, "that is out in the boonies where it's safe." She has no camping gear or camping experience, which probably doesn't matter much because she has no plans on what to do for shelter, food, or security after they arrive. The only thing she is certain of is that they must "head for the hills."

I asked about guns, already pretty sure what the answer was going to be.

"Oh, I have a .22," she said. Then she giggled. "But I don't know how to use it."

Just to be clear, if it all falls apart and she follows her plan, that lady is going to die very quickly. In fact, there will be a multitude of "cause of deaths" lining up for a chance at glory. I doubt she will make it a week. It's too bad; she is a nice person, just foolish and naive. There is not much we can do about people like that, except wish them well and make meaningful preparations for ourselves and our families.

Prepping means you must think ahead and make smart choices. Part of smart prepping is recognizing that the realities are going to be savage and brutal and that guns and ammo are the only tools that can help you keep what is valuable to your survival.

But which ones should you buy?

Well, I can say for starters that a .22 you don't even know how to load is not the correct answer.

I know you are interested in prepping and personal defense, otherwise you would not be reading this book. If you are like most intelligent people, you are looking to multiple sources of information on the topic of which guns and ammo are best for survival. But let me provide a little caution. Things have changed. Until recently if you were reading a book or a nationally circulated magazine, the text was likely written by a genuine expert in the field and was edited by a staff of professionals. For a gun writer to reach the point where he was publishing in the big national magazines or writing books for noted publishers, he would have paid a lot of dues. Back then a gun writer had to make his bones by proving his expertise. The editorial staff served as a filter to make sure the writer knew his stuff. Sure, an occasional article written by a fool slipped by, but any name that was in the magazine regularly belonged to a writer who had proven himself to be a true expert in the field. As for books, no legitimate publisher would make the investment necessary for a new book in a writer without a proven track record.

Today, everybody is an expert. The Internet gave a forum to thousands of people looking to publish. This is a great thing overall, but it opened the door to a lot of misinformation. I am not saying that only a print writer can be right; there are a lot of good writers on the Internet. Heck, I have my own blogs, including "Towsley on Prepping" and "Towsley on Tactical," and I regularly contribute to several other gun or hunting sites. Just be careful. Think about what you are reading and see if it makes sense.

One good example from the bloviating crowd that always sets my blood boiling:

"You only need one gun to survive. If you can shoot, you can get all the guns and ammo you want. Heck, give me one gun and I can get a tank."

Usually these guys will advocate for a simple gun like a revolver, which I suppose in their simple minds makes them superior. After all, if you can take a .38 Special revolver and attack a solider or even a well-armed civilian and take their battle rifle or their tank, well then you must be one hell of a man.

This misses several points. First, you must be willing to commit murder to take the other guy's guns. In my view, that's a very poor platform on which to base your survival strategy.

I recognize that this book is mostly about guns used to shoot other people, but I see a clear distinction. The guns I am writing about are for protection, survival, and defense. They are not used to murder other people and take their possessions. I have guns exactly because there are other people who are going to try to murder me for my stuff. I see a very clear moral distinction between the two. If you are the kind of guy who will murder somebody else in cold blood to get his guns, I see you as the problem, not the solution. You are the reason I have guns and why I am writing this book.

The second flaw in this argument is that you may well run into a guy who can shoot just as well as you can, or maybe even better. He has a rifle (or a tank), you have a revolver; the math is easy here. You will die for a stupid idea.

No matter how much you train, you are not going to be the biggest, baddest operator out there. If you approach survival with an aggressive and combative attitude, you will not last long. There are some truly badass guys in the world. Because I have worked in the gun industry for three decades and also because I am a competitive shooter, I know a bunch of the elite military operators. Trust me when I say we civilians, even those of us who train hard, would not last long against any of them. These guys have the best training and lots of combat experience.

I once played informal paintball with a longtime Delta operator. (He is also a consultant for this book.)

The set-up was two of us against him. We would head to the woods and see who "survived." I figured we had this one covered. After all, I am a hard-core hunter, and while it's bragging, I am pretty good at sneaking around in the woods and shooting stuff.

At one point my brother, Scott, and I had this guy pinned down behind a log right in front of us. There was no way he could escape. Yet, while we were arguing about which of us was going to draw his fire so the other one could take him out, he came up behind us and shot both of us in the back of the head.

I want to make two points about that.

First, forget any fantasies about fighting the battles of Armageddon. If you want to survive, learn to hide and evade. Stay below the radar and avoid fighting except as a last resort. But if you must fight, fight to win, fight like your life depends on it, because it will.

The second point? A paintball, shot point blank in the back of the head, hurts like hell.

Just saying.

There is a lot of other misinformation out there. Look at shotguns, for example: "You don't even have to aim, just point it in the bad guy's direction."

"The sound of racking the slide on a pump shotgun will scare off the bad guys."

"A shotgun is the perfect defensive gun for an inexperienced shooter."

All flawed, which you will see in the chapter on shotguns. In fact, as I will explain, a shotgun is a rather poor choice for a primary defensive long gun, no matter what Joe Biden might have to say on the topic.

Another I see all the time is:

"The .22 Long Rifle (LR) is the perfect survival gun. The ammo is light and it's easy to carry lots of it. It's all about bullet placement anyway; just shoot them in the eye."

There are a couple of flaws in this theory that are addressed in depth later. One is the shot placement argument. This one comes up all the time on the Internet; just Google anything about the 9mm versus .45 debate. You won't have to scroll through the comments very far before somebody will say, "It's all about shot placement."

Well yes, of course it is. Where you hit them is important. If you were in a fight for your life, only a fool would try to shoot the bad guy in the ass when his

▲ Is the .22 LR the perfect survival cartridge?

chest is available as a target. We train hard to be good shots and we learn anatomy so we know where to aim. But anybody who makes that "shot placement" argument has no idea what shooting under stress in a fast-breaking situation is really like. It is one thing to shoot at a static target on a square range and quite another to shoot at something that is moving, while you are also moving, and with the knowledge that your life is on the line because they are shooting back. Often you are just trying the best you can to get hits anywhere. The man who says he can hit them in the eye every time is a braggart and a fool.

The point is, a big tough guy may shake off a marginal hit with a .22 LR when a .223 Remington, .308 Winchester, or even a .45 ACP might have a different effect. Nothing is guaranteed, but the odds always favor a larger, more powerful cartridge. The .22 Long Rifle is never that cartridge. It is very low power in comparison. A .308 Winchester has about 2,600 foot-pounds of energy, a .223 has 1,300 foot-pounds, and a .45 ACP has about 450 foot-pounds. By comparison, a 36-grain hollow-point .22 LR has only 127 foot-pounds of energy. There are a lot of other factors in a bullet's ability to end a fight, but you get the idea here. Besides, none of those other factors enhance the .22 LR argument in any way.

The .22 LR is an important cartridge for preppers, but it's far from the ideal all-around survival gun. Falling for that argument, and a lot of others, can get you into a lot of trouble.

I risk repeating myself here, but this is very important. If social collapse occurs, it will be up to you to take responsibility for your safety and the safety of your family. You cannot depend on the government, society, the police, or the rule of law or to help you. You are on your own.

If you have prepared and put away food and other supplies, there will be desperate people trying to take it all away from you. As the cities empty and the number of hungry people increases, you must understand that at some point it will not be just one or two lost souls, but likely dozens or perhaps more who show up to take what is yours and possibly kill you and your loved ones. If you try to defend your home with your deer rifle or your shotgun, you will probably fail. Failure means death for you and your family. If the attacking hordes do not kill you, starvation or exposure will. There are plenty of reasons why trying to defend your home against an angry mob with your hunting guns will not work, but the primary reason you shouldn't use hunting guns for self-defense is simply that they do not hold enough ammo and are much too slow to reload. You will be overrun as soon as you run out of ammo and pause to reload.

That's one big reason why you never see a solider or a cop with a hunting-style gun.

Don't think that adding an aftermarket high-capacity magazine to your semiauto hunting gun is the answer. Hunting rifles are designed to fire a few shots at a time, not sustain a high volume of fire for a long time. They get hot and dirty and they seize up and stop running. The last thing you want (or likely will experience) is to have your gun go down in the middle of a fight.

A much better choice for defending home and family would be any of the guns that were originally designed as fighting rifles. This class of rifle was designed for battle, and most of them were originally designed with a full-auto option, so they can run sustained fire and continue to operate even when they are dirty and overheated.

Hunting guns are for hunting. While hunting and foraging are important to survival, and we will explore the guns used in other chapters, the primary focus of this book is surviving. The idea of living off the land is a bit of a fantasy for most people. Realistically, if society breaks down, a lot of really bad people will have the filters, governors, and restrictions lifted off their behavior, and the most difficult part of survival will be dealing with these people. It will be very hard to avoid these people, no matter where you live or where you may bug out to, they will be around sooner or later, and they will be your primary threat to survival.

Therefore *Prepper Guns* will deal mostly with guns for fighting. No matter what you may think or have been told, your .30–30 Winchester and double barrel shotgun are not the best choices to get you through to the end.

# Gun Guys Have a Tactical Advantage

*Why a prepper should learn to love all guns.*

▲ Shooters who learn multiple firearms have a better chance of survival.

The food is awful, but it feels good to sit down. A day of shopping at the local mall is not your idea of fun, but it keeps the peace with the family. Just as you are making that slurpy sound with the straw to annoy your wife (most men never really grow up) you hear full-auto gunfire and see a man spraying the food court with bullets as he screams "Allahu Akbar" over and over. The mall's rent-a-cop falls before he can get his pistol out of his triple retention holster, and the gun-man is working his way through the crowd toward you and your wife.

You grab your 1911 from its concealment holster and double-tap him. You believe in the old saying of "beware of the guy with one gun," and it feels like an old friend in your hand. It should; you carry it every

day and shoot it most days. You even use it to compete in IDPA matches on some weekends. You believe that by sticking with this one gun, you will shoot it well and always have the muscle memory to operate it no matter what happens.

That theory clearly works; the dead terrorist is proof enough for you. But as that guy falls, two more guys with rifles run through the doorway. You shoot, a little too fast, and miss the closest guy with the first shot. But you settle on the front sight and hit him with the second. You swing to the second guy and dump two to the chest and one in the head. The first guy is staggering around, so you double-tap him again. The magazine is empty so you reload with your one spare magazine just as you notice more guys coming from the opposite end of the mall.

▲ Putting all your trust and all your training into a single firearm platform like this 1911 is a mistake.

Jessica Stevens from Barnes Bullets shooting an MP5 submachine gun at the IC match. The more platforms you learn, the better your chances of survival.

Suddenly all that bragging at the range about, "if I can't handle a problem with two magazines and a 1911, then I deserve to die" rings a little hollow. There are a lot of bad guys coming your way and you start shooting at them. One falls and another staggers. You keep shooting and the others run for cover, giving you a window to de-ass the place. You tell your wife to run as you notice your handgun is at slidelock. When you run past the first guy you shot, you stop to pick up his rifle and a spare magazine. You notice a pistol in a shoulder holster, which you also grab and stuff in your belt.

You and your wife run down the main corridor, but you hear them coming behind you, so you duck into a store. Two guys follow just behind you, yelling and waving their guns. The AK-47 you picked up is empty and you try frantically to slam the spare magazine into the gun, but it will not stay. Dropping the rifle, you yank the Tokarev pistol from your belt, but it also will not shoot. You try to rack the slide, but it won't move.

It doesn't matter; it's too late and you watch as one of them grabs your wife's hair, yanks her head back, and pulls a knife.

Still think this "one man–one gun" thing is a good idea? If you knew that the magazine on an AK-47 had to be rocked in or that the pistol you picked up uses a half-cock on the hammer instead of a safety and that it locks the slide, you might have had a fighting chance. But you only know the 1911, because you thought it was more "tactical" to stick with one gun.

If you are serious about survival, you need to learn to run any and all of the most common guns you may encounter.

Dan Smith at International Cartridge used to put on a unique shooting match. He supplied all the guns and ammo and you never knew what would be waiting for you at any given stage. It might be a bolt-action rifle, pump shotgun, or a full-auto MP5. Or it could be an AR-15, AK-47, or a single-action revolver. We shot Glocks, S&W revolvers, Berettas, Rugers—you name it and usually there was one on a table somewhere. Dan's thoughts were simple: "I can run a standard match and some hotshot with a race gun will come in and win it, just like he expects to do every time. That's because he shoots that gun all the time and knows it well. But guys like that don't like my match. This is a match for gun guys, and if you are a true gun guy, you should be able to shoot anything they hand you well enough to compete."

It's not just competitors who shoot one gun exclusively. Time and again at self-defense courses I encounter people who believe that they should pick one "platform" (gun-speak for a particular gun design, like a Glock or a 1911 in handguns, or an AR-15 in rifles) and stick with that exclusively. Their reasoning is that in the fog of war and during a fight when you are full of adrenalin, you will run on muscle memory and still function with that gun. They believe that shooting other types of guns will confuse the subconscious and cause them to forget how to run their firearm.

I believe that is foolish thinking and the person promoting it has not thought the issue out far enough and considered all the possible scenarios. What happens if you no longer have access to your platform? How are you going to survive with a gun you have no idea how to operate and are in the middle of a fast-breaking situation with bad guys trying to kill you? The simple answer is: You aren't. You will die.

A true gun guy understands that the more you know, the better your chances are for survival. I know some of the most elite of the Special Forces in our military. These are the guys who have been in a lot of gunfights and in a lot of bad situations, and I can tell you that they can run any gun they pick up.

When I shot Dan Smith's match, I was one of two writers there as guests of Barnes bullets. The other was a retired Special Forces operator. I watched him, and every gun he picked up he either could run already, or figured out very quickly.

Todd Rassa, an instructor for the Sig Sauer Academy, addressed this issue during a class called "Civilian Response to a Terrorist Attack." In fact, the idea for the mall scenario above came from one of the drills we did in that class. Todd picked those two Soviet Bloc guns because they are popular with terrorists. I was a bit shocked to watch guys who were very serious about training and who had attended a lot of self-defense training classes struggle to operate these firearms.

Some of these guys were so convinced that they should only train with one gun that they would not even pick up and look at another handgun. One got mad because I even mentioned a 1911. He was a Glock guy and didn't want me talking about other guns because it might distract him.

I think what Todd was trying to do with this class was to show them how stuck on stupid they were. I am not sure if he succeeded, but I sure got the point.

When it comes to prepping, I would take it way past that. Instead of Islamic terrorists, it might be the next little snot shooting up a Colorado high school or movie theater, or it could be the guy down the street trying to get food for his kids. Or, in a survival situation, you may encounter any of a multitude of different guns.

This is not Hollywood and the bad guys won't all have a MAC-10 or a Desert Eagle like the bad guys in the movies always seem to carry. They will probably have guns they bought on the street or stole from somebody, and that means they could be anything.

Who knows what a bad guy might bring to his mayhem party? Can you run a Benelli M4, Ruger P85, SIG P229, FN FAL, S&W4013, UTS-15, Steyr AUG, Beretta CX4 Storm carbine or 92 series handgun, SKS, Marlin Camp Carbine, Winchester Model 94, Remington Model 750, or any and all other guns instinctively and without thinking about it?

Probably not; I doubt I could either. Not many people have the opportunity to become familiar with all the firearms on Earth. But I do know all of those listed, plus a lot more, and I probably can figure out the rest pretty quickly because I am familiar with so many different firearm platforms. That's because I work hard to put myself into locations where there are opportunities to try different firearms, and I always take advantage of those opportunities. It is always a shock when I see somebody at the range turn down a chance to shoot a new or unfamiliar firearm. It's foolish not to widen your horizons. It may even save your life someday.

I make it a point to try every gun I have an opportunity to shoot. Not just to pull the trigger, but to load the guns and make them ready to fire. That at least expands my experience and gives me a better foundation to figure out the gun I don't know a lot faster.

I shoot in a lot of matches, which teaches you to think and act under pressure, and to do it quickly. They also can expose you to many different guns. I have fired everything from an AK-74 to a grenade launcher while competing in shooting matches. I have shot Tommy Guns, MP5 machine guns, the Squad Automatic Weapon (SAW), M249 Light Machine Gun, a German MG42 machine gun, FN SCAR machine gun, M4 full auto carbine, and a lot more, including many different handguns. All of these were "stage" guns that were provided for us to shoot. It's a short and fleeting opportunity, but it's better than nothing.

You meet a lot of other gun people at the matches, and there are often opportunities to try guns you have not experienced. During downtime I have shot the Bren Ten (made famous by Sonny Crockett on *Miami Vice*), lots of suppressed rifles and handguns, precision long-range custom rifles, a bunch of machine guns, and dozens more.

I remember one small, local match in Massachusetts, of all places, where, once we were done shooting, a guy brought out a couple of machine guns. One was a Tommy Gun and the other was a Ruger AC-556. He said that if we had ammo, we were free to shoot them all we wanted. My buddies usually give me a hard time about all the extra stuff, including ammo, that I bring to a match, but that day I was the last man standing with those machine guns. I blasted hundreds of rounds that I just happened to have in my truck. I knew the Ruger pretty well already, but that was my first real experience with a Tommy Gun, and I left feeling like I understood the gun much better than when the day started. The point is, you just never know when opportunity will present itself.

It's not just competition. There are a lot of gun gatherings around the country—from machine gun blast fests to zombie shoots—and any of them will provide opportunities to shoot new and unfamiliar guns. Even something as simple as a visit to a public shooting range can provide opportunity. Be friendly and talk to people. They may have a gun you want to shoot and quite possibly they want to shoot a gun that you brought.

The smart, tactical approach is to be proficient with as many firearms as possible. That at least builds the foundation of knowledge that will help you deal with ones you are not familiar with.

You never know how a shooting is going to play out, and if you can pick up a gun and stay in the fight, you have a chance. If you run your gun dry and don't have a clue how to use the one the other guy was shooting at you with, or the gun the dead cop had in his hand, you will not have time to figure it out in the middle of a firefight.

The one true thing that is inarguable is this: *If you cannot shoot back in a gunfight, you will lose.*

Become a gun guy. Learn all you can about as many guns as possible. It's the tactical thing to do and it may save your life.

▲ Become a gun guy who loves to shoot.

Yes, I said "gun guy." That means anybody and everybody who likes guns and likes to shoot. I do not discount, disparage, or discriminate against any shooter. If you like guns and like to shoot, we are friends. We have to call ourselves something and "gun guys" has a ring to it. "Guys" has a generic connotation in many contexts anyway, like "you guys," for example.

"Gun gals" is going to make somebody mad, "gun people" sounds stupid, and if I try to insert every single social, economic, and gender identification I can think of into each reference in the book, I risk causing otherwise rational people to sit down, hold hands, and sing "Kumbaya."

I just ain't doing it; it's embarrassing.

If you are offended by such a benign term, then you are probably not the target audience. I suspect that you are not quite there yet, and your mindset is not ready for the serious and sometimes uncomfortable topics we are exploring. Let's face it, when the topics are survival, shooting other people, and even the end of the world as we know it, political correctness starts to shed the shroud that has masked its foolishness all these years.

So, if like all my female shooting buddies (most of whom can kick my butt in competition) you embrace the term and make it yours, welcome home.

The rest of you, please stick with the book; we have a lot of good information that can save your life and help you get through the bad times ahead. Be mad at me if you want, be offended, be horrified, be whatever; but read the book and be safe.

If we all survive and emerge from this intact, you can sue me then.

▲ Any one of these women can outshoot all of us, and they proudly call themselves "gun guys."

# What about Machine Guns?

*Rock 'n' Roll is fun, but do you need a full auto?*

This is a question that pops up sooner or later in every discussion about survival guns. So let's deal with it right now. Should you get a machine gun? Right now, as a citizen, it is possible; but is it important or even smart for a prepper to buy machine guns?

First of all, it's not easy or cheap. The trouble is, here in America, in "the land of the free," it is extremely difficult to own a full-auto firearm. Prior to 1934, there were no restrictions and it was very common for citizens to own these guns. But in 1934 the National Firearms Act was put into place, severely regulating machine guns and several other categories of firearms.

The NFA didn't ban machine guns outright, so I guess the guns weren't all bad in the minds of the politicians. Nothing is ever so bad that it can't be taxed, so instead of a ban, they put a $200 tax on machine guns, as well as short-barreled rifles and shotguns. Two hundred 1934 dollars is the equivalent of more than $3,500 today, so it amounted to a ban for most people. I guess the government deemed that only the rich had a right to these guns. But still, they didn't trust the rich all that much either. They had to register the guns with the government and get formal permission to own them.

Of course, government officials claimed that the law was due to the crimes being committed with these guns. But that's always their excuse, even today. Some believe that there was another reason.

Consider that Prohibition ended in 1933. First of all, that would have also ended most of the crime they claim they were addressing, as it was almost exclusively related to the trafficking of illegal alcohol, a fact that was largely ignored. But the end of Prohibition also put a lot of people out of work. All the government treasury enforcers, the guys whose mission it was to protect us from ourselves and make sure that nobody had any alcohol-infused fun, needed jobs.

Surprise, surprise. Now with the NFA, they had new taxes to collect and new laws to enforce. American jobs were saved and the world was again a good place to be a jackbooted thug.

Then along came the 1968 Gun Control Act. This one decided that only guns with a "sporting purpose" could be imported. That ended the importing of any machine guns, because no government official could ever conceive that shooting is a "sport."

In 1986, the Firearm Owners' Protection Act was passed. The bill was supposed to be a win for gun owners and was intended to prevent the federal government from registering guns or gun owners. But at the last minute, William Hughes, a Democratic congressman from New Jersey, added an amendment that called for the banning of machine guns. Charlie Rangel used some very sketchy and questionable maneuvering in Congress, and they adopted H.R. 4332 as an amendment to the final bill, which was passed and signed on May 19, 1986, by Ronald Reagan.

I'll get hate mail for pointing this out, but Reagan, who was said to be the most pro-gun president in recent times, also sold out gun owners by supporting the Brady Bill, although it was after he was out of office and no longer needed our votes. He was a great leader and one I miss, but he just proves the old adage, "The only enemies that guns have are rust and politicians."

No politician can ever be trusted with your gun rights, not even those we think are on our side. This was exactly the point of the Second Amendment to the United States Constitution. We just seem to have forgotten a few points that the founding fathers thought were important.

Other than being grossly misnamed, the result of the 1986 Firearm Owners Protection Act was that machine guns made after 1986 could not be sold to citizens of this country. Any made prior to that date could be sold and transferred under the NFA rules. So it was official. Exactly what our founding fathers feared had come to pass: Only the government and the police can buy newly manufactured machine guns. The rest of us apparently can't be trusted.

The pre-1986 machine guns have become known as "transferable" machine guns. According to the information available, there are only 182,619 transferable machine guns in the United States today and that number can only go down. So as might be expected, the prices for transferable guns have gone sky high. Ten grand gets you an entry-level piece of crap. For a high-quality gun in good shape, expect to pay double that or more.

It's often argued, and I believe not incorrectly, that all this is to ensure that American citizens do not have the ability to fight back against a tyrannical government, even though that was clearly the intent of the Second Amendment to our Constitution. But it doesn't matter; the government has spoken and machine guns are for all intents and purposes off the table for civilian home defense, so I will now get off my soapbox and get back to the business of guns for preppers.

If you have access to a machine gun, that's great. I would assume you know how to use it well and there is little doubt that it's a great fighting tool. As Randall Curtis, the long-time Delta operator who is consulting on this book, pointed out:

*There is something about a full-auto weapon going off in your direction that makes you think harder about "getting after it" than semiauto rounds going off. That full auto gets in your head.*

So it can have a deterrent effect.

Randall's job for the past several years has been to instruct military forces and police all over the world. He added more info related to the use of machine guns:

*I have been taught—and continue to teach—that the tactical use of the machine gun is the most casualty-producing weapon that can be immediately employed. It's basic "infantry tactics" when setting up an ambush that you initiate the ambush with the most "casualty-producing weapon," and that is generally the machine gun. Remember, an ambush is also not just an offensive operation—it is also used in defense of bases and with security patrols that are conducted to enhance security, by disrupting enemy offensive operations and/or to expand your perimeter.*

*The machine gun is considered an area weapon—meaning that it is not a precision weapon system—so to emphasize some points you mentioned, once it is used your intent is that any personnel in the given impact zone are "hostile" (bad guys).*

The point here is that we as civilian preppers play by different rules than the military. But if your home or compound is under attack, I think it's safe to assume that anybody downrange is your enemy. Here, a machine gun would prove to be a useful defensive tool.

*A machine gun's effective use is via six-to-nine-round bursts, and you are correct when you said it takes training to get guys to use them effectively. Then there are all the other issues of malfunctions, etc. For defense, they are a must for any perimeter and the ultimate Final Protective Line (FPL), where your perimeter is about to be overrun and you "rock 'n' roll" across the front axis of your perimeter in hopes of "mowing down" the assaulting enemy.*

Again, this is a predictable and possible scenario for preppers. If you are under siege and attack and it's a last ditch, do-or-die situation, a machine gun could be a very important tool.

*Another issue you hit on, but not in depth, was using controlled bursts. There are times that it can be beneficial—and trust me, we (where I used to work) had some debates over this. Using two-to-three-round bursts rather than semiauto fire can come in handy when there is a moving target, you are moving, or both you and the target are moving. It throws a "spread" or group of rounds out, increasing your chances of hitting the target.*

So, there is little question that a machine gun can be a very useful tool for a prepper. It's easy to assume that you may have access to them sometime after a crisis begins. The military and police use machine guns, and some of them will enter the black market or simply be

▲ The author shooting an MP5 submachine gun.

available to pick up. However, if you are in a location where there are dead cops or soldiers lying around for you to take their machine guns, you are in the wrong place. I would think the most important goal is to get the hell out of there.

So, the obvious question is should you, as a prepper, buy machine guns? Well, consider a few points. First, they are horribly expensive. You can buy a lot of semiauto AR-15 rifles for the price of one transferable machine gun these days.

Also, if you have a machine gun legally, the government knows you have it, because it must be registered. That can bring unwanted attention.

My advice is do not worry about buying machine guns unless you have so much money that you just don't care.

Besides, if you don't have a machine gun, I would not lie awake at night worrying about it. Randall made it a point to use exactly those words about the fact that he does not own one.

The good news is that it probably doesn't matter. Aside from being a lot of fun to shoot, machine guns are best used in war and not for civilian defense. They serve some important tactical uses on the battlefield, but for civilian defense they probably create as many problems as they solve. It really pisses me off that we can't have them, but the truth be told, in most circumstances, I would rather have a semiauto in a fight to protect my life, family, and property anyway. (The exception being the scenario explored earlier, where my position is about to be overrun.)

Consider also that our ammo resources in a survival situation will be limited, and the wasteful full-auto "spray the countryside mentality" can deplete it very quickly. Just look at the statistics from the Government's General Accounting Office (GAO) stating that in Iraq and Afghanistan the United States has fired an estimated 250,000 rounds of ammo for every insurgent killed. I don't know about you, but my ammo supply cannot sustain that ratio for very long.

Furthermore, unless there is total and complete collapse where there is no longer any form of government, you need to be mindful of the law. Even in a survival situation, we may be held accountable by the law, and as Charles Dickens pointed out so well, sometimes "the law is an ass." While it may seem to favor the bad guys more than the good guys, we must remember that we can't protect our families if we are in jail.

There are a couple of old adages here we should keep in mind: "You are accountable for every bullet you fire."

"Every bullet you fire has a lawyer attached to it."

That means you need to be aware of what your bullets are hitting. It's one thing to shoot the bad guys, but if an innocent person is hit, you can face legal charges and even jail. Even if there is a total collapse and there is no longer any law or government, we are still the good guys. We have a moral obligation to protect the innocent.

Full-auto guns make that accountability very difficult. When bullets are spitting out of the barrel at 600 to nine hundred rounds per minute, you can't be sure of where they are all going to end up.

Full-auto guns are not like what you see in the movies. Rambo standing there pouring fire from a belt-fed machine gun held in one hand is total Hollywood crap. Machine guns are very difficult to control. Each year at SHOT (Shooting Hunting Outdoor Trade) Show, during events like "Media Day at the Range," there are opportunities to shoot several guns the day before the show starts. I go because there are almost always some machine guns loaded with OPA (other people's ammo). One year there were a few guys from one of the gun makers with "Tactical" in its name who had some full-auto AR rifles and a pallet of ammo.

You know the type—Oakley sunglasses, shaved heads, and goatee beards, pumped-up arms covered with tattoo sleeves, and pants with way too many pockets. Late in the day one of them was spending more time flirting with a pretty girl than doing his job and he handed a loaded rifle to an older guy to shoot without paying any attention.

Proving that we men never outgrow it, the old guy was clearly trying to show off for the blue-haired ladies with him. He bladed to the target, tucked his left elbow into his waist and balanced the full-auto gun on the tips of his extended fingers, just like he had no doubt seen some 3-position rifle shooter do with a .22 rifle sometime in the past. When he pulled the trigger, the gun went full rock 'n' roll and the muzzle arched up and over his head. It probably would have shot one of the blue hairs behind him if "Mr. Badass" had not woken up and grabbed the gun.

The point is, full-autos have a mind of their own and they don't suffer fools very well.

Another time, I was in a firearms manufacturing plant in Russia. We were in an underground shooting tunnel, where the Russians were doing their best to embarrass us. I guess their idea of good PR was to bring in their best shooter to show up all the writers. It wasn't working out very well for them, as we were kicking this guy's butt pretty hard. Then they brought out a machine pistol. After their guy shot it a few times he handed it to one of our party, another older guy as it turns out.

He ignored any cautions about holding on tight to the pistol. He said, "I have been shooting guns for fifty years; you don't need to tell me anything." Or at least that's what we all heard. But when he turned loose with that full-auto pistol, the muzzle climbed like the national debt under Obama. I remember watching the impacts on the cement roof as they walked in a spaced pattern from downrange to directly over our heads, just like in the movies. There were Russians diving under the tables and screaming words in Russian that no doubt would have gotten their asses swatted with a wooden spoon if my mother had been there.

Finally, the magazine ran dry and it got very still in that tunnel. After about thirty seconds of silence, a very pissed off Russian took the gun and our handler led us out of the shooting tunnel and upstairs to the bar, ending the shooting for the day.

▲ Machine guns are very good at turning ammunition into empty cases very quickly.

The point is, except in very experienced hands a machine gun can become an uncontrolled animal. The recoil is not a one-time event, and the muzzle will try to climb off the target. Forget all that Rambo crap you saw on television; the best machine gun shooters work with bursts, not rock 'n' roll. Besides, at full rock 'n' roll, a stick magazine empties very, very quickly. Unless your gun is belt fed, you will be at slide lock, wondering what the hell happened, in a blink of an eye.

To become skilled with a machine gun requires hours and hours of practice, burning up thousands of rounds of ammo. Even if you do that, you will still have more control and probably be more efficient in a fight if you shoot with the select-fire option on semi-auto. This allows you to aim each shot and know with some precision where it will impact. Semiauto allows you to pick your targets and make each shot count. Sure, it's slower at going bang-bang than just spraying with full-auto, but if you want every shot to hit a designated target, semiauto is the way to go. Most of the experienced Elite Forces guys I know who have a lot of combat experience will almost always work with the semiauto setting when the goal is to kill the bad guys with some precision. Full-auto is fine for suppressing fire, but when you want to shoot and kill people who are trying to kill you, semiauto is usually better.

Don't assume it will be slow. While you will not be pouring as much lead out of the barrel, it's possible to do very fast aimed shots with a semiauto. For example, one of the practice drills we do is the 2x2x2 drill, proving that a semiauto can move bullets out of the barrel very fast.

The drill is three targets, usually about five to seven yards from the shooter, but that can vary. Start with the gun in the low ready position, the way you would have a rifle if you were exiting a vehicle or perhaps moving through a building. At the buzzer you raise the rifle and shoot each target twice, for a total of six shots. Almost any shooter can do it in two to three seconds and with practice can learn to do this in about 1.6–1.7 seconds. The very best will shave a few tenths of a second off that. My personal best is 1.3 seconds. Kyle Lamb, a former Delta operator with the Army and one of the top trainers in the country, has a video of doing it in 1.26 seconds. Remember, to count, every single shot must hit the scoring ring on the target, signifying a kill zone hit. That is, reacting to the buzzer and then putting six shots on three targets, all hitting the kill zone in 1.25 seconds. So let me ask you, do you see anything slow about that?

For the record, I recently participated in a 3-gun match that had a stage starting with a similar set up. There were three targets at about five yards. The shooter was given a full-auto AK-74 with ten rounds loaded. The goal was to have at least two hits on each of the three targets. An amazing number of competitors failed. Most of those who succeeded slowed down and worked the trigger for short bursts. Those I watched who flattened the trigger and emptied the magazine in a single burst all missed. Because the hits counted, I am sure that every single one of them could have gone faster with their semiauto competition rifles.

The great thing is that as long as you don't live in one of the more restrictive states, buying and owning the best semiauto fighting rifles is easy. If you do live in a place like California, New York, or Connecticut, my best advice is to move. You don't want to be there when the TSHTF anyway.

# RIFLES

## Battle Rifles

*Pay attention—this might be the most important chapter for preppers.*

O kay, so let's get this out of the way right now before you all start writing me letters or trashing my book on the Internet. I know that the traditional use of the term "battle rifle" is for 30-caliber, full-power, full-size military rifles. The purists won't even include the AR-10 and think it has to be an M1 Garand, M14, or some other huge gun that you can use for the center pole of a tent when you are not fighting.

It's all a matter of perspective, and the 30-caliber cutoff is arbitrary. When the Army switched to the .30–40 Krag and gave up on the .45–70, it might have been argued that the Krag was an intermediate cartridge by comparison and true battle rifles used 45-caliber bul-

lets. Now the 30-caliber is the big-bore and the 5.56 is the intermediate cartridge. It's just the times we live in, and those times are changing.

I once showed up for a "battle rifle" match with a DPMS AP4 in .308 with a Swarovski 1–6X scope. I called ahead and was assured it was fine, but when I got there a few people complained. One guy was dressed in full World War II battle uniform, including helmet and canteen, with a Garand, of course. He tried to stop me from shooting. In the end cooler heads prevailed and we started the match. I was on track to win when I made a big mistake and completely tanked a stage. I wound up in second and the guy with the Garand was below that by quite a bit. I think it proves

▲ The battle rifle of World War II is not the battle rifle of today.

▲ Who is to say that this DPMS AP4 .308 is not a battle rifle? It's more effective than a lot of the antiquated traditional battle rifles.

that mine was a better "battle rifle" than his. Also, he looked like a dork.

Besides, this ain't the US Army. We are civilians and we play by our own rules. You will find a bunch of stuff in this book that is not locked into the tactical-Nazis vernacular, particularly the military history side of things. Part of that is because I am not too deep into that world and don't know every nuanced term about every military gun ever made. But a bigger part of it is that I am not going to play the "me too" game. Too many writers just repeat what they read and that's how myths and misconceptions get started. I prefer to blaze my own trail and actually shoot the guns I am writing about, or at least I will tell you if I have little or no experience with them. In that case, I have a huge list of resources to research from, including some very knowledgeable people who are consulting on this book.

Besides, those guns are passé. No American uses those rifles in war anymore, except in very limited circumstances. The majority of our fighting forces use the M4 or other 5.56-chambered rifles for fighting. So are they not also battle rifles by definition? They sure see a lot of trigger time in battle.

Well, they are considered battle rifles in this book. For lack of a better term, that's what I am calling your personal defensive rifles, even those in sub30-caliber cartridges. If TSHTF, these are the rifles with which you will be defending your home, family, and your own life. If that's not the modern-day definition of a civilian battle rifle, I don't know what is.

This section will take a look at battle rifles, long-range sniper type rifles, scout rifles, and even some options like lever-actions. Yup, just like the cowboys used. Even today they still have their place with preppers.

I'll explore rifles from the .50 BMG to the .22 LR. You can't get much more diverse than that.

As you might assume, I offer some thoughts on the traditional "battle rifles" as well.

▲ This is what a modern-day battle rifle looks like from the business end.

# Basic Black

*A black rifle may be the key to survival for preppers.*

What exactly is a black gun? I think the conventional wisdom is that the term probably started out to define the AR-15 rifle and all its variants. But that definition is malleable and has mutated as these guns have become a bigger part of modern culture. Right now it has multiple meanings, many of which depend on the point of view of the person using the term. The media, the nanny staters, and the left-leaning weenies have a much different definition than I do.

For example, when I Googled *"black gun,"* the Urban Dictionary came up with this definition:

*In gun collector terminology Black guns are: AKs, ARs, MAC-10s, GSGs, etc. generally the "scary"* *assault/automatic guns normal people are afraid of.*

*"When my friend saw a black gun for the first time he wet his pants."*

Never mind that whoever wrote this doesn't have a clue. For example, the MAC-10 is the perpetual whipping boy of the anti-gun faction. They fail to understand that Military Armament Corporation (the MAC in MAC-10) went out of business almost four decades ago. The gun has been out of production in any recognizable form for almost thirty years and any transferable guns remaining are selling for as much as a used Prius. I can remember a member of Congress during one of the endless debates about banning guns saying the MAC-10 should be banned because it was the gun of choice for drug lords. When questioned on where he got that information, he proudly stated that he saw it on *Miami Vice*; so let's not let the antis define black guns for us. Besides, the MAC-10 was a pistol, so it's outside the realm of a black rifle.

The bigger point is that the anti-gun faction's almost universal lack of understanding of anything to do with guns would lead me to suspect that their definition of "normal people" will be much different than mine or yours as well.

We know that a normal person will not have an unrealistic fear of any inanimate object. I tend to believe that the circles I travel in are populated by pretty normal folks and when the people I know see a black gun, they do not wet their pants.

Well, that's not 100 percent true, one buddy starts to drool, which often will pool on his pants if he is sitting, making it look like . . . well, you get the picture. It's lust that's causing the wet spot, not fear.

My larger point is that the definition of a black gun belongs to the gun guys, not the media and the anti-gun people. Right now, black guns are hip and happening. They are gaining huge popularity with shooters and are probably the only rifle category that has recently seen their demand outstripping the supply.

So what's a black gun? Well, as I am the one writing this book, I suppose my definition is relevant. Of course, the term refers to the AR rifles, but I think it also includes guns like the AK, SKS, FAL, and any other magazine-fed, semiauto rifle. So guns like the Beretta CX4 Storm carbine or the Ruger Mini-14 might be included. I think we should include the M14, but if we are going to do that, shouldn't we also include the Garand, even though it's not technically magazine-fed? After all, that rifle was the father of the brood.

I believe in being all-inclusive, and I would think that any semiauto rifle designed originally for battle or defense would qualify. I think the primary black gun will still be the AR-15 and its variants, so this section will focus heavily on those guns, but the term is pretty inclusive within a given class of rifles.

They don't even have to be black! It's a definition, not a color scheme. AR-15 rifles come in a wide range of colors, including camo, but they are still black rifles at heart. Many of the other rifles will have wood furniture, but they still maintain black gun status.

Black guns were born in battle, but they have been proven to be the gun of choice in many circumstances for hunting, competition shooting, personal defense, and simple "plinking," or shooting for the sheer joy of shooting. But from a prepper's standpoint, they are a very important class of gun. The black gun is the primary gun for preppers. It's perhaps the only gun to consider during times of huge social unrest. If you are fighting off a large group of hostiles, the semiauto, magazine-fed battle rifle is your best chance for survival.

Well, I suppose your best chance for survival is to call in an airstrike or at least have a mini-gun or a SAW. But for civilians who for now must suffer under the repressive laws of this country, the best "legal" and affordable options are found in this category of guns.

The black gun is also versatile enough that in addition to being used for defense, it can work very well for hunting and foraging. The "black rifles" as we are discussing them here come as close to being universal survival guns as anything we can find.

Back in 1976 when Mel Tappan wrote his book, *Survival Guns*, the options for civilians were very limited. In fact, he only listed six semiauto battle rifles, and of those only one was AR-style: the Colt AR-15. Of the six, I think only the Ruger Mini-14 is still a viable option for civilians. Times change, but in this case they changed for the better. Despite our "of the people" government's efforts to disarm us, today we have so

▲ Black guns are the key to surviving TEOTWAWKI.

many options for black rifles that I would not even consider trying to list them all.

I can remember not so many years ago that the SHOT Show, the premiere gun industry trade show, would not allow any black rifles or banners or signs showing black rifles. They fought the trend, but the people spoke and black guns became too big to ignore. Today black rifles are a big part, perhaps the dominant part, of this huge show.

The black gun boom in this country has been enormous. The result is that we now have so many black gun makers that it would take half this book just to list their names and addresses. Somebody is buying these guns to keep all these companies in business. If you are smart about prepping, you will buy some too.

Shooting is fun, but it's always more fun with a black gun. I don't care who you are, if you can rattle off a magazine from an AR and not have a huge smile on your face, well then you are just not a normal person.

AR-style rifles have even become mainstream in hunting. They will work well for anything from prairie dogs to black bears. I shot an 1,800-pound Asian water buffalo with an AR-15 in .450 Bushmaster. My friend Randy Luth, the founder of DPMS, has hunted the world with AR rifles. Some of the game he has taken with an AR includes Dall sheep, African leopard, and, most recently, an Alaskan brown bear, on top of countless deer, bears, elk, and other game.

The AR is also just about the perfect rifle for culling coyotes or for hunting hogs, which proves its worth for preppers for foraging. I am going to be pretty damn hungry before any coyote steaks are on my grill, but hogs are delicious.

"Black" is the preferred rifle for 3-gun competition, as well as other shooting sports like High Power. They can be competitive in long-range precision shooting, as these black rifles have proven to be extremely accurate.

Competition is good training for preppers. You may read otherwise on the Internet, as it's become one of those perpetual arguments that seem to fuel cyberspace, but those arguing against it are almost always cops or trainers who are afraid to shoot in front of an audience. Read into that what you may. I would love to see one of the detractors of competition, the guys who keep saying that "competition will get you killed on the street," show up and shoot a few matches, but that never happens. They argue from a position of ignorance.

Most of the guys I know who make their living exchanging gunfire with bad guys think that competition is a good training ground for surviving a gun fight. Consider that many military and law enforcement agencies use competition as training for their people who go into harm's way. For example, the Army Marksmanship Unit exists in part to test guns and techniques in competition to assess their viability in combat. Some of the techniques that were developed and perfected in 3-gun competition were taught to soldiers fighting in Iraq and Afghanistan and are credited with saving a lot of lives in combat.

▲ The black gun is the best choice for hunting, foraging, and fighting.

▲ Competition shooting is excellent training.

▲ Building an AR-15.

In my never-humble opinion, when it comes to home defense there is no better rifle than a black gun, and when the zombie apocalypse finally comes, this is the only rifle that will see you through alive.

If you are a tinkerer, the black rifles, particularly the AR, are the ultimate kit guns. The additions, changes, parts, pieces, and bolt-on accessories are just about limitless. The guns are easy to work on and are user-friendly for a home gunsmith. You can build one from scratch or just switch out parts to show your individuality.

Check the sales records for centerfire rifle cartridges and you will find that the .223 Remington is number one, while the .308 Winchester is right on its heels. Any ammo maker will tell you that is because of the rapidly expanding popularity of black guns. But those two are hardly the limits of cartridge options, and black rifles can be chambered in cartridges ranging from the .17 HMR through fire-breathing dragon stompers.

As for the guns, it's not all ARs. I once had the pleasure of spending an afternoon with General Mikhail Kalashnikov at his home in Russia. His design, the AK-47, and its variants are probably the second most popular semiauto rifles in the United States. The relatively inexpensive surplus rifles on the market are fun to shoot and easy to work. Now that these imports are drying up due to the Obama administration's efforts to damage the gun industry, we are seeing a lot of AK-style guns being newly manufactured for the US market.

I recently built an FN FAL from parts and discovered another iconic black rifle. Actually, the list of black guns is almost as long as the list of cartridges. But the one universal truth for preppers is that these guns will be the key to survival.

The bottom line is simple. Every serious prepper should have at least one magazine-fed, semiauto, battle-born black rifle if they have any plans to get through what's coming alive.

# Your First AR

*Picking your personal long gun.*

 Your personal rifle is an important decision. It may be the single biggest factor for survival.

*M*ost gun guys know that Eugene "Gene" Stoner created the AR-15 rifle. Students of gun history also know that he developed the larger .308 Winchester–based AR-10 first. But what a lot of people don't know is that if the AR-10 submitted to the government for testing in 1956 had remained true to the Stoner design, things might have turned out differently.

Stoner was an engineer for ArmaLite, and the company president, George Sullivan, against strong protest by Stoner, insisted that they submit a gun for testing that was fitted with an unproven aluminum/steel composite barrel. The barrel burst during the test and the government rejected the AR-10 in favor of the M14 rifle.

It would be interesting to speculate about what would have happened if management had listened to their paid expert and submitted the gun with a steel barrel. Perhaps the AR-10 would have been chosen as the new battle rifle for the United States. It was shorter and lighter than the M14 and probably have received high praise from our fighting forces. If that happened and it became the military's standard fighting rifle, then perhaps the military never would have ended up with the M16 and we civilians would probably not be shooting the AR-15.

History, however, took a different course. No doubt the M14 is a great rifle, but some will argue it was antiquated for military use the day it was born. It wasn't long before the M16 replaced it and through a long and interesting journey that has accelerated exponentially in recent years, the AR-15 civilian version of that rifle has become the most popular long gun in America.

The name AR-15 is owned by Colt, but has come to be used as a generic term for any firearm of this type. When somebody says they have an AR-15, everybody knows the basic gun they are talking about. The accepted definition of AR-15 in common use today is the civilian semiauto version of the military's M16 platform.

The AR-15 is a lightweight (relatively speaking) intermediate-cartridge, magazine-fed, air-cooled rifle with a rotating locking bolt. The action is actuated by direct impingement gas operation or piston operation. It is typically manufactured with extensive use of aluminum alloys and synthetic materials.

The AR-15 was first built in 1959 by ArmaLite as a small arms rifle for the United States armed forces. ArmaLite had money troubles, so it sold the design to Colt. Colt redesigned the rifle and the government adopted it as the M16 rifle.

Colt started selling the semiautomatic version of the rifle for civilians in 1963 as the Colt AR-15. It took a while to catch on, but right now the AR-15 is the most popular rifle in America. Colt is not even a major player anymore in this market, where hundreds of different companies manufacture (or at least assemble) and sell AR-style rifles.

The design variations are almost infinite, and just when you think there is nothing left to change, redesign, or introduce in the AR-15 world, somebody comes up with something new.

To cover all of today's AR-15 rifles and carbines in a single book would be all but impossible. There are too many and the market is changing so fast that the information would be outdated before the book is published, and I will not be so foolish as to attempt to cover them all here. It doesn't matter anyway. Most of the guns being made today are good. They run well and have few problems. It is best left to the individual users to decide which gun maker is best for them. If you stick with a proven brand name, it's hard to make a mistake.

I truly believe that in a survival situation where we may be attacked by multiple attackers, terrorists, or an out-of-control mob, the magazine-fed battle rifle is the best tool for survival and an AR-15 is the best battle rifle of choice.

There are a lot of variations, but the most important AR that preppers can buy is their personal rifle, the gun they will carry every day—the gun that may be called on to save their lives.

## Your Personal AR-15

Each prepper will need, at the very minimum, a personal handgun and a personal rifle. Even as you buy more guns and build your survival battery, these will remain your primary guns.

▲ Your personal rifle is the key to survival. Learn to shoot it well. Learn to shoot it fast. Learn to trust it.

A general use rifle is something you will carry every day during a survival situation. It should be lightweight enough that it's not a huge burden. While the AR-15 concept was for a lightweight, six-pound rifle, weights have crept up over the years, and it's not unusual for a gun to weigh close to ten pounds today.

I find that unacceptable in an everyday carry and use rifle. In a survival situation you will probably already be carrying a pistol or two as well as extra magazines

▲ The M4-style of AR-15 is the most popular today and will serve well as a primary defensive long gun. You can customize it to fit your personal needs.

for both guns, a knife, Leatherman-style belt tool, and a lot of other gear. If your rifle is so heavy that you hate it, it won't be long before you are finding reasons to leave it behind. Rifles are like fire extinguishers; when you need one you really need one, and you cannot predict when that will be. If you left it behind because it's heavy, it's a good bet that things will not end well.

Probably the most popular design today mimics the military M4, and that is likely the best option for an off-the-rack personal long gun.

The civilian M4 style copies the popular, select-fire carbine used by the military and is probably the type of gun that most preppers should buy for their first primary rifle. The M4 has a short barrel, usually sixteen inches, so it's legal. Our government long ago picked that as an arbitrary allowable length for a rifle barrel. Any shorter and it falls under the purview of the National Firearms Act. That means you must pay a $200 tax and register the gun with the government.

A short barrel is good for moving in and out of vehicles or for use inside buildings, but I don't see the point in picking one shorter than sixteen inches for a prepper. It brings little to the table, and it will reduce velocity and increase muzzle blast. It will also require that the gun be registered with the government, which I think is a mistake. It's legal now, but the lower under the radar you can fly, the better. We cannot predict the future or what our government will do in a crisis. If they start confiscating guns, any registered under the NFA will be a good place to start. I would not risk being noticed just to have a legal short barrel rifle. There are other options, such as the AR-15 pistols explored in another section.

The adjustable stock works well with body armor or bulky clothing and can reduce the length of the carbine to make it easier to maneuver. It will also allow a wide range of shooters to use the gun, as any shooter can pick a length of pull that fits best. Usually in a personal gun, you will just set it and be done, but it does keep some options in reserve.

Most M4-style rifles will run on one side or the other of seven pounds, depending on who makes it and how much bling comes with it. For me, the closer to six pounds the gun gets, the happier I am.

Don't forget, you will be adding optics and a full magazine to the basic rifle's weight. Not to mention a

▲ This custom-built ultra-lightweight AR-15 is a good everyday carry gun. But, it's not designed for sustained firefights.

flashlight, laser, or any other accessory that you may want to bolt on. It all adds up.

I have a couple of lightweight rifles that I have built. One is less than five pounds and the other is a bit over. They are easy to carry, shoot well, and are not a bad choice for an everyday carry gun. In terms of how they shoot, I did the 2x2x2 drill with one of them in 1.5 seconds, which is about as good as it gets in terms of close and fast. Of course, these are custom guns that I built in my shop. You can buy similar guns commercially, but they tend to be expensive. One lightweight rifle I can highly recommend is the JP Enterprises SCR-11 Ultra-Light. This gun weighs only five pounds, twelve ounces, and like all JP Enterprises rifles it is superbly made and very accurate.

Just keep in mind that these ultra-light rifles will have very thin barrels and are not well suited for a sustained firefight.

If you are stocking up on rifles for uses other than to carry every day, then weight and a short barrel become less of an issue.

## Muzzle Brake or Flash Hider?

The uninformed often question why a recoil-reducing muzzle brake is needed on a rifle chambered in a low recoil cartridge like the .223 Remington. A muzzle brake will help keep your gun on target for fast follow-up shots. There was a time when I thought it was the best way to go in a fighting gun and actually wrote some articles about that, but I have since changed my mind. They do make the gun faster to operate, and in

▲ A muzzle brake at the moment of firing.

that aspect a muzzle brake is an advantage in battle. But they are loud—very loud—particularly for anybody off to the side of the shooter. This can be a huge problem in a fight. If everybody has ear protection it will be fine, but usually they will not.

I have come to the conclusion that the benefits of a muzzle brake do not outweigh the problems they create on a battle rifle. I have removed the brakes from my defense guns. Of course, I still have a brake on all of the competition rifles that I use for 3-gun shooting, but they are simply too loud for a fighting gun. The idea of ever firing an AR-15 with a muzzle brake inside a small room without hearing protection makes my eardrums spasm.

Flash hiders (often called flash suppressors) are also loud, but not as loud as muzzle brakes. Some of them also help to mitigate recoil and muzzle flip a little bit. Most of the guns in this M4 category are going to be equipped with a flash hider. I am not sure that they bring a lot of benefit to the table. They might help hide the primary flash if you have low-flash ammo to start with, but much of the ammo out there in 5.56 and .223 is anything but low-flash. I have seen muzzle flash in an AR-15 carbine ranging from barely noticeable to bright and big enough to sear your retinas. Some of the imported ammo looks like a solar flare when the gun fires. The good stuff might benefit from a flash hider; but much of the imported and cheap ammo is hopeless. Muzzle flash really comes down to ammo and the propellant used more than a flash hider. Other

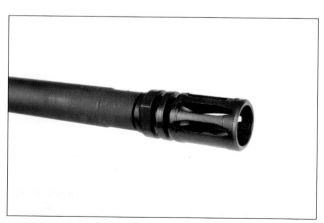

▲ Muzzle brakes are too loud for fighting guns.

▲ This is a typical "squirrel cage" style flash hider that is the standard for AR-15 rifles.

than making the gun a bit noisier, a flash hider doesn't hurt anything. They do help protect the muzzle from damage, which can be a big asset in a hard-working rifle. On the downside, they make the gun and barrel longer and add a slight amount of weight.

In terms of shooting I can't see that a flash hider changes much. My best time ever on the 2x2x2 drill was 1.3 seconds with a JP Enterprises JP15 competition rifle with a JP brake. I recently shot that same drill in 1.5 seconds, using a lightweight rifle with nothing on the muzzle except a cap to protect the threads.

Clearly a flash hider is absolutely necessary for marketing. Sales fall off when an AR maker takes them off a tactical gun. They might help a little in reducing flash, which might be an issue in a fight, and they may mitigate recoil-induced muzzle movement a little bit. But if you find a great deal on a gun that has everything you want except a flash hider, buy it; you aren't missing much.

## Triggers

▲ You can only shoot any rifle as well as its trigger allows.

I am a trigger snob. You can only shoot any rifle as well as its trigger allows, and most guns that come with a mil-spec trigger fail the test.

A lot of AR-15 makers are putting very good triggers in their guns today, but it's not universal. A mil-spec trigger keeps the price lower and in some cases it's actually a marketing point with uninformed "tactards."

However, to run the rifle at its potential, not just for accuracy, but for speed as well, you need a good trigger. If your gun comes with a trigger pull that is not clean and crisp and less than five or six pounds pull weight, you should replace it.

The glory of the AR-15 rifle is that it's the perfect "kit" gun for do-it-yourselfers. The single most important thing you can add to most AR-15s is a better trigger. There are a bunch of aftermarket triggers out now, and the competition is driving the price down on some of them.

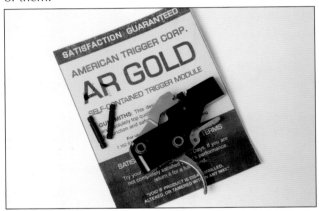

▲ There are a lot of aftermarket triggers for the AR.

A safe trigger does not mean a hard trigger. You can set up any AR-15 with a three-pound trigger that is safe. The difference is, when you need to make that 300-yard headshot with precision, you can.

## Slings

▲ The author's friend, Eric Reynolds, exits a truck with an AR-15 on a sling.

I like a simple, two-point sling on my AR, one like Kyle Lamb's Viking Tactics VTAC sling. Single-point slings are cool to stand around and look badass with, but they suck if you have to do anything else.

Some of the multi-point slings are just too damn complicated. You need a PhD to install, and use them, and they have too many straps running in too many directions.

A simple two-point with a quick release is, in my opinion, the way to go. It's also what Randall Curtis, a

consultant for this book and a long-time Delta guy for the Army, suggested. Who am I to argue?

When he said "None of my guys would use a single point sling in combat," I figured it was settled.

## Sights

▲ The Swarovski Z6 1–6X is a great all-around optic for any AR.

Your personal gun will need a good sighting system. There are a lot of optics on the market, and it's tough to say which is best. The 1–6X scopes that are popular with 3-gun shooters work well. Traditional battle optics include Trijicon ACOG or Aimpoint sights, which are both good choices.

I know that the "tactards" get apoplectic if you suggest that a rifle not have backup iron sights, or BUIS as they like to call them. (They do love their acronyms.) For most uses, I don't think you need them.

▲ EOTech and backup, flip-up iron sights.

▲ The best thing to spend your money on is ammo. Practice makes perfect.

That said, they do make sense on your primary survival rifle. I like the flip-up kind so they stay out of my way unless I need them. You can co-witness them if you have a non-magnifying optic and use them with the optic mounted. It's also a good idea to mount any primary sighting system with a quick release mount. That way you can jettison it in battle if it becomes disabled and use the irons.

## Ammo

The very best accessory for you to spend your money on is ammo. Practice and train with your gun until you know it backwards and forwards. Know the offsets from point blank range out to 600 yards, so you don't have to think when you shoot. (Offsets are where you must hold on the target that is over or under the expected point of impact, depending on the distance.) This is the gun most likely to keep you alive, so run it hard, and find any flaws or defects early. Make it prove itself to be dependable and then learn it like it's your best friend, because it may well be.

# The "Other" AR-15 Cartridges

*The AR-15 may well be the most important gun for preppers.*
*There is no doubt that the best cartridge is the .223/5.56, but there are other options.*

I think it's safe to say that the AR-15 is the most popular centerfire rifle in America today. By far the top cartridge for this gun is the .223/5.56. It dominates the rifle and it should be the first cartridge of choice for any prepper buying an AR-15 style rifle for survival. That's because it will be much easier to find ammo and magazines in a crisis situation, particularly ammo. This is the most popular centerfire rifle cartridge in America today, it's a NATO round, and it's used by law enforcement. That means if any ammo at all is available, it will likely be .223 Remington or 5.56 NATO. Smart preppers will have at least one gun for every member of their party chambered for the 5.56 NATO cartridges.

That said, the list of available cartridges for the AR-15 is pretty extensive. You may want to look at a few more options. It makes sense to have multiple uppers or

▲ L to R: .17 Remington, .204 Ruger, 5.45x39, .223 Remington, .223 WSSM, .243 WSSM, 6.5 Grendel, and 6.8 SPC.

extra guns to handle various chores like foraging for big game. Also, you never know what you will run into for ammo. Suppose you are out of .223 ammo, but you run into a black market guy with a boatload of 6.8 SPC or .300 AAC Blackout? It can happen; both are popular cartridges. However, if you don't have a firearm that can use these cartridges, they have no value.

Clearly you can't buy a gun in every cartridge available, but it makes sense to have some back up with one or more alternatives to the .223/5.56 mainstay.

Of course, you can find the AR-15 in rimfires like the .22 LR or the .17 Hornday Magnum Rimfire (HMR), but it's a centerfire gun at heart. Here is a look at some of the cartridges other than the .223 you can find in the AR-15.

## .17 Remington

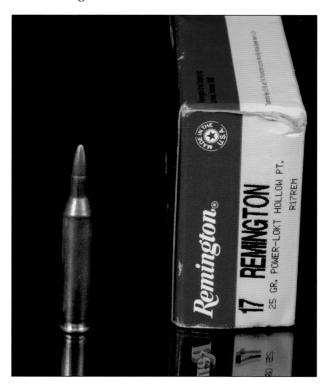

When this cartridge was introduced in 1971 it was the fastest thing anyone had seen. With Remington factory ammo, a 25-grain hollow-point bullet has a muzzle velocity (MV) of 4,040 feet per second (ft/s) while the newer 20-grain AccuTip load is flying at 4,250 ft/s.

Bullet impacts at this kind of velocity turn predators into puddles.

While not much of a fighting cartridge, the .17 Remington would be handy for pest control. However, the ammo is very expensive, very hard to find, and can't do anything that other cartridges can't do better.

The .17 Remington is notorious for fouling barrels, and it requires specialty tools to clean and maintain. It really brings nothing to the table for a prepper, and unless there are other compelling reasons, like an offer so good you can't refuse it, buying a .17 Remington makes little sense.

## .204 Ruger

The .204 Ruger is currently the highest velocity centerfire rifle cartridge in production by a major ammo maker. Hornady originated the cartridge and has the load with the fastest muzzle velocity. It's a 24-grain NTX bullet with a muzzle velocity of 4,400 ft/s. The 32-grain bullets run about 4,200 and the 40-grainers move out at 3,900. Hornady also has a 45-grain bullet with a MV of 3,625 ft/s.

My AR in .204 Ruger has a 24-inch barrel. It will put most bullets into less than ½ MOA (minute of angle) and it absolutely wrecks coyotes.

This cartridge has moderate popularity, so ammo is relatively easy to find. It's no better than a .223 for fighting, and the ammo is far more expensive. But if you are looking for an alternative, just to be different, it's a good cartridge that runs well in an AR-type rifle. Or perhaps you have another gun, a bolt-action for example, chambered for the .204 Ruger and have a good supply of ammo. Then it makes sense to buy a gun or at least an upper in .204 Ruger.

## 5.45x39

This was Russia's answer to the 5.56 NATO and was developed in 1974 for use with the new AK-74 rifle. Hornady, Wolf, and TulAmmo all offer newly manufactured expanding bullet ammo. Wolf and TulAmmo have 60-grain HP bullets with a MV of 2,960 ft/s. Hornady loads a 60-grain V-Max at 2,810. All of these loads use a Berdan primed, non-reloadable steel case.

This is a decent fighting cartridge and at times ammo is cheap and easy to find. Right now it's not, but that can change with the political winds. There are guns in AR-15 for this cartridge, and having one or an upper available is not a bad idea. Also, the AK-74 rifles are chambered in this cartridge.

Olympic Arms makes hunting rifles in all three of the Winchester Super Short Magnum Cartridges: .223, .243, and .25. Winchester makes the ammo.

Winchester and Browning no longer make rifles chambered in these cartridges, so the availability of ammo is limited and probably does not have a bright future.

All three would be deadly in a fight and can serve for foraging and hunting, but magazine capacity is limited. Also, in the guns I have used, reliability is a bit spotty with these cartridges.

If you happen to own the guns already, they will have a place in survival, but there is no compelling reason for a prepper to rush out and buy a new AR in a WSSM cartridge.

## .223 WSSM

Factory loads for the .223 WSSM drive a 55-grain Ballistic Silvertip bullet at 3,850 ft/s. That will stomp coyotes and bad guys flat where they stand. The 64-grain load has a MV of 3,600 ft/s and will work for hunting bigger game if you are so inclined.

I have taken several whitetail deer with this cartridge. While I do not recommend any 22-caliber for serious big game hunting, if I were to change that opinion this cartridge would be at the top of the list.

## .243 WSSM

With a 55-grain bullet at 4,060 ft/s this is a varmint- and predator-hunting machine. Turn loose a 100-grain at 3,110 ft/s and it's a death ray for deer and antelope.

## .25 WSSM

This is a .25–06 in an AR-15 rifle. The 115-grain bullet exits at 3,060 ft/s. Deer, antelope, or black bear, they're all covered. This could also work for long-range sniper defensive shooting if you have an accurate rifle.

## 6.5 Grendel

Created by Bill Alexander from Alexander Arms, the 6.5 Grendel is designed for precision long-range target work, but it's proven to be a good hunting and defense cartridge as well. Ammo is offered by Alexander Arms, Hornady, and Wolf. Bullet weights generally run 120 to 130 grains.

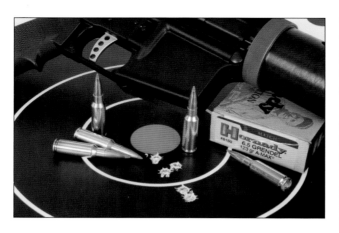

The popular Hornady ammo is available in two 123-grain bullets, the A-Max for targets and the SST for hunting. The MV is 2,580 ft/s from a 24-inch barrel and 2,350 from a 16-inch barrel.

This is a good cartridge, designed for the AR-15 platform. For long-range work using the AR-15, it's a top choice. It's also a good choice for battle as it hits harder than a .223.

Ammo is hard to find and expensive. But if you are willing to lay up a supply, this is a pretty good alternative cartridge for the AR-15. You will need magazines specific to the cartridge.

## 6.8 SPC

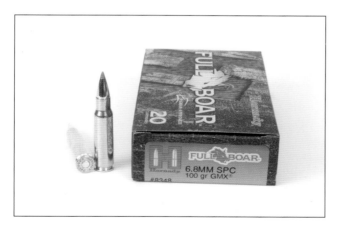

The 6.8 SPC has a checkered history, and as far as I can tell, there are currently four different chamber designs for the cartridge.

It uses a .277-inch bullet, the same as the famed .270 Winchester. The Hornady load with a 110-grain

V-Max bullet has a muzzle velocity of 2,550 ft/s from a 16-inch barrel. They also load a 120-grain SST bullet at 2,460 from a 16-inch. Remington, Silver State Armory, Wilson Combat, and others have other ammo available with a wide range of bullet options.

This cartridge was designed for battle by experienced military people. It brings a bit more "whack" to the AR-15 rifle with little compromise. It can reach out at long range reasonably well and it hits hard in a fight. The 6.8 SPC is an acceptable cartridge for foraging deer-sized big game, particularly if you pick good bullets. I have taken several whitetail deer and a mountain lion with this cartridge.

I think the 6.8 SPC represents a very good choice as an alternative cartridge in the AR-15. Ammo is reasonably easy to find and affordable. While it was initially said that standard magazines would work, this cartridge usually requires dedicated magazines to operate reliably.

## .300 AAC Blackout

This one is new and in vogue right now, and just about everybody is jumping on the bandwagon. It was originally developed by J.D. Jones to use with heavy bullets weighing 200 grains or more, running subsonic and suppressed. He called it the .300 Whisper. If you are looking for a subsonic, suppressed AR rifle to use for foraging, pest control, and defense of your property, this is the cartridge for you.

Advanced Armament took the design, claimed it as their own, and called it the AAC Blackout. With a lighter, supersonic bullet like a 125-grain at 2,250 ft/s, it is getting a lot of interest as a defensive and hunting round. While there are those who will no doubt disagree, I am not a huge fan of this cartridge for deer or hogs. It will work, but the chance of a wounding loss is too high to depend on it for survival. However, for smaller game or home defense it is excellent.

This is another cartridge that is a very good choice as a secondary gun in the AR-15 platform. It plays well with standard magazines.

## .30 Remington AR

This is a necked down .450 Bushmaster cartridge, which provides ballistics that are similar to the .300 Savage. Muzzle velocity for a 125-grain bullet is 2,800 ft/s, and it runs at 2,575 ft/s for a 150-grain bullet. This is the highest performing 30-caliber cartridge in commercial use in the AR-15 rifle.

Remington has not done a great job of supporting this cartridge, and no other major ammo maker has made ammo. Ballistically it's a good choice, particularly for foraging and perhaps for sniper work in defense of your home. But unless you stockpile ammo and magazines and/or handload for it, it might be better to pick a different cartridge for survival.

## .300 Olympic Super Short Magnum (OSSM)

Olympic Arms developed a 30-caliber cartridge by necking up the WSSM case. They are reporting 3,040 ft/s with a 150-grain bullet. That means the cartridge is outperforming the .30–06 from an AR-15 rifle. This is a proprietary cartridge available only from Olympic Arms and probably has little value to a prepper.

## 7.62x39

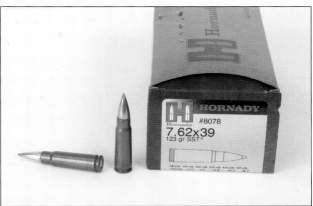

This is the cartridge that made the AK-47 famous. It's been around in AR-type rifles for many years. The 7.62x39 has a 125-grain, 0.311-inch bullet with a muzzle velocity of 2,365 ft/s from a 24-inch barrel. This makes it adequate for deer hunting if quality, soft-point bullets are used. Of course, its pedigree as a battle round is well documented.

This cartridge has always been a bit problematic in an AR-15 because the magazine design is incompatible with the cartridge design, but that is being addressed in guns like the new CMMG Mutant. The 7.62x39 is extremely popular, and ammo is plentiful and inexpensive. While it's designed for the AK-47, a fine gun every prepper should consider owning, when chambered in a gun like the CMMG Mutant the performance is elevated to the next level.

▲ CMMG Mutant combines the AR platform with AK-type magazines and positive feeding.

The Mutant combines the best of the AR with the feeding of an AK to really make this cartridge shine. I have one, and so far it runs well and is very accurate. The Mutant uses AK magazines, which solves the problems associated with the AR and this cartridge. If you have the resources to do so, buying a CMMG Mutant makes sense for a prepper. It allows you to access the 7.65x39 ammo that is common in the United States but stay with the AR-style rifle. That gun is much better suited for an optic than an AK, and it's inherently much more accurate.

I highly recommend that any prepper have a gun or two in this cartridge—either an AK-47 variant, an AR-15, or the Mutant.

From here we step up to the big-bores, which are covered extensively in another chapter. They have a place with preppers, as explained in detail in that chapter.

# .223 Remington vs. 5.56x45 NATO

*What's in a name?*
*Quite a bit, actually.*
*Make no mistake; these are not the same cartridge.*

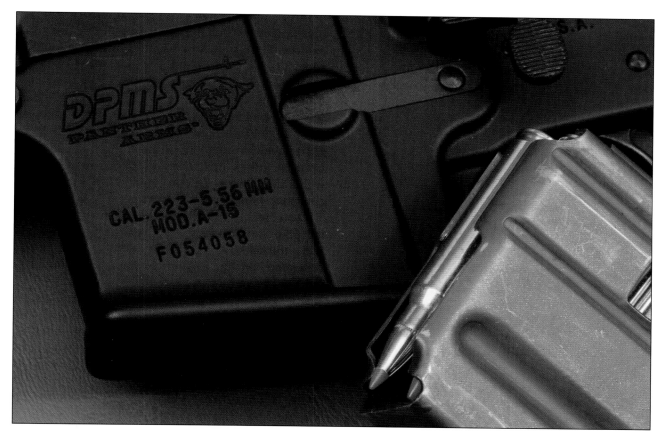

Most gun guys know the history of the .223 Remington and that, like so many of our popular cartridges, it started life in the military. Because the military switched to metric designations sometime in the '50s, this little 22-caliber cartridge was called the 5.56x45 NATO (commonly referred to as 5.56) when it was first introduced.

The 5.56 surfaced in 1957 as an experimental cartridge in the AR-15 rifle. The concept was to develop a smaller, lighter military cartridge that would still be traveling faster than the speed of sound at 500 yards, and they accomplished this by using a 55-grain boat-tail bullet. The Air Force was looking at the ArmaLite AR-15 rifle as a possible replacement for the M1 Carbine in 1960, and that probably opened the door to

the military. The AR-15 evolved into the selective fire M16 and was adopted by the military in 1964.

Even though it would ultimately all but kill off its .222 Remington and .222 Remington Magnum cartridges, Remington was quick to act and shortly after the military adopted the 5.56 cartridge, Big Green brought out the civilian version, called the .223 Remington.

Confusion followed.

The common misconception is that the 5.56 and .223 Remington are the same dance partner, but with a different dress. This can lead to a dangerous situation. The outside case dimensions are the same, but there are enough other differences to make the two not completely interchangeable.

One big difference is pressure. It becomes a bit confusing, as pressure is not measured in the same way for both cartridges. The .223 is measured with either copper units of pressure (CUP), or more recently with a mid-case transducer in pounds per square inch (PSI). The military 5.56 cartridge is measured with a case mouth transducer. The different measuring methods prevent a direct comparison, as a case mouth transducer gives lower numbers on identical ammo when compared to the mid-case transducer location. That's because the pressure is measured later in the event, after the pressure has already peaked.

Jeff Hoffman, the owner of Black Hills Ammunition, was a tremendous help in researching this subject. Jeff's company loads both 5.56 and .223 Remington, and he provided these pressure specifications for the cartridges. The .223 mid-case transducer maximum average pressure is 55,000 PSI. The 5.56 measured with a case mouth transducer has a maximum average pressure of 58,700 PSI. Jeff noted that 5.56 ammo can be expected to hit 60,000 PSI, if measured on a SAAMI (Sporting Arms and Ammunition Manufacturers' Institute) mid-case transducer system.

While the 5.56 chamber is slightly larger than the .223 Remington chamber in just about every dimension, the primary difference is throat length, which can have a dramatic effect on pressure. The 5.56 has a longer throat in the chamber than the .223 Remington. The throat is also commonly called the leade, which is defined as the portion of the barrel directly in front of the chamber where the rifling has been conically removed to allow room for the seated bullet. The leade in a .223 Remington chamber is usually 0.085-inch. In a 5.56 chamber the leade is typically 0.162-inch, or almost twice as long as in the .223 Remington cham-

ber. It is also notable that the throat angle is different with the two chambers and that can affect pressure rise and peak pressure.

SAAMI regulates cartridge overall length, but not bullet ogive design. The ogive shape can have a significant bearing on how far the bullet jumps before contacting the rifling. Some 5.56 bullets have an ogive suitable for 5.56 chambers with the longer throat, but if they were chambered in a .223 Remington, could result in very little, if any, "jump" to the rifling. This can drive up pressures. Remember, the 5.56 already starts out at a higher pressure. If the higher pressure 5.56 cartridge is then loaded into a .223 Remington firearm with a short throat, the combination of the two factors can cause raised chamber pressures.

If you are a handloader, you must also consider that the 5.56 cartridge case may have a thicker sidewall and a thicker head, designed to withstand the stresses generated by the higher chamber pressures. This reduces the powder capacity of the case. If the 5.56 case is reloaded with powder charges that have proven safe in .223 Remington cases, this reduced internal capacity can result in much higher chamber pressures.

**Bottom line?** It is safe to fire .223 Remington cartridges in any gun chambered for 5.56. However, *it is not recommended and it is not safe* to fire 5.56 cartridges in a firearm chambered for .223 Remington.

In fact, the 5.56 military cartridge fired in a .223 Remington chamber is considered by SAAMI to be an unsafe ammunition combination and is listed in the "Unsafe Arms and Ammunition Combinations" Section of the SAAMI Technical Correspondent's Handbook. It states, "In firearms chambered for .223 Rem.—do not use 5.56x45 Military cartridges."

There is no guarantee, however, that the .223 Remington ammo will work in the 5.56 rifle. Semiauto rifles that are chambered for 5.56 may not function with .223 Remington ammo, because they are designed to cycle reliably with the higher pressure and heavier bullets of the 5.56, particularly with short barrels. While problems are rare, they do not indicate that the ammo or rifle is defective. Like some marriages, they are simply incompatible.

It's likely that when shooting .223 Remington cartridges in a firearm chambered for 5.56 there will be degradation in accuracy and muzzle velocity due to the more generous chamber dimensions. That's not to say that a 5.56-chambered firearm won't be accurate with .223 Remington ammo, only that on average the .223 Remington–chambered firearms will be more accurate with .223 Remington ammo than the average of rifles chambered for 5.56 and firing .223 Remington ammo.

Another issue is the twist rate of the rifling. The SAAMI spec for .223 Remington is a 1:12 twist, and most non AR-15 type rifles will use that. But this is a cartridge that crosses a wide spectrum of use and as a result there is often a wide deviation from the 1:12 twist rate, particularly in the very popular AR-15 type black guns. There are bullets available for the .223 Remington that range in weight from at least 35 grains to 90 grains. With that wide of a spectrum, one twist rate is not going to be enough.

Firearms chambered for 5.56 often have a rifling twist rate of 1:7 to allow use of the long, sleek, heavy bullets for long-range use. This twist rate can cause lighter weight varmint bullets to spin apart in flight. The "hoop forces" generated by the high rate of spin on the bullet can cause the bullet to disintegrate soon after exiting the muzzle. I actually have a photo of a lightweight varmint bullet doing exactly that in flight from a 1:7 twist AR-style rifle. Any rifle with a 1:7 twist rate will work best with bullets heavier than 60 grains. On the other hand, a 1:12 twist rate (most bolt-action and other sporting .223 rifles) usually will stabilize

▲ The puff of gray downrange is a bullet disintegrating in flight. This is due to hoop forces generated by too fast a spin rate for the bullet and velocity.

most bullets up to 60 grains, although there are some longer 60-grain bullets that will not shoot well at that twist rate. Many firearms now use a 1:9 twist, which is a very good compromise that will work well with most bullets up to 70 or 75 grains. The great thing is that if you have a good barrel and quality bullets, the 1:9 works well with even the lightest bullets.

It's rare to encounter bullets that are heavier than 75 grains except in specialty ammo, but the light bullets are often loaded in varmint-hunting ammo, which is pretty common.

The best choice is a 1:9, as it will stabilize a wide range of bullets from the 75-grain down to the light 35- to 40-grain varmint bullets.

What does all this mean? If you have an AR-15 type firearm with a 5.56 chamber you can shoot .223 Remington or 5.56 safely. If your twist rate is 1:7 you should use bullets of 50 grains or heavier. If you have any rifle with a 1:12 twist you should shoot bullets of 60 grains or lighter for best accuracy. If you have a .223 Remington rifle of any type, it is not recommended that you use 5.56 ammo.

Any prepper should be aware of these issues when buying survival guns. All fighting guns should have a 5.56 chamber so that you can use any ammo available. It's also important that you be aware of the differences when reloading any cartridge cases. If you already have a .223-chambered rifle, don't rush out and trade or sell it. But if you are buying new guns with the primary focus on using them for defense, then you should consider getting them chambered in 5.56x45 NATO.

One other option is the Wylde chamber. This is a hybrid of the 5.56 and .223 Remington chambers. It is designed to shoot both cartridges while providing better accuracy than a 5.56 chamber. This is probably most important in a competition rifle or perhaps if you are planning on using your rifle for long-range shooting. I have tested two rifles from JP Enterprises using a Wylde chamber with .223 ammo, and the accuracy for both is outstanding. Both are capable of sub ½ MOA accuracy with Federal 69-grain factory ammo.

# Bludgeons, Brutes, and Thumpers: Big-Bore AR-15 Cartridges

*Cartridges that pound things that need pounding.*

▲ L to R: .450 Bushmaster, .458 Socom, and .50 Beowulf. These cartridges are the " sledge hammers" of AR-15 Cartridges.

In a survival situation it's always a good idea to have plenty of backup for every plan. Redundancy in your firearms ensures that you will always have something to work with. While the primary focus of our survival battle rifles should be those chambered for the most common and proven cartridges, a smart prepper does not stop there.

Clearly money is always a factor; most of us can't own one of every gun mentioned. The decisions for each prepper must be made on a personal level and based on the situation and expected needs. The goal of this book is to explore the options so you can decide what works best for your unique survival situation. Each of those is going to be different. Somebody who is way off the grid may have a lot more foraging options than an urban or even country prepper.

I have friends in Alaska who are so far off the grid that you truly can't get there from here. Visiting them means multiple plane rides and finding a boat to cover the last, very long leg. There are no roads and no commercial service of any kind. I expect that they will deal with foraging for game more than most of us. They will also have more problems with bears than with bad guys emptying out of the cities. My friend is a prepper, but his taste in survival rifles runs more to big-bore lever-action and bolt-action rifles than to AR-15s.

All preppers have to make their own choices, but the guns discussed in this chapter make a lot of sense on multiple levels for almost everybody. It's probably a good idea for any prepper to pick up a gun or upper and some spare magazines in one or more of these cartridges.

I see two big reasons to do that. First, depending on where you live, you may be foraging to find food. If part of that includes shooting wild big game or even cattle or hogs that have escaped captivity and become wild, then you should always bring enough guns.

If you are going to forage with your AR-15 in a fighting cartridge, it might end in disappointment. There is a lot of misinformation out there about hunting big game with typical AR-15 cartridges like the .223 Remington. Most of it is wrong.

The .223 Remington is, in my never-humble opinion, too small for any game deer-size or bigger under the best of circumstances. I base this on actually using it in the field a lot, not on what I read or on some internet theory. I have used the .223 on deer and hogs and found it lacking. Sure, using better bullets like the Barnes TSX, Hornady GMX, or Federal Trophy Bonded Tip will help, but you can't change physics and in the end it's a tiny bullet with a less than ideal amount of energy. I understand that a .223 Remington will kill deer or hogs, but it's not reliable.

It can and does kill these critters under perfect circumstances. But those promoting the cartridge for big game continuously and conveniently ignore the failures. If you are sport hunting and a wounded deer runs off, it's tragic, but you are not in danger as a result. If you are trying to feed your starving family and the deer, elk, wild cow, or whatever escapes after you wound it with an inadequate cartridge, it can be a very bad thing for all involved.

With the entire human population trying to survive and so many out hunting, game is going to become very scarce and very spooky. The longer a crisis goes on, the tougher it's going to be to find food by hunting. Every opportunity to shoot some protein will be very important. If you are sport hunting and blow it, you only have to deal with disappointment. This is called "survival" because failure means you may not survive. So, rather than forage with a marginal cartridge, it makes sense that on those days you know you are hunting to be using a rifle in a suitable cartridge.

So why not just use a bolt-action hunting rifle? If you are sure there is no possibility of running into problems, that might make sense. My buddy in Alaska will be pretty sure that he won't be facing a roaming gang of punks. But the rest of us, even those of us who live in or have retreated to remote areas, probably can't be sure.

We must assume that the world will still be dangerous, and this option will keep a battle rifle in your hands. It's still a magazine-fed semiauto, which gives you the best hope for winning a fight, far better than a bolt-action or other traditional hunting rifle. (One might argue that this is the concept for the Scout Rifle as designed and promoted by Colonel Jeff Cooper. There is some validity to that argument, particularly for those who are using a magazine-fed Scout Rifle and have practiced and drilled with it enough to be proficient in its use, although I would argue that a magazine-fed semiauto is still a far better choice. Scout rifles are explored in another chapter.)

Beyond that, the .223 Remington is far too small for elk, moose, bears, or cattle. It's a varmint cartridge suitable for prairie dogs and woodchucks that was adopted by the military because they wanted a smaller, lighter cartridge so ammo would be less expensive and so soldiers could carry more ammo. The shift in thinking with the military at the time led away from effective cartridges and precision marksmanship. When our forefathers fought the British for independence, every shot counted. That's why they won. The British lined up and fired "volleys" without picking targets. The Americans hid behind cover, picked a target, and made every shot count. I am not a military strategist, but it's clear that things changed after World War II. Today it's more like the British approach: Blast out a lot of bullets and hope a few hit something. For that, I suppose the .223/5.56 made sense.

If you doubt that, then explain why the US Government Accountability Office (GAO) found that the military fired 250,000 rounds in Afghanistan and Iraq for every insurgent killed. Clearly marksmanship is not key to today's style of fighting wars.

I recommend the .223/5.56 for survival for a multitude of reasons. When they are all considered together it makes a lot of sense, but it is not the most effective cartridge available for fighting, and it's not even in the running for the most effective big game hunting cartridge. You may wonder why, when deer are similar to men in body mass. Fighting and hunting are two very different things, with much different terminal ballistic goals. For both, the .223 is a compromise; but it's a much bigger one for hunting big game than for protecting your family. The .223 will work for foraging, of course. If you see a deer and it's the gun in your hands, shoot the deer. Odds are it will do the polite thing and die. But the cartridge is far less than ideal and in a hostile, threatening situation "ideal" is a goal you might want to keep in mind. This is true for many, if not most, of the popular cartridges used in the AR-15 platform (the exceptions being the three that are the topic of this chapter).

▲ Left to right: .450 Bushmaster, .458 Socom, and .50 Beowulf. .223 Remington in front. One look tells you that the big-bore cartridges pack more wallop.

Forget survival for a moment and let's consider hunting, because that's what you will be doing with these cartridges to survive. I have a simple test when choosing cartridges for hunting big game with an AR-15 rifle. It assumes that you have a working knowledge of cartridges and ballistics. The only requirement is that you be honest when you answer. Ask yourself: "If you were shopping for a non-AR rifle to hunt deer, bear, or hogs, would you pick one chambered for the cartridge you are willing to use in an AR-15?"

In other words, would you buy a bolt-action deer rifle chambered for .300 AAC Blackout over, say, a .308 Winchester or a .30–06? The honest answer is, of course, no. Otherwise gun makers would be flocking to build .300 AAC Blackout bolt-action rifles and they are not. Why not? Because there is no market. In fact, Remington tried this with the 6.8 SPC, but dropped the bolt-actions because they didn't sell. The .223 Remington is a good seller in a bolt-action, but not for big game hunting. The vast majority of .223 Remington bolt-action rifles are purchased for hunting varmints. The few .300 ACC Blackout bolt-action rifles I have seen were designed for tactical use, suppressed with subsonic ammo, not for deer hunting.

Big game hunters use the .300 AAC Blackout, 6.8 SPC, or .223 Remington in an AR-15 because of the platform, not the ballistics. Sure they can all kill game, but they are always a compromise and the hunter runs a higher risk of wounding loss than with traditional, more powerful deer, bear, or hog cartridges.

The trouble with the AR-15 platform is the limitations it puts on cartridge length. It's hard to make the gun work with a cartridge much longer than 2.26 inches. Of course, you can move up to the larger AR-L (AR-10) platform that is based on the .308 size cartridges, but the guns are bigger, heavier, and more expensive. That said, they are never a mistake. From a ballistic standpoint the .308 Winchester is a much more effective cartridge, both for fighting (which is covered at length elsewhere in the book) and for hunting. An AR-L rifle in .338 Federal is powerful enough to shoot just about anything you run into in North America. My friend Randy Luth proved that by shooting a large brown bear with a .338 Federal in an AR-L. However, this discussion right now is about the smaller AR-15 rifles, a gun that every smart prepper should own.

Oddly enough, back in the early days of self-contained metallic cartridges, new cartridge designers faced a similar dilemma but for very different reasons. The limitations of black powder and bullet construction pretty much topped out the bullet velocity at around 1,500 ft/s, give or take. So, to increase power, the cartridge designers made the bullets heavier and bigger in diameter. That's why the military's rifle cartridges were 45-caliber in the 1870s rather than the 22-caliber used today. I have read a lot of American history and while the trapdoor Springfield .45–70 used by the army had a lot of problems, I don't recall ever reading that a solider complained the cartridge was ineffective when shooting the enemy. Do a Google search on the 5.56 and its failings and then you will understand that with bullets, size does matter. There

▲ A .223 bullet next to a .500 bullet. The .500 clearly will hit harder and make a much bigger hole.

are a lot of complaints about the stopping power of the 5.56 on enemy combatants.

While the reasons are a bit different, today's hard-hitting cartridges for the AR-15 use the same concept as those old black powder cartridges. If you can't make the cartridge longer (or drive the bullet faster), then make the diameter larger and add bullet weight.

Just as the hunters using the old black powder cartridges understood, a big-diameter, heavy bullet at moderate velocity is deadly on big game.

For a prepper there is another big advantage to having guns chambered in these big-bore cartridges. Remember, you need to to envision every scenario and plan ahead to deal with the worst-case situations. No matter how much ammo you store, you may find it gone. You could be forced to abandon it, or it can be stolen or confiscated. You may even use it all. At some point you might be handloading your ammo, and if components are hard to find, you may be making bullets. If you are loading ammo and using cast bullets, those smaller AR-15 cartridges, like the .223 Remington, are not going to be very effective for much of anything. They will be poor fight-stoppers and even worse for hunting. As always, it's better to have them than no gun at all, but a non-expanding, small diameter bullet at a moderate velocity is not going to be very effective when compared to the full power, expanding bullet ammo the cartridge is designed to use.

These big-bore cartridges, even with cast bullets, will be one-and-done fight-stoppers. Just like the .45–70 that saw military duty in the 1800s, these big-bore cartridges toss a bullet that doesn't need to expand to punch a big hole. If there is a chance you will be fighting or foraging with cast bullets, size counts. Big bullets make big holes, even if they don't expand—and cast bullets rarely expand. Cast bullets do have some problems with the gas systems in AR-style rifles, but if they are your only option, they are workable.

Prepping is about backup plans. If one of yours is to have an AR-15 rifle, or at least an upper, in one of these thumper cartridges, it can help you deal with a lot of problems.

The lineup is not huge for big-bore cartridges on the AR-15 platform. In fact, from mainstream gun makers there are only three cartridges. But that's enough, as each one of this trio brings something impressive to the table.

## .450 Bushmaster

This is the smallest of the trinity of thumpers, with a bullet diameter of .452 inch. It uses a rebated rim cartridge case based on the .284 Winchester case.

The concept used to develop the .450 Bushmaster was initially put forth by Colonel Jeff Cooper. Cooper is best known for creating the Modern Technique of the Pistol, founding Gunsite Academy, and for his admiration of the 1911 pistol. Cooper was an avid hunter and loved to roam wild places in a "come what may" sort of way. He was a man of great experience in hunting all over the world, and he recognized that a big bullet

▲ Bushmaster rifle in .450 Bushmaster. Ammo by Remington and Hornady.

is a good thing when shooting big game. He thought that the perfect rifle for most "general" big game hunting would be a semiauto rifle, larger than 44 caliber and capable of taking big game out to 250 yards. He called this the "Thumper" concept.

Tim LeGendre of LeMag Firearms developed the cartridge and called it the .45 Professional. He licensed the concept to Bushmaster Firearms International for production and distribution, while Hornady developed the ammo. They modified the case a little so it would work better with their SST Flex-Tip bullet. The name was then changed to .450 Bushmaster with the blessing of LeGendre, and the cartridge was introduced in 2007.

The current Hornady .450 Bushmaster load uses a 250-grain FTX bullet with a factory-advertised muzzle velocity of 2,200 ft/s from a 20-inch barrel for 2,680 foot-pounds of energy. On my chronograph this load has a velocity of 2,090 ft/s fifteen feet from the muzzle when fired from my Bushmaster rifle with a 16-inch barrel. This produces 2,425 foot-pounds of energy at the muzzle.

The Remington Outdoor Group now owns Bushmaster, so it makes sense that Remington would start making ammo. Big Green currently offers a 260-grain Premier AccuTip load with an advertised muzzle velocity (MV) of 2,180 ft/s. Muzzle energy is 2,744 foot-pounds. This ammo produces 2,062 ft/s and 2,455 foot-pounds of energy from my rifle's shorter barrel.

I shot a bunch of hogs using some experimental ammo from Remington that was loaded with 275-

▲ The author shot this water buffalo with the .450 Bushmaster. This powerful AR-15 cartridge is good for hunting, foraging, or fighting.

▲ The Rock River Arms LAR-458 rifle in .458 Socom is a thumper!

grain Barnes XPB Bullets with an advertised MV of 2,175 ft/s and 2,889 foot-pounds of muzzle energy. From my rifle, the velocity is 2,009 ft/s and the energy is 2,465 foot-pounds. The addition of the Barnes X-bullet improves the terminal performance of this cartridge over the lead-core bullets. They were primarily designed for deer size game, where this bullet can be used on bigger game with good results.

There have been a few delays in getting this ammo to market, but we should see it soon. Meanwhile, the bullet is available from Barnes to handload. It's listed as a bullet for the .460 S&W handgun cartridge.

I also shot an Asian water buffalo that weighed more than three-quarters of a ton with the .450 Bushmaster and that experimental load. I was very impressed with all of the results on hogs and the buffalo. I will admit, this cartridge is probably a bit on the light side for hunting buffalo, but it's the gun I had with me when opportunity knocked, which is exactly the concept that Cooper envisioned.

## .458 Socom

The .458 Socom was developed for military applications after the fighting in Mogadishu in 1993. That battle left a lot of participants disappointed in the performance of 5.56 NATO cartridges, and they wanted some serious, .45–70 class thumping power for the M16/M4-style rifles.

I might point out that hogs, bears, moose, elk, and even some deer tend to run bigger and tougher than underfed insurgents. If the guys in the fight think that the .223/5.56 is not enough cartridge, then perhaps we should reevaluate the use of that cartridge, at least for big game hunting. The fact that they were not happy with the performance on bad guys speaks for itself. That is a common complaint with our military. Better ammo has helped alleviate the problem for the military, but they are still stuck with non-expanding bullets. As civilians we are not forced by foolish politicians to use ineffective ammo, and the .223/5.56 cartridge is much more effective as a defensive round when loaded with high-quality hunting bullets.

(As a cautionary note, much of the "price-point" .223/5.56 ammo is also loaded with non-expanding bullets. It is fine for practice, but a very poor choice for defensive use. You should keep that in mind when stockpiling ammo. Look for expanding bullets loaded in ammo you plan to use for defense.)

History has shown that a heavy .458 bullet at modest rifle velocity is effective both on bad guys and on big game. The .45–70 was the US Military cartridge for many years. Back then they had non-expanding lead bullets. Not because some politician decided to risk the lives of our military with ineffective projectiles, but because it was state of the art at the time. That's why the military used a .45 and not a .22. Now we have bullets that will expand at those velocities very reliably. With high-quality expanding bullets, the .45–70 is a one-and-done fight-stopper and an outstanding big game cartridge.

The .458 Socom was designed to duplicate .45–70 performance. The cartridge came out in 2002, and while it didn't gain widespread acceptance as a military round, it has proven to be a great hunting cartridge.

It uses a lengthened .50 Action Express case with a rebated rim and is necked down for a .458-inch bullet. Unlike the straight-walled cartridges, which must headspace on the case rim, the .458 Socom has a shoulder to headspace off. This is a more positive approach to headspacing, and it allows the bullets to be crimped in place.

One big advantage of the .458 diameter over the .452 diameter is there is a wide selection of rifle style bullets on the market. This is reflected in the multiple factory load options, and it opens a lot of doors for handloaders. One of the best bullets for any use, short of the largest African dangerous game, is the 300-grain TTSX that Barnes developed specifically for this cartridge.

I have found factory-loaded ammo currently offered by three companies: Wilson Combat, Southern Ballistics Research, and CorBon. Rifles are from Rock River Armory and Wilson Combat. My current rifle is a Rock River with a 16-inch barrel.

CorBon has ammo using the Barnes Tipped TTSX 300-grain bullet. The advertised muzzle velocity is 1,825 ft/s. They also have a 300-grain HP at 1,900 ft/s and a 400-grain JPH at 1,600 ft/s. These velocities are reported from a 16-inch barrel.

From the 16-inch barrel on my Rock River test gun, MV for the 300-grain Barnes load was 1,894 ft/s, which is slightly higher than advertised. The 400-grain Speer JSP load has a MV of 1,580 from my gun. Given the chronograph screen at 15 feet, and if you extrapolate back to the muzzle, it's pretty much what they claimed. That load produces 2,218 foot-pounds of energy.

I have used this same 400-grain Speer bullet at about the same velocity from a .45–70 for years to hunt black bear, hogs, and deer. To say that it has always been impressive on game would be an understatement. I once shot a black bear with this load, and another hunter sitting in his stand almost a mile away said that the bullet impact sounded like Hulk Hogan had clobbered the bear with a two-by-four. He was so impressed by the sound that he left his stand and walked to mine just to see what kind of gun I was shooting. The bear was even more impressed, and his big skull is on a shelf watching over me as I type these words.

The Wilson Combat 300-grain Barnes TTSX load produced 1,834 ft/s and 2,241 foot-pounds of muzzle energy from the Rock River rifle.

Southern Ballistic Research offers twenty-one different loads for the .458 Socom, with bullets ranging from 100 to 500 grains. I tested the 300-grain JHP load and got 1,831 ft/s and 2,234 foot-pounds of energy.

After testing two different Rock River .458 Socom carbines, the LAR-15 CAR A4 and the new LAR-15 X-1, I have been very impressed with the accuracy. Both shot right around the MOA mark with just about any ammo I tried.

It might have a military background, but the .458 Socom is a big game cartridge capable of taking anything in North America. I think this cartridge deserves a look from any serious prepper.

## .50 Beowulf

As you have probably figured out by now, I am not a fan of small cartridges for hunting. I have hunted big game with most of the popular cartridges, from the .17 HMR to .500 Nitro Express, as I think experience is the best way to gain knowledge. But I have come to believe that each category of game has a list of spe-

▲ The .50 Beowulf is a beast that can fill the dinner table or stop a fight with one shot.

cific cartridges that are appropriate for use. I tend to gravitate to the upper 50 percent of that list in size and power. I like a cartridge that hits hard and removes the doubt. The .50 Beowulf epitomizes that concept. With a 325-grain, half-inch diameter bullet at 2,000 ft/s, it moves the power level up a notch, and there is never any doubt when you hit something.

Bill Alexander of Alexander Arms was one of the pioneers of big game hunting cartridges in the AR-15 style rifles. He developed this cartridge and named it after Beowulf, a legendary literary warrior who slayed the undefeatable Grendel by ripping his arm off. The day after that battle, Beowulf fought the horrible monster that was Grendel's mother. He killed her by cutting off her head with a mighty sword from her own armory. A sword of which it was said "no other man could have hefted in battle." Years later, in his doddering old age when he was worn out and feeble, Beowulf fought and killed a dragon.

In short, Beowulf was big and bad and backed down from no fight—the perfect namesake for this cartridge.

When it was introduced in 2001 the .50 Beowulf was the first of the AR-15 specific, ultra-big-bore cartridges to be offered by an AR manufacturer. It is based on a lengthened .50 AE case with a severely rebated rim so that it fits a bolt head designed for the 7.62X39 cartridge. This bolt face size works well with an AR-15 style rifle.

From a 24-inch barrel, the .50 Beowulf pushes a 325-grain bullet to 2,010 ft/s and 2,916 foot-pounds of energy at the muzzle. The 400-grain load has a muzzle velocity of 1,875 ft/s and 3,123 foot-pounds.

The bullet is half an inch in diameter and can expand to more than an inch. Compare that to a 55-grain .223 Remington at less than half the diameter. The 325-grain Beowulf has almost 500 percent more bullet weight and an unexpanded diameter that is larger than a .223's fully expanded bullet. Once it has expanded, the Beowulf bullet has a 123 percent larger frontal area, not to mention that the Beowulf has about three times more energy than the .223 Remington. This is a serious step up in power for the AR-15 platform.

Even from the stubby 16.5-inch barrel on my rifle, the .50 Beowulf loads are moving at 1,950 ft/s for 325-grain and 1,800 ft/s for the 400-grain. That is 2,745 foot-pounds of muzzle energy for the 325-grain and 2,878 foot-pounds for the 400-grain load. Considering the 7.5-inch difference in barrel length, the velocity loss is minimal. Clearly, this is a cartridge that is well suited to the shorter barrels often used on the AR-15.

I have used the cartridge on multiple hogs and a few deer, always with very good results. With the right bullets it hits hard, penetrates well, and leaves a very large hole in its wake. Just as Sir Samuel Baker said about his two-bore rifle, "Baby," I can honestly say that I have never lost a single animal hit with this cartridge! I don't even need to rely on exploding bullets for that result, as he did with Baby.

The first time I shot my Beowulf, we were blasting at a piece of steel that had been on the range for a while. I had shot it with a lot of different medium velocity cartridges, with little or no real damage. But when after two or three shots the Beowulf knocked it off its stand, we walked the 100 yards to hang it back up. We were shocked to see that the big bullets were making craters. Not the eroded-out craters that high-velocity bullet impacts make, but huge, deep bowls reshaped into the metal that left bantam egg–sized bulges popping out of the off side of the steel plate. Most steel target damage is a result of high-velocity impacts or steel-core bullets making holes or divots, but these were caused by the brute force, bludgeon-type power of these big bullets smacking the steel and pushing it out of shape.

The Beowulf has been used for some military applications, including one that's a bit on the secret side, so I can't get into specifics. (I know I sound like every other douchebag that has ever wrote about AR-15 rifles and wanted to impress you with his "connections," but it's true. I swore to the guy I would never reveal the details. Trust me, though, the guy who told me about it was the real deal and was in a position to know the truth.)

Following an overseas terrorist attack, the military identified a previously unknown situation. Until they could get this problem addressed they needed a short-term solution that included a way to break stuff like the engines that were propelling attack vehicles. They armed a bunch of military guys with Beowulf AR-15 rifles and lined them up to deal with any attack. I honestly don't know if any more attacks happened during that time, but if they did, the Beowulf stopped them because we would have heard about it if they did not.

Obviously, these cartridges are not designed for long-range. But, all the recent "sniper" hype aside, the truth is that most big game (and bad guys) is shot at well under 200 yards anyway.

So to answer my own question, "Would I buy a non-AR-15 rifle for hunting if it were chambered in these cartridges?" I would welcome any of these cartridges in any rifle. A short-action bolt gun would be very interesting, and I think they would be great in a lever-action. In fact, I have hunted for years with cartridges with similar ballistic performance, such as the .444 Marlin, .45–70, and .450 Marlin. So the answer is pretty much, "been there, done that," only now I get to use an AR-15, which is very hip and happening these days.

These cartridges are very specialized, but they do have a strong place with preppers. I would not make them your first gun purchase or consider them as a primary long gun. But if you are well into your prepping and have several AR-15 rifles already, I would consider buying one or more of these guns, or at least an upper and some magazines that you can use with your current AR lower. They will make foraging more successful and safe. They also can be handy in some defensive situations, particularly if you are going to be using cast bullets. Plus, they are just friggin' cool! Shooting this much power out of an AR-15 is fun!

▲ Bigger bullets are never a mistake.

# AUG Option

*This may be the coolest rifle ever for zombies, survival, or just looking good at the range.*

▲ Photo credit: Eric Poole.

*I* am not sure how many *Walking Dead* fans will read this, but I am sure that, like me, they spend an unhealthy amount of time yelling at the television. The characters' choice of weapons on that show is absurd. It has gotten better in recent years, but it's still enough to make true gun guys foam at the mouth with frustration.

Daryl's crossbow is my biggest pet peeve. It looks cool and no doubt it has all the basement warriors who watch the show pumping their fists and drooling in their laps, but it's a foolish choice that would have left him dead in the first days of the zombie apocalypse.

I have used crossbows a bunch and I can honestly say that I can't think of a worse choice for fighting off a zombie horde. Any crossbow is extremely slow to load, impossible to carry, and has limited range. A compound bow is much better in every respect, except maybe for exciting those mall ninjas who, when they

are not watching *The Walking Dead*, hide in their mom's basement and fantasize about Lara Croft. (Not that there is anything wrong with that.)

That said, anything that shoots a stick is a poor choice to fight off a zombie horde, or any rioting, murderous mob for that matter.

Then there is Rick's Colt Python. The Python may be one of the coolest handguns on the planet, no argument, but it's a poor choice for surviving TEOTWAWKI. Like most revolvers, it only holds six rounds and it's very slow to reload compared to a magazine-fed pistol. No good for a zombie horde, unless there is a director to yell "cut" and save your ass every time they are about to overrun you.

Rick's limp-wristed, wimpy style of holding the gun makes me think he got beat up a lot as a kid. I suppose, like the crossbow and the Python, the producers think that looks "badass." But to a gun guy, it looks like Rick doesn't have a clue how to run a handgun.

I get it; it's TV. Clearly they pick the guns for their visual appeal rather than any true tactical advantage. I suspect that's how they ended up equipping their über-bad guy, "The Governor," with his gun. His bullpup carbine may well be the most badass-looking gun ever on the show, but the producers probably didn't know that the Steyr AUG is also an excellent choice for any zombie apocalypse or, I suppose, to raid a prison full of survivors. That's not to condone The Governor's actions—I would have liked to shoot him myself if he had not already had a Japanese Katana run through his guts.

My point is simple. While his rifle, the Steyr AUG, has an on-camera profile that makes any nerdy producer or fanboy pop wood, it's also a serious fighting firearm.

I know for a fact that the European management at Steyr wanted to stay out of the whole zombie thing when it was in vogue and they were a bit upset that their gun showed up on *The Walking Dead*. That is, until demand went through the roof for the AUG; then it was okay.

The AUG (*Armee-Universal-Gewehr*—universal army rifle) is a piston-driven, Austrian bullpup, 5.56 NATO rifle. It was designed in the 1960s and has seen extensive use by military and law enforcement all over the world.

The AUG feeds from thirty-round magazines that fit behind the trigger. The bullpup design ensures that it is a short firearm, which has lots of advantages in close quarters battle (CQB), when riding in a vehicle, or even when hiding it in a diversion bag so you can carry unnoticed. It is also much easier to carry on your body every day than a longer gun. The AUG is reliable and accurate enough that I have seen them used in 3-gun matches with targets out to 400 yards.

In early April of 2014, I had the pleasure of visiting the grand opening of the Steyr Arms facility in Bessemer, Alabama. While I was there I was able to burn up a bunch of ammo with the AUG. As a hardcore AR-15 shooter, it took a few shots to adjust to the different feel of the gun. But by the time I was into my second magazine I was ripping off double-taps and keeping them in center-mass at 25 yards. The gun is very controllable, easy to operate, and notoriously reliable. The AUG is very left-hand friendly, and it has ejection ports on both sides of the gun. The controls are very simple to use.

The gun is available with either a 1.5X or 3X scope. The scope also has three Picatinny rail sections so you can mount a laser or other bling. The front of the sling attaches with Quick-Disconnect while the rear is a fixed swivel. As a bullpup, the AUG A3 M1 is only 28.15 inches long, even with a 16-inch barrel. The short-stroke gas-piston exhaust vents gas out of the front of the rifle. The gun has dual gas-adjustment settings to run a wide range of ammo.

Conversion to left-hand operation requires replacement of the standard bolt with the optional left-eject bolt and swapping the ejection-port cover. The gun has a quick-change barrel with a collapsible forward grip.

I ordered one with their integral 1.5X sighting system. I also had them send another rail mount so I could attach my own optics if I decided I didn't like theirs, but I never did because the scope that came on the gun is fine.

The AUG uses its own magazines. You can order the gun configured to use NATO-style, AR-15 magazines, and it might make sense to buy the gun with the AR-15 magazine option.

The AUG is an alternative choice for a primary, personal long gun. It has seen decades of military use and has proven to be extremely reliable and durable. The short, bullpup design is much easier to manage on a sling. The problem with any rifle or carbine is that it becomes a huge pain in the ass if you try to carry it every day. They bounce and swing around on the sling,

▲ Steyr AUG.

they get in the way when you are trying to do anything, and when you squat or kneel they hit the ground. That's not going to go away, but with a shorter bullpup gun all those issues are somewhat mitigated. If you can do that without any tactical compromise, as with the AUG, why not consider it as an option?

It's worth a look for any prepper looking for something just a little different.

# AR-L Introduction

*Why mess with little guns? If you are going to be a bear, be a grizzly.*

This is another of many contradictory chapters. The concept that there is a single best option in any firearm category for preppers is condescending, because it assumes that only one opinion matters and that all preppers have exactly the same needs and issues. Guns are not "one size fits all," and preppers must make their own informed choices. There is no single "best" in any category. If there were, there would be no need for this book. I could write up a short list and be done.

The nature of firearms today is that we have a lot of options. The function of this book is to explore those options, and often they will contradict each other. For example, some say the best pistol for a prepper is a Glock. But, is it? Many others believe it's the 1911, which, after all, is the best-selling pistol in history. Some progressive thinkers believe the best pistol for preppers is the 2011-style handgun, which combines the best of both; except that the 2011 is expensive and you can buy multiple Glocks for the price of the 2011, so now the frugal prepper is in a quandary.

So which is the best choice of pistols for every prepper?

Hell, I don't know. All of them? None of them? It all depends on your personal guidelines. What's the best for me is not necessarily the best for you.

It's the same with rifles.

I still believe that the best personal long gun, battle rifle for preppers is the AR-15 and its variants. That said, nothing is perfect, and I have a concern with the rather small cartridge. The 5.56/.223 is a bit on the small side when compared to historically successful battle rifle cartridges.

That is mitigated somewhat because as civilians we can use advanced-design expanding bullets, so many will argue that some of those concerns have been addressed. That may be true, as long as we have the ammo we want to use, not the ammo we are forced to use. Still, when you weigh all of the variables, in spite of its flaws, the AR-15 remains the best choice for preppers. At least in my never-humble opinion.

Except I am of the opinion that there is another best choice: the AR-15's older, bigger brother. Eugene Stoner came up with the .308-chambered AR-10 first, so it has been around longer. In our current civilian rifles, this larger .308/7.62x51-chambered rifle is very similar in design to the AR-15 except it's scaled larger.

When it comes to trying to kill things that are trying to kill me, I always follow the guideline that bigger bullets are better bullets. The .308 Winchester is much more powerful than the .223 Remington and uses a

▲ Some of the most common cartridges for the AR-10 type rifle, L to R: .234 Winchester, .260 Remington, 7mm-08 Remington, .308 Winchester, and .338 Federal.

much bigger bullet. That's a fact and nobody can dispute it without ignoring math, physics, and logic.

While I still truly believe that the AR-15 in .223 is the best choice for a prepper's primary long gun, in a lot of ways the .308 is just as good, maybe better.

Am I not being clear? I suppose not, because there is no wrong answer here. I can make just as strong an argument that the larger .308 rifle is just as good of a choice for preppers as the AR-15. The larger gun has its flaws too, but the cartridge and its ability to stop a bad guy from continuing to be a bad guy is not one of them. When you may be defending your life it is never a mistake to pick a larger cartridge.

I also believe that even if you decide to go with the AR-15 as your primary long gun, a smart prepper should always have one or more of the larger .308-chambered rifles as well.

The trouble is, I am not sure what to call them. While Colt technically owns the rights to AR-15, the term has become generic to describe a rifle style. While rifle makers have to use a different name on their guns, the term AR-15 has become accepted as descriptive of a class of rifles. When you say "AR-15," everybody knows what you mean. The same goes for the AR-10, except Armalite owns the trademark to the AR-10 and apparently they are strident in protecting that name. So, the rest of the makers have to get creative if they want to avoid problems.

DPMS calls their rifles LR, as in LR-308, LR-338, etc. Even the new Gen II DPMS guns are called LR. Rock River Arms calls theirs the LAR-8, with JP Enterprises it's the LRP07, and Ruger calls theirs SR-762. The list goes on, and to avoid confusion a lot of shooters just call them an AR-308. But that's not correct either, as there are other cartridge options beyond the .308 Winchester/7.62x51 NATO.

The apologists in the gun industry came up with "modern sporting rifle" as a name for all AR-style rifles so we would not "offend" our anti-gun enemies and to try and hide that we are talking about black rifles. Sorry, but I am not getting on that bandwagon; and if you ever see "Modern Sporting Rifle" or "MSR" under my byline, rest assured it was put there by an editor. I am not of a mind to apologize or try to hide the truth about the guns I am using or writing about. Besides, it does nothing to address the issue of how to differentiate the AR-15 from the AR-10 size rifles.

So, I think I'll just invent my own term: AR-Large, or AR-L for short. It should keep me, and this book, out of trouble and you will all know what I am referring to as a rifle platform.

But it still doesn't settle the matter completely. That's because there are some other differences between the AR-10 and many of the other .308 rifles based on Stoner's design. Most of the new firearms makers entering the field are following the DPMS concept, and that has become the standard, more or less. Magazines and some other parts are interchangeable among this group, whereas the AR-10 and some others use a different magazine and some parts are not interchangeable with the DPMS-style guns.

Confused?

Me too.

To simplify for now, the primary difference between the ArmaLite AR-10 and other AR-L rifles is the magazine. There are two magazine types: the DPMS pattern and the AR-10. Both rifles are designed around the .308 Winchester cartridge and are chambered primarily for that cartridge or one of its offspring.

When you move up to the larger AR-L style of rifle, the cartridge options open way up in terms of horsepower. This rifle is designed for the .308 Winchester, so any variant of that cartridge will run well in the gun. The cartridges are covered in depth in another section.

Preppers, of course, should consider having their first AR-L only be chambered in .308 Winchester (7.62x51 NATO). This is an extremely popular rifle cartridge with civilians of all kinds, from hunters to long-range shooters, so ammo is easy to find. It's also a NATO round and is used extensively by law enforcement. That means that in a crisis there will always be ammo, either from people who no longer need it or on the black market. If you already have a few .308s, it's a good idea to look at the other options outlined in the section about cartridges for this platform.

The downside of these rifles is that they tend to be heavier than the smaller AR-15. Plus they are bigger and everything, including the springs, is beefed up so they may be more difficult for a smaller person to operate. Another issue is that the magazines generally hold nineteen or twenty rounds. Larger magazines are available, but they are not as common as large-capacity .223 magazines. The AR-L magazines are larger in dimension than the AR-15, so a lot of load-bearing vests or other gear designed to carry spare magazines for the AR-15 will not accept the AR-L magazines.

On the other hand, the .308 is a far better fight-stopper than the .223 and is an infinitely better choice for foraging big game or feral livestock.

Every serious prepper should have one or more of these guns. If you need to find ammo, the odds of .308 being in the pipeline, including the black market, is very high. If the only ammo you can find is in .308, it does you no good without a rifle to shoot it through. Even if you don't select the AR-L as a primary, personal long gun, you should probably have one or more waiting in reserve along with a bunch of magazines. I would rank it very high on the list as you are prioritizing the guns you will purchase.

▲ If you are hunting for survival and there is a chance of trouble, an AR-L is the best choice in rifles.

# "Big Brother" AR-L Cartridges

*The AR-15's big brother handles some very powerful cartridges.*

As with the .223 in the smaller AR-15 (AR-S?) platform, it makes sense to have one or more guns chambered for the most common cartridges in the AR-L platform. With all the options, it might be in a smart prepper's interest to have a few alternatives available too.

Most of these cartridges were designed for hunting, but they have crossover applications as well.

## .243 Winchester

The .243 Winchester is simply the .308 Winchester necked down to take a .243-inch diameter bullet. The 20-degree shoulder is maintained and the case length is slightly longer at 2.045 inches, versus the .308 at 2.015 inches.

The strength of the .243 Winchester is in its versatility. It is a true "dual-use" cartridge that will perform equally well on deer-size game and on varmints.

Bullet weights run from 55-grains at 4,000 ft/s to 100-grains at 2,950 ft/s.

As with any of these cartridges, I would not hesitate to use this rifle in a fight. Any cartridge designed on the .308 case is powerful enough for self-defense.

The .243 Winchester is a hugely popular cartridge and any sporting goods store that sells ammo will have some on the shelves. That makes it a good candidate as a secondary choice for your AR-L rifle.

## .260 Remington

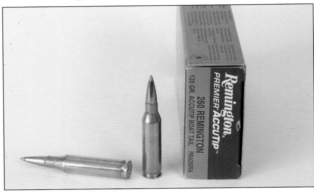

The .260 Remington bridges the gap between the .243 Winchester and the 7mm-08 Remington, while retaining much of what is good about both. Recoil is manageable, making it a good choice for young or small stature shooters, but it has more bullet weight and a larger frontal area than the .243 Winchester for improved terminal performance.

Popular bullet weights are 120-grain at 2,950 ft/s and 140-grain at 2,750 ft/s.

This cartridge is not as popular as some others, so ammo might be a bit more difficult to find. It is starting to see some use for long-range shooting. Right now that's mostly a handloading proposition, but it's expected that some of the big-name ammo makers will start producing target ammo in this cartridge.

## 6.5 Creedmoor

Think .260 Remington, but with better marketing. The two are very close ballistically, and the major difference

is that ammo makers for the .260 Remington have focused mostly on hunting, while the 6.5 Creedmoor is targeted (pun intended) more at the long-range target crowd.

Right now Hornady and Nosler load ammo in both hunting and target bullets. Hornady's 120-grain Superformance load has a MV of 3,010 ft/s. The 129-grain Superformance loads hit 2,910, and the 140-grain A-Max has a MV of 2,710 ft/s. Nosler also makes a few loads in 140-grain: Ballistic Tip or HPBT Match.

This is a very accurate cartridge. My custom precision rifle is capable of 0.3-inch, five-shot, 100-yard groups with factory ammo. I also have a Ruger Predator rifle that's nipping at its heels in terms of accuracy with ½ MOA groups. I have used the cartridge in bolt-action rifles to make one-shot hits on 1 MOA targets from 200 to 1,200 yards. In an accurate AR-L, it can easily do the same.

Ammo is a bit limited now, but this cartridge is growing in popularity at a very rapid rate. I would expect it will be easier to find in the next few years. If you stockpile ammo and/or handload, this is a very good choice if you are looking for a long-range AR-L rifle to protect your home.

### 7mm-08 Remington

Every family of cartridges must have a 7mm—this is the law of Remington. In general, the American public does not give great acceptance to metric cartridges, except if they are promoted by Remington. The 7mm Remington Magnum is popular, as is the 7mm RUM and the .280 Remington. Pretty much no one else has

been successful with the .284 bullet diameter. The 7mm-08 is Remington's contribution to this class of cartridges.

Popular bullet weights run from a 120-grain at 3,000 ft/s through the 150-grain at 2,650 ft/s. The most popular is a 140-grain with a MV of 2,850 ft/s.

Like the .260, it's a fine cartridge, but ammo may be a bit tougher to find than some of the other cartridges.

### .308 Winchester / 7.62x51 NATO

What can I say here that hasn't been said already? This is the cartridge the gun was designed around.

It is the preferred cartridge for fighting with AR-L guns and it's also one of the best for long-range shooting, even out to 1,000 yards. As with all 30-caliber cartridges, the bullet options are too huge to list here. My choice for long-range work is the Federal Premium load with a Sierra 168-grain MatchKing. For hunting

and foraging, I really like the Barnes VOR-TX ammo with a 150-grain TTSX bullet.

For a fighting gun, any expanding bullet ammo will be a much better one-shot stopper than anything you can put in a .223.

The guns and ammo are heavier, there is a bit more recoil, and the magazine capacity is lower when compared to a .223 Remington, but when it comes time for a serious, save-your-life fight, you can never go wrong with a .308 in an AR-L rifle. Nobody who survived a gunfight ever said, "Gee, I wish I had brought a smaller cartridge." There is a reason for that. We explore some of that in other chapters, but in the end this cartridge and an AR-L rifle make a great fighting package.

## .338 Federal

This is one of the best short-action hunting cartridges offered in any gun and particularly in an AR-L rifle. It also brings a new level of power to the AR-L platform.

While ammo is hard to find, this cartridge is worth a look for a prepper. It is the best option for hunting and foraging. It also has some tactical advantages. It's a good fight-stopper of course, but it also has the capability to penetrate barriers and to break stuff like car engines. I am a huge fan of this cartridge in any platform, but it stands alone in an AR-L. Of course, you will need to stockpile ammo and/or handload, but it's worth it for the performance you can get.

As we discussed in the big-bore AR section, if you are going to hunt or forage for feral livestock you need a powerful cartridge. But you also need a platform and a cartridge capable of saving your life if you run into trouble while hunting. While magazine capacity is an issue with the big thumper cartridges in the AR-15, the magazines for AR-L hold the same number of cartridges for a .338 Federal as they do a .308, so there is no compromise for the more powerful cartridge.

Federal and Fusion offer a wide range of ammo options, but I am partial to the 200-grain Fusion load with a muzzle velocity of 2,700 ft/s for hunting most game or for defense. Some years back I used an early engineering sample of this ammo to shoot my best ever black bear, and I have nothing but confidence for its use hunting hogs or deer. I have seen this cartridge perform on elk, moose, mountain goats, and a bunch of other game. It's very impressive. With the new Federal 200-grain Trophy Copper bullet, it can handle any ungulate in North America.

My choice of rifle is the incredibly accurate JP Enterprises LRP-07H Long Range Precision Hunting Rifle. With the Fusion load, three-shot, 100-yard groups average 0.71-inch. The best group was a ragged hole that measured 0.3 inches. That's about as good as it gets.

This cartridge is surprisingly good at long range and you can use it to reach out to 400 yards or more with confidence.

# .308: Is Bigger Better in an AR Battle Rifle?

*A look at the .308 option.*

▲ This DPMS .308 is a lightweight rifle that is very accurate. It lacks a flash hider, but that's not important.

of another AK-47. He survived that, but the lingering physical effects of the war killed him while he was still relatively young. I might note that he was a medic during the war and saw the results of many bullet strikes from a wide range of cartridges. I knew him for two decades, and he never wavered about the fact that a bigger bullet is better.

Even today, more than half a century after the military selected the 5.56 NATO, the controversy still rages and a lot of reports from the sandbox are critical of its stopping power. Of course, the arguments peck away at lesser issues like barrel length or bullet design, but the bottom line is that with a bigger cartridge there would be no argument at all.

While our fighting forces have to use what they are told to use, we civilians have a choice. Certainly we have an advantage that the military does not in the choices about which bullets we can load in our magazines, as we are not bound by foolish convention agreements made by politicians. The non-expanding bullets the military is forced to use are banned in most states for hunting because they are ineffective and cruel, yet we let our men and women of the military trust their lives to them. It makes no sense to me. But if we were forced to use a military style, non-expanding rifle bullet, then clearly a bigger bullet would be more effective.

That is a distinct possibility for a prepper. While we may plan to use better bullets, what's that old saying? Man plans, while God laughs? We may be separated from our ammo, or we may use it all up. With NATO

*L*ike most gun guys, I think a lot these days about how to protect myself and my family. When it comes to my defensive rifle, the choice is clear; it will be an AR of some sort. This is the fighting gun I am most familiar with and one that, after many thousands of rounds, I have learned to trust. But the .223 Remington cartridge is a concern. There is a school of thought that wonders, "Do I want to trust my life and the lives of my family to a varmint cartridge?" The .223/5.56x45 has always been controversial. When it was first used extensively in combat during Vietnam, there were a lot of critics. One good friend of mine got so frustrated with its failures that he dumped his M16 and picked up an AK-47 off a dead enemy soldier and used that for the rest of his tour. A tour, incidentally, that was cut short when he was on the receiving end cartridges you can be sure that ammo will show up on the black market. If we are forced to use non-expanding military ammo, suddenly the bigger bullet of the .308 has a lot of appeal over the .223.

As a hunter, I am a firm believer in bigger, heavier bullets. While I have hunted deer and other game with .22 centerfires many times, the results ensured that I am not an advocate. The fact that .22 cartridges are illegal to use for big game in many places supports my opinion. So why defend your family against bad guys who are about the same body weight as whitetail deer, or even a bit bigger on average, with cartridges and bullets you would not hunt with?

(I am not trying to disparage the .223 here. I feel it's an important cartridge and the AR-15 is an important firearm for preppers. But I am willing to play devil's advocate a little to explore the issues. I am not trying to talk you out of your AR-15, as that would be foolish; but I am trying to make you think.)

One thing that is important with any home defense rifle is ammo availability. In days past the issue of social collapse was mostly fodder for interesting theoretical barroom discussions. Today, it's much closer to reality. With the threat of terrorism growing ever larger, the possibility of economic collapse on a world scale very real, rogue nations building nuclear arsenals and questionable leadership in Washington, there has never been a more dangerous time in America.

There are two approaches to this. One is to pretend it's not real, scoff at those who believe it is, and bury your head in the sand. That's what most of my neighbors are doing. Or you can prepare for the worst case scenario and hope it never happens, which is what I am doing.

In a simple home invasion scenario, ammo availability is not an issue and you should have plenty on hand to deal with the problem. But if there is social collapse, you will probably be using your rifle not only for defense, but also to feed your family. It's like Hank said, "a country boy can survive," but only if he has the tools. In a long-term survival scenario, sooner or later you will need more ammo.

A military cartridge makes sense because the odds are much higher that you will be able to locate ammunition in times of crisis if it's used by multiple governments. The problem, as noted already, is it will be non-expanding. If you are forced to use non-expanding military ammo for foraging and protection, a bigger bullet is insurance against failure.

All this is leading down multiple paths which all converge on the .308 Winchester, or 7.62x51 NATO as the military calls it. We can, of course, consider other cartridges, but something always rules them out. For example, the 6.8 SPC might be a good choice from a ballistic standpoint. After all, that cartridge was spawned by the military; but they rejected it in the end and ammo is now available only through civilian channels. When is the last time you saw cases and cases of 6.8 SPC on a shelf in a gun store? The 7.62x39 is an effective cartridge, except it's not a NATO cartridge, which could lead to availability problems in stressful times.

Sure, there is a lot of 7.62x39 ammo floating around, but it's strictly a civilian cartridge in America. If it shows up in military hands on American soil, we will have very big problems. As in Russia invading. It is also not friendly in an AR-type rifle. I know; I own one, and over the years I have collected a drawer full of high-capacity magazines that do not work. This cartridge was designed to work in the SKS or AK platform, and its tapered case doesn't play well with AR rifles, with the exception of the new CMMG Mutant. That gun uses AK not AR magazines.

Most other common cartridges are eliminated because of the ammo availability issue. Unless it's a military cartridge, you are at great risk of ammo shortages. When you look at all the arguments, a .308/7.62X51 rifle is the only one that makes sense.

One potential downside of a .308 is magazine capacity. Most magazines top out at twenty or twenty-five rounds, but .223 AR magazines are standardized at thirty rounds and larger capacity magazines are very common.

While I suppose the current lack of high-quality, high-capacity magazines could be an issue if you are holding off an advancing zombie horde, I can't see that it is truly a big issue for a home defense rifle. You can get a lot done with twenty rounds. If that's not enough, a magazine change can be accomplished very quickly with practice, so with multiple magazines on your person you are not hugely disadvantaged. Besides, let's not lose sight of why I picked a .308 rifle. It's the same reason I often choose a 1911 in .45 ACP for my carry handgun instead of a high-cap 9mm; because I don't plan my defensive strategy around how many times I am going to miss or how many times, other than once, I need to shoot the bad guy to make him behave. I fail to see the value in sending a swarm of little bullets to accomplish the same thing as one big bullet.

Clearly, power is the primary advantage of this rifle cartridge. The popular 168-grain .308 load has more than three times the bullet weight of the common 55-grain .223 load and more than twice the muzzle energy. In fact, the .308 has more energy at 400 yards than the .223 has at the muzzle. Not to mention that the frontal area of the expanded bullet is much larger with the .308, so it pokes a bigger hole. It will also penetrate much deeper in any material. If you must shoot through a car door, windshield, or building wall, the .308 has a huge advantage. And let's not forget that zombie thing; everybody knows that they are tough buggers and sometimes take a lot of killing. No point in taking chances with a little prairie dog bullet.

Sure, the recoil is heavier in a .308, but with a muzzle brake it is still a mild recoiling rifle. In fact, I was surprised at just how easy a shooting rifle the .308 turned out to be.

I was concerned that the higher recoil of the .308 would negate any tactical advantage the extra power brought to the table. But a properly configured fighting gun is pretty fast. Part of that is because it is a semiauto rifle. While recoil can be a big issue with the military when shooting full auto, civilians are limited by law (with a few notable exceptions) to semiauto rifles. It is much easier to deal with recoil when using a semiauto,

as the shooter has full control over when the rifle fires and can bring the sights back on target before firing the next shot.

During the test outlined in the following sidebar, the .308 made a good showing. While the results in the sidebar are compiled averages for all the shooters, I would note a few points. I think that one of the toughest comparisons between cartridges, as far as the effect of recoil, would be the close range, double-tap, multiple-targets test. My best time on my first run-through with the three different rifles was with the .308 Win. After my second run-through, that time was only eight-tenths of a second slower than my best time for all six runs with three different cartridges. Also, my splits, which are the time between the two shots on each target, were virtually the same. Considering that I have been seriously training with .223 rifles for a few years and this was the first time out with the .308 Win. rifle, these results put to rest any lingering doubts I had about the recoil becoming a huge factor. In total, with all the scenarios we ran, my average time with the .308 was actually three-tenths of a second faster than with the .223. The bottom line, in my opinion, is that with equally equipped rifles and plenty of practice, a good shooter will give up very little speed in a fight by selecting a properly set-up .308 over the .223.

One more point. Most 3-gun competition is centered around double-taps, particularly on the close shots. I know that a lot of operators rely on them as well. I have a friend who is a professional hunter in Africa, but in his younger years he was in the South African Special Forces and he saw a lot of action. He told me that they always double-tapped.

The point of a double-tap is to hit the bad guys twice because you cannot be sure that one hit will eliminate the threat. If you hit them with a .308, the odds of the first shot eliminating the threat raise exponentially over a hit with a lesser cartridge, probably making the double-tap an unnecessary redundancy or much better insurance that the guy is out of the fight, depending on your point of view. I hunted in Zimbabwe some years later with a veteran of the Rhodesian war. He used an FN FAL rifle in .308 during the hostilities and told me that it was a very effective, one-shot fight-stopper.

With shooters of equal ability and similarly configured rifles, the .223 may always be a little bit faster for repeat shots or multiple targets. But the difference is smaller than you might think and it all comes back to that swarm of little bullets versus one big bullet thing. Me? I know from painful experience that the heavyweights hit harder. That's true in boxing, martial arts, and in rifle bullets. I'll put my trust in the big guy every time.

That's why an AR-L in .308 is such a good choice if my family is ever in danger.

I still think that the AR-15 in .223 is the best primary defensive long gun a prepper can have, but when building your battery of guns it makes a lot of sense to also have an AR-L in .308 Winchester. It's a better fight-stopper and much better for hunting and foraging. Also, as with the 9mm pistol, it's one of those cartridges that show up in any ammo source, including the black market. Finding a bunch of .308 ammo will do you no good unless you have a rifle or two to shoot it.

## Testing the Cartridges

▲ The three cartridges used in the test: .223 Remington, 6.8 SPC, and .308 Winchester.

In the interest of finding out how the .308 stacks up as a fighting gun from a user-friendly point of view, some years ago I conducted a long and loud test.

I set up three DPMS M4-style carbines (in .223 Remington, 6.8 SPC, and .308 Winchester), all similarly equipped with a 16-inch barrel, a muzzle brake, and an adjustable stock. They were all equipped with good triggers; the .223 and .308 both had JP triggers while the 6.8 had an American Trigger Corp. AR15 Gold trigger.

Leupold was kind enough to loan me three of their Mark 4 CQ/T scopes. These are a 1–3 variable with an illuminated circle-dot reticle. This optic is very popular with military and law enforcement and is a good option on any fighting rifle. By having the same optic on all three rifles I tried to eliminate as many variables as possible, and to direct the focus on the differences in the cartridges.

I assembled a team of five shooters who varied both in age and experience. This gave me a good cross section to test the cartridges, not only with experienced old gray beards but also with young, new shooters. I think it is important to note that not one of us had any measurable experience with the .308 AR-L rifle at that point. While the amount varied, we all had past trigger time with the .223 prior to the test. If anything, this skewed the test slightly against the .308.

I set up three scenarios and we shot them with all three rifles, running through each scenario twice, but not consecutively. All the shooting was measured with a PACT timer and the results were recorded on the back of a couple of cardboard USPSA (United States Practical Shooting Association) targets. You know when you drive to the range with that nagging feeling you forgot something? In this case it was my notebook.

We used Remington ammunition during the test. Remington is one of only two companies that offer ammo for the .223 Remington, 6.8 Remington SPC and the .308 Winchester. Hornady is the other.

The .223 Rem ammo was Express 55-grain PSP. The 6.8 SPC was Premier Core-Lokt Ultra with 115-grain Core-Lokt Ultra Bonded bullets. Finally, the .308 Winchester ammo was Express with a 150-grain Core-Lokt bullet. Each represents a popular bullet weight for these cartridges.

▲ The three cartridges tested, .223 Rem, 6.8 SPC, and .308 Win. The advantages of the .308 in terms of power are obvious in the size difference.

## Stage One

The shooter is standing, the rifle on his shoulder, muzzle down. There are five bowling pins at 35

yards. At 85 yards there is an Action Targets Hostage target, which is a metal target the size and shape of a USPSA target. At 90 yards there is an R&R Racing swinging target with an eight-inch diameter plate.

At the buzzer the shooter knocks down all the bowling pins, then double-taps the hostage target before shooting the eight-inch circle to stop the clock.

The idea is to have some smaller and more difficult targets at moderately long range for an offhand shooter. This calls for speed and precision. Most did well until the last, when hitting the eight-inch target off hand proved elusive for some shooters. That has the some of the raw times higher than expected and skewed the results a bit.

With no misses, this stage can be completed with eight shots. While we did have a bunch of nine-shot runs, a clean run was accomplished only once when I did it with the .308 in 10.32 seconds.

The trouble was that the bowling pins proved tricky, as well as the R&R Racing target. The fastest time was 9.4 seconds, by Brendan Burns shooting the 6.8 SPC. That means he beat my best time by just over half a second. If he keeps that up I might not let him marry my daughter.

(Update, we did this test several years ago. They have been happily married for several years.)

### Results

#### .223

| | |
|---|---|
| Raw Time—average for all shooters: | 19.009 seconds |
| Splits—average for all shooters: | 1.03 seconds |
| Number of shots to complete average: | 13.375 |

#### 6.8 SPC

| | |
|---|---|
| Raw Time—average for all shooters: | 15.346 seconds |
| Splits—average for all shooters: | 1.122 seconds |
| Average number of shots to complete: | 10.75 |

#### .308 Winchester

| | |
|---|---|
| Raw Time—average for all shooters: | 19.567 seconds |
| Splits—average for all shooters: | 1.3765 seconds |
| Average number of shots to complete: | 10.875 |

If you look at the splits you can see that on average the shooters had little problem dealing with the extra recoil of the .308. The lower the recoil, the faster the splits; so the .223 was best, the 6.8 next and the .308 last as expected. But check out the differences; there is less than 0.35-second difference. Remember, this is for aimed fire at relatively small targets at longer range.

### Stage Two

This was a cardboard USPSA target set at fifty yards. The shooter begins by lying prone with his sights on the target. At the buzzer he shoots the target five times, as fast as possible.

The concept here was simply to measure the effect of recoil on speed, but with purpose; as all five had to hit the target to score. The splits between shots as well as the raw total time are both telling.

My son, Nathan, turned in the fastest time with a .223 at 1.12 seconds. He also had one at 1.13 seconds. That edged my 1.25 seconds, also with a .223, back to third place. I hate it when that happens.

### Results

**.223**

| | |
|---|---|
| Raw Time—average for all shooters: | 1.505 seconds |
| Splits—average for all shooters: | 0.285 seconds |

**6.8 SPC**

| | |
|---|---|
| Raw Time—average for all shooters: | 1.774 seconds |
| Splits—average for all shooters: | 0.388 seconds |

**.308 Winchester**

| | |
|---|---|
| Raw Time—average for all shooters: | 2.778 seconds |
| Splits—average for all shooters: | 0.60 seconds |

Again, the difference between the cartridges follows the expected path. I think that the prone position made a difference here as the lighter recoiling rifles could be "tripoded" with the magazine and both of the shooter's elbows contacting the ground. With this technique, the sights stayed on the target and once the shooter realized that, it became a matter of how fast he could pull the trigger. But with the .308,

the recoil was just enough to require some sight correction between shots. Still, five shots into the center of mass in less than three seconds on average is not bad. Nathan did it in under two seconds with the .308.

### Stage Three

Four USPSA targets were placed in a semi-circle at distances from five yards to fifteen yards. The shooter started with the rifle on his shoulder and the muzzle down. At the buzzer he double-tapped the targets. On the first run we shot right to left and then reversed the direction for the second run.

This measures shooting speed, both in the splits between the shots on targets and on how fast the transitions from target to target are completed. The targets must be hit to score.

Once again, Nathan was fastest. Using the .223, he did it in 4.28 seconds. Between him and Brendan they had four runs that beat my best time, which was with the 6.8 SPC at 4.66 seconds. Three of those were with the .223 and one with the 6.8. I will note that on my first run through my best time was with the .308 Winchester, 5.49 seconds. My splits with the two shots on target were almost identical between the .223 and the .308, with only 0.0025 seconds difference. The .308, by the way, was the faster of the two.

### Results

**.223**

| | |
|---|---|
| Raw Time—average for all shooters: | 5.672 seconds |
| Splits—average for all shooters: | 0.3 seconds |

**6.8 SPC**

| | |
|---|---|
| Raw Time—average for all shooters: | 5.916 seconds |
| Splits—average for all shooters: | 0.273 seconds |

**.308 Winchester**

| | |
|---|---|
| Raw Time—average for all shooters: | 5.984 seconds |
| Splits—average for all shooters: | 0.434 seconds |

This is a good simulation of a fight when your position is being overrun and speed, power, and

▲ We turned a lot of ammo into empty brass with this test.

accuracy are your only hope for survival. The difference in raw time between the .223 and .308 is only three-tenths of a second for the four targets and eight shots, but the odds of taking out all the bad guys with two hits each from the .308 are astronomically higher than with the .223.

# The DPMS GII Recon

*Innovation and engineering have improved the AR-L rifle and made it an even better choice for preppers.*

There are far too many rifles on the market to cover them all. The best I can do is tell you about some favorites. Before this rifle came along in an AR-L, my first pick would have been my DPMS AP4. This is a .308 version of the M4 carbine. I have had mine for several years and have used it in battle rifle competitions as well as for hunting and a lot of training and practice. It's the gun used in the test described elsewhere in this book when we pitted the .308, 6.8 SPC, and .223, all head to head in M4 style semiauto rifles. I still highly recommend that rifle, but now there is an ever better choice.

This is the one that broke the mold with AR-L rifles. The DPMS GII Recon is a gun that deserves a hard look from any prepper. It's lighter, runs faster, and has backup redundancy built into problem areas like the extractor. The gun I tested ran like a well-tuned machine and was very accurate.

The GII is almost as small and as light as the AR-15 rifle. Current GII models start at 7.25 pounds, with

▲ The Recon in action.

the AP4. There are two ejectors on the GII. The gun will operate with one ejector, so even if one were to break, the gun will remain in the fight. The extractor is made of some new high-tech metal. DPMS says that in testing it is almost impervious to failure. Instead of

the standard wound-wire extractor spring, the GII uses an elastic, polymer button that has been nicknamed a "tactical Skittle." Again, extensive testing has shown it to be just about failure proof and far less prone to problems than a conventional spring.

The lower receiver has an integral trigger guard and a beveled magazine well. The trigger is standard and can use any of the current AR-L triggers if you wish to upgrade. The GII rifles will, of course, take DPMS pattern magazines.

Currently DPMS offers six different models of the GII. The AP4; MOE; Recon; Hunter, Bull and SASS, in .308 Winchester. From a tactical standpoint the Recon model is pretty much a do-all gun, more than accurate enough for long-range shooting, fast enough for CQB and at 8.5 pounds it's light enough for a prepper to consider it as a primary long gun.

The Recon has a bead blasted, stainless steel 16-inch barrel with a low profile gas block and a mid-length gas tube. The three-pronged flash hider on the end of the barrel is designed to accept a silencer from AAC, a sister company. The forend on the Recon is a four-rail, free-float tube so you can add all the accessories you wish. While the four-rail design has fallen a little bit out of vogue recently, I like the positive feel in my hand this forend provides and still think it is one of the best options on a fighting rifle. The Recon has an adjustable Magpul buttstock and a Magpul grip. My Recon features a DPMS two-stage trigger that breaks nicely at five pounds, five ounces and feels even lighter.

The Recon I tested was very accurate. With the NRA's tough testing protocol of five, five-shot groups it ran just over one MOA across the board. It is not a fussy eater and shot well with all the ammo tested. The best group was with Fusion 150-grain MSR ammo designed for AR-L rifles. That logged in at 0.65-inch for five shots at 100 yards.

The GII Recon has proven that an AR-L rifle does not have to be big and heavy, but rather it can be light and responsive and still function flawlessly.

This is a gun that I think is worth a look from a prepper who is thinking of adding a .308 AR-L battle rifle or two to the gun locker.

# AR-15 and AK-47 Pistols

*Godsends or gimmicks?*

▲ Eric Reynolds with an AK-47 and an AR-15 pistol.

National Firearms Act, these guns are only allowed if you get permission from the government and pay them bribe money.

You must register the SBR and pay a $200 tax. In the times we live in I think each prepper must ask himself if he wants to do that. Having a registered NFA gun, no matter if it's a short barrel rifle, machine gun, or even a suppressor, which is considered a firearm by the government, is not a good idea. It puts you on the radar with the government; and the bureaucrats in charge of that sort of thing often see people who own these guns as problem children and not law-abiding citizens with an interest in firearms.

If things go bad, I think it's safe to say that the government is going to go after gun owners. There is plenty of

▲ Eric Reynolds exiting a truck with an AR-15 pistol. In some places it's legal to have a loaded handgun in a vehicle, but not a long gun.

I have to admit, when I first saw an AR-15 pistol the word "useless" came to mind.

What was the point?

But I am not one to form opinions without actually learning something about the topic, so I got a few of these guns and started using them. I must admit, my mind was changed.

Here's why.

First off, the government.

Short-barreled rifles (SBR) are all the rage right now and a lot of people believe that they are much better for close-quarter battle (CQB.) There is no question that an SBR has some tactical advantages in a multitude of situations. The problem is that, due to the history to back up this assumption, so do you want to take that risk? It's not just Obama. Citizens' guns were confiscated under a Republican administration during Katrina. Yes I know, it was not the Feds; but they didn't stop them, either.

If we are forced into a survival situation, you will not make it without your firearms. Do you really want to take the risk that the government will follow the law? Besides, if they declare martial law, there is no law except what they decide is the law. I seriously doubt that they will be bothered by the Second Amendment and I damn sure don't want to be the test case who finds out.

Your other guns are not registered with the federal government—at least not if we can trust the government to follow the law. The 4473 form you filled out stays with the dealer and when he calls the NICS num-

ber for the FBI to run a background check on you, they are supposed to destroy the records of the gun you are buying. Many people don't believe they do, as the government has blatantly broken the law for years without consequences. For now, we have no option except to believe they follow the law, which means you have not registered any guns with the federal government.

But if you register a NFA gun, you are on record with the government as a gun owner and they do have a track record under multiple administrations of attacking and arresting gun owners while confiscating their guns. Yes, there are plenty of other ways for them to track gun owners, and yes, they probably know you have guns, but why chance it? Why give the government a reason to come and search your house in a time of crisis?

An alternative to a SBR is an AR-15 pistol. It's short and compact just like a SBR, but is legal to own on the federal level and does not require that it be registered with the federal government.

The BATF has made some bizarre rulings on the use of these guns recently, mostly around the Sig SB15 Pistol Stabilizing Brace, which is an attachment that goes on the buffer tube. First the BATF said it was fine. Then they decided it was fine unless it touched your shoulder; at that point it became a felony. That was important because they were no longer regulating the firearm; they were regulating the user of the firearm and how they used the firearm. Later there were reports that this was reversed. I honestly don't

▲ Eric Reynolds with a CMMG AR-15 pistol in .300 Blackout.

▲ This is a full-auto AR-15 pistol chambered for .300 ACC Blackout. The author is using it to "clear" a shoot house during training at Gunsite Academy in AZ. Shooting well with this kind of firearm takes a lot of practice.

know what's what with this issue at this time. I doubt anybody is clear on it.

So what follows is strictly hypothetical and is something I have heard through the gun guy grapevine. I have no actual personal knowledge of it, only what I have heard. With AR-15 handguns, particularly those with the Sig Brace, you can place the buffer tube on your shoulder like a stock and control the guns pretty well. If you pick a sighting system with no eye relief issues like an Aimpoint red dot the gun is pretty easy to shoot fast and accurately. I have heard that they can manage CQB-type drills very well.

I will also note that if you install a laser sight, they are very easy to shoot. I have run the 2x2x2 drill with an AR-15 pistol and a laser sight and can do it in 1.6 seconds, which is very fast. That's reacting to the buzzer and putting two shots on each of three targets in 1.6 seconds. That makes these guns a good choice for close defense work.

▲ Eric Reynolds with a Century Arms AK-47 pistol.

▲ Windham Weaponry AR-15 pistol with a Meprolight Tru-Dot RDS sight.

Another issue, at least in my home state and probably other places as well, is carrying loaded firearms in a vehicle. In Vermont, and perhaps other states, we can carry a loaded handgun in a vehicle, but not a loaded long gun. The idea is that we are adults trusted to follow the law and should be able to have a self-defense handgun. But if Big Brother were to also allow us to have a loaded long gun, we would all instantly become poachers and would decimate the wildlife.

I believe that it's very important to have a semiauto, magazine-fed rifle in your vehicle these days. You can't

▲ Eric Reynolds exiting a truck with a Century Arms AK-47 pistol.

predict the future and if the world crashes and burns while you are on the road you will need to get back to your home and family. Given the possibility of riots or terrorism, a handgun might not be enough.

It takes time to get an unloaded gun into action. A loaded AR-15 handgun is faster to get into the fight and is almost as effective.

The AK-47 handguns do not have the buffer tube in the back. This makes the guns shorter and more compact, but you lose that theoretical shooting technique. Hollywood loves this gun and you always see actors shooting from the hip. I suppose there might be somebody who can hit things that way, but it ain't me or any of my shooting buddies. A full-auto with tracers can use the spray-and-pray technique, but for us mortals with semiautos, any handgun needs to be aimed.

The AK-47 handgun I have from Century Arms has four rails on the forend. It's easy to mount a red dot or similar sight and/or a laser on the gun. Now you have a short, easy to carry, concealable firearm with a high-capacity magazine that is chambered for a high-powered cartridge. They are still tougher than a rifle to shoot well, but they are a lot easier to carry and conceal.

These handguns are no substitute for your battle rifle, but they do make some sense for certain applications. If you already have rifles that use the same ammo and magazines, it might be smart to pick up a handgun or two to supplement them.

# Pistol-Caliber Carbines

*With roots in the Old West, this concept makes sense for preppers.*

▲ The author with the TRESNA JAG9G BU Tactical Rifle. This is a 9mm-chambered AR-15 type rifle.

A lot of the cowboys in the Old West embraced the concept of having their handguns and their rifles chambered for the same cartridge. That way they only had to carry one kind of ammunition. Many of them reloaded and they only needed one set of tools in their saddlebags. In a fight, they didn't have to worry about segregating ammunition; they could feed both guns from the same source.

Granted, some of that was because the repeating rifles of the time were not all that powerful and most were chambered for pistol-caliber-type cartridges, so why not match the rifle and pistol? If you had a Winchester Model 1873 rifle in .44–40 and were looking for a Colt pistol, a .44–40 made more sense than a .45 Colt. But in the end, it worked out for convenience and cost savings as well.

I am not suggesting that you get a pistol caliber carbine as your primary long gun. As a prepper, you really should have some serious battle rifles. That's not a pistol-caliber-carbine forte. They are personal defense guns and do not have the power or the long distance capability of a true battle rifle.

But pistol-caliber carbines make perfect sense for self-defense. They are great for everyday carry when you want to have a companion gun to your pistol. They also give a prepper the ability to shoot pistol ammo in a long gun. So, if the ammo supply dries up and all you can find on the black market is handgun ammo, you now have a long gun that can use that ammo. There is little question that a long gun is easier to shoot than a handgun.

One other consideration is for use inside a building, like your home. Shooting a short-barreled .223 or .308

carbine inside a building is not a good idea. The blast from these guns is so loud that without hearing protection they can stun the shooter and will certainly cause permanent hearing damage. With a pistol caliber cartridge in a carbine, the blast is less and might be a better option when fighting a home invasion.

There was a time some years ago when these guns were all the rage. I remember Ruger and Marlin both had carbines in pistol cartridges. But I guess they didn't sell all that well because they are gone. I think it was because they were ahead of their time. I suspect they would sell very well today, as people are more aware of the need for personal self-defense.

The cowboys loaded their cartridges into both their rifles and their handguns one at a time. They didn't have magazines that could be replaced. Of course, we have that option, so the smart thing to do is to match the carbine to your handgun so that they can both use the same magazines. That way you can reload either gun in a fight without the need to think about which is which. Just grab a new magazine, stick it in the gun, and get back in the fight. Also, you only need to carry one set of magazines, not two.

There are a lot of different pistol-caliber carbines on the market, including several AR-15 variants. Again, I can't begin to cover them all but here are a few I have tried and like. They represent three "classes" of these guns.

## Kel-Tec SUB-2000

▲ The Kel-Tec SUB-2000.

Yeah, I know, cheap guns right?

Yes, they are inexpensive, but those I have tried work pretty darn well. The only Kel-Tec that ever gave me a problem was a .380 handgun that broke after several years of shooting. The company just sent me a new one, no questions asked. Considering that the original gun was pretty inexpensive, it really didn't owe me a thing. This kind of customer service is rare today.

Please do not take that as an endorsement for all inexpensive guns. Most are a mistake. But these Kel-Tec guns, at least those I have owned, are a good value for the money. It's probably best to buy high end for your primary guns, but getting a few inexpensive guns for backup and barter makes sense.

That was my idea here—an inexpensive carbine for backup or barter. Then I tried the gun and was very pleasantly surprised. I wasn't even going to cover it until David Fortier, the editor of the prepper magazine "Be Ready," told me about this carbine. I am glad that he did.

This little carbine has the option of using several different pistol magazines. I ordered mine to use Glock 9mm magazines. I wanted a .40 but they were back ordered, so I got a 9mm and left an order for another in .40 when they are available. Fortunately, I have several Glocks in both cartridges and have collected a lot of magazines for both. Glock magazines are not expensive to buy and there are a lot of aftermarket magazines that often cost even less than Glock brand.

The coolest thing about this gun is that it folds in half to reduce it to a size of 16.25 x 7 inches. That means you can put it in a bag like the Blackhawk Diversion

▲ The Kel-Tec SUB-2000 folds up for easy carry and concealment.

Wax Canvas Messenger Bag from BLACKHAWK! or the Vanquest Envoy 2.0 bag. You can put the folded carbine, several magazines, and even a pistol in these bags and just look like any other hipster headed to the coffee shop.

If you get the dorky haircut, Buddy Holly glasses, and skinny jeans, nobody will ever suspect you are armed. It's the perfect urban camo until TSHTF. Except, I am not sure it's worth the hit on your self-esteem and sex life. They call those birth control glasses for a reason.

With this carbine folded and inside one of these messenger bags or a backpack, it's completely hidden but ready for action very quickly. Just take it out, snap it shut, and go to work. The downside is that it is difficult to mount an optic because the sight will block the gun from folding up all the way. There is a peep rear and a protected front sight which work fine. I added a rail-mounted laser sight from LaserLyte on the bottom rail. All I have to do is slide my hand down the rail to hit the activation switch. Another option would be to mount a small red dot on an angle on the side of the forend using an M-Lock mount. Then the gun can be turned sideways to use the optic. This is a common technique in 3-gun shooting for Open Class rifles and is very effective for defense as well.

The stock is adjustable to three different positions and includes a single-point sling loop attachment, a slot for adding a nylon sling loop, and a Picatinny rail on the bottom for adding small accessories.

The safety is a push-bolt located behind the trigger on the grip. The bolt can be locked in the rear position by the operating handle. The rear sight is an aperture and the protected post front sight can be adjusted for windage and elevation. The thread protector on the muzzle covers ½–28 threads on the 9mm and 9/16–24 threads on the .40 S&W so you can add muzzle accessories if you wish.

This little gun only weighs 4.25 pounds, so it is comfortable to carry on a sling. I have shot it a bunch and so far it's very reliable. This is an interesting little gun. I don't honestly believe it's of a design or quality to be your only gun for survival, but I sure think that buying one or two to have around is a great idea.

### TRESNA JAG9G BU Tactical Rifle

▲ The TRESNA JAG9G BU Tactical Rifle is a 9mm-chambered AR-15 type rifle. It uses the Glock magazines so you can interchange with a Glock 9mm handgun.

This 9mm is an AR-15 based gun. It uses a dedicated milled billet lower receiver that uses Glock magazines and comes with a thirty-three-round high cap magazine. They say any Gen 4 Glock magazine will fit.

The gun is more or less the M4 design, with a 16-inch barrel that even has a cut for a grenade launcher. It has a birdcage flash hider, of course. The forend is a four-rail that is a little short for my style of shooting, but is easily replaced. The stock is adjustable. The gun has a decent trigger and pretty much the same controls as any AR-15. I have been shooting it for a few weeks and so far it has digested every 9mm cartridge I have fed it without any bitching. I have tried multiple factory loads and a few hand loads and the gun just runs them without drama. I like that in a rifle.

The gun is relatively light as AR-15s go at 6.5 pounds. It carries and handles like any M4 with a collapsible stock.

I have a Vortex Strike Fire red dot sight mounted on the gun and it's very fast for multiple target drills. I can rip through the 2x2x2 drill and run my MGM plate rack probably as fast as with any rifle I have. The recoil of the 9mm cartridge is so minuscule that split times for aimed fire are fast.

The 9mm also picks up a little more velocity in the longer barrel than with a handgun and so is more effective with terminal ballistics. This is a gun that a serious prepper would do well to consider as a companion to a 9mm Glock handgun.

### Beretta Cx4 Storm

▲ Beretta Cx4 Storm.

I got this carbine many years ago because of New York. We were shooting USPSA at a club not too far from my home in Vermont, except that my son was a teenager and New York would not let him even touch a handgun. No kidding. As I understood the law, if I asked him to hand me my pistol and he did, we both would be committing a felony. I think if they had their way it would be illegal for a teenager to look at or even think about handguns and that was before New York got bad about gun laws.

So I talked the guys at the club into letting Nathan compete with a carbine and that's how this Beretta Cx4 Storm came to live here at Camp Towsley.

Of course, the club disbanded after we shot one match. Now, with the new and improved gun laws

▲ The author with a TRESNA JAG9G BU Tactical Rifle. This is a 9mm-chambered AR-15 type rifle.

in New York, I no longer do any competitions in that state.

But I still have the Storm. This little 9mm carbine takes Beretta pistol mags and has controls that are similar to running a pistol. For a right-handed shooter, the safety is a push button that you run with your trigger finger. The slide release is easy to reach with your thumb. The bolt is pulled back by a lever on the left side. You can reverse it all for lefties.

The rear sight is a peep with a post-style front. The adjustments are on the front sight. The gun has a rail on top and I have an Aimpoint red dot mounted on it so that I can also use the iron sights by looking through the Aimpoint.

The gun comes in 9mm or .40 S&W. It has a 16.6-inch barrel, is 29.7 inches long and weighs 5.7 pounds. The two-stage trigger is not what it could be. It's hard to pull at almost 9-pounds pull weight and kind of mushy feeling. But other than that, this is a great little carbine.

I once had a buddy visiting my house who had been in the South African Special Forces for many years. He did some amazing shooting with this gun! If you are a Beretta fan and carry a Beretta handgun, this might be a great companion gun.

The idea of a pistol-caliber carbine is one that every serious prepper should check out. Using the same ammo in their pistols and rifles helped a lot of cowboys survive the lonesome prairie. It might help you survive the lonesome apocalypse.

# The AK-47

*Let's start by playing the game in "real time."*

▲ The author with General Mikhail Kalashnikov, the creator of the AK-47 rifle.

There is a game that's fun to play with your friends. It is simply to pick a historical figure that you would like to spend some time hanging out with.

Most quickly pick Jesus, but he is eliminated for a bunch of reasons. First, he's too obvious. Second, there is no mystery. He will simply do a couple of water tricks; you know, walking on it and turning it into merlot. Then he will raise a dead man back to life and unless you are a total fool you will become a true believer. The next thing you know, you are at the airport handing out flyers and Jesus is back hanging with the apostles; much too predictable, makes the game boring.

Hitler is another popular choice. Everybody wants to go back and kill him so they can save the world all that

trouble. Again, not fair; in this game you can't change history. The point is to find out who you want to hang with, not how you can change history or the course of your own life.

Personally, I can think of several people. Teddy Roosevelt might be fun. The man did a lot of remarkable things in his life. But as a writer, a hunter, and an adventurer with a thirst for life (and other things) I think Hemingway would be an interesting buddy. He wasn't afraid to grab life by the shirt and shake what he wanted out of it; and he had the talent to put the results into words that got your attention.

But then, as a gun guy, I have to look at the men who left their marks on the industry. Sam Colt and John Browning are two who come to mind. They were not only geniuses in the designs they came up with, but also in the timing of those designs. A couple of decades one way or the other and those guns that are so well known today might not have caught on with the market. I would love to meet these men and to learn about how they came up with their ideas and why. The closest I have come was to sit in the room where John Browning's body was laid for viewing at the FN plant in Belgium. I felt the same eerie connection with history then that I felt when standing on Hitler's reviewing platform in Nuremberg or at Custer's death site at Little Big Horn. I wondered what the men who created the destinies of these places were like.

Except it's only a game; we can't travel back into time no matter how much we would like to. Until we get that one figured out we are stuck with our little game of sitting around the campfire and discussing which men we want to meet and why it would be important to us, if not to them.

But what of the men our children might pick when they inevitably play this same game in the future? (Of course, I suspect that with the way it's going the "do-gooders" will have prevailed and they will be discussing the prospect over a tofu, wheat-grass blended nature drink rather than good bourbon. Somehow I doubt it will be the same.) What men will they be discussing and, if those men are alive today, would it be interesting for us to meet them now?

Well, from a gun guy's perspective there was at least one legend who had the ability and insight to create a rifle design that not only was genius in its simplicity, but one that has unquestionably left an impact on the

▲ General Mikhail Kalashnikov, the creator of the AK-47 rifle, signs a book for the author.

bites of cake and the General continued his story like he had never been asked to tell it before. That display of family and humility is universal with good people throughout the world.

"I had grown up on a remote farm," he said, "and I was a tank commander in World War II when I got wounded. As soon as I was able to walk they transferred me to another hospital deeper into Russia and away from the front. During my long recovery I heard again and again from the other wounded Russian soldiers how the Germans were kicking our butts because they had automatic rifles and we did not. I had an idea for a gun that could change all that. The Germans wounded me and while I was recovering from my injuries I started making drawings. Later, I created my first machine pistol, which has since been lost. The second pistol, though, is now in a museum in St. Petersburg. From that, the AK-47 rifle evolved. Because I was a simple tank driver, the military committee didn't want to even consider the design, but with persistence and help from some powerful friends they finally relented and decided to take a look. The design spoke for itself from then on and they couldn't ignore it and it was adopted as the new Russian military rifle."

I have several military friends, guys from multiple generations and multiple wars who have all told me pretty much the same thing about the rifle. In a nutshell it was this:

"The AK-47 has a very distinctive sound that I hate because I usually heard it when somebody was shooting at me. However, as a solider and a shooter I have to admire the design of the rifle and the man who created it."

That kind of respect is usually well earned.

I asked the question that I am sure the General was sick of answering, "Do you have any regrets?"

"I designed this gun to help my country. It's a tool, that's all. I designed the gun; the politicians start the wars. I designed it to help protect and save my country and I do not have any regrets."

After we finished our drink he sent his granddaughter to get a book he had written, which he signed and gave to me. Then we went outside and took some photos. At five feet, eight inches it's rare when you see me towering over any man in a photograph, but I had him by almost half a foot. Mikhail Kalashnikov might have

world. With all politics aside it would be an honor to meet that man and discuss the merits of gun design.

Well, I did that.

It was my pleasure to have spent an afternoon some years ago with General Mikhail Kalashnikov, the creator of the AK-47 rifle.

"I owe it all to the Germans," he told me through our interpreter. We were in the kitchen of his dacha located on a lake outside of Izhevsk, Russia. Other than for the language difference, I could have been sitting in any kitchen anywhere in the world. His wife and daughter were serving us tea and cake while he slipped out a bottle of cognac, because he didn't think the women had the drink part quite right. His young granddaughter skipped around the room between

▲ The AK-47 has a very distinctive look.

been small in stature, but when he passed away on December 23, 2013, he left a huge footprint behind.

The AK-47 is probably the most recognizable rifle on the planet. That's partly because Hollywood loves the gun, but it's also because there are so damn many of them. According to the Internet, there is an estimated 875 million firearms in the world. Of that, 100 million are AK-47s, which makes it the most popular firearm on the planet.

The AK-47 is a select-fire, gas-operated assault rifle that is chambered for the 7.62x39 cartridge. The rifle has distinct profile with its curved magazine and when it fires on full-auto it has a very distinctive cadence. The AK-47 is the battle rifle of choice for much of the world. We Americans are for the most part not allowed to own the full-auto version (unless you can locate and afford a transferable gun), but we can have the semi-

auto version, which has pretty much all the benefits; only without the fun switch.

The 7.62x39 cartridge uses a bigger, heavier bullet than the 5.56 NATO cartridge and many believe it's a more effective fight-stopper. Typically, the AK-47 is not a highly accurate rifle and the slower velocity of the cartridge is not an issue within the effective range of the gun. However, just yesterday I watched some young guys pounding a steel IPSC (International Practical Shooting Confederation) target at 300 yards using an AK-47.

The AK-47 is a peasant's gun, one that can stand up to use and abuse by a less than refined class of solider. The AK-47 has earned a reputation throughout the world as a gun that will run and run no matter what and that will stand up to hard use. Those are important qualities for a prepper.

In Africa I have seen the government game scouts with AK-47 rifles that look like a week-old road kill. They toss them in the back of a truck, which is often filled with blood, dirt, and stuff you don't want to think about. They rest their feet on the gun to keep their truck tire sandals out of the gore. While in the bush, they sit on the gun to keep their butts out of the mud and sand. The guns are passed from scout to scout and there is no pride of ownership, which shows. Yet, when a lion charged, our scout ripped half a magazine into the dirt in front of him and changed his mind. The AK had survived all the abuse and still worked. While it's

▲ The AK-47's 7.62x39 cartridge is more powerful than the 5.56 NATO.

▲ This FN FAL was carried all week by our game scout to "protect" us. When we tried to shoot it, the gun would not fire.

an example of one incident, which means nothing, on the same safari, another game scout had an FN FAL that was pretty much treated the same way. When we tried to shoot that gun, it would not function. The gun that the government sent to keep us "safe" would only fire one shot before stopping. That didn't bother the guy with the rifle one bit. Later he tricked one of his buddies into trading with him so he had the AK and his buddy had the gun that didn't work.

That's Africa.

Should you as a prepper have an AK-47? I believe you should. For a long time it was easy and relatively inexpensive to find imported guns that had been converted to semiauto and were civilian legal. My son and I bought a couple of them from Century Arms a long time ago. I don't know how much we have shot them, but it's a bunch. I don't think either one was ever cleaned, and I don't think either one has ever jammed. When you consider that most of that shooting has been with imported, surplus Russian ammo with steel cases that I bought based on price alone, it's remarkable performance; except they are AK-47s and that's what they do.

Politicians hate this gun and have been using every back door trick possible to dry up the supply for civilians to buy. At one time they were cheap and easy to find; now, not so much. Most recently, the Obama administration has used its power to stop the import of most of these guns so that sources are drying up even faster. There are still a lot of guns on the used market, but the prices are going up and more people are hanging on to their guns, so it's harder to find them at any price.

As a result, some companies are starting to make new AK-47 rifles for sale. This is a bit of a change, as we have always depended on converted surplus rifles. But it's also a chance to get a handle on manufacturing quality and to introduce the AK-47 concept to new materials and modern manufacturing techniques. The result should be better rifles.

The only gun I can comment on is the Century Arms. I talked to other manufacturers and they failed to send guns as promised. That could simply be a supply issue, or it could be that they didn't want their guns looked at too closely and written about. I honestly don't know; so proceed with caution before writing a check for any gun you are unfamiliar with.

What I can tell you about is the Century Arms C39v2. This gun is a 100 percent American-made AK rifle. The one I have is well made, with the fit and finish excellent. The gun is all American with no imported parts. It's built on a milled receiver, machined from a solid block of 4140 ordnance-quality steel.

According to Century Arms, some of the enhancements include a T-shaped magazine catch, compatibility with AKM furniture, a bolt hold open safety, an enhanced dust cover, and standard AK sights. The C39v2 is finished with black nitrite and uses a new RAK-1 enhanced trigger group. The trigger pull on mine is surprisingly clean and crisp and breaks at 5-pounds 10-ounces.

The 16.5-inch barrel has a 1:10 twist rate and comes with a muzzle brake that is installed on a left hand 14x1 metric thread so you can change it out with other muzzle attachments. The gun is 37.25 inches long and weighs 8.2 lbs. Century Arms even has a pistol version of the gun, which I cover, in another chapter.

Century Arms C39v2 is an excellent choice for a prepper who is looking for a newly manufactured, yet affordable, AK-47 style carbine.

The AK-47 is chambered in 7.62x39, which is a cartridge that has more than proven itself in battle. It's not a NATO cartridge and it's not used in the United States by the military or law enforcement. However, there are thousands and thousands of AK-47 and SKS rifles out there in civilian hands and, for a long time, millions of rounds of ammo were being imported. Combine that

▲ Century Arms C39v2 AK-47.

with the US-manufactured ammo and there are a lot of 7.62 bullets out there waiting for their ride.

If we find our country under terrorist attack from radical Islamic forces, odds are they will have AK-47 rifles and I highly advise taking all the ammo you can find off their dead bodies.

While finding ammo will probably not be as easy as it will be for .223 or even .308 chambered rifles, it's going to be pretty close and I suspect that 7.62x39 ammo will be in the top five of available rifle cartridges.

The AK-47 is probably second only to the AR platforms in suitability for preppers. Magazines are easy to find and are inexpensive. There are plenty of newly manufactured magazines as well as surplus military mags. I just picked up a few surplus magazines at a local gun shop for ten bucks each. They were brand-new and still packed in Cosmoline.

The downside of the AK is that the iron sights are difficult to see. They hide in poor light for anybody and if you are on the downhill side of age forty they will be almost impossible to use, even in good light. The gun was never designed to be used with an optic and it's a bit harder to mount a glass sight on the guns than it is on an AR flattop with a rail. There are some mounts out there and which one works best depends on the gun you have. I have a mount from Texas Weapons System that replaces the top cover on the receiver. This mount has a rail for mounting an optic such as a red dot. They offer a peep sight to mount there if you would rather not use an optic. I find I can use a peep sight much better than open sights.

I can't think of any rifle with more accessories and bolt-on goodies on the market than the AK-47. You can run it out of the box as God and the General intended, or you can add an infinite amount of bling to your rifle.

▲ Texas Weapons System scope mount for an AK-47.

Of course, there is that perpetual argument that a prepper should have the guns needed to avail themselves of the current ammo available. You can't buy a gun in every cartridge, but you can play the odds. If times get tough, the 7.62x39 is a battle rifle cartridge, with very high odds that it will show up on the ammo market. Even if you do not elect to use the AK-47 type rifle as your primary long gun, it makes sense to have a gun or two and some magazines in your collection of survival guns. These are not expensive rifles and an AK-47 should be high on any list of prepper guns to buy.

## AK-74

The AK-74 is the newer version of the rifle. It was designed to use the smaller 5.45x39mm cartridge, which is very similar to our 5.56/223 cartridge in performance. I suppose most of what you can say about the AK-47 you can also say about the AK-74; except there are a lot fewer of them, it uses a less powerful cartridge, and ammo is much harder to come by here in the United States.

My personal experience is a bit limited and no doubt, I am biased. The few times I have used the full-auto version of this gun it has not run well. We experienced way too many jams. It is probably an issue specific to those guns or perhaps the ammo, but it soured me a bit. AKs are not pretty and they are not accurate, but they are supposed to run. That's what makes them what they are.

I know gun guys who love the AK-74, but I am not one of them. I may well be wrong on that, as I am the first to admit my experience is limited with this gun.

But even beyond that, I don't see a lot of reason for preppers to stock up on guns with a cartridge that is similar in performance to the 5.56/.223, but with ammo that is much harder to find. Any gun a prepper buys has to bring something to the table other than just its "cool factor" and must offer something you can't find anywhere else. I don't see that the AK-74 does that. It probably makes sense to buy at least one if you have the resources and have already purchased everything else on your list. Or, if you want a gun handy to fire the cartridge, buy a much less expensive upper for your AR-15 that is chambered for the 5.45x39mm.

I think a prepper should have every gun on the market, if possible, and I'll never discourage buying any firearm, but this one is pretty low on my list. You, of course, may disagree, but I think that the AK-47 is the much smarter option of the two.

# SNIPER GUNS
## The Long-Range Option

*Sometimes you just gotta reach out and touch someone.*

 prepper who is "sheltering in place," as the latest buzzwords like to call it, may see a strong need for a long-range rifle.

If you have a home or compound that is remote enough to survive a social or economic meltdown and have been smart enough to create open space around it, then you will need some rifles capable of long-range use to defend that space.

Here is how I handled that in my novel *The 14th Reinstated*. I think this illustrates an example of why some preppers will need long-range precision rifles.

After a devastating attack where the protagonist and his family lost control of their home for several days and were robbed of guns and provisions, they decided that they needed better security. Here is a passage from the book on that:

*I realized that we needed a more defensible position. We cut every tree around the house for several hundred yards. My neighbors had moved and abandoned their house a few years back. We heard that they were all killed soon after they left, so we reluctantly tore it down, salvaged the lumber and filled in the cellar hole so it could not provide cover for the bad guys. To get to my place then, anybody had to cover four hundred yards of open ground in any direction.*

*My son, son-in-law and I spent several weeks traveling to farms in the area left empty after the owners left or were killed, collecting the barbed wire and fence posts from the abandoned fields.*

*We ringed the house, starting at the four hundred yard-line with a six-foot-high fence with ten strands of tensioned barbed wire, strung too close together to climb through and too high to step over. We then looped several strands of loose wire another two feet* above that so that anybody trying to climb up the tensioned wires would not be able to make it over the top. Then we repeated that every fifty yards to the one hundred-fifty yard line. That meant we had six fences, one every fifty yards.

For the next fifty yards we scattered random coils of barbed wire, sort of like military concertina wire, for a tangle foot. In random places, we held it up a foot or so on posts or by stapling it to blocks of wood so that it formed a big mess that was impossible to walk, let alone run, through without stumbling.

We planted crops between the fences, but no tall growing plants like corn. I didn't want any place to hide.

I put signs every ten feet on the outside fence stating that it was private property monitored by armed guards and anybody approaching past the fence would be shot.

We installed gates through the fences using big thick steel pipe that I had traded for years earlier, set deep in concrete. I traded a thousand rounds of .223 ammo to a guy with a diesel-powered welding rig in exchange for putting the gates together. These gates were too big and tough to crash through with a truck. Besides that, we staggered the gates twenty-five yards off center, so that the second gate was twenty-five yards to the left and the third twenty-five yards to the right, or fifty yards apart. It was a pain in the neck for us, but with six gates to get through, this staggering arrangement would prevent any truck ramming the gates from building up enough speed to get through them all.

The gates were triple locked with the locks hidden under welded brackets so that they could not be cut with bolt cutters. When things started to get bad I had the foresight to order three dozen hardened locks. Half of them were keyed alike so one key opened them all and the other half all required their own individual keys.

The gates have spikes sticking up on top to discourage climbing over them and were strung with barbed wire. They were all easily visible from the bunker we made on the roof of the house, so we could shoot anybody trying to breach them.

We kept a .50 BMG rifle loaded with armor piercing ammo at the ready to take out any vehicle. We also kept a bolt-action sniper rifle in .300 Winchester ready to deal with anybody trying to cut through the locks. Plus, we all practice with our AR carry rifles out to five

hundred yards. Any one of us could easily handle a problem along the fences with those rifles if the need came up.

We surrounded the house with a double row of sandbags to stop any bullets, leaving shooting ports at strategic locations. I welded up metal doors and window covers in my shop and installed them before it became impossible to get materials or electricity to run the welder. Of course, I had gun ports through them, which could be closed and locked from inside when not in use. We installed a double metal roof to prevent anybody from tossing a torch on the roof to burn us out.

When it came to our guns, we picked wisely. Each of us carried a semiauto handgun and several spare magazines at all times. After that first incident, we also never left the house without a long gun. We didn't use deer rifles, even though I had a lot of them, or the shotguns that so many others thought were the answer. We picked AR-15 rifles because of their thirty-round magazines and the fact that the empty magazines can be replaced in about a second if you practice; giving you another thirty shots, so shooting was virtually uninterrupted. Our current guns were the best in my collection and they were tested to be sure they would keep running when they were hot and dirty.

We also had a few highly accurate bolt-action "sniper" type rifles with removable magazines to handle any long-range precision problems such as a sniper or some jerk on a machine gun. We kept several extra magazines with each rifle so it could be reloaded very quickly.

In addition to carrying one of the AR rifles whenever we stepped outside, we also kept at least one more in every room of the house and plenty of loaded magazines near each one. It was a risk because we might lose them again, but the benefits outweighed that risk.

What a bolt-action precision rifle primarily brings to the table is power. The secondary benefit is accuracy. There is no doubt that some semiauto rifles can be incredibly accurate and there are times when they might be the better choice. But the semiauto guns that provide that level of accuracy are limited in the size of the cartridge, usually to the .308 Winchester and similar cartridges. These don't have the ultra-long-range capability that some bolt-action rifles can provide.

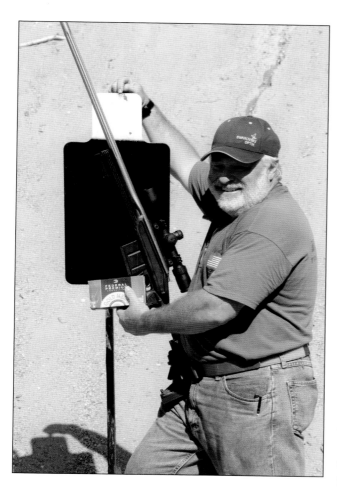

▲ This is a head shot at 1,000 yards. Rifle is a Remington Sendero converted to tactical use. Cartridge .300 Winchester, Federal ammo with 190-grain Sierra bullets.

other barriers, something to stall them at longer range so that you can defend your property and family without letting them get closer. They may be wearing body armor and will certainly be using any cover they can find, so the need for precision and power is critical.

The second need for preppers defending their homes in this situation is the ability to disable vehicles or other machinery, perhaps even something like a machine gun.

I can see the eyes rolling now. But we need to think this through and try to predict every possibility as best we can. In a total melt down, if the government breaks down there is no predicting where any of the military gear will end up. It's a very plausible scenario for a gang of bad guys to have a black market or stolen, vehicle-mounted machine gun. This calls on a big powerful cartridge with a bullet that can break stuff.

On the other hand, if they show up with a tank, run away! You are out-gunned on that one.

I suppose we probably should look at the possibility that you are under attack by government forces as well. It's hard to think about that happening in America but we must, because it is a very real possibility. The truth is, you can't win that one either. If you try, they will kill you. Again, run away. It's better to live.

Nothing is ever completely off the table and we must try to consider every possible scenario, but we are not fighting an offensive war and we will rarely be justified in shooting at any threat that's not on our property. Of course, that is a very wide-ranging list of possibilities. My property is probably not the same as your property.

For example, I know several different people who live in remote locations, more or less in the center of a large property. Most of them are in western states where the terrain is relatively open. In most situations, their land is fenced and the boundaries are well marked. Anybody on their property is knowingly trespassing, and in a survival situation I suppose anybody trespassing on the property is probably there with bad intentions and could be considered a threat.

For those preppers, it makes sense to have a rifle capable of shooting at ultra-long-range and delivering a bullet with enough whack to do the job. Somebody on a remote ranch in Texas with open terrain will probably need more long-range capability than a prepper

The short-action carbines also do not have the power needed to penetrate some barriers or stop a vehicle.

On average, the precision bolt-action rifles will have a bit more practical accuracy than a semiauto rifle—partly because of the design of the gun and partly because they will generally have a better trigger. Finally, a bolt-action rifle is very reliable, can function under conditions that will stall a semiauto and will run poor ammo that a semiauto won't tolerate.

The prepper defending his home against a long-range threat will have two types of targets. The first is bad guys making an attack. If you planned well with your location there will be something to keep them at a distance, at least temporarily—open space, fences, or

▲ .50 BMG rounds.

in northern New Hampshire living on fifty wooded acres.

Once again, it comes down to knowing your situation, trying to envision every reasonable possibility, and then customizing to your needs when buying guns for prepping.

If you are defending a smaller compound, say, something more like what is described in the book excerpt above, you may be legally and morally bound to not shoot past the boundaries of the property. In that circumstance, a cartridge that's very capable at 500 yards is adequate, where the prepper in Texas may have use for a rifle and cartridge capable of ending a threat at twice or even three times that distance.

Unfortunately, a civilian does not have the options of the military. We can't call in an airstrike and we are not allowed to own weapons like a rocket launcher or Claymore mines. Besides, this is a firearms book and guns are the only options we are exploring here. There are other sources of information on other methods to defend the perimeter of your property, but I am not going to get into them here. This book explores the firearms that a civilian can own and what are the best firearms to protect your property. For that, a precision rifle is a critical tool.

If you are a prepper living in a remote or semi-remote area you should probably look at getting one or more of these rifles.

# The Workhorses of Precision Rifles

*There is a lot that goes into making a rifle that can hit a target half a mile away.*

There is no doubt that the most popular precision rifles today are usually chambered in the .308 Winchester and similar short-action cartridges. Much of that is due to the lower recoil when compared to some of the larger cartridges.

Of course, the .308 Winchester is important because it's a NATO cartridge and it's used by law enforcement. It's also one of the most popular centerfire rifle cartridges for civilian use. Of any of the precision rifle cartridges, you have the best chance of finding ammo for the .308 after a meltdown.

Actually, any accurate cartridge can be considered for precision work. In fact, many preppers may already have deer rifles that are fully capable for limited use here. The main issue with using a hunting rifle is the very limited magazine capacity. In most hunting-style bolt-action rifles the magazine will hold four standard, non-belted cartridges. The belted magnum cartridges are usually limited to three. That's not a lot of ammo for a rifle that will be used to defend your life. Reloading will be slow, as you must insert each new cartridge into the magazine one at a time. However, it is possible to change out the bottom metal on most guns to use removable box magazines. That way you can have a supply of extra magazines loaded and ready to use. With most systems you can also get magazines that hold ten or more cartridges. The better magazine systems are a bit expensive, but it's money well spent.

The other issue is accuracy under sustained fire. Most precision rifles are designed and tested to maintain their accuracy even when the barrel is very hot from a lot of shooting. Hunting guns often will not maintain accuracy when the barrel gets hot. Group sizes can open up or the point of impact may change and may even continue to change as the heat increases.

Of course, not all guns are prone to changes and some very thin-barreled guns can shoot well hot. For example, I have a Remington Custom Shop 40X rifle in .280 Remington with a very thin barrel. In fact, it's the prototype for their "triangle" shape barrels seen in later production on many factory guns. This gun is designed for sheep hunting and is extremely lightweight. Yet, it is very accurate and will maintain accuracy and point of impact even when the barrel is very hot.

I've tested a lot of guns over the last thirty years as part of my job as a gun writer for NRA Publications and other magazines. While I have seen a lot of hunting guns that cannot manage a hot barrel, I think the trend today is slowing down. I am not sure why, except I know that barrel making has changed and I suspect they are finding ways to make less stressed barrels or at least to do better stress relief.

The reason a barrel loses accuracy or point of impact as it heats up is usually due to stresses in the barrel. When the metal heats up, these stresses change the dynamics of the barrel. It is a common practice with some barrel makers to straighten the barrel. That is, if the barrel is not straight after manufacture, they bend it until it is straight. But if it is not stress relieved correctly, the metal tries to return to its old position when the barrel gets hot and the point of impact shifts. The key is to not stress the barrel to start with, or to stress relieve it correctly. I don't know the reason for sure as a lot of companies keep their secrets tight to their chests, but I am seeing fewer and fewer factory hunting guns that react negatively to a hot barrel. A lot of the newer rifles now shoot very well when hot and sometimes I even run into a gun that gets more accurate as the barrel heats up.

So, how do you tell? Shoot the gun. Run it until it's hot and dirty. If it's still accurate and hitting to the correct point of impact, you lucked out. If not, keep it for hunting or trade it to a hunter and try again. It is not a bad gun; you are asking it to do something it was not designed to do.

Or better yet, buy a precision rifle. The best ones are designed and built to maintain accuracy with a hot barrel. They also are designed with removable box magazines for fast reloading. These tend to be heavy rifles designed primarily for shooting from a rest or from prone. They have good triggers and often

an adjustable stock so that you can fit the gun to your body shape and shooting style.

Here is a look at some of the most popular cartridges for precision long-range rifles. I am not going to cover every cartridge used, just the most popular in each category.

## Short-Action Rifles

### 6.5 Creedmoor

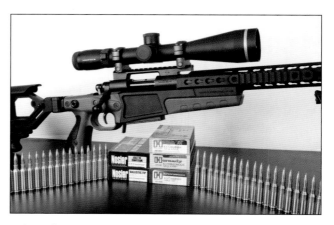

When the creative people at ammo companies actually spend time pulling triggers, good things can happen. During the 2007 Camp Perry matches, Hornady engineer Dave Emary and High Power National Champion Dennis DeMille were talking about the 6.5 wildcat cartridges that are popular in the sport. As can happen with any wildcat cartridge in the hands of shooters who think they can beat the laws of physics, the lack of standardization was leading to problems. They thought it would be great if there was a cartridge that followed current popular design, was accurate enough to win, and was available from a commercial ammo manufacturer. So Emary and fellow Hornady engineer Joe Thielen pooled their talents and in 2008 announced a new Hornady cartridge designed for long-range shooting called the 6.5 Creedmoor.

The 6.5 Creedmoor can trace its roots back to an odd parentage, one far from the long-range target game. The .307 Winchester was introduced in 1982 and was designed for the lever-action Winchester Model 94 rifle. Not exactly 1,000-yard competition ready. The .307 Winchester never achieved much success and is no longer chambered in any commercial rifles. However, that case was used to make the .30 TC, which was introduced in 2007. Thompson Center had commissioned Hornady to design a proprietary 30-caliber cartridge for the introduction of their bolt-action Icon rifle. Emary used the .307 Winchester case, although it was modified and modernized. The case was shortened, the thick case walls thinned, and the rim removed. The result was the .30 TC. When necked down to take a .264-inch bullet, the .30 TC gave birth to the 6.5 Creedmoor.

Emary said that the cartridge was designed around the 140-grain A-Max bullet preferred by long-range target shooters. They looked at other short-action .264 cartridges and made some changes to the chamber throat angle and other specifications to accommodate a long-ogive, high-ballistic-coefficient bullet of that weight. As a result, Hornady was able to extract better long-range performance than is commonly seen from other 6.5 mm short-action cartridges.

The 6.5 Creedmoor cartridge has a .473 diameter case head, the same as the .30–06 family of cartridges. It has a 30-degree shoulder and the case length is 1.920-inch. The overall cartridge length is 2.825-inch, so it will fit in a standard short action. With a difference of 0.905-inch, or almost a full inch between the case length and the overall cartridge length, there is plenty of room for the long 140-grain 6.5mm, VLD-type bullets to extend from the case. This means they can be seated properly without intruding into the powder space.

The listed muzzle velocity for the 140-grain Hornady load is 2,710 ft/s.

This cartridge is hugely popular in precision rifles. I have used it to make first shot hits on one MOA targets out to 1,200 yards while shooting at the FTW long-range shooting school in Texas.

### .260 Remington

I first saw this cartridge when Remington gave some writers a sneak preview at their 1996 gun writers seminar and then "officially" introduced the cartridge at the 1997 SHOT Show. Credit was given to Jim Carmichael of *Outdoor Life* fame for developing the .260 Remington and no doubt influencing Remington to make an honest cartridge out of it. Carmichael developed the cartridge for use in IBS 1,000-yard benchrest competition and called it the 6.5 Panther.

▲ The .260 Remington will fit in any AR-L rifle and can reach out for long range.

Part of the "family" of .308 Winchester-based short-action cartridges, the .260 Remington bridges the gap between the .243 Winchester and the 7mm-08 Remington while retaining much of what is good about both.

Even though the .260 Remington started life as a long-range target cartridge, Remington ignored that aspect and pushed it as a hunting round, which is the primary reason why it's not more popular for long-range shooting. There is a serious lack of factory ammo with long-range bullets from any major ammo maker in the .260 Remington, as in none. While the 6.5 Creedmoor has lots of long-range-oriented ammo from multiple ammo makers, most have ignored the .260 Remington in this area.

Handloaders don't have those restrictions and the .260 Remington has become very popular with long-range shooters. It has more case capacity than the 6.5 Creedmoor so if the gun has the chamber cut for long 140-grain bullets and the magazine is large enough to handle the cartridge, it actually has a slight ballistic advantage over the 6.5 Creedmoor.

### .308 Winchester

Like so many other great cartridges, the .308 Winchester was spawned by the military. In the 1940s the United States Government started searching for a new rifle cartridge to replace the .30 Carbine and .30–06 Springfield. The resulting cartridge was initially called T65, later to become the 7.62X51mm NATO, which the military accepted in 1954.

Winchester actually beat the military to the punch and brought out the civilian version of the cartridge, the .308 Winchester, in 1952. They also offered rifles in the Model 70 bolt-action and the Model 88 lever-action chambered for the .308 Winchester.

Although it was nearly half an inch shorter than the .30–06 Springfield, the .308 Winchester almost duplicated the performance when introduced. This is often attributed to the new ball powder that was developed for the cartridge, but it's notable that the .308 Winchester is loaded to slightly higher pressures than the .30–06 Springfield, which is a factor in performance. The SAMMI Mean Average Pressure for the .308 Winchester is 62,000 PSI while the MAP for the .30–06 is 60,000 PSI.

The .308 Winchester has been one of the most successful cartridges ever introduced. It has been offered in just about every rifle style made. Bolt-action, single-shot, lever-action, semiauto, full-auto, pump-action, straight pull and single-shot—all have been chambered in .308 Winchester. The cartridge is also perpetually in the top ten for sales of rifle ammunition for every single ammo maker. This is a big factor for preppers as it means you can find ammo just about everywhere.

The .308 Winchester is extremely popular with hunters and it's a good cartridge for all but the largest North American big game. Some believe that the .308 Winchester may be the most inherently accurate 30-caliber commercial cartridge ever produced. This accuracy has made it a top choice for shooters of many disciplines.

The cartridge is used in just about every type of long-range or accuracy-oriented competition shooting. It's also extremely popular with tactical shooters as well as in the "heavy" classes of 3-gun shooting. The .308 Winchester is perhaps the favorite chambering for "tactical" bolt-action rifles designed for law enforcement and favored by accuracy and long-range shooting buffs. I doubt there is any other rifle cartridge claiming so large and diverse a resume. The .308 Winchester is one of the most historically significant rifle cartridges ever introduced and will continue to be extremely popular for the foreseeable future.

For tactical use, the two most common bullet weights are 168-grain and 175-grain. Palma shooters often use a lighter 155-grain bullet so it will stay supersonic to 1,000 yards, which may also be applied to tactical use if you plan to shoot that far.

The trouble with any short-action cartridge is that they really start to run out of whack at about 500 yards. Of course, you can hit a target much farther with them. I have shot my .308 out to 1,000 yards and have hit targets at 1,400 yards with a 6.5 Creedmoor, but when you really stretch out the range they are lacking the energy and velocity to be effective.

At 1,000 yards all three are down around 600 foot-pounds of remaining energy and, more importantly, the velocity is below what is needed for positive bullet expansion. If your defense scenario calls for being able to effectively shoot past 500 yards, you may want to look at a larger cartridge.

But if your defense scenario is that they will be used to stop an attack at 500 yards, or less, this class of cartridge is fine for shooting bad guys and will be very effective.

## The Middle Ground

The middle level of power for precision rifles would be cartridges in the .300 Winchester class. That would include any of the cartridges with similar ballistics, like the .300 Remington Ultra Mag, .300 Weatherby or any of the various 7mm Magnum cartridges.

## .300 Winchester Magnum

There is no doubt that the .300 Winchester Magnum is by far the most popular of this class of rifle cartridges for long-range shooting and in truth it pretty much stands alone here. The other cartridges are, of course, capable enough, but the .300 Winchester has a long history as a sniper round, going back to when it was introduced in the early '60s. It was also once the darling of the 1,000-yard competition shooters when it set world records. As a result, there are many more options for rifles and ammo used for long-range work.

Back when it was first adopted by the military for use in Vietnam there were not many other options in this class. The .300 Winchester was available in rifles like the Remington 700 and Winchester Model 70. That made the cartridge and those rifles the logical choice as sniper guns used by the military. Even today, the M-24 Sniper rifle in .300 Winchester is based on a Remington Model 700 rifle.

This means that of the cartridges in this class, the .300 Winchester has the best chance of keeping ammo in the supply chain in times of trouble. It's also a hugely popular hunting cartridge so every Mom-and-Pop store in East Podunk probably has ammo on its shelves.

The .300 Winchester is one of the preferred sniper cartridges with the military because it brings more energy to longer ranges. Where a .308 drops below 1,000 foot-pounds at around 600 yards, the .300 Winchester makes it to nearly a 1,000 yards before dropping below that threshold. Most expanding bullets need around 2,000 ft/s on impact to work their magic and the .308 drops below that threshold at just past 300 yards. The .300 Winchester maintains 2,000 ft/s until more than 500 yards. So it effectively extends the useful range of the 30-caliber bullet.

But even with a 190-grain bullet at 2,900 ft/s muzzle velocity, the .300 Winchester is mostly for shooting bad guys, not breaking their tools and toys.

## The .338 Lapua

The .338 Lapua cartridge started life in the early '80s and had a rocky road for many years. Due in part to its performance in Iraq and Afghanistan, today it is one of the most popular long-range rifle cartridges around.

When it comes to ultra-long-range shooting the .338 Lapua has emerged as a fan favorite. Of course, holding the world record for the longest sniper shot ever made is a pretty good marketing trick.

According to the *Guinness Book of World Records*, the longest successful rifle shot in history was made in Afghanistan by a British sniper named Craig Harrison using an Accuracy International rifle in .338 Lapua. Three hits at 2,707 yards, or 1.54 miles.

Harrison and his colleagues were providing cover for an Afghan National Army patrol south of Musa Qala. When the Afghan soldiers and Harrison's troop commander came under enemy fire, Harrison, whose vehicle was farther back on a ridge, set up on a Taliban compound in the distance.

He started shooting with his .338 Lapua rifle. Not every bullet hit the target, but enough did to get the job done. One round hit a bad guy running a machine gun and killed him. Another insurgent stepped up to the machine gun and another bullet killed him. A third shot took out the machine gun.

The distance was measured by a GPS system at 8,120 feet. That is 2,707 yards, or 1.54 miles. It is so far that it took the bullets nearly three seconds to get there, and it's 1,000 yards past what was thought to be the effective range of the firearm.

▲ The author makes an adjustment to the scope on a Blaser .338 Lapua.

My grandfather had a saying about when somebody made a spectacular shot, "Well, the bullet had to go somewhere." Meaning the guy probably got lucky. One shot can simply be luck, but three effective hits? That's not luck, that's shooting at the highest level. Even at that extreme distance the big, heavy bullets managed to kill the bad guys and break their machine gun.

For ultra-long-range shooting, the .338 Lapua fills the gap between the .300 Winchester and the .50 BMG. It's proven to handle wind better and hit harder than the 30-caliber cartridges. But unlike the .50 BMG, the .338 Lapua rifles are light enough to be carried by a normal human. Even in the comparatively lighter rifles, the .338 Lapua has much less recoil and muzzle blast than the .50 BMG.

The .338 Lapua is very effective for shooting bad guys as it is accurate and powerful, but still controllable enough to shoot relatively fast. The 250–300-grain bullets normally used in this cartridge are edging into the power level needed to break things and disable machines.

The .338 Lapua is perhaps the very best choice for shooting at ultra-long-range. It brings a level of power that can get things done out in the nether regions but is still a reasonable cartridge that is easily manageable in a rifle. The guns are light enough to carry and move, yet the recoil doesn't shift body parts to new locations and the muzzle blast doesn't smash stuff in its path.

The popular 250-grain load still carries almost 1,500 foot-pounds of energy at 1,000 yards. At 1,500 yards

it has 763 foot-pounds, which is 225 percent of a .308 and 164 percent of the .300 Winchester at that distance. Plus it has a large, heavier bullet so it carries a lot more momentum. Even if the bullet does not expand due to the low velocity at long range, the .338 diameter is going to make a bigger hole.

The downside is that factory ammo is very expensive for the .338 Lapua, so it's a pricy gun to practice with unless you handload your ammo. That said, there are some outstanding factory loads from a wide range of ammo makers. There are also some great bullets for handloading. If you are going to buy just one long-range gun to do everything, this is a great choice.

## .500 BMG, The Bludgeon

▲ Lee Houghton shooting his home-built .50 BMG.

There is something almost religious about turning loose more than 14,000 foot pounds of energy from a rifle you fire from your shoulder. When you consider that's about three times the energy produced by most guns used for hunting elephants, it all kind of comes into perspective. The .50 BMG is a special kind of rifle and shooting it is a vastly addicting experience.

The .50 Browning Machine Gun cartridge was developed by John Browning for the Browning 50-caliber machine gun and was adopted by the military in 1921. It was initially to be used as an anti-aircraft round, but it proved useful for a lot of warfare, including sniper work.

▲ .50 BMG cartridges next to .223 Remington cartridges.

The .50 BMG is simply a scaled-up .30–06 cartridge. It's a NATO cartridge, so ammo should be available for it after TSHTF.

It is the big boy of long-range cartridges. The .50 BMG has no shoulder-fired equal when it comes to breaking things at any range. It can fire a 750-grain bullet at nearly 3,000 ft/s muzzle velocity. Where a .308 Winchester has about 2,600 foot-pounds of energy at the muzzle, the .50 BMG has almost 14,500 foot-pounds of muzzle energy and the big, heavy, high B.C. bullet carries well out to ultra-long range. Size matters with bullets and this is as big as it gets in a shoulder-fired rifle. The .50 BMG has no peers when you want to smash stuff and end problems.

The guns are heavy, the recoil stout, and the muzzle blast is fearsome, but when you absolutely, positively must get the job done, there is nothing you can legally own and fire from the shoulder that even comes close to the .50 BMG.

For stopping vehicles or punching through barriers, the .50 BMG stands alone. If you have property to defend, it is highly recommended that you have one of these guns.

Nothing says, "Go away and leave me alone" quite like the .50 BMG.

# Long-Range Rifles

*Rifles for reaching out.*

There are so many guns on the market that fit this category that it would be impossible to cover them all in a single book, let alone suggest what to buy. I will, however, tell you about some that I have and what I like or don't like about them. That may help you when it's time to buy your own rifles. I will also make some suggestions on ways you can procure a long-range rifle or two without breaking the bank.

I will point out that these are not guns you should just buy and stick in a closet while you wait for the world as we know it to end. First off, long-range shooting is a skill that takes a while to learn and can erode rather quickly. The time to find out you suck at long-range shooting is not when your life is on the line. You need to build your skills and then keep practicing to stay sharp.

That's not a punishment.

Shooting is fun, long-range shooting in particular. There is something that builds smiles when you can reach out an impossible distance and ring a steel target.

These guns are made to shoot, so shoot them. You may even find yourself entering some of the precision rifle competitions that are popping up all over the country. If nothing else, just spending a Saturday afternoon with your friends busting targets at long range is great therapy for whatever is ailing you. If more people did that it would become a better world and maybe the need for this book would abate.

There is not enough room here to cover all the aspects of long-range shooting. I wish there were, but this book has already doubled in size from the original proposal, and we had to end it someplace. There is a lot of good information out there and some that's not so good. The best way to learn is to get some professional instruction. If you have the time and resources I highly recommend that you attend a class on long-range shooting.

When it comes to long-range shooting instruction and opportunity, the best place I know is the FTW ranch in Barksdale, Texas. It's about a two-and-a-half-hour drive from the San Antonio airport, but the winding road will take you to a whole new world. As the owner Tim Fallon pointed out, the ranch was the last stronghold of the Comanche and once you see this country you understand why. It is wild country with deep canyons and steep hills. It's a perfect place to evade the cavalry or to learn about long-range shooting.

The facility has a wide range of targets out to 1,800 yards and even farther. In fact, the world record 3,600-yard (two miles) shot was done at the FTW ranch. The many targets are set in diverse terrain, including at angles up and down and in long, deep canyons where the winds get screwy. The military trains here, partly because of the various target opportunities, but also because the rough and broken terrain simulates the wind conditions found in Afghanistan's mountains.

FTW Shooting School
1802 Horse Hollow Rd
Barksdale, TX 78828-1134
(830) 234-4366
www.ftwoutfitters.com

## The Guns I Know

### 6.5 Creedmoor

▲ The author shooting his custom-built 6.5 Creedmoor.

Of course, there are a lot of factory-produced guns available and chambered for the 6.5 Creedmoor, both in bolt-action precision rifles and AR-L rifles designed for long-range shooting.

At the FTW Ranch shooting school I hit targets out to 1,400 yards with the Ruger Predator FTW rifle. That gun is designed for hunting, but is a great low cost option for a long-range rifle. I have shot with two of them and both are great shooters: very accurate, good triggers, and shot well when hot. This rifle is a good option for this cartridge at an affordable price. It lacks the extras of a tactical rifle like a removable box magazine and oversize bolt handle, but those can be added later.

Recently I decided to have a precision rifle built for long-range competition shooting and to use for defense of my home if it ever comes to that. To be honest, I went back and forth on the cartridge. I already had long-range rifles in .308 Winchester, .300 Winchester and .338 Lapua. I was going to pick the .260 Remington because I have had years of experience with that cartridge as a hunting round and already had all the tools I needed for reloading. I like the idea of the better performance possibilities over the 6.5 Creedmoor, due to the slightly larger case. But it would be an all-handloading situation as currently no major ammo maker offers factory-loaded ammunition with long-range target bullets in the .260 Remington. I

can live with that, I have been a hard-core handloader since my grandfather taught me how to make .243 Winchester ammo when I was thirteen years old.

Part of the deal was I was going to do a magazine feature on the gun for NRA's *Shooting Illustrated* magazine. When I was discussing the details with the editor, Ed Friedman, he was pretty adamant about picking the 6.5 Creedmoor. The cynic in me thinks it's because of all the factory ammo available for this cartridge and the fact that all those ammo companies are potential advertisers. But he also pointed out that it's the hottest cartridge for precision shooting in the country and that the "cool factor" was off the charts. After all, we have to inspire the readers to buy the magazines, so I ordered the rifle in 6.5 Creedmoor.

That was the best move I have made in years. While there is nothing wrong with the .260 Remington and I am sure I would have been very happy, the 6.5 Creedmoor is one hell of a cartridge.

This is a great cartridge choice if for no other reason that there are a bunch of factory ammo options available for long-range shooting. While I love to reload, I don't always have the time I need to do that. It's great to have the option of using factory ammo from companies like Hornady and Nosler. What I discovered is that even with factory loads this is the most accurate rifle I have ever owned.

I should explain that while factory ammo is very good today, it's still mass produced to fit in any rifle chambered for that cartridge. Handloads can be custom tailored and tuned to the specific rifle. Typically, when doing that, the ammo will be more accurate than

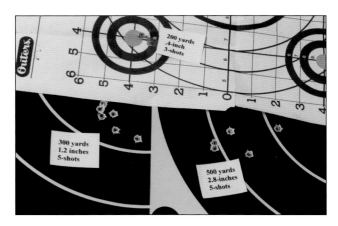

▲ Targets shot with the 6.8 Creedmoor custom rifle.

factory ammo from that rifle. This rifle is new to me and with the deadline for this book hanging over my head like the Sword of Damocles I have not had time yet to develop any handloads. Doing that is very high on my "to-do" list starting the day I ship this manuscript. It's likely that handloads will shoot the best in this rifle. But the bar is set very high and it's going to be very hard to improve on the outstanding accuracy of the factory ammo.

The accuracy in this rifle is off the charts. I have shot 200-yard groups that are ¼ MOA. Even at 500 yards it's holding half MOA.

My rifle uses an Accuracy International Chassis for its foundation. It has a Bartlein Barrel fitted into a Stryker Ridge action from Brownells. The trigger is a XTSP. Dave Tooley of Gastonia, North Carolina, built it, and he did one hell of a job with this rifle. I mounted a Leupold V6 4–24X52 scope with a TMOA reticle in Leupold rings.

The very first time I shot it at the range for record I was using the NRA Publication's protocol of five, five-shot groups at 100 yards. By the end of the day I believed that it might well be the most accurate rifle I have ever owned. Now, after multiple range sessions shooting as far as 500 yards, I am sure. Many guns can shoot a good group now and then, but to maintain it for five, five-shot groups is tough. Yet, this gun performed incredibly. In fact, the more I shoot it the better it is getting. No doubt as it breaks in and everything settles, the accuracy will only improve. I may repeat

the formal test after a few hundred more shots to see if there is any change.

Here are the results of that first session at the range for an average of five, five-shot groups. These are just as I shot them; there was no cherry picking or tossing out groups I didn't like.

Hornady 140-grain A-Max 0.56-inch. Best group: 0.4-inch.
Hornady 129-grain A-Max 0.61-inch. Best group: 0.4-inch.
Nosler 140-grain HPBT 0.64-inch. Best group: 0.35-inch.

That was with a brand-new rifle that was not even broken in yet. I am sure that a lot of the larger groups are my fault and are due to my inability to shoot better. Shooting groups is an art. At the risk of bragging, I am pretty good at it because I have had years and years of practice testing rifles for magazine articles. But when the groups are this small, things like your heartbeat start to have a larger influence on the result. At some point even the best shooters will reach the point of their limitations. We are not shooting from a machine rest and the shooter still must aim and fire the rifle. It's all but impossible to do that with the same precision of a machine rest. When I know I am doing it all right and I break the shots correctly, they snuggle into one ragged hole. If you wobble enough to open a group two-tenths of an inch it doesn't matter much with a normal rifle. But when your gun is shooting this well, a tenth of an inch has the potential to open the groups by 50 percent or more! This is truly amazing accuracy.

This rifle is well suited for a prepper wanting the best of the best for long-range defense. It's also a great way to go for a serious long-range shooter who wants to get into competition, or just wow his buddies on the weekend. It's not an inexpensive rifle, but the performance is at the highest level possible.

I cannot say enough good about this gun, so if you want one of your own, contact Dave Tooley at tooley-rifles@carolina.rr.com.

## Ruger Precision Rifle

I had a chance to shoot a prototype of this rifle last spring and was very impressed. I just received my sample, too late to shoot it for this book, but I have little doubt that based on the performance level we are seeing from Ruger rifles in the past few years it will

▲ Shooting a prototype of the Ruger Precision Rifle before it was announced. This was at the FTW Ranch and shooting school in Texas.

be a great shooter. This is a ground-breaking rifle as is a chassis-based precision rifle that will be available street price for about a grand. That's a game changer. Mine, of course, is in 6.5 Creedmoor.

## .308 Winchester

This is by far the most popular of the short-action cartridges in precision rifles. If a rifle maker is offering a tactical rifle, odds are it's available in .308 Winchester. The AR-L class of semiauto rifles uses this cartridge, and there are some outstandingly accurate rifles. I have a DPMS LR308 with a heavy 24-inch barrel that's extremely accurate. I also have a JP Enterprises JP LRP-07H Long Range Precision Hunting rifle that is an outstanding shooter. The DPMS GII Hunter in .308 is a tack driver and the DMPS GII Recon is hot on its heels, averaging sub MOA. I can go on, but what's the

point? If you get a good AR-L rifle in .308 Winchester from a name-brand maker and it has a good barrel, it will probably be a sub MOA shooter. The heavy, long barrels will extract the most velocity and be best for long-range work, but the carbines can also serve as defensive carry guns, so they are more versatile.

In fact, this style of rifle makes a lot of sense for a "carry" carbine while you are around your home or compound. They work well for combat at medium-to-close range, but can also reach out with some authority for long-range work. If trouble shows up you will likely be fighting with the gun you have, not the gun you wish you had, so a multi-tasking AR-L makes sense.

As I said, what you give up with the shorter barrel is velocity. The 168-grain Federal target load produces 2,630 ft/s from my 24-inch barrel DPMS, while the 18-inch barrel on a DPMS carbine has a MV of 2,488 ft/s with the same load. However, if you are shooting at 300 yards or less it's not enough to matter.

When it comes to bolt-action precision rifles in .308 Winchester they are as common as teenage girls with iPhones in their hands. You can go the best-of-the-best route and order a JP Enterprises MR-10 bolt-action chassis-style rifle with a guarantee of ½-MOA accuracy. This rifle is less expensive than a full-blown custom gun, but will shoot right there with any of them. J. P. is a serious long-range competition shooter and he knows how to build a rifle that works. Or, for less money, you can pick one of the production guns from brand-name companies like Remington, Ruger, or Savage. It all comes down to budget.

In a nutshell, the guns are defined as heavy barrel with a removable box magazine and with a large bolt handle. Other features may include things like an adjustable stock or tactical rails mounted here and there to hang bling on the gun.

A longer barrel is a good choice if you are going to use it in a fixed position to defend your property. If you set up on sandbags or a tripod and plan to stay dug in there, a bigger gun makes sense. The extra velocity is always a bonus and the weight of the longer barrel helps to dampen recoil, which helps get back on target for the next shot.

There are a couple of common approaches to the precision rifles in .308 Winchester. The longer barrel

▲ Savage Model 10 FCP-SR. This rifle has a 20-inch barrel and is useful for defense at moderate range.

to extract more velocity from the cartridge is one. The other is a rifle with a short, usually 20-inch, barrel that is designed for sniper work in urban settings. The planned shots are no more than 200 yards as a rule and are usually much closer. The short barrel makes it easier to use the gun inside a building or to maneuver in a vehicle. If you are on the move, this is a good option.

One that I have been using lately is the Savage Model 10 FCP-SR. This gun is sold as a "law enforcement" rifle, but it's a great choice for defending your property when the shots are 500 yards or less. One huge advantage of this is the price. The gun sells for about half of what a high-quality AR-L sniper gun will run. Like most of the new Savage guns this one has the AccuTrigger and is very accurate. The barrel

▲ Savage Model 10 FCP-SR.

is threaded for a brake, flash hider, or a suppressor. I have mine fitted with a Weaver Tactical 1–7X24 scope with Dual-Focal Plane, illuminated, mil-dot reticle. The ten-round double-stack hybrid magazine is a mix of polymer and metal.

With a few extra magazines, this is a good rifle for defense of your property at a very reasonable price.

**The Long View**

▲ Nathan Towsley shooting the "homemade" .308 Precision Rifle.

My long-barrel .308 Winchester precision rifle is one I made myself. My "safe place" is my shop. I love the concrete under my feet as I mess around with guns, and my shop is where I go to unwind and get away from the world. One of my do-it-yourself projects a few years ago was to build a long-range rifle.

If you like DIY projects, here is one that will result in a very nice long-range rifle and you can build it with hand tools. While I have lathes and a milling machine, I wanted a project that anybody can do without those expensive machines.

I used a Remington action and fitted it with a 1:10 twist rate 26-inch Shilen barrel in the heavy Remington "Varmint" contour. It comes with all the lathe work done, which means it's already threaded and chambered. The chamber is left about .010-inch "short" so you can fit the barrel to the action and then use a chambering reamer by hand to carefully finish to exactly the headspacing you want.

The stock is an H. S. Precision Series 2000 tactical stock with an adjustable cheekpiece. The stock is

▲ Nicknamed the "Snake" because of the coating on the barrel, the author built this .308 Winchester rifle.

also adjustable for length of pull. It's fitted with H. S. Precision Detachable Magazine bottom metal. This comes with a four-round magazine and I added a couple of additional ten-round magazines.

The action comes with a bolt that would have worked fine, but I wanted stronger extraction, so I ordered a spiral-fluted bolt from Pacific Tool and Gauge with an M16-type extractor and the oversize tactical bolt knob.

For a metal finish, I coated the barrel and action with DuraCoat spray-on finish, doing a "snakeskin" pattern on the barrel. I installed a Timney 1.5-pound pull trigger and a Swarovski Z6 5–30X50P scope, using Brownells Tactical Rings.

At the 100-yard range I fired the first five-shot group and was pleasantly surprised to see the holes were all touching. Rather than a fluke, this proved to be common for this rifle. Like all rifles it has its ammo preferences, but I didn't try any ammo that it hated. With Black Hills 175-grain Match and Federal 168-grain Match, it shoots sub MOA. With handloads it will approach ½-MOA on average with five-shot, 100-yard groups.

Every time I shoot this gun and look at the snug little groups on the target I think, "I made this," and I smile.

## .300 Winchester Magnum

The main reason I am getting into do-it-yourself options is that I found it to be a good way to get into a long-range rifle without spending a ton of money.

Once again, there are a lot of great rifles on the market chambered for .300 Winchester Magnum. I can't begin to list them all and don't want to; this is not a gun catalog, it's a book about guns. For the most part, I am writing here about guns that I have used and know, not trying to make a 120,000-word list of guns.

For just Remington alone, I see six guns listed as "tactical" in the Model 700 line up. In .300 Winchester they range from the synthetic stock Model 700 XCR Tactical Long Range to the Tactical Chassis model. That's only one gunmaker! Now consider the number of gun makers out there, including the custom market. See what I mean? Lots of .300 Winchester tactical rifles to choose from and most of them are pretty damn good.

### The Nesika Tactical Rifle

▲ The Nesika Tactical Rifle in .300 Winchester with Schmidt & Bender 5-25X tactical scope. An accurate rifle is only part of the key to long-range precision shooting; you also need high-quality optics.

One .300 Winchester in my vault that I can recommend is the Nesika Tactical Rifle. The Remington Outdoor Group owns Nesika, a company long famous for their actions.

I first tried this gun at a Remington Gun Writers' Seminar. To be honest, it's tough to tell much about any gun at these events. There are dozens of writers all shooting at the same targets. Half of them feel compelled to mess with the scope adjustments on the gun and the other half see it as their mission in life to wear the gun out with Remington's ammo. It isn't long before guns are hot and dirty and the targets are poked full of holes. Where they are hitting is often anybody's guess.

When you try to do anything serious with the gun there will be a line of guys with annoyed looks waiting their turn. So I did what I always do with a rifle that has some potential; I asked them to send one for me to play with at my range, where I am King and nobody messes with me. (Except maybe the Queen.)

This rifle has a Nesika Stainless, Tactical Action Receiver made from 15–5 stainless steel with a one-piece bolt made of 4340 CM Steel. The action is fitted with a one-piece, stainless 1913 Rail with 15 MOA Taper. What that means is there is fifteen minutes of angle of elevation already built into the scope mount. This allows the shooter to reach out farther with any given scope.

The gun is fitted with a Douglas Air-Gauged stainless steel 26-inch barrel in what they call "Tactical Contour." It's fitted with an AAC Blackout Muzzle brake/Suppressor Adapter. The gun has a Timney trigger, which surprisingly is the three-pound version. I am sure the corporate lawyers nixed the 1.5-pound version. The gun uses a five-round removable box magazine.

The stock is their tactical design. It's a composite stock with aluminum bedding block. It has spacers for adjustable length of pull and an adjustable cheekpiece.

They "guarantee" MOA accuracy at 100 yards, which seems a bit foolish to me. This is a high-dollar, high-end rifle that had better be able to shoot a lot better than that if they want serious people to buy it. I am sure that they are a bit wary of an accuracy guarantee and they padded their hand a bit here. This is an excellent long-range rifle in a very versatile cartridge. Any serious prepper trying to defend a fixed position would do well to check it out.

**My Personal Solution**

*There is another path to a "Poor Man's Sniper Rifle."*

The topic of survival guns for preppers is pretty wide ranging. If you buy all the guns you need it's a huge investment. You need a battle rifle and a primary carry pistol at minimum, then maybe a backup pistol, a shotgun and maybe a .22 LR. Now I am telling you that you need a sniper rifle?

▲ Remington Model 700 Sendero converted for long-range tactical use.

That's just for one person and it does not include any overlap or spares. If you are a family of preppers these needs are multiplied by each member. Plus, you need ammo for all of them. It's daunting, I know. For most of us it's very expensive and is probably putting a strain on a family budget that's already taxed to its limits. If you are prepping you are also buying food, tools, seeds and all the other things necessary to survive. Most of us are struggling just to pay the bills these days and it means sacrificing something else to buy more guns.

Normally it could take years to build up all the guns you need, but the way the world is going we don't have years. You need to get at least the basic guns sooner rather than later, as it's highly possible that they will not be available later. Or if they are, the price will be so high that it won't matter. Look at what happened to AR rifles a few years ago when panic buying dried up the market. Prices skyrocketed. That was just a reaction to the government's attempt at more gun control. Just imagine what will happen if they do ban guns or if we have a major event. It's likely you will not be able to buy a gun at any price. The trouble is, we can't predict what will happen or when; we can just prepare for it.

I understand that you need to take a pragmatic approach and sometimes we need to cut corners, set priorities and figure out another way.

Here is one way to go.

Prepping is about ingenuity. It would be great to buy every gun suggested in this book, but who can afford that? If you can, you can hire private security or better yet buy a remote island, staff it with workers and ride

▲ The M70 Laredo.

out the end of the world as we know it. For the rest of us, we need to improvise. If you have a good shooting rifle, why not tweak it a little bit to make it viable for defensive long-range use?

For two of my .300 Winchester long-range rifles, I took a different approach. I dusted off a couple of old guns I had in my collection that were designed for long-range hunting. You can take this approach with any cartridge, not just a .300 Winchester. It just happened that I had these guns hanging around and not seeing much use. If you don't have the option of already owning an appropriate rifle, there are a lot of guns on the used gun market that will cost a lot less than a full-blown long-range rifle.

A lot of hunters bought heavy barrel rifles when long-range hunting became popular, only to discover that they are a bit heavy for lugging around the woods. They soon traded them for something easier to carry. But it doesn't need to be a heavyweight; even a "standard" weight barrel will work if it's a good shooter. If you prowl the gun shops, particularly before Christmas when people are strapped for money, you can often find some bargains on used rifles. In my part of the world, New England, the magnums go cheap because hunters are not interested. Put a Remington pump action .30–06 on the used gun rack and stand back so you won't get trampled. But stick a heavy barrel .300 Winchester up there and watch it gather dust. Gun shop owners lose money if inventory is not turned over, so if you are patient you can sometimes find a bargain donor gun for a project.

I used two rifles to do two different levels of modification for long-range work. For the most part, the guns were designed for long-range shooting anyway, so it was just a matter of a little fine-tuning.

The first one is a Winchester Laredo rifle with the BOSS system that lets you tune the harmonics of the barrel for the best accuracy. Winchester introduced this rifle back in 1997 when long-range hunting was getting a lot of coverage in the magazines. It just didn't sell well enough to continue manufacture and it was only made a few years before they discontinued it in 1999. Mine has been gathering dust for a long time and it was ready for some action.

I installed a 1.5-pound Timney trigger. I put a rail scope mount on top and mounted a Leupold VX6 4–24 scope. That's it, done.

It's not a full-blown tactical rifle, but it is capable of ¾-MOA accuracy with factory ammo. The gun sits well on sand bags or a bipod and it can reach out to long-range targets just as well as any other rifle.

I may add a tactical bolt handle and a removable box magazine someday, but probably not. With a high-end tactical scope and a better trigger I took a dust collector and made it a viable long-range gun. I am happy with that result.

I also had a Remington Sendero in .300 Winchester that got a bit more advanced tweaking. This is pretty much Remington's competition for the Laredo as a long-range hunting rifle. It's the heavy barrel "varmint" gun that Remington made for years for shooting prairie dogs, but with a grown-up cartridge. Rather than let it keep gathering dust in my gun vault, I decided to "trick" it out for long-range shooting. Of course, I wrote an article about that project. Here is the condensed version.

### Long-Range Rifle Makeover

Each generation likes to think they discovered everything great, but it's simply not always so. Sometimes those things have been around a while. For example, the son of one of my wife's co-workers came home all excited from a high school dance several years ago.

"Dad," he said breathlessly, "you *gotta* hear this new song they have been playing! It's called *Stairway to Heaven* and it is so awesome!"

It's the same with long-range rifle shooting. It's been around a long time. It just changes faces to match

▲ This modified Remington Model 700 Sendero works well for long-range tactical use.

the times and every generation starts to think they invented it.

My personal hard-start introduction came fifteen years ago when long-range deer hunting was all the rage. Soon enough, every rifle company had a gun designed to reach out and smack something. For the most part, they were line extensions of their heavy-barrel varmint rifles chambered for powerful "big game" cartridges. It seems the Texas theme was hot and Winchester called theirs the Laredo, while Remington's was the "Sendero." Being a true gun nut, I wound up with one of each, but they don't see a lot of use these days. Newer guns came along and those "long-range" hunting rifles have been gathering dust in my vault for years.

What I needed now was a long-range "tactical" target rifle for a lot of reasons, one being "just because."

The trouble is, as with most households the Obama economy has left Camp Towsley a bit short on discretionary funds dedicated for new rifle acquisitions.

So I dug out the Sendero, blew off the dust, and started playing with it on some long-range targets. As always, it shot well but it just wasn't "tactical" enough for today's shooting world. So, in discovering something great all by myself, I thought, "Why not turn this unused hunting rifle into a long-range 'tactical' shooting machine?"

Here's how it all went down.

First I removed the stock, bolt, scope, and mount from the rifle, stripping the rifle naked and ready for a makeover.

While Remington is capable of making some very good triggers, this rifle did not have one of them. I know the Remington trigger inside and out and have tuned dozens, perhaps hundreds of them; but I could not make this one behave. So the first step was to replace the factory trigger with a Timney trigger that is preset at the factory with a 1.5-pound pull weight. A pull weight, by the way, that is unattainable safely with a Remington trigger. If you want a light trigger pull, you must replace the trigger.

I replaced the rifle's stock with the Knoxx Axiom Ultra-Light Rifle Stock from BLACKHAWK! This unique stock has a spring-loaded recoil-compensation system to take the sting out of the .300 Win Mag. The stock is a fiberglass-reinforced injection molded polymer design with aluminum pillar bedding. The adjustable buttstock has length-of-pull options from 11.25-inches

▲ A modified Remington Model 700 Sendero. The .300 Winchester Magnum cartridge is one of the best choices for tactical long-range use.

to 15.25-inches, a feature that alone makes this stock a great choice. The barrel is completely free-floated so the stock fits all barrel diameters with zero barrel channel fitting work needed. This means you can install it on that slim-barrel hunting rifle you have hanging around as well as on heavy-barreled guns like mine.

The stock actually took a lot of work to fit to this gun, which was a surprise. While I was at it I decided to fit Accuracy International bottom metal to this stock so that I could use their outstanding removable box magazines. That too turned out to be one heck of a project, but I got it done and it was worth the effort.

I mounted the Weaver Precision Tactical Bipod using the Weaver Swivel Stud Picatinny Rail Adaptor, which clamps on the existing swivel stud and allows mounting the bipod.

I replaced the standard bolt handle with an oversize "tactical" knob. That required some lathe work and a jig from Pacific Tool and Gauge Company. Once it was set up in the jig, I turned the old bolt handle down until it was the correct size and then threaded it so I could screw on the new, oversize bolt handle. No lathe? No problem. There are replacement handles that you can do with hand tools. Brownells has an assortment to pick from.

I installed a Weaver Tactical Multi-Slot Picatinny scope mount base designed for the Remington 700. It features a recoil lug that mates to the action at the front of the ejection port to help keep the recoil forces off the mounting screws. With the heavy weight of tactical scopes and rings this is a good feature. It also mounts the scope a bit lower than some other rails I have tried.

I have had a bunch of scopes on it over the years, as this gun is so accurate I often use it to test new tactical scopes when writing about them. I started with a Nikon and right now it wears a Weaver Tactical.

My first day at the range it was spitting snow and very cold. The wind was gusting just a little and with a deadline looming I was more interested in getting finished than in the process. This all usually adds up to a bad day of gun testing, but with tactical ammo from Federal, Cor-Bon, and Black Hills, my three shot groups were running on average just under one MOA. With the factory ammo it liked best, they were ½-to ¾-MOA. Since then I have made head shots on USPSA-style targets at 1,000 yards with this rifle. I have shot

▲ The author and Scott Ballard, an instructor at the Sig Sauer Academy. This is a five-shot group that the author shot at 1,000 yards with a tricked-out Remington 700 Sendero in .300 Winchester Magnum.

sub MOA groups at that distance as well. It's a goofy looking thing, but when it shoots this well, who cares?

If you have a rifle sitting around collecting dust, or can find a used gun at a bargain price, this is a great way to get into a long-range gun without spending the kids' college funds. Just find one that's chambered in a cartridge suitable for tactical long-range use, which is pretty much any bottleneck centerfire, and it's a candidate for a makeover. For a lot less than the cost of a complete, new "tactical" sniper rifle you can get into this "long-range tactical" shooting thing and put a neglected rifle back in service. Then you can excitedly tell all your friends about the great *new* shooting sport you just discovered.

## .338 Lapua

▲ This Accuracy International .338 Lapua will really shoot.

Several years ago I tested seven different .338 Lapua rifles extensively at the range and most of them failed to impress me with their accuracy.

Except two.

One was an Accuracy International AX, a version of the gun used to set the record for the longest sniper shot ever. It's a fantastic gun and in my next life I hope I'll pick a better paying profession so I can buy one. While it's worth every penny, with a base price in the neighborhood of the cost of a good used car, it's out of my league. But it is to this day the most accurate .338 Lapua I have tested. For the record, the list of .338 Lapua rifles I've tested is well into double digits now.

▲ Savage 110 BA in .338 Lapua. This gun is fitted with a Zeiss 6-24X56 scope with a Rapid-Z reticle. A rifle this accurate deserves the best optics.

The other gun—the one that was and is in a very close second place for accuracy, almost, but not quite matching the high-dollar AI rifle—is a Savage 110BA, which sells for about 1/3 of the price. The 100-yard groups were outstanding and at long range it just gets better. I shot a five-shot group at 1,000 yards that measured 5.9 inches. I had the first three shots in two inches. The average for multiple five-shot groups at 1,000 yards was 6.45 inches. That is nearly ½-MOA at 1,000 yards!

▲ Shooting the Savage 110 BA .338 Lapua at 1,000 yards.

Not bad, considering that one arrogant gun magazine editor told me I was "slumming" by using that rifle.

For the record, I don't think there is a better bargain in a precision .338 Lapua rifle and I bought the rifle after finishing the magazine articles.

▲ Outstanding accuracy from a Savage 110BA in .338 Lapua.

The rifle is also available in .300 Winchester Magnum and comes in right or left hand.

### .50 BMG

I have to confess, I don't really enjoy shooting a .50 BMG all that much. It's probably because in a moment of stupidity I took a handloading assignment for that cartridge a few years back. I wound up shooting hundreds of rounds in just a few range sessions. I have always said that once the novelty wears off, this cartridge is kind of a beast. Well, it wore off very quickly with that assignment.

The .50 BMG might be a beast, but for the job at hand, nothing else can compare. There is a huge selection of guns on the market, ranging from uppers you can put on an AR-15 lower to full-blown, high-dollar precision rifles. The only limit is your budget.

I did most of that handloading work with a Barrett Model 99. This is a heavy-duty, bullpup-style, single-shot, bolt-action rifle. It is a reasonably priced rifle. With a 32-inch tapered bull barrel the gun weighed twenty-five pounds, and my sample, equipped with a Leupold scope and BORS system, weighed two ounces shy of 30 pounds.

The arrowhead-shaped muzzle brake is clamped on the barrel and is very effective at reducing recoil, but the blast was close to life altering. By most standards the gun was a good shooter and was certainly accurate enough to hit a car engine block at 500 or even 1,000 yards.

Perhaps the most pleasant .50 BMG to shoot is one my friend Lee Houghton built himself, using a machine gun barrel. This beast is nearly as tall as I am and weighs 48 pounds. With the long barrel and a brake Lee designed and made, it puts the blast out away from the shooter. Recoil is very light due to the brake and the weight of the gun. On top of that, it's a good shooter! But it's one of a kind.

### Accuracy International AX50

Accuracy International AX50 .50 BMG with Schmidt & Bender 5–25X tactical scope. You must be able to see a distant target to hit it, so a good rifle deserves high-quality optics.

I just received an Accuracy International AX50 rifle on loan from EuroOptic for a feature article in NRA's *Shooting Illustrated* magazine. This is a battle-proven gun that may well be the apex of bolt-action,

▲ Accuracy International AX50 .50 BMG with Schmidt & Bender 5-25X tactical scope. You must be able to see a distant target to hit it, so a good rifle deserves high-quality optics.

▲ Accuracy International AX50 .50 BMG.

magazine-fed .50 BMG rifles. Its barrel is twenty-seven inches and the rifle weighs 24.6 pounds. If you want the best of the best in a .50 BMG, this is your gun.

Their website says, "This Accuracy International 50-caliber is designed for military use as an anti-material weapon system." That means it's a good choice for breaking stuff that needs breaking.

The gun has a flat-bottomed steel action that is bolted to a full-length aluminum chassis. The two-stage trigger is the best trigger I have seen on a .50 BMG and it breaks at four pounds, six ounces. However, the first stage is three pounds, three ounces, so the effective trigger pull is only one pound, three ounces. This is a big asset in precision long-range shooting.

The double chamber muzzle brake is both screwed on and tension clamped, which should tell you something about what happens at the end of a .50 BMG barrel. They advertise that it effectively reduces recoil, muzzle flash, and dust eruption (all of which a .50 BMG is very good at generating). The barrel can be changed in less than ten minutes using the barrel change kit, but if you shoot it out, you are a better man than me!

I have not had a lot of time with this gun yet, but so far I am impressed. I believe that there is no better choice than this rifle for defending your property, family, and life from a fixed position, particularly if you expect the need to break things and disable vehicles. It's not a cheap gun, but it's probably priced lower than you might expect. EuroOptic sells the Accuracy International 6800B AX50 for $11,082. It's a serious investment. But if you live in a place where you will need a rifle like this, it's an investment that may well keep you alive.

# OTHER RIFLES
## Scout Rifles

*A look at the legacy rifle from one of the great gun guys in history.*

▲ Jeff Cooper. Photo courtesy of Gunsite Academy.

eff Cooper (May 10, 1920–September 25, 2006) was a bit of a renaissance man in the modern gun world. He was instrumental in starting action pistol shooting, which lives on today with USPSA and IPSC competitions all over the world. Cooper developed and taught the "modern technique" of pistol shooting, which changed how we shoot defensive handguns and is the foundation for much of the technique used in pistol shooting today. He founded Gunsite Academy, one of the top firearms training centers in the world. Cooper was a prolific writer, leaving behind several books. He was also a hard-core big game hunter with worldwide experience.

One lasting legacy to the gun world is the continuing popularity of the scout rifle, which he first began to develop in 1968. He wrote about the idea in his book, *The Art of The Rifle*.

"Back in my high school days the scouting and patrolling manual in the R.O.T.C battalion stated as follows: 'The scout is a man trained in ground and cover movement from cover to cover, rifle marksmanship, map reading observation, and accurately reporting the results of his observation.'"

He continued, "The scout, therefore, was a man by himself or possibly with one companion. He was not supposed to get into fights, but if he could not avoid contact, he was expected to shoot quickly, accurately, and hard. His weapon, therefore, should be somewhat more specialized than that of the line soldier."

Cooper thought the Winchester Model 94 and the Mannlicher 1903 Carbine both had attributes useful for this idea. In 1968 Cooper was shooting a Remington Model 600 Carbine in .308 Winchester. He was intrigued with this light, short rifle and after using it during a couple of backcountry trips to Central America he thought it would make a good basis for the scout rifle concept. He used that Model 600 carbine to build "Scout One," the first of a series of scout rifles.

(Cooper was also a fan of the .350 Remington Magnum in the Model 600-style rifles for hunting big game, which reinforces that he understood terminal ballistics. He was never a fan of "small" for the applied-use cartridges and no doubt would scoff at today's trend in that direction.)

Cooper first introduced the scout rifle concept in the early 1980s. It was a bolt-action carbine chambered in 30-caliber, less than one meter in length, and less than three kilograms in weight. The gun is fitted with iron sights, a forward mounted optic, and a practical sling. (The Ching sling later came to be identified with the scout rifle.)

▲ Jeff Cooper shooting a scout rifle. Photo courtesy of Gunsite Academy.

Cooper defined the scout rifle as "a general-purpose rifle that is a conveniently portable, individually operated firearm, capable of striking a single decisive blow, on a live target of up to 200 kilos in weight, at any distance at which the operator can shoot with the precision necessary to place a shot in a vital area of the target." The scout rifle concept, as it evolved over the years, was not a hard set of specifications, and Cooper kept it fluid. However, simply put, today's concept of a scout rifle is a short, bolt-action carbine weighing seven pounds or less, typically chambered in .308 Winchester and with a forward-mounted optical sight.

Cooper thought that the .30–06 would be the perfect scout rifle cartridge, except that it required a long-action rifle, which made the gun heavier and longer. With advancements in factory-loaded ammo the .308 Winchester comes very close to the .30–06 in performance and he proclaimed that to be the best cartridge for the scout rifle concept. He conceded that the 7mm-08 might also be a good choice for a rifle in countries that ban .308s because of the cartridge's military applications. He even mentioned the .243 Winchester for the recoil-shy or for places that do not allow the .308 Winchester.

For any prepper, the .308 Winchester is clearly the best choice in a scout rifle. It's a NATO cartridge, it is very popular with law enforcement, and it's one of the top civilian rifle cartridges. That means, after TSHTF, if any rifle ammo is available anywhere at all, the odds favor highly that it will be the .308 Winchester.

The .223 Remington/5.56 NATO might well have even better odds of being available and you can buy a scout rifle in that cartridge. But doing so may risk the ghost of Jeff Cooper haunting your nights. Cooper disdained the cartridge in a scout and said, ". . . to reduce a scout to take this cartridge is rather like putting a Volkswagen engine in a Porsche. You can do it, but why should you?"

I must say that I agree with him 100 percent on that. If you are to use your scout rifle for hunting and foraging and for defense, the much more powerful .308 Winchester is a far smarter choice than the .223 Remington.

Cooper initially thought that a ghost ring rear sight with a post front sight was fine and that optics were optional at best. He later revised that when Bushnell came out with a pistol scope that could be mounted forward on the gun. This allowed easy access to the action for top loading and kept the scope away from the shooter's face. One of the biggest issues then was the quality of the optics, as many of the early scopes could not stand up to the recoil of the rifle and were prone to failure. They were also designed for use on a pistol; so anytime they were mounted on a rifle, compromises had to be made both in the optics and the mounting system. Today there are several outstanding riflescopes designed just for scout rifle use. Companies like Leupold, Weaver, and Burris all make high-quality optics designed to be mounted in the forward, "scout rifle" position. These optics have put to rest the reliability problems that plagued the early scout riflescope sights as the quality is excellent. Today the forward-mounted scope more or less defines the "scout rifle" concept.

The rifles have developed a bit of a cult following in recent years. But, when looking at how the options have changed over the years I have to wonder if Cooper would have refined his concept further. He was a very smart man who developed his own ideas and didn't follow the pack. But he was a bit old school as well. With the advancements of semiauto rifles that remain true to the scout rifle concept in terms of performance and use, I have to wonder if he would embrace those as part of the scout rifle family?

I was recently discussing the possibility of having a scout rifle competition with another writer who was

▲ Some of Jeff Cooper's scout rifles. Photo courtesy of Gunsite Academy.

trying to develop the match. The issue of how fair it would be to allow semiauto rifles came up and I wrote: "I cannot think of a single scenario that you can reasonably have in this match where the semiauto will not dominate." That's true. Unless the match designer comes up with some oddball scenario specifically designed to punish the semiauto user, the semiauto will dominate the match.

The number-one issue brought up by scout rifle disciples when I approach the question of an AR-L semiauto as a scout rifle is the weight. The very popular Ruger Gunsite Scout Rifle weighs 7.3 pounds with a laminated wood stock and is 40-inches long. The DPMS GII AP4 AR-L carbine weighs 7.25 pounds and is only 34.25 inches long with the stock collapsed. Both of these guns are a bit heavier than Cooper's seven-pound limit, but not by much. Both

are in .308 Winchester. As a fighting rifle, it might be argued that the AP4 has the advantage by virtue

▲ The question of if Cooper would have embraced the new lighter, .308 AR-L rifles like this DPMS GII Recon as a scout rifle will remain unanswered.

of being semiauto and having a higher magazine capacity.

But the question is moot as Cooper died in 2006, before the boom in civilian AR-type rifles took off. Back when he was developing the scout rifle concept in the '70s and '80s, the options for civilian-owned .308 battle rifles were very limited and none of the guns matched the criteria he put forth for a scout rifle. The recent surge in popularity for AR-style guns led to the advancements and developments that make some of these rifles strong candidates for the "scout rifle" concept. But we will never know if Cooper would have approved. I saw the man around the SHOT Show in his later years, but I never formally met him. I only know him from his writing and do not presume to know his mind. I know that he did not like the AR-15, but that was mostly because of the 5.56 cartridge. I like to think that he would embrace this new generation of lighter weight, .308-chambered semiauto carbines, both as battle rifles and as members of the scout rifle family.

However, with that question remaining in the company of "the number of angels dancing on the head of a pin," and just as unanswerable, we will stay true to his original concept of a scout rifle in this chapter.

Although it could be argued that the scout rifle idea is a bit dated, everything that was true about the scout rifle when Cooper was developing the idea is still true today. There are some tactical advantages to a bolt-action rifle. Reliability and the ability to use damaged or corroded ammo that will not feed in a semiauto is an example. A bolt-action is much quieter to load and chamber a round, even if stealth techniques are employed with the AR-type rifles. The bolt-action has the potential for a better trigger than can be safely used in a semiauto. On average the bolt-actions are lighter than most semiautos and the bolt-action rifle design is friendlier to carrying with a shoulder sling.

For "crossover" use—that is, a rifle used for defense as well as foraging and hunting—the scout rifle makes a lot of sense. In truth, Cooper designed it for this situation with it weighted toward being a hunting gun. He recognized that the needs of a scout are different than a typical military man and that the scout rifle was for solving problems, not fighting battles. As for the hunting aspect, he wrote, "The best weapon for the military scout may also be the best weapon for the private citizen stalking the deer."

If you are a bolt-action guy and are familiar with running that style of rifle fast and smooth, then the scout rifle may be what you need for personal and home defense. For a rifle to be used while "scouting" when you are out and about, foraging or checking the road ahead, it is a great choice. After all, that's what it was designed for.

I like shooting these guns and find that there is a certain kind of confidence to be found in mastering the scout rifle. I embrace the history and the fighting spirit of the man who conceived the scout rifle design. He and I think a lot alike when it comes to gun, cartridges, bullets, and philosophy of life; so how can I ignore his signature rifle?

While the scout rifle is a bit of a niche category when it comes to survival guns for preppers, it's a competent rifle for our use. Those preppers who buy a scout rifle are never making a mistake, if for no other reason than each time you fire the gun, the spirit of Colonel Jeff Cooper will be watching over you and guiding the bullet to its destination.

## The Rifles I Have Used

There are currently four production-grade scout rifles that I am aware of being manufactured and sold today. Steyr made the first commercial scout rifle and worked with Cooper on the design. It is the only scout rifle made today that had his hand on the tiller as it was designed, and it's the only one with his stamp of approval. That's not to say Cooper would not approve of the others—he likely would—but this is the only rifle introduced with his blessing while he was still alive.

Ruger designed its scout rifle in conjunction with Gunsite Academy, but years after Cooper had passed away. Savage and Mossberg both have more recently introduced versions of the scout rifle.

I have experience with all but the Mossberg. I can't comment on that design. It may be fine, or may not be; I can't say because I have not had one here to test.

▲ L to R: Savage Model 11 Scout rifle with a Weaver fixed 4X Scout Scope; Steyr Scout with a Burris fixed-power 2.75 Scout scope; and Ruger Gunsite Scout with a Leupold VX•R 1.5-5x33mm Scout FireDot scope.

## Steyr Scout

The Steyr Scout was the first commercial scout rifle. It was developed by Steyr Mannlicher of Austria in conjunction with Jeff Cooper and released in 1998. It's a bit different design than most Americans are used to seeing in a rifle, but is full of innovation and European-style engineering.

The gun has a five-round removable box magazine with a "magazine in reserve" setting for manual loading. It is designed with a double click when inserting it into the magazine well. If you push the magazine into the rifle until the first click, it is held in place but will not feed ammo into the gun. This is, in effect, a magazine cut-off. This allows you to single load ammo

▲ Jeff and Janelle Cooper with a Steyr Scout rifle. Photo courtesy of Gunsite Academy.

while maintaining a full magazine, if you want to use a different specialty load. It also works if you are in a situation where you feel you have time to single load the rifle while keeping the full magazine at the ready in case the situation deteriorates or changes. There is a second magazine stored in the butt of the rifle where it is easily accessed.

The gun is lightweight, 6.6 pounds, due to the aluminum receiver and the polymer stock. It has a 19-inch hammer-forged, fluted barrel. There is a Weaver-style rail integral to the rifle for mounting optics, either conventionally or in the forward "scout" position. There is a UIT rail on the bottom.

The unique roller tang safety locks the bolt shut in the safe position. It also has a midway position that allows the bolt to open while on safe or fully forward in the fire position.

The two-stage trigger is user-adjustable. Mine is factory set for a total pull weight of three pounds, ten ounces. The first stage is fourteen ounces. There are backup, flip-up sights. The rear is a ghost ring and is adjustable for elevation. The front post is adjustable for windage.

One unique feature of this rifle is the integral folding bipod. The legs are cleverly hidden in the stock, but by pushing a button on the bottom they are released to open. There are three points of attachment for a sling, the third being for the Ching sling.

I have the Burris fixed-power 2.75 Scout scope on mine. A gun writer friend who is a disciple of the scout rifle and has tested everything on the market related to these guns told me it's the best scout optic on the market. I'm not sure if I agree with such a definitive statement as there are some other outstanding scopes, but on the other hand, I have nothing to argue against it, either. It seems to be a great scout scope.

The Steyr Scout was the first commercial scout rifle and remains as a category leader today.

## Ruger Gunsite Scout

In 2011, Ruger introduced the Ruger Gunsite Scout, a re-designed scout rifle based on their Model 77 action and developed in cooperation with Gunsite Academy. Mine is matte finish stainless steel with a black, wood-laminate stock. This gun has an 18.7-inch barrel and weighs 7.3 pounds. If you order the Ruger Scout Rifle

with a synthetic stock and a 16.1-inch barrel, it reduces the weight by more than a pound to 6.25 pounds. The extra weight on my gun is an asset when shooting the rifle as it aids in reducing felt recoil, but in truth if I had it to do over I would do as Cooper suggested and go for the lighter weight. But, that was not available at the time I got my gun. With the removable flash hider installed, my rifle is forty inches long.

The receiver is a typical M77 with a three-position safety. The single-stage trigger is clean and crisp and breaks at four pounds, fourteen ounces on my rifle.

The forward-mounted Picatinny rail allows mounting scout-style scopes. I have a Leupold VX•R 1.5–5x33mm Scout FireDot scope mounted in Leupold quick-detach rings on my gun. This big, bright 30mm tube scope has a huge eyebox, which is important in a scout scope. The FireDot illuminated center dot is visible in daylight and is intensity adjustable. For the scout-style of shooting with both eyes open, this dot draws your eye to the center of the scope and provides a positive aiming point. This variable-power scope is an excellent choice for a multi-use scout scope. Leupold was in early with the scout scope concept. In fact, their early pistol scopes were often used for scout rifles. Leupold was the first optics company to introduce a dedicated scout rifle scope, the M8 2.5x28mm Scout, back in 1996, and they have remained a strong leader in the scout rifle category ever since.

The Ruger M77 receiver has integral scope mounting locations for conventionally mounting a scope and my gun came with scope rings for that option as well as the scout position.

The rifle comes with a ten-round, detachable box magazine with a release just forward of the trigger guard.

There is a soft rubber recoil pad with buttpad and three half-inch spacers that will allow adjusting the length of pull. There are backup sights, with an adjustable ghost ring and a protected ramp front sight. The action has a controlled round feed extractor.

Like all Ruger guns, the Scout is well built and should prove to be very dependable during years of hard use.

### Savage Model 11 Scout Rifle

In 2015 Savage announced a Model 11 Scout rifle. It's a .308 Winchester of course, built on the famous 110-style action. This gun has an 18-inch barrel with another 2.5 inches of muzzle brake. Personally, I question the reasoning behind a muzzle brake on a scout rifle. Muzzle brakes are very loud and, if you are adhering to the scout concept in its use, you probably will not be wearing hearing protection when you shoot this rifle outside of the range. A muzzle brake is a great thing at the range where you are always wearing hearing protection. It will reduce muzzle flip and recoil, allowing fast follow-up shots. But if you need this gun in the field for defense or hunting, there may not be time to put on hearing protection.

Anybody who has fired a short-barrel .308 with a muzzle brake without hearing protection will tell you it's a one-and-done kind of thing. It only took one time for me shooting at a big Florida hog with a brake on my .308 AR-L to decide that the next one could be the

▲ Is a muzzle brake a good idea on a scout rifle?

world record, but he was safe until I got some muffs on my ears. I am very glad I didn't make this discovery during a fight for my life. In a short-barrel .308 a muzzle brake can be so loud that it's disorienting to the shooter, which could lead to bad things in a defensive situation.

It might make sense to remove the brake for true scout work. On the other hand, that's why muzzle brakes are usually threaded on. You can remove them and install a thread protector.

The stock on the Savage is injection molded synthetic in a tan color they call "natural." The stock has three sling attachment locations, per Cooper's design: front and rear, with a center attachment for a Ching sling. There is an adjustable comb on the stock to adjust for the best cheek weld, depending on the sighting system used. The length of pull is also adjustable, with spacers between the stock and the 1-inch black, recoil pad.

The rifle comes with a detachable, double-stack, ten-shot magazine. There is a fully adjustable Williams peep-style rear sight and a protected, blade-style front sight. The gun comes with a rail that is mounted forward so it bridges the barrel and action, attaching to both. My gun is fitted with a Weaver fixed 4X Scout Scope.

Like most new Savage rifles, the Scout has an AccuTrigger. Mine breaks sharp and clean at 2.75 pounds, which makes it the best trigger on any scout rifle I have tried.

The bolt has a large, oversize handle that's a big asset in running the gun fast and while wearing gloves.

The safety is tang-mounted, three-position and it does lock the bolt closed when it's on. The gun is a bit heavy at 7.8 pounds, at least if we use Cooper's guidelines of three kilograms, or 6.6 pounds. The overall length is 40.5 inches, which also misses his one-meter-in-length guideline, but not by much—a meter is 39.37 inches. If the brake is removed the length is within Cooper's specs.

The Savage Model 11 Scout rifle is priced lower than any of the three scout rifles I have tried. Time will tell, but Savage rifles are tough and durable. This gun represents a great value in a scout rifle.

# The Lever-Action Alternative

*If you are politically oppressed and can't own the gun you want, this might be the gun you need.*

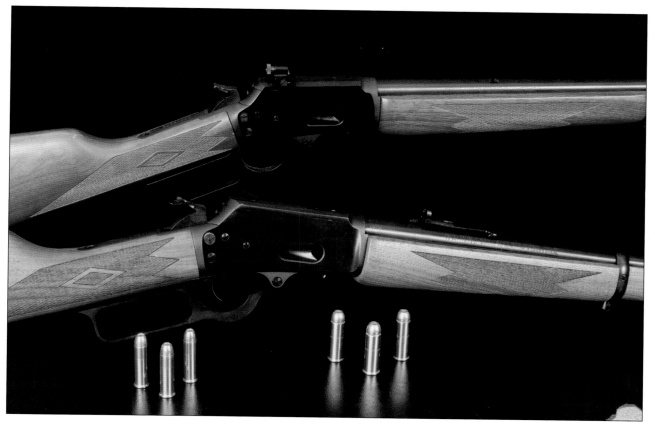

▲ Marlin 1894 carbines: front is .357 Mag., back is .44 Mag.

There is no question that a magazine-fed, semiauto rifle is the best tool a prepper can have for survival. But what if you are one of those poor unfortunate souls who live where the government doesn't trust you enough to own one? Well, the obvious answer is to move. Those places almost always have high population densities and that means trouble after TSHTF. Even if you live in a more rural part of your state, you are close to huge populations of people and when the cities empty, they will find you.

Easy enough to say, but believe me, I am the first to understand that moving is not always as easy as it sounds. Sometimes we get "stuck" for reasons out of our control, like jobs or family. I also recognize that for some people it's home and they don't want to move.

But that doesn't mean you have to break the law to protect yourself or to prepare.

One alternative to consider is a lever-action carbine in a revolver cartridge. These guns provide an interesting and surprisingly effective alternative for those politically repressed poor souls who can't legally own an AR-15, AK-47, or similar rifle. A lever-action may be the best alternative where it's the only alternative.

Because these guns are an old design and were seen in every cowboy movie ever made, they fly below the radar. The anti-gunners are motivated by emotion and they tend to go after scary-looking guns. Nobody except those deeply afflicted with hoplophobia (fear of firearms) thinks that Gene Autry's gun is scary looking. It's much easier politically for the gun-banners to go after a black gun than the one John Wayne used to keep the West safe. So, for the most part, lever-actions are legal and socially acceptable even in locations that do not embrace the concept of the Second Amendment.

The history of the lever-action is uniquely American. It started with Walter Hunt in 1848 when he developed the "Rocket Ball and Volition Repeater." This was a lever-action, breech-loading repeating rifle with an under-the-barrel tube magazine. Sound familiar? It should; that's the basic premise for the lever-actions we use today. That rifle used a cartridge of sorts that featured a hollow base, conical bullet with the powder charge contained in the base. A separate primer ignited it, so it wasn't exactly a self-contained cartridge, but the bullet and propellant was one single unit—an underpowered, wimpy single unit, which is why sales were dismal.

Hunt later teamed up with George Arrowsmith (no relation to the "Dude Looks Like a Lady" guys) and Lewis Jennings. They were granted a patent for the Jennings improvement in 1849 and they changed the name of the gun. They also got a contract to make five thousand Jennings Repeaters in Vermont, but the rifle was too complicated and underpowered for commercial success. Only a handful were made in repeaters and the rest were produced as single-shots. The foreman in that factory was Benjamin Tyler Henry, a man who became very important in the development of the lever-action rifle.

In 1854 Horace Smith and Daniel Wesson developed a lever-action pistol with an under-the-barrel-tube magazine. Their shop foreman? None other than B. Tyler Henry. After the production of about one thousand of these guns, the name of the company was changed to Volcanic Repeating Arms Company. (If you are lucky enough to have one of the original pistols hiding in your attic it might be worth as much as a small, new car—maybe even more. Find a Volcanic Model Pistol with a detachable stock and you may be able to pay off your mortgage.) Joining this company as an investor was a men's garment maker named Oliver F. Winchester.

Henry later developed a successful rimfire .44 cartridge and a brass frame lever-action called the Henry Rifle. The first fifteen-shot Henry rifles were shipped in 1862 and soon gained a reputation as formidable fighting tools. One Confederate officer called it "that damn Yankee gun they load on Sunday and shoot all week."

One widely publicized incident helped to sell this rifle. Captain James M. Wilson of the 12th Kentucky Cavalry was accosted by seven guerillas while dining with his family in his home. He convinced them to kill him outside so his family wouldn't have to watch. On the way out the door he grabbed his Henry rifle and killed the seven bad guys with eight shots. In an era of single-shot rifles, this proved beyond all doubt that the Henry was the gun to have when your life depended on shooting fast and well.

I suspect that, like me, Wilson got grumpy when he was hungry. Clearly, they should not have interrupted his dinner. Telemarketers, take note.

The Henry rifle was the launch pad for all modern lever-action rifles. What followed was a revolution in rifles. The single-shot cartridge rifle was now passé and the repeating lever-action would dominate American gun culture at least until World War II. Even today, the lever-action rifle is alive and well. When we explore the current new lever-actions on the market chambered for revolver cartridges, it pretty much means the Marlin 1894, Winchester 1892, or Henry Big Boy. However, production on the first two guns is a bit uncertain at this writing and they may be difficult to find.

There are also some imported copies of the old Winchester guns like the 1892, 1873, and others. Some are okay, but many others can be pretty spotty on quality and function, so check the gun out thoroughly before you buy it.

You may also find some used guns on the market. Winchester made the 1894 in .44 Magnum for years. I have a couple of them and they are fine guns. Also, the Marlin 1894 was pretty popular and you can find used guns, usually in .44 Magnum, for a reasonable price. A lot of the Marlin .357 guns were snatched up by the Cowboy Action Shooters. Be very wary of any of those on the used gun market as CAS shooters often modify the guns to the point of stupidity and those changes can be detrimental to use as a defensive rifle. Have a gunsmith check it out before you buy.

These lever-action carbines are usually chambered for .357 Magnum, .44 Magnum, or .45 Colt. The .357 and .44 Magnums are the best choices as they will

▲ With modern ammo the .45 Colt can be effective in a handgun or a lever-action carbine.

offer the most options for functional ammo designed for self-defense.

While never traditionally chambered in a lever-action rifle, modern gun makers put the .45 Colt in lever-actions to appeal to CAS shooters. Most factory ammo is underpowered, but at least one major ammo company, Hornady, is making defensive ammo for the .45 Colt. I checked with Hornady and their spokes-man said the company's Critical Defense ammo is well suited for use in lever-action rifles. In fact, another .45 Colt load from them, LEVERevolution, is designed for lever-action rifles. Hornady ammo is some of the best on the market and in this situation it can make a .45 Colt lever-action into a viable defensive carbine. There are not as many defensive ammo options as for the .357 or .44, but that .45 Colt punches a big hole.

▲ The .357 Magnum is a versatile cartridge and is handy in a lever-action rifle for defense.

Some of the imported guns will be chambered for old cartridges like the .38–40 or .44–40. Avoid those guns, as there is no good defensive ammo available. They are marketed to the Cowboy Action Shooters and their ammo is very underpowered. These two are also a bit tricky to reload so they are not the best choices for a prepper.

Why use a revolver cartridge? Primarily because of magazine capacity. These little carbines will hold ten rounds in the magazine. The longer cartridges like the .30–30 will limit a carbine to seven cartridges. Plus the .30–30 kicks more, so recovery time is slower between shots. Also, a powerful rifle cartridge like the .30–30 will run a higher risk of over-penetration. That is when the bullet exits the target and can cause unwanted damage to whatever is beyond. This is a bad thing when you have friends, family, or neighbors lurking about whom you would prefer not to shoot.

▲ The .44 Magnum is effective for defense in a handgun or a carbine.

Several manufacturers offer .357 Magnum and .44 Magnum cartridges with bullets designed for self-defense. Part of that design is to help minimize over-penetration.

While not even in the same class as a magazine-fed, semiauto rifle, these carbines can be reloaded relatively quickly and a partially empty magazine can be topped off. With practice a shooter can hit multiple targets surprisingly fast with these guns. Check out any Cowboy Action match and you will be amazed how fast those shooters can work a lever gun.

The lever-action, revolver-cartridge carbine can also be used for hunting as these cartridges can take deer-size game, although the .44 Magnum is more powerful and better suited for that. I can attest to that with personal experience: I have shot several deer, hogs, and black bears with the .44 Magnum and my uncle Butch Towsley used a Marlin in .44 Magnum exclusively for years, shooting a lot of deer. It's an amazingly effective cartridge.

The lever-action also gives you a long-gun option for those revolver cartridges. You never know what will show up in the ammo supply stream during a survival situation. These are very popular revolver cartridges and the odds favor that you may find ammo available even when things are bad. These carbines give you an option beyond the revolvers. They also respond very well to cast bullets so if you are making your own bullets and reloading ammo, these guns are a very good option. Some of the older Marlins had micro-groove rifling that was not the best for cast bullets, although they will work if you cast them with a hard alloy. The more recent Marlin guns have deep cut Ballard rifling designed for cast bullets. Because lever-actions are not gas operated like semiautos and don't have a gas port to plug up, they won't have the problems associated with most semiauto rifles and cast bullets.

I prefer a peep sight over the traditional open sights that come with the gun. One of my Winchester 94 .44 Magnum carbines and my Marlin 1894 in .44 Magnum both have Williams rear peep sights. Lyman also makes peep-style sights for these rifles. My Winchester has a brass-bead front sight while the Marlin has a fiber-optic front sight. I like the high visibility of the fiber optic and find it's very fast when doing drills on the range or hunting. If you go that route, make sure you store some replacement filaments for the fiber-optic sight as they break now and then. It's probably a good idea to stock up on a few extra sights, including a few brass-bead front sights, as front sights tend to break with hard use. You may want to install a red-dot or even a low-power scope. The modern Marlins are drilled and tapped for optics. With their side-ejection design they work very well with any top-mounted optic. The later production Winchester Model 94 carbines in .44 Magnum made before the New Haven plant closed were drilled and tapped as well. They have the angle-eject feature for mounting a scope. The current reproduction Winchester Model 92 rifles do not allow easy scope mounting. Most of the imported guns follow the original Winchester design and will be difficult to fit with an optic.

These lever-action carbines are a lot of fun to shoot, which means you will be inclined to train with them more often.

The lever-action first gained recognition as a self-defense gun during the Civil War. Even today, a century and a half later, this historically all-American design works fine for defense of hearth and home.

Make no mistake; the lever-action is old technology, and these guns are not even close to being as effective as a magazine-fed, semiauto like the AR-15. But if you live where American freedom is no longer recognized and realize that you must have something to protect yourself and your family, consider the lever-action alternative.

Even if you live in a free state, any serious prepper should consider one or more of these guns because of possible ammo availability and because they are one of the best long-gun alternatives to use with cast bullets.

# The "Other" Rifles

*Rifles that just don't fit in.*

▲ The .351 Winchester SL was once the cutting edge in a fighting rifle; today, not so much.

*I* am reluctant to open the door to this topic. "Other rifles" can encompass a very wide range of firearms and the chapter could get out of hand pretty quickly.

This is kind of an end of the section, end of the book catch-all for all those other rifles and concepts that didn't quite fit into any of the other chapters.

I can't begin to cover all the "other rifles" out there. I don't want to, and you don't want me to. Do you really want to hear about my antique L Ehennec MLE rifle? How about the Trapdoor Springfield .45–70 or my 1907 Winchester semiauto in .351 SL? They were all fighting guns at some point, but that point is in the past. They are irrelevant to any prepper today.

This is more of a random collection of the leftovers. Some like the Mini-14 are here because I had planned a long chapter on the gun, until the word count got

out of hand and those chapters not yet written became abbreviated. Had I started with this gun you would have probably read a long, historic dissertation of Bill Ruger's gun, one he never really wanted to be a fighting gun, but became one anyway. It had the unfortunate position of being one of the last guns I wrote about. No reason—it just was. Even in abbreviated form, you will see it's a great gun. If you need more detail, wait for Volume II of this book, or just Google it as a lot has been written on the Mini-14 in the forty years it has been around.

The SCAR is much of the same; I wanted to give it a much bigger word count, but couldn't. Again, it's a great rifle with a strong history. I wish I could have explored it more, but you get the point that it's a good choice for preppers. It was one of the last guns to show up, so it got a bit short changed.

Finally, you didn't think I would forget the .22 LR, did you? It may well be one of the most important guns a prepper can have. Once you deal with your personal protection firearms, you need to look at the guns that will help you live and survive the issues beyond fighting. The .22 LR is an important piece of that puzzle.

For lack of a better choice of words, here are some of the leftovers.

## Ruger Mini-14 and Its Variants

*Spawned from America's last battle rifle, this Ruger is a good choice for preppers.*

▲ Ruger Mini-14.

▲ The Ruger Mini-14 is an iconic American-made, magazine-fed, semiauto rifle.

In 1975 Sturm Ruger introduced the Mini-14, which is, as it was described in the book *Ruger and his Guns*, "a scaled down version of the M14—but not exactly."

The M14 was the last true "battle rifle" as defined by using full power 30-caliber ammo. It was a big, long, and heavy rifle. Ruger trimmed it down, chambered it for our current fighting cartridge, and developed a rifle for those looking to be a little different. For those who love the M1 or M14 designs or who are simply looking for an alternative to the AR/AK rifles, the Ruger is a well-proven rifle.

The Mini-14 rifle has been offered in multiple variations over the years in 5.56/.223 chambering. They also offer a .300 ACC Blackout. The Mini-30 is chambered for 7.62X39. They made a Mini-6.8, in 6.8 SPC, for a while, but it's discontinued.

My Mini-14 is a tactical model with a 16-inch barrel and a birdcage flash hider. It's stainless steel with

a synthetic stock. The gun comes with an adjustable rear peep sight and a protected blade front sight. The receiver will accept Ruger rings for mounting a scope. There are also rails and mounts for mini red dots available aftermarket.

▲ The author shooting the Ruger Mini-14. This is a good choice for a personal-defense long gun.

The Mini-14 comes with two twenty-round magazines, but aftermarket magazines are available and thirty-round mags are common and affordable. There are some reports of poor-quality aftermarket magazines, so if you go outside of the Ruger factory options, do some homework and make sure you are getting high-quality magazines.

The Mini-14 magazine might be an issue for preppers because it's not interchangeable with the AR-15. The gun has been around for a long time and there are a lot of magazines out there, but they will be harder to find than AR-15 magazines if TSHTF. So it's always a good idea to stock up on extra magazines.

This is a gas-piston-driven rifle and it is reliable. Some of the older Mini-14 rifles had a reputation for horrible accuracy, but the new guns are vastly improved. As with any Ruger, they are tough and dependable.

These guns deserve a hard look from any prepper and can provide a good alternative to the AR-15 as a personal, primary long gun.

## FN SCAR 16

The Special Operations Forces Combat Assault Rifle (SCAR) is a modular rifle made by Fabrique Nationale de Herstal (FNH) for the United States Special Operations Command (SOCOM) to satisfy the requirements of the SCAR competition.

These full-auto battle rifles are a lot of fun to shoot. I have been lucky enough to use them several times, including at a 3-gun match as a guest of FN. For the record, I did use the "fun switch" on one stage—the

▲ The author shooting an FNH SCAR.

temptation was too great to resist—but a threatened DQ changed my mind on doing it again. Of course, I had plenty of time between stages to play with it. I have also fired the SCAR full-auto at night with a laser sight. Great fun.

The SCAR-L, for "light," called the SCAR 16, is chambered in the 5.56×45mm NATO cartridge. The SCAR-H, for "heavy," called the SCAR 17, is chambered in 7.62×51mm NATO. Both are offered in several different configurations.

One way to describe the SCAR 16 is that it's the next generation of the AR-15. While a different gun, the controls are similar with the safety, magazine release, and bolt release all in the same location and operated the same. The mag release and the safety are ambidextrous.

▲ Mark Hanish from FNH shooting a SCAR in a 3-gun match.

My SCAR has a rail for mounting optics as well as folding iron sights. The SCAR is a tough, battle-proven, piston-driven rifle. I have seen them used a lot in 3-gun competition with my friends on the FN 3-gun team and other shooters. It's a reliable rifle that can stand up to tough conditions. Anything an AR-15 can do, this rifle does just as well or better.

My only complaint is the charging handle is on the left side and reciprocates as the bolt operates. This can cause problems if it hits your hand or when shooting through a doorway or window if it hits the frame. When that happens, it will jam up the gun. I have hit my thumb multiple times with the charging handle while shooting this gun. When that happens it not only jams the gun, it hurts like hell and makes me say words that would get my bottom swatted with a wooden spoon if my mother was alive.

The SCAR uses NATO-style M16 magazines so that any AR-15 magazine will work. This is a huge advantage for a prepper, because magazines should be relatively easy to find.

The .308 chambered SCAR 17 uses a proprietary magazine, so it probably isn't as good a choice for preppers. During a time of crisis magazines will be very hard to find as these guns are not as common as many other .308 rifles. It's a fine rifle; but if you buy one, stock up on magazines.

And after TSHTF it might be harder to find parts for the SCAR than the more common AR-15 rifles. Other than that, this is a very good choice for preppers looking for a personal long gun.

## FN FAL

The FN FAL or Fusil Automatique Léger (Light Automatic Rifle) is a selective-fire battle rifle produced by FNH, the same people who now make the SCAR.

Most NATO countries adopted the FN FAL, but not the US military, even though it was at the insistence of the United States that the standard cartridge be 7.62×51mm NATO (.308). As a result, this rifle is one of the most popular guns in history. It has been used by the military in more than ninety countries. The rifle is nicknamed, "The right arm of the free world." In many ways it is to the Western world what the AK-47 was to the Communist bloc.

During the late 1980s and 1990s, many countries replaced and decommissioned their FAL rifles. Many

▲ Nathan Towsley sighting in a FN FAL.

of them were sold to US importers as surplus and the upper receivers were destroyed under American law, so they were no longer full-auto guns. They were then sold as "parts kits" and used with a different receiver to build legal semiautomatic rifles.

In fact that's how I got mine; I built it with a Coonan receiver. (They are the same folks who make a 1911 pistol in .357 Magnum.)

There are a lot of these guns out there on the American market. Even as a semiauto, they are serious battle rifles in a serious cartridge.

The trouble is they are commanding a high price on the used gun market. The guns now are going for more than the price of a new AR-15, so I am not sure that this is the best gun for a prepper.

If you can find an FAL at an affordable price it's a good functional rifle and is a good long-gun option.

But it's probably not a gun that a prepper should seek. You might be better served to spend the same money on an AR-15 or an AR-L in .308 and have a new rifle that easily accepts modern optics. Also, parts and magazines will be easier to find for these rifles.

## "Other" Military Rifles

General Patton is quoted as saying, "In my opinion, the M1 rifle is the greatest battle implement ever devised."

People still cling to that, even though the military has long since given up on the rifle. In 1945 it was true, but today it is not the best option. It's not even in the top five. I love the rifle. I think it's on the list of guns that every hard-core gun guy should own, but mine is for something other than prepping.

No matter how cool it looked with Clint Eastwood pointing it at gang members and snarling "get off my lawn," the M1 is an old, outdated rifle. So are the M14 and any military rifle like the Mauser or Springfield bolt-actions.

## Mosin Nagant Sniper

If you think a Mosin Nagant is the ultimate survival rifle, you are not thinking this through. (I have seen that statement on the Internet many times.) Sure the Soviet Union held off the Nazis at Stalingrad with that rifle, but that was back when the Nazis were also using bolt-action Mausers. Don't get me wrong, I love the Mosin Nagant; I own several and shoot them often. But they are for fun and nostalgia, not protecting my life. It is an 1890s Russian-design bolt-action rifle with a clip-fed magazine and is long enough to serve as a support pole for a circus tent. Only a fool would think this is the best gun to survive TEOTWAWKI.

Of course, any gun is better than nothing, but if you are serious about prepping, you should be looking at serious guns for that serious business.

## Hunting Rifles

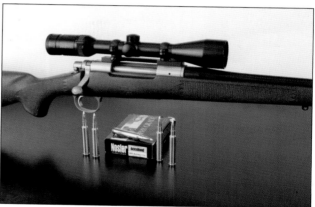

▲ Custom Remington Model 700 in .280 AI.

I suppose the same might be said about hunting rifles. They are better than no rifle at all. But most hunting rifles hold very limited ammunition, are slow to reload and are not designed to hold up to sustained firing.

What about hunting? Well, that could be a big part of survival. Foraging and hunting may be important to making sure you have enough food, but keep it in perspective.

There is this romantic notion that we can "head for the hills" and live off the land. I can tell you this much: I have been a hard-core hunter, both as my personal passion and as my profession as a hunting writer for all of my life. I have hunted with just about every type of firearm and with most of the archery gear that can fling an arrow. I have even hunted hogs with a knife. I have hunted almost every legal species in North America and a bunch of different critters in Africa, Russia, Europe, Mexico, and South America. I am also a trapper and made my living trapping for a couple of winters back when fur was bringing a good price. I am an experienced fisherman and I pride myself on being a woodsman and on my skills in the wilderness.

*I do not want to live off the land!* I am not even sure I could live off the land. Even if I were successful, it would be a very tough life. A lot of food is seasonal and will be very difficult to find at times.

The hunter-gatherers in history lived hard and short lives.

Beyond that, think it through. If the crisis drags on very long, wild game will become scarce. Most of it will be shot, the rest will develop skills at not getting shot.

▲ Remington R25 in .038.

Finally, you can hunt with most of your personal protection rifles. An AR-L in .308 is good for most any game in North America. The exceptions might be the polar or grizzly bears, neither known as good table fare. Law and order may be a thing of the past and a lot of people will be desperate and hungry. If you run into trouble while hunting, you are much better equipped with an AR-L in .308 than with a bolt-action .308.

If you are in the extremely remote wilderness where hunting game like moose or elk will truly be a big part of survival and where the odds of running into packs of bad guys are remote, then a bolt-action rifle might

be a good idea. In that situation, I personally would pick a big cartridge to help remove any doubt about the critters I shoot, at least a .300 Winchester or larger. If there are bears with attitudes around, particularly the grizzly kind, I would pick a .338 or larger. But for the vast majority of preppers who are going to be trying to survive in the lower forty-eight states, I can see little use for a bolt-action hunting rifle, at least not as long as you have better options.

If you have hunting rifles, by all means keep them. They are backup guns and excellent barter items. But if you are buying guns to build your survival battery, it might be best to put your money into guns that are more diverse in their use than a hunting rifle.

## The "Survival" Guns

▲ The AR-7 Survival Gun breaks down and stores in the buttstock.

The concept of a "survival" gun has again taken on a bit of a romantic notion with the prepper movement. Like I have stated many times, I think the best survival gun is an AR-15 or AR-L in .308. There is not much that these guns can't do. They are outstanding for defense and adequate for hunting and foraging.

But for many, the concept of a "survival" gun is some minimalist firearm that you take with you as you bug out and head for the hills. It's a gun that when mated with your scary ninja skills will keep you fat and happy for the rest of your long life. Or at least that's what I keep reading on the Internet. Heck, the best of the best of them say they plan to bring a flintlock. They will make their own flints, powder, and balls, relying only on the resources of God's bounty and their superior intellects.

I wish them luck, but that sounds like a hard way to go when there are so many great guns out there and plenty of cartridges to run them. Why take a flintlock when you can have an AR? Remember too that the bad guys will have ARs or AKs. Good luck fighting them with your flintlock. You might also want to check out how using those old muzzle-loaders worked for Lewis and Clark when they ran into grizzly bears. Here's a hint: It didn't end well.

Then again, if you believe all the television shows about TEOTWAWKI today, all you need to survive is a sword. Or maybe a crossbow. Hollywood and the fan-boys love them both. I think it's now a law that you can't have an end-of-the-world show unless the people in it are using swords and crossbows. Seeing that, you start to understand how the term "survival gun" has morphed in today's Internet and television-driven society.

I think the concept of a "survival" gun goes back to the idea of something small, compact, and inexpensive. It was to put under the seat of an airplane, snowmobile, truck, or boat, and forget until you needed it. If your bush plane crashed, you dug out this survival gun and a few cartridges and used it to feed yourself until you walked home or were rescued. It was not intended to fight off hordes of hungry zombies or to shoot a moose, but rather to plug a grouse or rabbit or maybe even a deer if conditions were right.

This concept has a place with preppers as well. Much of this book focuses on fighting guns. I think that should be the number-one goal for preppers. Staying alive, particularly in the early years, is going to be mostly about keeping what you have. There will be a lot of people trying to steal your food and equipment and possibly trying to kill you. This is what you need to prepare for.

But there will be other considerations. If you move to a retreat or are lucky enough to already live in the country you will need to look at long-term survival. Eventually, you will probably have chickens and other fowl, as well as livestock. You will have a garden. The meat, eggs, milk, and vegetables will be what sustain you and your family. Sure, you may have food stored away and you will hunt and forage, but in the end you will need to have a multi-tiered approach to survival.

What people are prepping for today, a lot of us who grew up rural and poor just called "life." Part of that is solving your own problems.

It seems like today people call the government for everything. If there is a raccoon raiding the garbage, they call animal control. If a fox is in the neighborhood and acting sick, they call the cops. If a deer is eating their shrubs, they call the game warden.

Those people are not going to do well in the new reality. Self-reliance is a trait that will be required. The solution that is obvious to most of us is to trap the coon, shoot the fox, and eat the deer.

You will also have rats, woodchucks, rabbits, squirrels, and other varmints eating your food. They might be cute now, but when the rabbits have trashed the garden that you need to survive the winter, cute doesn't cut it. I think that a .22 LR rifle or maybe a shotgun are critical tools preppers need to deal with these problems. Besides, rabbits are tasty.

I live in a rural area now and we have some problems with pests that I have to deal with pretty regularly. I can tell you it's a lot of fun to open the kitchen window and blast a property-damaging varmint with an AR-15. There is a certain satisfaction in the "overkill" on a red squirrel that just caused hundreds of dollars of damage to the gear stored in my shed, but in a survival situation it's prudent to stay a bit lower key. You don't want to call attention to your home with loud noises and it's best not to scare off any other edible game that might be around.

(Take note, if you continue to train with your defensive guns, and you should, it might be best to find a spot some distance from your living quarters.)

The survival guns can be a good choice here. These are generally low-cost, simple guns that you can stick where they might be needed, like by your back door, in the barn, or in a boat.

There are a lot of guns that will work, but here are a few suggestions of new guns that have caught my eye.

### Savage Model 42

For years Savage has made the Model 24, over/under with a rifle on top and a shotgun on the bottom. The most common was a .22 LR over a .410 shotgun. But they also made the rifle in cartridges like the .30–30 Win. or .308 Win., both suitable for big game. The

▲ Savage Model 42 in .22 LR and .410 shotgun.

rifles chambered for these cartridges usually had a 20-or 12-gauge shotgun barrel underneath. That model is no longer made, but you might find some on the used gun market.

▲ Savage Model 42 in .22 LR and .410 shotgun.

Today Savage makes a modern version called the Model 42. You can get a .22 LR or a .22 Magnum on top and a .410 shotgun underneath.

This is a break-action single-shot. (Well okay, two shots, but a single shot in each barrel.) It's short, handy, and only weighs about 6.1 pounds.

This is a perfect gun to keep by the back door or in your barn to shoot targets of opportunity like a garden-raiding rabbit or a rat stealing your cattle feed.

## Break It Down

Semiauto .22 LR rifles are as common as dirt. They are not horribly expensive to buy new and the used market is full of these guns. It's a good idea for any prepper to have one or two .22 LR rifles around. They work well for this "survival" gun concept. When I was growing up everybody had a deer camp and they all had an old .22 that was left there to deal with porcupines and other problem varmints.

I keep hearing how the .22 is the perfect survival gun, mostly because you can carry a lot of ammo with you. But again, I am hearing it from foolish people with foolish notions about how survival will be after TSHTF. I know there must be a lot of them because indications are that they are the driving force behind the .22 LR ammo shortages that have gone on for years.

However, the concept of fighting for your life with a .22 LR is a very bad idea. This is not a stopping cartridge. It's easy to say you will "shoot them in the eye" but that ignores the fact that you are not fighting paper targets on a square range. That eye you are planning to shoot is attached to a guy who will be moving and hard to hit. He will also be shooting at you, probably with a much bigger gun.

Another thing I keep hearing is, "I'll just shoot him a bunch of times." While you are shooting the bad guy over and over, his buddy will be shooting you.

Forget it; the .22 is not a fighting gun, just as it's not for foraging big game. I suppose it might work for either in an emergency, if you are lucky, but that's not what it's good for. It's useful for pest control and hunting small game, or perhaps for training with cheaper ammo and less noise.

But make no mistake; a .22 LR rifle is one of the most useful guns a prepper can have in "true life" survival scenarios.

I highly recommend that any prepper have a magazine-fed semiauto .22 LR with several spare magazines. Or, like I said before, two would be better.

Two interesting guns in this category are the takedown models offered by Ruger and Marlin. They come with carry bags and break down to smaller packages that are easier to store under a seat or in a backpack. They embody the "survival" gun concept as it was originally intended. These would make great rifles to have in a boat, at your remote cabin, or even in a bug-out backpack.

They are also good guns to keep around your place for dealing with problems. You can leave them ready to go, or break them down for travel.

### Marlin Model 70PSS Stainless

▲ Marlin Model 70PSS Stainless takedown .22 LR.

This stainless steel, synthetic stock, semiauto comes with an all-weather case. You can take it apart and put it back together in a matter of seconds. The barrel is held on with a knurled nut that you tighten or loosen with your fingers or the supplied wrench. It comes with open sights and the receiver is grooved for a tip-off-style scope mount.

The gun comes with a seven-shot magazine and the padded case has built-in flotation. The gun only weighs 3.25 pounds.

### Ruger 10/22 Takedown

▲ Ruger 10/22 takedown.

The Ruger 10/22 might be the best-known and most popular .22 rifle on the market. It has earned a reputation as a tough, reliable, accurate rifle. It is not all that expensive and a prepper would do well to consider the 10/22.

The gun is also offered in a takedown model that is easy to transport. The gun slides together and a slight twist locks it together. A spring-loaded lever releases the two halves and a slight twist in the other direction takes it apart. It is stainless steel with a synthetic stock and a Ruger ten-round rotary magazine. You can even order it with a threaded muzzle and a flash hider. The gun comes with open sights and is drilled and tapped, with a base included for mounting a scope.

▲ Ruger 10/22 takedown with Ruger BX-25, twenty-five-round magazines.

The ballistic-nylon case has pouches for each of the two parts as well as cleaning gear and ammo. One pocket is designed to hold six loaded Ruger BX-25, twenty-five-round magazines. As I pointed out before, a .22 is a poor choice in a fight, but if you get caught in a fight and all you have is a .22, you'd better hope it's this one with those magazines!

# HANDGUNS
## Picking a Handgun

*Which defensive pistol is right for you?*

▲ S&W 1911 in a Galco holster.

Prepping for survival is different than the concept of a carry gun in good times. We must plan for any contingency and the worst-case scenario will probably be much different than we found back before the world took a turn to the crazy side.

We may still have to deal with someone trying to rob us of our wallets, just like in the old days, but we may just as well find ourselves fighting for our lives against an angry mob or a terrorist attack. In that light, the higher-capacity handgun argument makes some sense. Not just because of what's in the gun, but also because of the amount of ready-to-use ammo we will have with us. If we have our gun and two extra magazines, it will be argued that the amount of ammo with a high-capacity "Wonder Nine" will be much higher than for a 1911 .45. With a Glock G17, for example, you will have one in the pipe and three fully loaded seventeen-round magazines for a total of fifty-two rounds of ammo, or more than double what a 1911 shooter will have with the same two reloads.

Of course, you can always carry more magazines and that's advisable if you are in a true survival situation. But part of prepping is being prepared before problems occur. For most, that includes buying and carrying a handgun now.

One of the popular platitudes of modern-day gunfighters is, "two is one and one is none." I am not really sure that makes a lot of sense from a grammatical standpoint, but the concept is that you should always carry two guns: a primary and a backup. Not horrible advice, but it can open the door to some extreme ideas. I know people who carry two handguns and multiple magazines for each. They will be well prepared for a fight, but that's a lot of weight to lug around every day. There must be a balance that lets you operate each day within the boundaries of current society. If you are in a survival situation, that makes complete sense. In fact you are probably under-equipped. But if you are carrying every day in our current, "mostly" functioning society it might be a bit of overkill to have multiple guns and hundreds of rounds of ammo in magazines all stashed on your body. I am not saying they are wrong, just that we all need to find the balance that works best for our unique situations.

If you subscribe to this idea honestly, then you should have a rifle with you, as that's better in a fight than a dozen handguns. But if you start carrying a fighting rifle everywhere you go, you will become well acquainted with your local SWAT team. The point is that as this concept of backup escalates, at some point the amount of guns and ammo you are lugging

around becomes a burden. You need to find a balance between your everyday carry needs as they stand today and the load-out you will bring to war.

This relates to what you carry on your person, not what is in your vehicle.

For me and many others, everyday carry is a primary handgun with two extra magazines. There are times when I will add another backup gun, but they are pretty rare. I know that I could well regret that if I am caught in a complete SHTF situation, but I have judged the odds and decided I can live with the risk. Your results, as they say, may vary.

Often the gun I carry is a 1911 or a S&W Shield in .40 S&W, both with relatively low magazine capacities. In fact, I often carry a S&W J-Frame Model 340 revolver. It's a five-shot .357 Magnum, so even with two reloads I have less ammo than one magazine for a Wonder Nine. That's what I carry now, in our "sort-of-functioning" society. But if problems continue to escalate with more riots and social unrest, or if we experience a catastrophic change where society fails and it becomes survival, I will change my carry guns to reflect those times.

I recognize that there is a flaw in my logic with my current carry guns. My friend Scott Ballard made his living in harm's way for many years. These days he is an instructor at the Sig Sauer Academy in New Hampshire. When talking about carrying a gun because it's convenient or because it's the best tool, he said this:

"I will not disparage those who do, but I am not able to make convenience a primary deciding factor for the weapon I carry. I find that capacity is a close second to shoot-ability on my list. Finding a solitary hunter is a rare thing amongst the predatory human animal."

As a gun guy who makes his living writing about this stuff, I buy a lot of guns and as a result I have lots of options. I am lucky enough that I have multiple guns and can carry a lightweight gun like the Shield today, but can switch to a full-capacity handgun at any time. If you are buying your first, and perhaps only, carry gun, you need to study the issue and find the balance that works for you.

If you are prepping and/or buying your primary carry gun and can only afford one gun right now to protect you in any survival situation, then some kind of a high-capacity handgun makes sense.

▲ S&W M-340 .357 Mag.

I know I suggested elsewhere that it be a 9mm for reasons of expected ammo supply, but it doesn't have to be a 9mm. This book is going to be filled with contradictions and this is one of them. That doesn't mean they are wrong.

The 9mm makes sense from an ammo supply point of view, but from a performance aspect it's lacking. The main argument on the performance side is for high capacity and that argument has evolved and changed. Thirty years ago the 9mm was pretty much the only option for high-capacity handguns. Today you can get big magazine guns in almost any chambering. If we put the .45 in the same double-stack design pistol, most of the full-size guns have a magazine capacity of thirteen or fourteen rounds. Most .40 S&W pistols will have fifteen-round magazines while the Wonder Nines usually have seventeen in a magazine. At least that's what the gun that started all this, the Glock G17, holds. Some might argue for the Browning Hi-Power, which was around long before the Glock and is a fine handgun. The Hi-Power magazine holds thirteen rounds. So I'll give the argument all the help it can get and go with the Glock's seventeen-round capacity.

While many will still argue for the higher capacity of the 9mm, I think the logic of their arguments is often flawed or at least incomplete. First, I don't think you should plan your strategy around how much you are going to miss, which seems to be the theme of a lot of the guys arguing for a high-capacity handgun. It's also poor strategy to pick a gun with a less powerful cartridge just because it holds more ammo. This is another common argument, "I have seventeen shots; I'll just keep shooting." The problem with that is the other guy might have the same idea and he might actually hit you. The goal is to strike the bad guy with the first and every shot you fire. That may not be the reality, but it damn sure should be the goal. That first hit may well be the only hit and so it should be as powerful a blow as you can strike.

Shooting under stress is far different than shooting at the range. It's folly to think you can just keep shooting and hitting the bad guy. He is going to react and move, probably attacking you. A moving target is difficult to hit, particularly if you are moving too, and you should be. Forget multiple shots or precise shot placement; you will be lucky to get any hits at all in a

fast-breaking, stress-filled, panic-fueled fight for your life. I think it's a far better idea to use the more powerful cartridge with a better chance to end the threat as fast as possible with that one hit.

The .40 S&W wasn't around thirty years ago when the Glock G17 began a revolution in handgun design. Today it is, and it is chambered in guns with high magazine capacity. That revolution in double-stack handguns has also prompted new high-capacity pistols in .45 ACP that we didn't have then. With the bigger, more powerful cartridges logic says you will not need as much ammo. If you pick a .40 S&W double-stack you are only down six rounds total with a loaded gun and two extra magazines from a 9mm, but you have a more powerful handgun so you should be more effective. If you go with a double-stack .45, you are down nine rounds.

I will point out that most .40 S&W and 9mm handguns use the same basic grip frame size while the .45 ACP (and the 10mm) need a longer, front-to-back magazine which results in a larger grip frame. While for many that's not a factor, it is for short-fingered guys like me, and I have trouble reaching the trigger correctly with some striker-fired guns like the Glock in .45 ACP. Many women and small-statured shooters may find the same problem with a double-stack .45 ACP. This does not apply to all guns, as I can shoot the single-action trigger guns like the STI 2011 .45 ACP handgun just fine. Where I struggle is with double-stack .45 ACP guns with striker-fired actions, which usually have the trigger positioned farther forward than a single-action

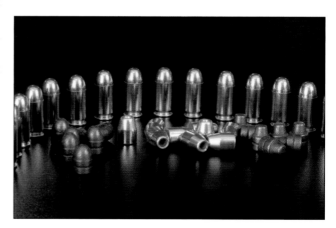

▲ .45 ACP.

handgun. Bottom line, try a gun on for size before you write the check.

So, let's get back to the cartridges. In an increasingly partisan world, if there is a gun-related subject that is sure to create an argument today it is defensive-pistol cartridges. This saga plays out on the Internet every day with the arguments running the gauntlet from reasonable and concise to total dumbass mode. The "full-retard" side is often argued by those who mistake their opinions for fact. Those people usually have developed those opinions based on reading the crap posted by foolish little boys hiding in their mom's basements and blogging about guns they have never shot.

At the other end of the spectrum, I have some elite military friends who have seen a lot of combat, includ-ing with handguns. Almost to a man they do not like the 9mm because they have to shoot the bad guys too many times. (Yes, I know, they have different ammo. But remember, it's the ammo you may be using in a survival situation.)

If you are just not sure, learn all you can about as many guns as possible. Then try as many guns as you can. Go to shooting ranges and shoot other people's guns. Prowl the gun stores and handle a lot of different handguns. Find one that fits and functions for your specific needs.

Then buy two of them. It's going to be a tough ol' world out there and you can't take any chances.

# A Clear-Eyed Look at Handgun Stopping Power

*Unless you're stupid, you can't ignore physics or facts.*

▲ It's a fact, heavyweights hit harder.

There is no question that the Internet is the greatest invention of our time, although Al Gore trying to take credit was one of the sleaziest acts ever.

The trouble is that there is no filter on the net. I was talking with the editor of a very large gun magazine recently about a test I am doing on a defensive shotgun.

"Don't do like (name withheld to protect the stupid) and test a smooth-bore, defensive shotgun with sabot slugs designed for rifled barrels," the editor said with what I hoped was an ironic laugh. Then he told me, "That guy will not be writing for us again."

The point being that with magazines, the writers have a filter and the fools and dumbasses don't make it into print, at least not regularly. If you are a writer for any of the major magazines, you made your bones first. You had to work your way into that position by proving you knew your stuff.

With the Internet, not so much. Anybody can start a blog. If what they are writing catches the fancy of the reader, it doesn't have to be true. If that reader has a blog, maybe he repeats it like it was his idea. Then one of his readers posts it on Facebook, where 1,000 people "share," then all their friends share and so on, until pretty soon people start to believe it's the truth.

This is why much of the misinformation about the effective stopping power of defensive handguns is being repeated over and over. In fact, the term "stopping power" is disparaged and distorted today. I am amazed at the total BS out there.

Let's take a look at reality. I am a big game hunter and I have been lucky enough to spend up to 150 days a year for decades hunting over most of the world. I have shot a lot of stuff including Cape buffalo, elephant, hippo, and hundreds of smaller critters. I have watched other people shoot hundreds more. With the exception of the very big game like those mentioned, we use rifles that are proportionally much more powerful than defensive handguns.

▲ The author shot this Cape buffalo with a .500 NE double rifle.

For example, a whitetail deer is similar to a man in size. The .30–06 Springfield is one of the most popular cartridges used to hunt them. With a 150-grain bullet at 2,910 ft/s, it produces 2,801 foot-pounds of energy. A 9mm 124-grain bullet at 1,150 ft/s has 364 foot-pounds of energy. So in effect we are shooting a deer with a bullet carrying 670 percent more energy than that popular self-defense cartridge carries to stop a bad guy the same size as the deer.

Contrary to what you see on outdoor television, big game rarely just falls down when it's hit. For television, most people are using a high-shoulder shot that shocks the spine and causes the animal to fall. It's great for the camera, but is not the best shot from a hunter's perspective. The more common and less risky shot is to double-lung the deer by shooting behind the shoulder, center of mass. It's always fatal, but the deer will almost always run before they die, even when hit with

a powerful rifle bullet that does an incredible amount of damage.

If a .30–06 doesn't drop a deer in its tracks every single time, how can we expect a 9mm or even a .45 ACP to drop a man instantly?

We can't.

The elephant or Cape buffalo is perhaps a better comparison. We use big guns with about 5,000 foot-pounds of energy, but they are big critters. So in the case of a big buffalo we are hitting it with about three foot-pounds of energy per pound of body weight. With an elephant it's about 1:1, or even less. Shooting a 200-pound bad guy with a 9mm is hitting him with 1.8 foot-pounds of energy, per pound of body weight. With a .45 it's just over two foot-pounds of energy per pound of body weight. So, this is a fair comparison.

Heart shots are effective, as is a double lung for buffalo. They run away, you wait a while and then follow. In a short distance you find them dead. If he had decided to attack during the time he spent running away, a "dead" buffalo could do a lot of damage to a person.

Nobody with a brain messes around with dangerous game and little guns, even though a double-lung shot with a small rifle might well kill a buffalo or elephant. That's because when an elephant or buffalo charges, you need to stop them before they turn you into a bloody puddle. In that situation, you shoot for the brain, to take out the control center, but it's a tough shot on any charging critter. That's why we use big, heavy bullets with as much horsepower as we can get behind them. The idea is, if you miss the brain or spine, you want to break bones, take out the structure so they can't keep coming. A big bullet also does more tissue damage, which is what ultimately kills anything being shot with a firearm. Plus, they impart more shock; this may stun the attacker and perhaps buy you a little time for another shot. Every fraction of a second counts here. Bullets through the heart, lungs, and other important stuff will kill them, but you need to stop them long enough for that to take effect; so you take out the structure with deep penetrating, big, and heavy bullets with lots of power pushing them. Little guns may well kill dangerous game, but only a fool chooses to bring one on a dangerous game hunt.

The same concept applies to defensive handguns. You should be planning for the worst-case scenario, not what's adequate most of the time. There are no do-overs when you are fighting for your life. Sure, a small cartridge may kill the guy who is trying to kill you, but the goal is not so much to kill him as to stop him from trying to kill you as quickly as possible.

No handgun is going to be an instant man-stopper 100 percent of the time on any bad guy. If a .30–06 is not an instant stopper, a 9mm or even a .45 ACP will not be either. However, a .45 will do more tissue damage and break more bones than a .380 or 9mm. Bigger bullets mean a bigger hole and more energy on impact. That's simple physics.

The only shot that will be a 100-percent instant stop on a bad guy is one that shuts down the central nervous system, even temporarily. Always shoot for center of mass because it's much easier to hit in a stress situation. If you have options, forget head shots; they are Hollywood bullshit. The brain is small and easy to miss. The skull is tough and, with a glancing blow, can deflect a pistol bullet. Besides, the head is usually moving. High, center mass puts you into important tissue to damage and a bullet with enough penetration may hit the spine for an instant stop. If not, just as with the hunting TV's high-shoulder hit, it may cause enough tissue displacement to disrupt the spinal cord's function long enough to stop the fight. Remember, the bone structure is all connected and a big, heavy blow to the sternum or ribs is going to have effect. You are playing the odds with any shot, but with a bigger bullet and more energy the odds are swayed in your favor.

The laws of physics still stand and a more powerful handgun with a bigger bullet carrying more energy is always going to be a better option than a smaller cartridge. There are other considerations when choosing a defensive handgun, but shot for shot, bigger is always going to be better. We can distort the argument with anecdotal evidence, emotion, and other non-scientific arguments, but it doesn't change reality. The laws of physics remain intact.

▲ A .380 in your hand is better than a 1911 .45 ACP back home.

Granted, a .380 in your pocket is better than a .45 at home on the kitchen table when it comes time to fight for your life, but nobody can argue that the .380 is a better man-stopping cartridge than a .45 ACP.

When choosing a defensive handgun, look at terminal ballistics as well as magazine capacity, recoil, and the other critical factors. Pick a gun that works for you. It may well be a 9mm, but make your choice based on a solid foundation of scientific information, not what the latest instant expert on the Internet is spouting as "fact."

# Striker-Fired Double-Stack Handguns

*This relatively "new" category of handguns may be a prepper's best friend.*

▲ Glock G17.

t's funny sometimes how life works out.

In 1980, a fifty-year-old manager for a car radiator factory happened to be visiting the Austrian Ministry of Defense. He was there because of his part-time, home-based business where he made door fixtures, curtain rods, and knives. He sold the knives to the military. By coincidence, he overheard a conversation between two colonels about the Austrian Army's need for a new pistol. The man interrupted and asked if he could bid on the contract. Knowing that he didn't make guns, own guns, or know a thing about guns, the colonels laughed and said, "Sure, knock yourself out, buddy," or whatever condescending German phrase carried the same meaning.

They laughed when the man asked for the details of the requirements for the new gun and replied, "It shouldn't be too difficult to make such an item." He was too naive to even understand that gunmaking is a complicated, difficult process. In Europe handguns were made by companies that were often hundreds of years old. The thought that some guy who made curtain rods in his garage could come up with a workable handgun design and then manufacture the guns was beyond absurd.

But Gaston Glock was not just "some guy." Love him or hate him, you have to admit he had the brains and the balls to shake up the world. The fact he knew nothing about guns actually worked to his advantage. Even something as simple and as long established as the grip angle was new territory for him. Rather than copy the other pistols, he nailed a couple of wooden sticks together and asked people to tell him which angle felt more natural. Turns out it was 108 degrees, which was a departure from other, established handguns.

Everybody knew that handguns had to be made of metal, but Glock didn't get the memo. He used injection-molded plastic to make handles and sheaths for his knives, so he thought, "Why not make guns out of plastic?"

Not being a gun guy, Glock picked the brains of people who were. He also did a self-educating crash course on handguns by buying every gun he could. He took them apart and studied their engineering and he shot them until he knew them well.

Another thing he decided was unnecessary was a safety. Safeties caused problems, mainly when people under stress forgot to disengage them in a gunfight. Revolvers didn't have a safety. The long, hard, double-action trigger pull was their safety. So he reasoned, why did a semiauto handgun need a safety?

Glock hired some engineers, including a plastics expert from the camera industry, and went to work. Legend has it that he designed the gun in six months, but Glock himself said it took a year. Either way, it was remarkable. Most new handguns from established companies take several years to develop and bring to market.

Glock called his new pistol the Glock G17. Not because the plastic magazine held seventeen 9mm cartridges as most people think, but because it was his seventeenth patent.

The simple gun had only thirty-four parts. Everything except the barrel, slide, and a few small internal parts and springs was made of plastic. Even the magazine was plastic. The gun was cheap to manufacture and even when priced well below the competition, it created unprecedented profit margins.

Glock won that Austrian military contract, beating out long-established handgun makers like H&K and Beretta. Later he partnered with a guy named Karl Walter to introduce the gun to America. Walter agreed to a small salary and a percentage of the US sales. Ironically, several years later, when Glock was a billionaire, he tried to change the contract to remove the percentage of sales clause and cut Walter's income drastically. When Walter refused, Glock fired him.

Walter had been brilliant in marketing the gun. He focused on law enforcement at first. Fueled in part by the disastrous FBI Shootout in Miami, there was a transition in law enforcement from revolvers to higher-capacity semiauto handguns. Walter used some unique marketing ideas, such as taking the old revolvers in trade, to arm police with the new Glock G17.

The Glock G17 became controversial when some foolish people thought the plastic would make it undetectable at airports. The hysteria reached alarming levels as Congress tried to ban the gun. Walter just used it all to get the name out there. Time and again, Walter found new and innovative ways to turn lemons into lemonade in marketing this gun.

Of course, it's easy to sell something that works. The Glock G17 was unfailingly reliable and its durability became legendary. The trigger has a small metal lever in the center that must be depressed before the gun can fire, essentially acting as a safety. But due to the location, there was no need to remember to activate the safety as with other semiauto handguns; it was automatic when you pulled the trigger. The firing system, called "striker-fired," was different than the conventional, hammer-fired guns. The trigger kind of split the difference between the long, hard, double-action trigger pull of a revolver and the light, *some say unsafe*, single-action trigger pull of more conventional semiautos. The striker-fired trigger required about 5.5 pounds of pull weight and half an inch of movement. This system proved to be safe and reliable, but easy to shoot accurately.

With the gun control frenzy of the Clinton years, Glocks became a huge seller in the civilian market as well. That sealed the deal and Glock became the best-selling handgun in America. It continues to hold that position to this day.

This new and innovative handgun design didn't just rewrite the book on defensive handguns; it burned it and stomped on the ashes. The Glock G17 changed everything. Almost every other company making handguns today has copied the design.

The thing about Glock handguns is most shooters love them or hate them, with little middle ground. The traditionalists disdain the plastic parts, calling them "Tupperware" guns, but even the most hardcore of critics will admit that the plastic guns are incredibly rugged and durable.

That grip angle has resulted in one of the more controversial aspects of the Glock handguns. Proponents claim, and probably correctly, that the grip angle makes the gun point more naturally. Those who use Glocks exclusively love this aspect. But the grip angle is challenging to those of us who shoot a multitude of handguns. There is always a learning curve when switching from a Glock to a traditional-grip-angle pistol or back to the Glock. I find it frustrating when making that switch for at least a few magazines of ammo. The different feel between the guns and the difference in where they point takes a little "getting used to" and when you go back and forth, it can be frustrating.

That said, the reason we all complain about this is that we all own Glocks. So I guess you can easily see the irony in that point.

The bottom line is that the Glock handguns and the multitude of Glock clones, copies, and competition—the striker-fired, polymer-framed handguns—are arguably the best choice for survival handguns. They are relatively inexpensive, extremely reliable, and very durable. Plus, they hold a lot of ammo. They are easy to repair using simple tools and have few parts, making inventory of spare parts easier. For the most popular models like the Glocks and S&W M&P handguns, magazines are easy to find and inexpensive.

Glock changed the handgun world and launched a revolution that has spawned clones from every major gun maker in the market and inspired several other gun makers to enter the market.

There are far too many striker-fired, polymer handguns for me to review all of them here. But, that doesn't mean if you don't see your favorite gun here that it failed. It's far more likely that for any number of reasons I didn't already own one and for any of a multitude of reasons I did not get one to review for the book.

There are so many striker-fired, double-stack handguns on the market today that testing them all would almost become a full-time profession. One thing that I think is relatively safe to say is that you get what you pay for with these guns. If you find a handgun that is far less expensive than the going rate of other guns in that category, there is usually a reason. Be cautious, because to reduce the price, they had to cut corners at some point. Something, somewhere on that gun is different than all the more expensive guns. Not a big deal if you are just blasting targets at the range, but

remember this is a gun that you are choosing to protect your life and the lives of your loved ones. Because we may well be dealing with the end of the world as we know it, the gun has to hold up and keep working. It's also a gun that may need to last the rest of your life. So, choose carefully. In my way of thinking it is far better to buy an established brand-name handgun and spend a few more bucks than to go cheap and buy on price alone. These are not expensive handguns to start with; a brand-name, top-shelf, double-stack, striker-fired, polymer handgun will cost about half of what you will pay for a top-name, production-grade 1911 handgun.

While there was a time when Glock owned the category, that is no longer true and the double-stack, striker-fired, polymer-frame handgun marketplace today has a list of excellent handguns that is quite large.

Probably the biggest competitor is the S&W M&P. That handgun has made huge inroads into the market, both with civilians and law enforcement. But it's not alone, as there are several other brands of guns that are doing well.

The following looks at some of the striker-fired guns that I have shot and can recommend. This book is not intended to be a catalog of all the guns available that may interest preppers, but more of an overview of the category of handguns. I can't and won't test every gun on the market. The number is too huge, which is mind boggling when you consider that these handguns first came into the market nearly a decade after home computers and several years after Ronald Reagan became president.

▲ Glock G17 in a Front Line Quad Holster. A prepper can't go wrong with a brand-name striker-fired, double-stack handgun.

# Glock Handguns

*The gun that Gaston built not only started a revolution, but is a top choice for preppers too.*

▲ Glock G34 in 9mm top and Glock G35 in .40 S&W bottom.

While there have been uncounted new guns introduced over the years, not very many can claim that they changed the world. The Henry rifle, Colt's revolver, Browning's 1911, and the AK-47 did that, maybe a few more, but this is a pretty small and exclusive club. By any account it must include the Glock handgun.

The Glock G17 is the gun that shook up the world. It changed the way we look at defensive pistols and it's one of the best options available for a prepper.

While there may be other striker-fired guns that I like better, I will always own a G17. It's an icon in the handgun world. This pistol was a serious game changer and it launched a revolution that inspired a brand-new direction for defensive handguns. The G17 is high on my list of guns that every gun guy should own.

The compact version in 9mm is the G19, which is a smaller frame with a slightly lower capacity of fifteen rounds. The G19 will also take seventeen-round magazines as well as the extended thirty-three-round magazines and any of the multitudes of aftermarket magazines for the Glock 9mm handguns.

The G26 is the subcompact which holds ten rounds. The G34 is a longer-barreled version designed for competition. However, it's also a good defensive pistol and I know several serious guys who carry this gun.

I prefer the .40 S&W in a fighting gun and the .40 S&W guns are identical except for the chambering and the magazines. The standard-size .40 S&W is the G22, which holds fifteen rounds in the magazine. This was my first Glock pistol. I was a bit slow to jump on the Glock bandwagon and I bought this gun in 1994. It has handled thousands of rounds of ammo and I

▲ The author shooting his Glock G22.

▲ The Glock G17 Gen4 and G22.

think I might have cleaned it once, but my memory is fuzzy and I may be mistaken. I have had the gun long enough that the night sights have run through their life cycle and dimmed, yet I can't remember a single problem with this gun. The only work that's ever been done to it is a trigger kit, which to be honest I kind of regret. Now I suppose I'll need to replace the night sights, damn . . . it's always something. Kidding aside, this is as far from a "high maintenance" handgun as I have ever owned and in twenty-one years the G22 has given me zero problems.

The compact model in .40 S&W is the G23. Its magazine holds thirteen rounds. I bought a G23 as a carry gun some years back and I have logged a lot of miles with that gun on my hip. I added some Trijicon HD

night sights. The HD front sight has a large, colored luminescent dot that stores light and glows in the dark. In the center is a tritium capsule that is always visible in the dark. The wide-notch rear sight has two tritium dots. I am a believer in night sights; I have these HD sights on several other guns as well, including a 1911 that I built and a S&W Shield.

I have a LaserMax guide rod green laser in the G23. This activates by pushing on the slide stop with your finger. It fits completely inside the gun so there are no holster fit issues. The green laser is visible in brighter light than red lasers, so it's visible in most daylight situations. My G23 also has a Crimson Trace Lightguard light that fits on the rail and over the trigger guard of the pistol. The activation button is positioned under your ring finger so it comes on as you grip the handgun. With the night sights and laser, this light completes the pistol for bedside home defense use as well as carry. Unlike some bulky units, the slim light is very holster friendly and Galco has holsters to fit most handguns, even for a lefty like me.

## Why My Favorite Carry Gun Is the Glock G23

*Here is an edited and shortened piece I wrote for the annual* Glock Magazine *and catalog. Remember this was for a Glock publication, so I couldn't really tell them that I am a fickle gun guy and I have a lot of "favorite" carry guns. The G23 is just one of them, but it's high on the list.*

There is something very personal about picking out a new carry gun. You will be spending a lot of time with

▲ The Glock G23.

your pistol so it must be comfortable. There is a big difference between when you put it in the holster first thing in the morning and later, when it's been there for fifteen hours. Little things that you think you can ignore become very big things as the day moves on. Comfort is important because most people will find excuses not to carry an uncomfortable handgun; or they will replace it with a little gun because it's lightweight and small.

It's important to remember that you are carrying this gun because you may have to use it to defend your life or the life of others. Sure, the little pocket pistol, mouse guns are comfortable to carry around, but stop and ask yourself: Do you really want one of them in your hand when you are fighting for your life?

There is a balance between the little mini-guns and a full size rock 'em sock 'em pistol that is too big and heavy to carry all day. For me, the compact size Glock G23 is the perfect balance. For starters, the Glock design has no sharp edges or protrusions to poke and prod me all day. The safe-action trigger ensures the gun is always ready for action. Your fine motor skills and cognitive thinking may both disappear in a high-stress situation. The simplicity of the Glock design means you have less to think about and nothing other than the trigger to manipulate. There is no need for you to worry about pushing off a safety, just pull the trigger. Also, a striker-fired trigger system is ideal for a carry gun. They are easy to master and shoot well with, yet they are much safer in a high-stress situation than a light,

single-action trigger and will reduce the possibility of a tragic unplanned discharge.

The G23 is compact and at 21.3 ounces (31.32 ounces loaded) it's light enough to carry comfortably all day. Yet, it's large enough so that I can shoot it very well. The grip is big enough for good control over the handgun. The sights are clear and easy to see and with a 4.02-inch barrel length the gun has a 6.02-inch sight radius for more accurate shooting. In fact, this gun shoots so well that my son-in-law, who works in federal law enforcement, competes exclusively with his G23 in IDPA, 3-gun, and USPSA matches. This is the same gun he carries when he is off duty and has a choice in carry guns. (At least he did until my daughter commandeered it for her carry gun! That just meant they had to buy another Glock.)

Oddly enough, I never see a shooter with a pocket pistol at any of the matches. Why is this important? What good is a carry gun if you can't hit the bad guys? (The IDPA BUG backup gun matches changed that, but this was written before those matches were introduced. It's important to note that the BUG guns need their own match and own rules, as they cannot compete head-to-head with the big guns. There is a lesson in that when carrying a gun for defense. You will be competing head-to-head with whatever gun the bad guy brings, and in this competition there is no second-place winner.)

I am a firm believer that when it comes to defensive handgun cartridges, bigger is better. At least within reason. Unfair or not, the 9X19 does not have my trust. I shoot thousands of 9X19 cartridges every year in competition, but when it comes to defending myself or my family, I hold to the old adage that fighting pistol cartridges should start with a four.

The .40 S&W cartridge will fit in the same size handgun as a 9X19 because the cartridge overall length is actually slightly shorter than for the 9X19 cartridge. That means that the .40 S&W is the largest cartridge that will fit in the Glock handguns designed for 9X19 and similar size cartridges.

So if big bullets are the key, why not a .45 Auto? That goes back to the "personal" part of choosing a carry gun. The .45 Auto or 10mm Auto cartridges are longer and because the magazine is in the grip, a handgun chambered in those cartridges will require a longer grip size. If you have big hands that's not an issue, but my wide hands have stubby fingers and I find the larger grips in any double-stack, striker-fired, .45 Auto handgun difficult to manage.

This brings up another very important point. Your carry gun should fit your body style well so that you are comfortable not just carrying it, but also shooting it. If you are struggling to reach the trigger, you will never shoot it well. In the end, if you miss, it doesn't matter what cartridge or bullet you are using. With a gun that feels like an old friend in your hand, you will want to shoot it more often. Practice is critical if you choose to carry a handgun for defense. Handgun shooting is not a storable skill and it erodes fast. You must train often and if you enjoy the training experience you will be much more willing to do that.

Of course, a single-stack .45 Auto may well fit your hand with its smaller grip, but then the issue is magazine capacity. It's often pointed out that most gunfights are over in a few shots, so a single-stack has plenty of ammo. But that conventional wisdom does not consider the times we live in and the changes that have occurred. The threat of multiple assailants is all too real now. Possible scenarios include terrorist attacks, a gang attack, home invasion, or angry mobs due to

social unrest or the aftermath of a natural or man-made disaster. A higher magazine capacity means more ammo to deal with these things, not only in the gun, but with your spare magazines as well. The old saying that it's better to have it and not need it than to need it and not have it applies to ammo. It would be tragic to lose your life over something you can so easily control as the amount of ammo you are carrying with you.

In the end, after I examine all the options and issues, logic keeps pointing at the Glock G23, which is why it's my carry gun of choice.

The competition model in .40 S&W is the G35 and the subcompact is the G27 with a nine round capacity. They also make the standard, compact, and subcompact sizes in the .357 Sig, and .45 GAP.

Glock has a full range of larger-framed pistols in .45 ACP and 10mm as well as long-slide pistols in 9mm and .40 S&W, not to mention the full-auto and LE-only line of handguns. They also have introduced pocket size single-stack guns in .380 and 9mm, which are covered in another chapter. In the end, detailing all of them will start to make this look like a Glock catalog.

I think, to put this in the simplest terms possible, you can't go wrong with a Glock. They run well, rarely break, and are affordable.

# S&W M&P

*Striker-fired guns from America's pistol maker.*

he Smith & Wesson M&P (Military and Police) is probably the second most popular handgun in the polymer-frame, double-stack, striker-fired pistol category. When you consider that the M&P was introduced in 2005 and that Glock had a twenty-year head start in the market, running a close second to the Austrian wonder pistols is a pretty remarkable achievement.

There are many features on the M&P that I prefer over the Glock. One is the grip angle. There is nothing wrong with the Glock grip angle if all you shoot are Glocks. But I am a hard-core gun guy and I move from pistol to pistol with regularity. Most of those transitions are relatively easy, except when there is a Glock in the mix. It might just be me, but I find that when switching back and forth in either direction, it always takes a while for me to get command of the pistol.

The S&W M&P uses a grip angle that is "normal," or at least more common with today's handguns, so I do not encounter this small but important issue when I first pick one up after a lay off from shooting that gun. I also find that the adjustable S&W grip fits my hand very well with the medium grip panel installed. Of course, the Glock Gen 4 handguns offer this same option now as well. I like the feel of the trigger on the M&P. I have seen some amazing aftermarket triggers in these guns. I must admit, I am a bit of a trigger snob and I love a good single-action trigger on a handgun. My single biggest complaint and the source of constant aggravation for me is the striker-fired trigger. I never shoot them as well as I would like and any improvement that does not change reliability is a good thing. Some of the best triggers I have tried in a striker-fired gun have been on worked-over M&P handguns.

▲ M&P C.O.R.E. with a Trijicon sight.

I also I like that I can install a Crimson Trace Laser Grip easily. I have lasers on all my carry guns and the CT-style of grip laser is one of the most intuitive designs around. (Although I wish they would make a left-handed version as my thumbs sometimes block the laser.) The CT laser for the Glock clamps on the outside of the grip, changing the dimension, while the CT laser grip for the M&P simply replaces the grip panel in the rear. Of course, there are other laser sight options for the Glock, but none that I've tried have the on/off switch as well placed as the Crimson Trace design.

I like the metal magazines for the M&P because they drop clear of the gun better when empty. I find that plastic magazines sometimes stick in the gun and require that they be pulled free. This breaks your rhythm and focus if you are expecting the empty maga-

▲ A Crimson Trace Laser Grip on a S&W M&P.

zine to fall free when you push the release button. Obviously, it also extends the time it takes to reload.

I own and shoot several different M&P handguns, including a C.O.R.E. model which is fitted with a red dot sight. Most are in 9mm, but as you might have guessed, I like a bigger cartridge for serious defense. My preferred carry for the full-size M&P (I do love the scaled-down M&P Shield) is a variation on the M&P40 handgun. It has a few "extra" features from the factory and a few more I added.

## The Viking Tactics/Smith & Wesson M&P40 VTAC Pistol

*A tested warrior and America's best known handgun manufacturer team up for the ultimate fighting pistol.*

At the risk of dating myself, I remember all too well the war in Vietnam. It seems like every guy I met who spent time there claimed he was a Green Beret. Today, it seems like everyone I talk to who's been to the sand box in the early years was a sniper, now everybody is a SEAL.

I wonder how we can fight wars when nobody is driving the trucks, emptying the latrines, or peeling potatoes?

Those posers are also represented well in the recent rise in the number of training schools. As a friend of mine pointed out, there are a lot of guys running schools who have never fired a shot in anger or been shot at themselves.

While they may or may not be able to teach, it's those who have "been there and done that" who teach it best. Kyle Lamb is one of those guys. He is the real deal and like most who are, he doesn't need to brag about it. Kyle was one of the elite Special Forces: perhaps the most elite, Delta Force. He has survived years of bad guys all over the world trying to kill him. He is retired now, runs Viking Tactics and is one of the top trainers in the country for those who want to learn how to use their guns to defend themselves.

In a world where more and more guns are hitting the market that are designed by people who don't even shoot, it might be smart to use the skills and experience of a guy like Kyle to design a fighting pistol. Smith & Wesson thought so and they teamed up with Kyle Lamb and Viking Tactics to create the ultimate fighting handgun, the S&W M&P VTAC.

The S&W M&P is one of the most successful striker-fired handguns on the market and it's the basis for the

▲ The .40 S&W is a good compromise round between the 9mm and the .45 ACP. The VTAC is offered in 9mm and .40 S&W.

VTAC model. The VTAC has a distinctive look as the gun's polymer frame and bumper pads on the magazines are in Flat Dark Earth color. The slide is finished with PVD coating that is a metallic version of the FDE. It creates a slightly different hue and a pleasing contrast.

The trigger, slide release, take down lever, and sights are black. So is the slide end cap and the exposed chamber section of the barrel and the extractor. This makes for a very interesting contrast and a striking-looking handgun. It's the kind of gun that invariably gets an initial "wow" response from anybody I show it to. Same response with the ergonomics. When a shooter picks up the gun, they always comment about how good it feels to them. Like any well-designed firearm it seems "alive" in your hands. It is well proportioned and well balanced. After carrying it many days, weeks, and months I can also say that with a weight of 24.25 ounces (empty) it is comfortable to have on your belt with no sharp edges to rub, gouge, and aggravate you.

The M&P's hinged trigger breaks at a stiff 6–1/2 pounds, although smooth and with a well-defined finish. I know that the thought for most combat guns is that they need a stiff trigger pull, but that's at least two pounds more than I like in a striker-fired pistol. The good news is that the trigger can be improved easily by a competent gunsmith.

As with all M&P Pistols there is a "viewing window" on the top of the gun to see if there is a round in the chamber. It makes the cartridge visible through this small port, so you will see brass or nickel when the gun is loaded. I like this, as it eliminates the need for a "press check," a practice I have always been wary of because I worry that some pistols may not go back into battery correctly.

The gun features the unique Viking Tactics sights that are different from any other sight on the market. The Viking Sight has both fiber optics and night sights built into one system, but separate from each other. The front sight is tall and the rear notch is deep, this is to accommodate the dual system. The other benefit is that the long sight is easy to see and fast to acquire. There is a three-dot, green fiber optic system on top. Underneath is a three-dot, tritium night-sight system. The sights are tall and the front sight is tapered. This taper will help draw your eye to the top of the sight. It's wide at the bottom, but narrow enough at the top for more precise shooting at long range than some other battle sights. The rear sight notch has also been cut lower than normal to enhance speed to allow the use of the tritium vials that have been inserted below the fiber optic. The night sights show up well in the dark and they only change the point of impact slightly, not enough to make a difference in a low-light, close-quarters situation. I tested this at the range and found that the difference in point of impact at ten yards between the fiber optic and the night sights was only 2.5 inches. That is statistically zero in a close range gunfight.

There is a lot of light on both sides of the front blade and I found that I could acquire these sights very quickly, even with my aging eyes. My only complaint with the sights is that I would prefer a contrasting color for the front and rear, both in the fiber optic and the night sights.

In doing some close-range, five yards to twelve yards, multiple-target speed drills I amazed myself at how fast I could acquire and double-tap each target. I also used the pistol to run several other drills, to test the skills needed for defensive situations. One drill uses an MGM Texas star and a speed plate. This tests target transitions as well as tracking and hitting moving targets. It also requires some precision, as the moving plates on the star are only eight inches in diameter. The drill is simple; from fifteen yards, draw from the holster at the buzzer and shoot the Texas star. Sometime between the first and last plate on the star, shoot the speed plate, which is set at twenty yards and is some distance to the side of the star so the shooter has to shift position. My best time is with a 9mm with an optical sight, but with the M&P40 VTAC I was only 0.4-second slower. It was my fastest time with any open-sighted gun I have tried on this drill. That trend held up over the course of many other shooting drills. The gun's shooter-friendly design and high-visibility sights allowed me to transition targets fast and to track moving targets easily and make precision shots.

I have about five hundred rounds though this handgun. I experienced one failure to fire. But, that was with ammo using hard, "military-grade" primers that have also exhibited problems with several other .40 S&W guns, so I don't consider it a gun problem. With all other ammo the reliability factor has been 100

▲ The VTAC M&P with Crimson Trace Lightguard rail and the trigger guard and Crimson Trace laser grip.

percent. (Note: I have well over one thousand rounds through the gun now, with no further issues.)

The frame has a rail in front of the trigger guard. In fact, I tricked out one pistol with a Crimson Trace Lightguard light which attaches to the rail and the trigger guard. I also added a Crimson Trace laser grip. I figure it's now the ultimate carry and home defense pistol, with three sighting options and the light. Best of all, the three sighting options are all available instantly and do not intrude on each other, so there is no hesitation.

Galco and Columbia Firearm Services both have holsters that fit the gun with the Lightguard installed. Of course, every holster maker on Earth makes holsters for the standard M&P.

The gun is shipped with three different size grip panels so that grips can be adjusted to fit a wide range of hand sizes. I find that with some striker-fired guns the reach is too long for me to properly place my finger on the trigger, which results in low-right impacts on the target. (I am left handed.) The medium grip panel for the M&P VTAC fits me perfectly and places my finger correctly on the trigger. The grips can be easily swapped out by turning the half moon–shaped piece behind the mag well ninety degrees and pulling the "frame tool assembly" locking pin out. Change the grip panel, insert the pin, and turn it back in place to lock everything. It took you as long to read this as it does to make the change.

The VTAC model M&P is, in my never-humble opinion, a sensible, simple design. It does not have a safety or magazine disconnect or any other foolish, lawyer-inspired additions that can get you killed in a fight. The simplicity and safety of a striker-fired trigger system is all you need. The gun can't fire unless the trigger is pulled—all you need to do to fire the gun is pull the trigger. Simple and safe.

This pistol is extremely left-hand friendly. The slide release is ambidextrous and the magazine release is reversible. Although, after more than four decades of working the magazine release with my left index finger I left it alone on my pistols.

The M&P VTAC comes with two magazines and is offered in 9mm with a seventeen-round magazine capacity and in .40 S&W with a fifteen-round magazine capacity.

Things are changing in the world and today we are not just faced with the possibility of one or two guys trying to rob us at the ATM. With terrorism and the increasing threat of social collapse due to man-made or natural disasters, I don't think the idea of a higher-capacity magazine is flawed thinking. If nothing else, it adds to the amount of ammo most of us carry. If we carry the loaded gun and two mags, a single stack with eight-round mags will have twenty-five rounds (three mags, one in the pipe). But this VTAC .40 S&W will have forty-six rounds. If you are trying to get out of a shopping mall full of terrorists, that's an advantage for you.

I think there is one simple test for any gun that a writer reviews. What happens to the gun after the test? I send most of them back because I simply can't afford to buy every gun I fall in love with and still pay the mortgage, but with this M&P40 VTAC I see one of the best designed and well-thought-out carry guns I have ever reviewed. I added this one to my personal collection. Read into that what you may.

*You will note that this gun shows up in other chapters. I actually have two of them. The one with the laser and the light stays beside my bed. The other has a laser and no light. When I am not carrying it, it lives in a tactical vest that stays with my bug-out gear. This is the pistol that will go with me if I have to abandon my home and make a run for safety. The reasons I chose it are covered in the chapter on bug-out guns. But it's important to note that the M&P in .40 S&W is my choice for the handgun that goes out the door with me when TSHTF.*

# The Other Polymer-Frame, Striker-Fired, Double-Stack Handguns

*The "Not a Glock" handguns.*

**W**ell, some of them anyway. This category is like buying a new computer that's obsolete before you get it home. There are so many new guns hitting the market that anything I write as being "complete" today would be as pathetically out of date when you buy this book as your drunk uncle trying to show his "dance-floor cool" at a wedding.

Here are a few of the guns that I either own or have tested and can recommend. If a gun is not here that may mean it's crap, or it may mean I just didn't get a chance to test one. There are a lot of good guns out there in this category that are not included here. If you are thinking of buying one that's not covered here, all I can say is *Caveat Emptor*.

## Sig Sauer P320 Handgun

▲ The Sig Sauer P320 handgun is pretty much a "kit" gun. The serial number is on the trigger group, which is removable and portable. So you can switch frames, slides, barrels, and grips to configure the pistol any way you want.

You know how they say that the three most important things about real estate are: "1: Location. 2: Location. 3: Location"?

Well, for a defensive pistol it is: 1: Reliability. 2: Reliability. 3: Reliability.

Sig Sauer's latest entry into the double-stack, striker-fired, polymer-frame handgun market impressed me with its reliability.

Although it's new and lacks the long track record of some of the other guns, I think this is a good choice for a prepper. The gun is clearly well built and reliable. The modular approach allows for switching and swapping parts to configure the gun to suit your current needs. It's a very simple gun to work on, which is important in a survival situation. Repairs are easy and you do not need to inventory a lot of parts.

But reliability trumps everything. All those endless arguments about cartridges, bullets, ballistics, sights, triggers, magazines, accuracy, and ergonomics don't mean spit if the gun fails to go bang when bad things are happening.

There are several protocols to determine if a pistol is reliable, but I used a rather unique approach with Sig Sauer's new entry to the polymer-frame, striker-fired world of defensive pistols. In late summer 2014 I completed a multi-day training course at the Sig Sauer Academy, during which I fired about 1,500 rounds of 9mm ammo from the Sig Sauer P320 handgun. I shot with my strong hand, weak hand, and both hands. I shot while on the move and when seated in a chair. I fired the gun from a locked, standing, modified Weaver stance and from a limp wristed, barely clearing the holster, hip-shooting position and everything in between. I did man-on-man drills when speed was more important than anything else as well as some slow "precision, shoot-for-groups" techniques. I did all this with a borrowed Sig Sauer P320 pistol and it never once even hinted at failure.

Most of the ammo was lead-free with frangible, lightweight bullets, which can be finicky in some pistols. I later used a different, new-out-of-the-box P320 for more range testing. In addition to a couple of FMJ target loads, I shot a dozen different defensive factory loads, including most of the popular bullet weights and designs from every major manufacturer. The ammo ranged from low recoil "home defense" through full-blown +P barn burners. I even picked two ammo products that I know are prone to feeding problems in other guns and, again, I experienced zero failures. I am closing in on 1,800 rounds with two different guns, which is a pretty extensive test protocol for a new pistol. Actually, it's something like ten times the normal amount of ammo used in most gun evaluations for magazine articles, yet I have experienced zero failures. From what I can see, the Sig Sauer P320 pistol is one of the most reliable designs I have ever pulled a trigger on.

"So what?" you might ask. "Lots of striker-fired, polymer-frame guns are reliable." And you would be correct. This is where all those other things become important.

Ergonomics, for example. The P320 is pretty much a "kit" gun from which you can design a pistol that works best for you. The serial number is on the trigger group, which is removable and portable. So you can switch frames, slides, barrels, and grips to configure the pistol any way you want, even switch cartridge chamberings. There are three grip-frame sizes: small, medium, and large. Then there are variations of those for full size, carry size, and subcompact. By my count that's nine current options on the grip size alone. If like me you like the inexpensive 9mm ammo for training, but prefer something with a bit more whack for defense like the .40 S&W or .357 Sig, you can switch back and forth easily.

The gun is lefty friendly. The magazine release is reversible and there is a slide release lever on both sides of the gun. Tritium night sights are standard.

The P320 comes with two magazines. About the only downside I can think of is that compared to other, similar handguns the P320 is still new on the market and finding magazines will not be as easy as it may be for some other guns in a crisis situation. I expect that will change as the gun gains in popularity. But for now, if you buy a P320, just be sure to buy plenty of extra magazines. Of course, that same thing would be said of any of polymer-frame, striker-fired, double-stack handgun, except perhaps the Glocks and M&Ps, because of their widespread popularity.

In the full-size 9mm I tested, the magazine holds seventeen rounds. The .40 S&W and .357 Sig magazines hold fifteen. The carry size is the same and the compact size magazines hold fifteen for the 9mm and thirteen each for the .40 S&W and the .357 Sig.

Sadly, the included holster is right handed only, so their commitment to all shooters has its limitations.

(We lefties tolerate so much discrimination in a world designed for the comfort of the commoners.)

The P320 is designed with a grip angle the same as a 1911 pistol, which is familiar to most shooters. The trigger on my gun is a bit stiff at seven pounds, eleven ounces. However, it breaks clean and crisp (by striker-fired standards) and with very little overtravel, so it feels lighter. I find the gun much easier to shoot than other mushy-trigger, striker-fired guns with a pound or two less pull weight.

This gun is extremely easy to break down and unlike some other polymer-framed, striker-fired guns, the P320 can be disassembled without pulling the trigger. That makes it just a little bit more "idiot proof" and a lot safer.

While the striker-fired, polymer pistol field is pretty crowded these days, I suspect that with a suggested retail of $713 and a street price well south of that, the Sig Sauer P320 handgun will shoulder its way to the top of the category pretty quickly.

## Springfield Armory XD Series

▲ The Springfield Armory XD(M)-9 5.25 pistol. Hornady Critical Defense 115-grain FT. 25 yards.

These Croatian-made handguns have gained a good market share within the double-stack, striker-fired, polymer-frame handgun marketplace. They are well made, reliable, and reasonably priced. I bought an XD in .45 ACP for my son, Nathan, when he graduated from high school almost a decade ago. He has shot that gun silly over the years, including using it for USPSA and 3-gun competition. If you have never been around a gun-crazy teenager then you probably don't understand the passion they can bring to depleting your ammo supply. I don't know how many rounds he has fired through that pistol, but it's in the thousands. The only part he has replaced is the bushing for the cocking indicator. He broke the plastic part while disassembling the gun, and it was not a malfunction or a bad part from the factory. Nathan made a new one out of aluminum in our machine shop and it has lasted for years.

I also reviewed the XD(M) competition model 9mm when it was introduced for NRA's *Shooting Illustrated Magazine*. I will note that when I was finished with this article, rather than my sending the gun back to Springfield Armory, Nathan bought it and it is his primary competition pistol today.

Any handgun that can stand up to years of competition shooting is well suited for survival because it is rugged and dependable, not to mention accurate and fast.

## Steyr Mannlicher L-A1

▲ Steyr Mannlicher L-A1.

I first ran into this new pistol when I was in Bessemer, Alabama, in April of 2014 for the grand opening of Steyr's new US-based facility.

At first I thought it was "just another Glock clone." Then we shot some early production models of the gun in Steyr's indoor range and I discovered it was a lot more than that. This gun has a few unique and innovative features. I was impressed and intrigued enough with the handgun that I ordered one of my own before

I left. It took a while to get it as they were ramping up production, but late in the year it arrived.

The L-A1 is a full-size, duty-style, double-stack, striker-fired, polymer-frame handgun. The gun is available in .40 S&W, .357 Sig, and 9mm. Mine is a 9mm. That means the metal magazine holds seventeen cartridges. The .40 S&W and .357 Sig versions will hold twelve cartridges. I am not sure why there is this discrepancy, as the magazines should easily hold fifteen, but that's what the website says. I confirmed it with a company representative who also didn't know why. The gun will fire without the magazine inserted, which is important in a self-defense handgun.

The gun has a 4.52-inch barrel and is not particularly heavy at 28.8 ounces. It's 7.9 inches long, 5.1 inches high, and 1.2 inches wide.

The handgun has a massive slide that is big and square in the European style. That helps control recoil with the mass and weight. The grip is square and boxy in the back, with finger grips in the front. It is a great fit for my hand and is very comfortable under recoil. It also lets you get your hand up high and close to the axis of the bore so, again, recoil is mitigated and controlled.

The trigger has a center-lever safety (like a Glock). The trigger points down, at close to ninety degrees to the bore axis, rather than angling forward as with some other striker-fired guns. Although the distance from where the web of the hand contacts the backstrap to the trigger is 2.9 inches, which is consistent with Glock and perhaps other handguns, this design makes it feel like the trigger is easier to reach. The trigger doesn't "rock" on the axis as much as you pull it, making the feel much different and more like a conventional trigger. This is one of the features that I really like. I have wide hands with stubby, Irish fingers. Most striker-fired handguns put the trigger far forward on the gun and they just don't feel right for me. This gun puts the trigger so it feels like my finger is pulling it correctly. I point this out so that other shooters who have trouble with the striker-fired trigger position might want to take a look at this gun. The trigger has a short travel for a striker-fired handgun, with a total travel of 0.2-inch. The two-stage trigger divides exactly in half. The first stage travels one-tenth and the second stage is one-tenth of an inch of travel. The reset is at the center point, one-tenth inch back. The total pull weight for the trigger on my gun is five pounds, ten ounces. The first stage is one pound, nine ounces, so the second stage is just over four pounds. The trigger breaks clean and crisp for a striker-fired gun.

The trigger guard is large and is actually larger in front, so it allows the use of gloves. There is a rail on the bottom of the frame for mounting accessories like a light or laser.

The gun has the slide release and the magazine release both on the left side for right-handed shooters. As a lefty I am used to that, and use my index finger to run both the mag release and the slide release when I use it. The truth is I rarely use a slide release when shooting, preferring instead to rack the slide with my weak (right) side hand. However, I can easily manipulate the slide release with my finger.

The loaded chamber indicator sits flush in the rear of the slide when the chamber is empty and is raised slightly when the chamber is loaded. This allows the shooter to check both visually and by feel for a loaded chamber.

The takedown lever is on the right side of the gun. There is a lock on the side that can be activated with either of the two keys provided that will lock out the gun and prevent it from being used.

▲ The Steyr Mannlicher L-A1 has very unique sights.

Perhaps the most unique features of this pistol are the sights. The front sight is a triangle with a white triangle insert. The rear sight is a trapezoid with two white trapezoidal inserts, one on each side. Both sights are in dovetails so they can be drifted for windage adjustment. There is no elevation adjustment. It takes a little getting used to, but once you understand the sights and train your eyes and mind not to be surprised when they appear on the target, this system works surprisingly well.

I used this pistol to do a lot of speed drills on paper and with my MGM plate rack. The first few times I presented from the holster these odd sights threw me a bit of a curve, but within just a few minutes of practice I could draw and shoot amazingly fast. Target-to-target transitions were also very fast. These sights inspire a "what-the-hell" reaction when you first see them, but after shooting a little you start to get a warm and fuzzy feeling about them.

But if you are one of those guys who hate anything different and if you just can't stand change, there are optional traditional sights.

I have a few hundred rounds through the gun so far and it has been very reliable. Of course, I would expect that from this company; it has been building guns for very long time and has an excellent reputation for reliability.

The gun comes with a spare magazine, a lockable case, two keys, and of course, the Clinton-inspired and required padlock.

One great feature is the price. The MSRP is only $560. That should put the street price below $500.

# 1911

*John Moses Browning's masterpiece is, and always will be, a viable fighting pistol.*

▲ 1911 handguns in holsters by Galco.

For a lot of hard-core gun guys one fighting pistol stands alone, the 1911. It's controversial today and a lot of the Internet experts believe it's an antiquated design chambered for an unnecessarily large cartridge and that it does not hold enough ammo.

I believe that everyone is entitled to his opinion . . . even if it is wrong and stupid.

Speaking of opinions, you might be questioning mine in a minute. In a book as wide ranging as this one, you will see contradictory statements. My goal is to provide information about as many guns as possible and let you, the reader, make up your mind. If you have read the section on polymer-frame, double-stack, striker-fired handguns, you saw that I believe that design may well be the best choice for a prepper's primary defensive handgun. I'll stand by that . . . but the

1911 may well also be the best choice for a prepper's defensive handgun.

*"Do I contradict myself? Very well, then I contradict myself, I am large, I contain multitudes."*
—*Walt Whitman*

This concept of "the best guns for preppers" is large and contains multitudes. The new generation of high-capacity plastic guns has a lot going for it. But too, there is a lot to be said about the 1911 as a fighting handgun as well. Being in favor of both is not contradictory. It shows that you are large and have multitudes.

The fact that so many hard-core, in-the-know gun guys pick the 1911 as their defensive carry gun speaks volumes. Or at least it should.

As for the Internet instant experts, they are full of crap on all aspects of their criticism of the 1911, except perhaps one. This is a single-stack handgun chambered for a large cartridge and as a result the magazine capacity does not approach the volume of a double-stack Tupperware gun in 9mm. But I would counter that by saying that if you are planning your handgun strategy around how many times you are going to miss, the 1911 is probably not your pistol.

I know that I wrote elsewhere about magazine capacity, the changing world, and the new threats we face. I understand that we may be facing multiple opponents and that a larger magazine capacity can be important. I stand by that, so this is one of those "contradicting myself" situations.

No gun is perfect. For example, I am not a big fan of the striker-fired trigger and I much prefer the more controllable single-action trigger pull on a 1911. Every gun has compromises and the trigger pull is one you must make when you choose a plastic high-capacity gun. With the 1911, the compromise is magazine capacity.

(The obvious solution is a double-stack 1911 with a higher magazine capacity. We will get to that later.)

Still, the 1911 brings a lot to the table and sometimes compromises must be made. It's a metal gun, which, in theory at least, is tougher and will last longer. The trigger pull is excellent on most 1911 guns, which makes it easier to hit what you are shooting at, and the design has been proven in trial by fire more than any other current fighting handgun. The 1911 served through two world wars and one hundred-plus years

▲ The 1911 is one of the best fighting pistols ever produced.

of use by military, law enforcement, and civilians. This gun has won every type of handgun competition on Earth. The inarguable truth is that the 1911 has more than proven its durability, reliability, stopping power, and its accuracy.

Yes, I said "stopping power." I know that term is out of favor with the Cheetos-encrusted, basement-bound fanboys these days, most of whom have never witnessed a bullet strike living flesh in their lives. They have no idea about how a bullet actually works other than what they have read, but currently their flawed opinions are driving the conversation.

The term "stopping power" has been distorted and prostituted until its true meaning has been lost in the cyberspace arguments. Stopping power is not a myth as some would have you believe. They think it means that if you shoot somebody they instantly stop, fall down, and die. That is a myth with any cartridge; but that's not what stopping power has traditionally been defined as during all those dark years leading up to the age of Internet enlightenment by keyboard warriors.

Stopping power is about the cartridge's ability to stop the fight, to make the aggressor stop "aggressing." How that happens is subject to a lot of variables and many of those variables are not in your control. But at least one is—the bullet you use and the cartridge that launches it. The bigger the bullet and the more energy it carries, the more effective it will be when it strikes an aggressive and dangerous target. That's just simple physics and denying it is just proof of ignorance.

Remember that old joke when the reporter asked the Texas Ranger, "Why do you use a .45?"

"Because they don't make a .46," was the deadpan reply.

He was right. You can't rewrite the laws of physics just because you read it on the Internet. While other cartridges may or may not be effective, to claim that one with a smaller, lighter bullet carrying less impact energy is "just as effective as a .45" is stuck on stupid.

As for "stopping power?" If the bad guy trying to kill you stops trying to kill you, then "stopping power" has been applied. The .45 ACP has a long history of making that happen more effectively than just about any other defensive pistol cartridge.

If you think that "stopping power" is the ability for any cartridge to stop a bad guy instantly with one shot, you spend way too much time indoors in front of an electronic screen. That doesn't happen in real life with pistols or rifles.

Well, let me back up; yes, it can happen, but there is no way to predict it 100 percent of the time and, in truth, it's rare. We can shoot a 200-pound deer with a .300 Winchester Magnum rifle and odds are that it's going to run several yards before it dies. The only way to avoid that is to damage or impact the central nervous system, which is the brain or spinal column. That's what the television guys do on the hunting shows to make the critter fall on camera. They go for a high shoulder shot that shocks the spine. That's a risky shot with a higher potential for failure than other target areas, but if you pull it off the result is dramatic, which is all that counts on TV. If you shoot a bad guy in the brain with a pistol you get the same result, but that's not stopping power.

Stopping power is the ability of a cartridge and bullet to stop a fight with a wide range of various impact locations. The .45 ACP was developed due to a failure in stopping power of the cartridge the military was using at the time and it has proven its worth as a competent "fix" for that problem over the last one hundred years.

It wasn't until the Internet came along and created all the basement experts that anybody even questioned the effectiveness of the .45 ACP. If you value the opinion of people with zero experience who just mimic each other like a bunch of trained parrots, then those guys have your back. However, if you value over one hundred years of battleground experience with the military, law enforcement, and civilian defensive shooters, then the .45 ACP has proven its worth.

One thing that bothers me greatly with the new generation of Internet bloggers is that they rely on criticism and complaint. They always seem to take the negative approach with articles like, "The five worst guns on Earth" or "Ten cartridges you need to avoid." They thrive on tearing down rather than building up. That's the foundation of all this criticism of the .45 ACP and the 1911. It was the king and so it must be crushed.

I think that the world would be better served by making a positive case for whatever cartridge and gun they wish to promote (if they can), rather than attacking the traditional mainstays. The .45 ACP can take the hits, but they are unnecessary.

▲ The 1911 was developed for and works best with the .45 ACP cartridge.

On that note, I was recently going over the specifications for a new custom 1911 handgun that I was having made. A friend was standing with me and asked, "What cartridge are you getting?" I was a bit shocked he even had to ask and took a minute before I replied, "There is only one cartridge for a 1911, the .45 ACP."

Of course, the truth is the 1911 is offered in a lot of different cartridges. I have 1911 handguns in 9mm and .38 Super. You can also get .40 S&W, 10mm, and a few others. But those cartridges represent a fraction of a percent of the 1911 handguns sold. The overwhelming majority of 1911 handguns are chambered for .45 ACP. So as this chapter progresses let's make it easy and, unless otherwise stated, you may assume any 1911 mentioned is chambered for .45 ACP.

My novel *The 14th Reinstated* is an action adventure story that is set in New England a few years after the world has suffered a total economic and social collapse. It's written in first person and the unnamed protagonist is an aging gun writer living in Vermont. (Write what you know, right?) Anyway, he has survived what we are prepping for and attributes most of that to having the right guns. His pistol of choice is the 1911 for a lot of reasons.

He thought the worst was over, until he has to shoot his way out of an assassination attempt and then stumbles onto a plot to take over the remains of the world.

Here is an excerpt from the book where he and his friend Davy are going into the bad guy's compound to rescue his kidnapped niece. It explains a little about the 1911:

▲ The author draws a 1911 handgun from a shoulder holster.

I am a believer that lots of ammo can solve any problem. It's not always the outcome you want, but the problem can be solved. (I once said that to a buddy of mine from Austria who ran the US sales division for one of the European sporting optics companies. "How about stinky feet?" he said with a smile. Then the smile disappeared. "Oh," he said. "I guess you can fix that too.")

I also believe that ammo is very possibly the one thing you can control as you go into a bad situation. There is no way to predict what is going to happen in a fight. Once the shit hits the fan, the splatter pattern is anybody's guess. But if you control any variable you can, the outcome is weighted more to your favor. If you bring a lot of ammo there is no guarantee you will win the fight. But, if you run out of ammo in the middle of a fight, it's a sure bet that you will lose.

My knees were complaining about the weight, but let them bitch. If they wanted to keep their jobs, we had to come out of this thing alive.

I still had my doubts about that happening, but I did know one thing for sure. If they wanted to see my dead body, they were going to have to wade through a lot of empty cartridge cases to get to it.

I was carrying my M4 semiauto carbine and two pistols. One was my 1911 and the second was another 1911 Jack had loaned me. His was a compact gun called an "Officer's Model" and smaller than my pistol. But, like mine, it was chambered for the best fighting cartridge ever put in a pistol, the one the 1911 handgun was designed to use, the .45 ACP.

Actually, that cartridge dates back to a war the United States fought in the Philippines from 1899 to 1902. The US forces were using double-action revolvers chambered in an anemic cartridge called the .38 Long Colt. But too many of our fighting men were getting chopped to pieces with machetes even after hitting the drug-crazed natives with every bullet in the gun.

This experience, combined with the dubious Thompson-LaGarde Test of 1904, led the Army and the Cavalry to decide that a minimum of 45-caliber was required in the military's new handgun. John Browning developed the .45 ACP in 1904 and it was adapted to the Browning designed semiauto pistol in 1911.

That confirmed a concept that dates back to at least when Sammy Colt first sent his hoglegs west, a concept

that most gun guys still believed in, "If you bring a handgun to a fight, make sure it starts with at least a four."

While both the pistol and the cartridge have undergone some modernization, the 1911 remains, at least in the minds of many gun savvy people, the best fighting pistol and cartridge team available. The only downside is the relatively small magazine capacity. The standard magazines I was carrying hold eight cartridges. Considering that some 9mm handguns hold as many as nineteen cartridges, that's not a big number. But, I'll accept the need to reload more often in exchange for using a handgun I shoot well and trust. Besides, I never saw the point in sending a swarm of little 9mm bullets to do what one grown-up .45 can accomplish.

While there are mechanical differences, from a shooter's standpoint the 1911 differs from the striker-fired guns as it uses a traditional cocked hammer and has a lighter, single-action trigger pull. It also has a manual safety and a second, redundant, grip safety. The grip safety is disengaged by correctly holding the gun while the thumb pushes down on the mechanical safety to disengage it and allow the gun to fire.

▲ The proper condition for a 1911 is cocked and locked.

The correct way to carry a 1911 is cocked and locked. That is, with the hammer fully cocked and the safety engaged. It's no different than carrying a rifle, shotgun, or pistol with an internal hammer that is cocked and with the safety on, except that the hammer is visible on a 1911. This will often frighten the uninitiated into thinking the gun is unsafe.

Another old story tells how a little old lady stopped a crusty sheriff and said:

"Excuse me sir, but are you aware that your pistol is cocked?"

"Yes ma'am, I am," he replied.

"But isn't that gun dangerous?" she asked with no little amount of indignation.

"You damn betcha it is!"

The truth is that with both a mechanical safety and a grip safety, the 1911 is one of the safest carry guns you can buy.

Many of the accidental discharges that are hurting people with carry guns are from striker-fired guns that catch on bunched up clothing when holstering. This can pull the trigger on a striker-fired handgun as it is shoved into the holster and has resulted in a lot of people shooting themselves. It's a huge reason why I don't carry appendix style. Nobody plans to shoot himself, but if it happens I would rather be shot in the ass than blow off pieces of my man parts.

No matter, a correctly cocked and locked 1911 cannot fire when holstering like a striker-fired gun—another check mark in the win column for the 1911.

The 1911 handgun is made today by far too many companies to even think about mentioning them all. Traditionally, there are three basic sizes: The "full" size, which has a 5.03-inch barrel. The "Commander" size is in reference to Colt's designation, which has long since gone generic. This gun has the same grip frame as the full-size 1911, but uses a shorter 4.25-inch barrel and shorter slide. The "Officer" size is again a Colt designation. This scaled-down handgun has a 3.5-inch

▲ 1911 handguns, top to bottom: full-size Kimber; Commander-size S&W; and Officer-size Kimber.

barrel and corresponding shorter slide. This gun also has a shorter grip and uses a shorter magazine.

There can be a little mixing and matching. For example I recently built a 1911 for myself using a Caspian frame. It had the Commander-size slide or upper with a 4.25-inch barrel and an Officer-size frame and short grip. The frame is titanium so this is a lightweight, easy-to-carry handgun. I also have a Para 1911 handgun that took the other approach. This one has the short, Officer-size 3.5-inch barrel and slide, but on a full-size frame. So, nothing is really cut in stone.

## Full Size

▲ Remington R1 1911, full-size.

The full-size 5-inch 1911 has pretty well ruled the roost for years. There is not much more I can say about this gun that hasn't been said a thousand times over. I have several full-size 1911 guns ranging from cheap imports through some top of the line models from the best names in the business.

▲ A Kimber full-size 1911 in Desert Warrior mode. The barrel is threaded and the sights are set high for use with a silencer.

I carry a full-size 1911 for defense quite often. Which one I carry is subject to whimsy and is often the one that is new and shiny so it has caught my eye. Lately it's been a Remington R1 Enhanced that I have worked on a little bit, including the addition of an ambidextrous safety.

Indulge me a sidebar on that subject for a moment, if you don't mind. For years I refused to buy a 1911 because back when I started shooting pistols nobody was offering ambidextrous safeties on a factory gun. It was an inexpensive add on that required a gunsmith to fit. (That was long before I learned how to do it myself.) I thought I was making a statement that if the gunmakers (mostly Colt at that point) were going to ignore the left-handed market, then I would ignore them. It was probably stupid on my part and it kept me from enjoying this fine pistol for decades, but it pissed me off.

It still pisses me off.

I was discussing ambi safeties with an executive from a very well-known 1911 manufacturer one night during dinner. After he had a few drinks he started to get belligerent. At one point he blurted out, "Fu*# you left-handed guys, as long as I am in charge we will never put ambi safeties on the 1911."

I wish I could say he stopped there, but he didn't. He went on to address his female boss in front of a group of shocked gun writers, commenting on her "saggy tits." Needless to say, he didn't last long. So for all the other people making 1911 handguns, including my friends at Remington, Ruger, and the other 1911 handgun makers, listen up! The message is clear. Put an ambi safety on all your 1911 pistols, or risk Chapter 11 bankruptcy.

Besides, not doing so ignores and insults fifteen percent of your customers. Would you go out and deliberately drive away fifteen percent of your business? Would you run an ad campaign that alienates fifteen percent of your customers? Of course not. An ambi safety costs essentially nothing extra when making the gun and it subtracts nothing from the "commoner's" market, where you sell to right-handed shooters. Besides, you should be able to run a fighting handgun with either hand, no matter who you are. If your right hand is disabled or busy, you must shoot with the left, which will be easier if the gun has an ambi safety. Even if you are a commoner and shoot right handed, you should have an ambi safety on your fighting guns. It should come as standard equipment on any serious fighting handgun.

Okay done, off the soapbox.

Anyway, I installed an ambi safety on my Remington R1, smoothed out the trigger, and opened up the gap in the back sight to let in a bit more light. I carry this gun often, including when I am hiking or hunting as well as in urban settings. I also shoot it in USPSA competition now and then.

I have several other full-size 1911 handguns from Kimber, Smith & Wesson, and a few other companies, and they have all served me very well for IDPA, USPSA, and 3-gun competition as well as for carry and lots of shooting practice.

I even had good luck with the inexpensive Taurus PT 1911. Mine was good enough that I bought another for my son-in-law when he graduated from college. I don't know what it would take to wear that gun out, but I know how much of my ammo he used trying, and it was a lot! (I don't care. It was a good investment. He is a federal agent today and may well depend on his handgun shooting skills to stay alive.)

## Commander

▲ The Commander-size 1911 is perfect for carry.

The Commander-size 1911 is very popular for concealed carry. It's often made with an aluminum frame to reduce weight. My first 1911 was a Kimber PRO CDP lightweight frame Commander size. I added adjustable night sights and a set of Crimson Trace laser grips. This has been my primary carry 1911 since the mid-'90s. I have shot thousands of rounds through this gun and it's never given me any sass or backtalk.

▲ The Ruger SR1911 Commander size.

As mentioned earlier, my first attempt at building a 1911 was with a Commander, 4.5-inch barrel and slide with the smaller Officer's frame in titanium. It's still a bit of a work in progress as I have some cosmetic work left to do, but it's replacing the Kimber as my go-to carry gun.

I have a Ruger SR1911 in the Commander size. It's my first experience with Ruger 1911 handguns, as they are relatively new to that market. However, I can say that, as expected, it's a fine handgun; it runs boringly well with just about any ammo. My only issue? Right-hand-only safety. I sent a note to Ruger, perhaps they will listen, but probably not. This is a "loaner" gun, so I can't modify it. If I could, I would carry this gun in a heartbeat.

That new custom gun I ordered? It's Commander size. Designed for carry and defense. It has night sights, an ambi safety, of course, and not many other frills. The 1911 doesn't need a lot of bling to do the job.

## Officer

▲ Officer-size Kimber 1911.

This is the smallest of the 1911 handguns. It makes for a nice carry gun, particularly if the gun has a lightweight alloy frame. The downside is, some complain about the recoil with the smaller gun.

Another issue with this scaled-down 1911 is that it uses different geometry inside and can be very finicky about ammo. If you look around, the odds are good that you can find a decent self-defense load that runs well in the gun. This is fine for everyday carry, but from a prepping point of view you need a gun that can run just about any ammo available.

I have had two 3.5-inch 1911 handguns and both are picky eaters. I have had people tell me that they have 3.5-inch 1911 handguns with no modifications or tuning that will run any ammo presented right out of the box and never jam. The way I see it, guns like that are like unicorns. They may or may not exist, but I have yet to ever see one personally. If you find such a gun, treasure it.

The 1911 is more of an expert's handgun in that it's more complicated to use than a lot of newer designs. The biggest complaint I hear is that you must remember to move the safety to the off position before you can shoot. I have a retired police chief friend who teaches handgun classes now. He tells me about a training film in which a cop had his newly acquired 1911 when he walked in on a robbery. Used to his double-action revolver, the cop pulled the 1911 and tried pulling the trigger over and over without releasing the safety. The security cameras caught it all as the bad guy killed him.

The 1911 has also fallen out of favor for law enforcement and in some personal defense circles due to the single-action trigger. The thinking is that it's easier to make a mistake when covering a bad guy in a stressful situation due to the lighter trigger pull.

Clearly both of these are training issues, not design flaws. The 1911 is not as simplistic as a point-and-shoot DA revolver or striker-fired pistol that requires nothing more than pulling the trigger, so I suppose the argument that the 1911 is an expert's gun has some validity.

Then again, if you are prepping and you want to survive what's coming, you need to be training with any and all guns you select for your defense. Not just a time or two, but with regular practice and a lot of it. It's like the guy said, "buying a gun does not make you a gunfighter any more than buying a piano will make you a musician." You need to practice and train. You need to become an expert.

If you practice and train with a 1911, then those "issues" raised by the critics are null and void.

It's as simple as that.

▲ This little Browning in .380 ACP is a scaled-down 1911.

# The "Other" Double Stacks

*Single-action, double-stack, hammer-fired guns—it's what Glocks want to be when they grow up.*

▲ Top to bottom: Sig Sauer P225 X5 Competition, Sig Sauer P225 X5 Tactical, STI Tactical DS in .45 ACP, and STI Marauder.

hat if you could have the best of both worlds in a defensive handgun? The magazine capacity of a double-stack, striker-fired handgun, but with the slick, single-action trigger of a hammer-fired pistol like the 1911?

Perfect, right? Well, you can.

This style of handgun dominates most serious, action shooting competition. In those competitions where the style of handgun is pretty much open to the shooter's choice, and not dictated by the rules, these guns are used almost exclusively by the shooters who have the option and resources to buy one. That's because there is no other high-capacity handgun that is as easy to shoot fast and accurately.

So if they are the best at winning shooting competitions, then it stands to reason that from a purely techni-

cal, shooting standpoint they are also the best option for defense. One upside to a user like me, they are the guns I compete with so I know them well and shoot them better than any other handgun I own.

Some will argue that a striker-fired or even a double-action only trigger is safer. But that is a training issue, not an equipment issue. Remember, for years before the striker-fired guns came into prominence a lot of law enforcement types carried 1911 handguns. Funny, they were considered safe enough then. The only thing that really changed was that the nanny state grew stronger and the hand wringing old ladies of the world are now in charge and making way too many decisions.

If you are willing to train and stay sharp with your handgun, these single-action pistols may be a better option. Except for one thing. As a rule, the guns and magazines are much more expensive than a polymer gun, and they can be heavy. (Well, okay, I guess that was two things; math was never my best subject.)

As always, I can only comment here on the guns I have used, so if you don't see one, it's not an indication of anything other than I can't cover every single gun on the market. Here are a few of the guns I have tried and can recommend.

## STI

With handguns, like most things in life, you get what you pay for. Take the STI 2011 series for example. STI is a leader in double-stack, single-action handguns and they are some of the finest handguns made.

This is the gun that most serious competition shooters use. STI's top-of-the-line Open Class guns go for as much as $3,700 (MSRP in 2015). Shooters pay that for a reason; these guns win. They are not only superbly accurate and easy to shoot, but their reliability is near-

ly 100 percent. Remember, in action shooting sports, just as in life, there are no alibis or reshoots allowed. The gun must run.

Many of the 2011 handguns designed for competition can make great carry guns. I have a custom STI with two uppers so that I can switch between 9mm and .40 S&W. All I have to do is change the upper and the magazine to switch from one to the other. I got it for competition shooting, but this gun is 100 percent reliable and holds a bunch of ammo. I would not hesitate to carry it in a survival situation. If it can survive several years of hard-core 3-gun competition, including tough matches like the MGM Iron Man, it's tough enough for survival.

▲ STI Marauder. This gun is designed for 3-gun competition, but would work well for defense as well.

One of my friends, Eric Reynolds, has an STI Edge 2011 in .40 S&W that he uses in USPSA competition. More recently, for 3-gun, I am shooting the new STI Marauder in 9mm. These guns can pull double duty as a defensive pistol and would be an excellent carry gun during a survival situation. With their flared magazine wells, they are a bit difficult to conceal, but those can be removed and the guns are easily configured for concealed carry.

They all have relatively light, three-pound or less triggers, but so what? They are still safe handguns that will not fire if you do not pull the trigger. If you train with them they are as safe as any other handgun but they can perform at the highest level—performance levels that other guns may not be capable of achieving. In a survival situation, isn't performance pretty high on the list of good things in a handgun?

STI makes guns for a wide range of use, not just competition. The STI Tactical handguns are for defensive use and are considerably less money than an Open Class race gun. Sure, they are still expensive, but you get what you pay for. They might not be for everybody, but the hard-core gun guy who wants the best possible fighting handgun and isn't concerned about the price would be hard pressed to find a better option.

The STI Tactical DS in .45 ACP that I have been using retails in 2015 for $2,199 with night sights. The lightweight aluminum frame model adds one hundred bucks to that. You can buy three or four plastic guns for that price. You can also buy three or four maga-

zines for a plastic gun for the cost of one steel STI magazine. But for the prepper who wants the best in defensive handguns and for whom cost is no object, these pistols are works of art. The fit and finish are superb, they balance perfectly, and they run like a Swiss watch.

There are multiple magazine options, but the high-capacity magazines can hold as many as twenty-six 9mm cartridges, twenty-two rounds of .40 S&W, or fourteen .45 ACP cartridges. The grip frames are small enough, even in the .45 guns, and with the position of the single-action trigger even stubby-fingered hands can manage the guns easily.

They also make a 2011 in 10mm, but as covered elsewhere, it's probably best for a prepper to stay with the more common cartridges because ammo will be easier to find in most circumstances.

If money were not a consideration I think that I would be hard pressed to find a better handgun for survival than the STI Tactical in .45 ACP. I have been shooting one quite a bit this year and have really come to like this gun a lot. My only serious complaint is that the trigger is too stiff, a bit over six pounds on the gun I have. That's to appease the political side of the LE departments that will not allow a light trigger because of perceived safety issues. It's a problem that is easily fixed by a competent gunsmith. If I owned this gun I would do a trigger job, but alas, it's a loaner that will need to go back unaltered to STI one sad day.

While the STI guns are very well represented in the competition world, they are not by any stretch as common as, say, a Glock with the rest of the gun world. While Glock magazines might be pretty easy to locate on the black market, not so much with these more specialized handguns. It makes sense for a prepper to buy extra magazines and to stock up on a few spare parts.

## Sig Sauer

The Sig Sauer, single-action, double-stack guns are in a bit of flux as I write this. Due to political pressures, the Germans stopped exporting handguns to the United States in 2014, so Sig is ramping up production in their new factory in New Hampshire. The upside is that most of these new US-made guns will cost considerably less than the imported handguns.

▲ This STI .45 ACP holds a lot of ammo.

▲ Sig Sauer P226 X-5 Tactical 9mm.

▲ Sig P226 X5 Competition.

That aside, the Sig Sauer double-stack, single-action handguns deserve a serious look from any prepper.

Once again, if you go this route, pick up lots of magazines and have a spare parts kit. These are fine handguns, but not common enough in the world to depend on the black market supplying any replacement parts or extra magazines.

## Browning Hi Power

Of course, the old standby here is the Browning Hi Power. This was John Moses Browning's final gun design and he was working on it when he passed away.

The 9mm Hi Power, introduced in 1935, is small and compact, so it carries well. Unlike some Walthers

I shot a P226 X5 Competition in 9mm for several years of serious 3-gun competition. These are big, heavy guns that shoot well and manage recoil for very fast split times. I also have one of the P226 X5 Tactical model guns that is about ten ounces lighter. These are both 9mm handguns and share the same twenty-round magazines. They are very well made and reliable. The only issue I experienced with thousands and thousands of rounds through four different P226 X5 Competition guns over a five-year period was the external extractor would wear out and stop working. I am happy to report that the new US-made guns will change to a stronger external extractor. With that, there is not a single serious complaint with these guns, except that they are expensive and heavy.

▲ The Browning Hi Power.

of that era, the Hi Power maintained a single-action trigger.

The Hi Power was available in .40 S&W for a while, but Browning dropped that cartridge. I always liked this gun in .40 S&W and I regret not buying one when they were being made. You might find some on the used-gun market and those I have seen are priced well below what the 9mm Hi Power is commanding on the used market.

The double-stack 9mm magazine holds thirteen rounds and some aftermarket magazines will hold fifteen rounds. The gun I have has an ambi safety and three white dot (actually rectangular) sights. Browning also offers the gun with adjustable sights.

The gun is not without its critics. It has a magazine safety that prevents the gun from firing without a magazine inserted. This is undesirable and unnecessary in a fighting gun.

Most serious students of defensive pistol shooting advise never shooting your gun dry and having a pistol that can fire without a magazine so that you are still in the fight during a mag change, at least with one shot. If there is a magazine safety that prevents the gun from firing and something happens during a mag change, you are screwed. This feature is also said to contribute to the heavy trigger pull common to the Hi Power (almost eight pounds on my gun). Both, of course, are correctable by removing the magazine safety and tuning the trigger. That probably voids the warranty, but who cares; in a survival situation there are no warranties. Also, the hammer can hit the shooter's hand, as the short beavertail does not protect the shooter from the hammer spur. A bloody hand is a common complaint from Hi Power shooters.

This gun has a very strong following and is very popular with hard-core gun guys. I suspect it's second only to the 1911 in terms of a cult following from the traditional defensive pistol guys. The Hi Power has also seen a lot of service with law enforcement and military, particularly in Europe. While not as common as a Glock or even a 1911, parts and magazines should be available for the Hi Power due to the sheer number of handguns on the market.

The design is a bit old and antiquated by today's standards, but the Hi Power is still a relatively small, all-metal, high-capacity handgun with a long history of reliable performance.

It's a little expensive when compared to a polymer-frame gun, but the Hi Power will always be a viable defensive handgun. If you are the kind of prepper who would like to be just a little bit different than the other guy and you have a strong sense of tradition, this gun might be just what you need.

## DA/SA

In my never-humble opinion, double-action/single-action pistols are an abomination. They are the Bruce Jenner of handguns, a gun that can't make up its mind what it wants to be. To my thinking, they were designed by fools to appease the lawyers and politicians and from a technical and tactical standpoint DA/SA is a ridiculous concept.

Am I being too subtle here?

I hope not.

If I am, just to be clear, I don't like these handguns.

Most advocates I know are cops who were forced to use them by their departments and just kind of got used to the design. No one I know who is gun savvy and has a choice picks a DA/SA as his number-one choice for a defensive handgun.

That said, there are a lot of them on the market and most are a double-stack, high-capacity design. They are often sold at a reasonable price. They are, for the most part, serviceable handguns and they will work. It's sort of like buying a VW bug; it will get you where you are going, but there are much better options.

I have several DA/SA handguns and I shoot them often so I can stay sharp with the design, but if TSHTF and you want one, come see me; they are the first guns I will barter away.

The DA/SA design goes back to the European-made Walther handguns introduced in the 1930s. This was well before the surge of striker-fired handguns and their rise to popularity here in the United States. As far as I have been able to find out while researching the issue, the DA/SA concept was based on fear and ignorance. There were those who believed that a cocked-and-locked hammer-fired handgun looked "unsafe," which led to much wringing of the hands with the sheep. So they decided that if the gun could be carried hammer down with no safety to worry about, it would accomplish two things. First, if there were no safety, an untrained shooter would not forget to disengage it in a fight. Secondly, they believed that the first shot with a hard, double-action trigger pull would somehow be safer. I suppose it would be, at least for the target. Compared to a single-action handgun or even a striker-fired pistol, these guns are difficult to shoot well out of the holster with a fast first shot. There is a third reason too (that math thing again). With this design, the uninformed public would not be wetting their collective pants about a "cocked" firearm visible in a cop's holster.

I think it was Jeff Cooper who suggested that it might be best to just deliberately dump that first round from a DA/SA into the ground and get it over with. I think he said it in jest, but he is often criticized even today for that statement, although he had a point.

When I put out the question of why this gun was created, one crusty, unfiltered gun writer posted this on Facebook about the design and its roots:

*To understand Eurotrash pistol designs, it must always be remembered that Europeans consider a pistol as something to be used to shoot people who are bound, kneeling and facing away from you.*

He is probably right, but I guess I'll just go with the more PC explanation of the design that it is so the gun can be carried in public without spooking the sheep.

A shooter can do well with a double-action trigger; millions of revolver shooters have proven that time and again. The trouble is that the DA/SA gun uses that long, double-action trigger pull for the first shot and then shifts modes to a single-action pull. It's a two stage with a very long take up, but with a lighter single-action-type trigger at the end. It has a much different feel than the trigger pull from the first shot.

So the first shot will be a long, hard, double-action pull, while the next and all subsequent shots will have a much lighter single-action trigger pull, usually following a long take up. As if you don't have enough else to worry about in a crisis situation, remembering that transition will be a chore. Often the first shot will miss because of the horrible trigger pull and then the second shot will also miss because the much lighter pull startled you and the gun went off prematurely. If you are lucky, the bad guy might give you a third chance to get it right.

I believe that this design was conceived and used by people who do not really understand guns and shoot-

ing. It's a political compromise to appease the public who may be frightened by cocked-and-locked guns and those who advocate minimum training for cops. It's better to risk the cop's life with a poor handgun, than to risk a poorly trained cop shooting somebody because he can't keep his finger off the trigger. The political police chiefs, politicians, and the lawyers all love these guns; gun guys generally do not.

If you train with them, you can master the DA/SA handgun and shoot reasonably, but why? You are far better off to pick a consistent trigger system and stick with it. While I am also not a fan of double-action only, semiauto pistols, at least they are consistent. They, too, were conceived to be used by people who do not train and to appease the politicians, lawyers, and police chiefs. It's thought that the hard trigger pull will make the bad guys safer from a negligent discharge. It also makes them safer from being hit by a bullet intended for them. The double-action only might make a little sense in a cheap, small carry gun because it keeps the manufacturing cost down and the function simple. If you are fighting with one of these at powder-burn distances they work fine, but they are a compromise at best. A full-size, DA-only semiauto pistol makes little sense for a civilian looking for a defensive handgun because there are so many better options.

## An Exception

FNH has a unique approach to this concept with its polymer-frame FNX-45. This is a DA/SA gun, but with a twist. The decocker is also a safety. So you can carry

▲ FNX-45.

the gun "cocked and locked" with the safety on, or you can decock the gun and use the DA/SA mode with the hammer down during carry.

Of course, there is a bit of a downside. First, there is no grip safety like with the 1911 or 2011 handguns. I know a lot of shooters think a grip safety is an unnecessary redundancy, but in a single-action, hammer-fired gun I kind of like that redundancy. Safeties can work their way off and a little backup insurance is not a bad thing. I understand that some guys, including guys I respect and listen to, pin the grip safety to deactivate it on a carry gun. I prefer to tune it so it will release easier and keep working. Not a huge issue, but something to think about.

(Note: A few days after writing this I witnessed a 1911 with the grip safety deactivated fire three times as the shooter attempted a magazine reload. He hit the trigger with his finger while gripping the gun to release the magazine, causing the gun to fire. Then the recoil caused the trigger to bounce on his finger and fire twice more. It was 100 percent shooter error, but if he had not taped the grip safety down to deactivate it, it would not have happened. This was during a pistol match and he was disqualified. But it could have had a more tragic ending, as the gun was out of control. That grip safety is on there for a reason. In retrospect, maybe it is a huge issue.)

The other downside of the FNX-45 is that if you push hard on the safety when the gun is cocked and locked, it will go past the center detent stop and decock the pistol, so now you are in DA/SA mode. I suspect that in a fight, your adrenalin-fueled thumb is going to do just that.

On the other hand, this is a .45 ACP with a fifteen-round magazine and an adjustable grip with interchangeable backstraps that accommodate most hand sizes. The gun is reliable, powerful, and holds a lot of bullets. It's also affordable, with pricing in line with most of the better polymer-framed guns.

Like I have said elsewhere in this book, I will often contradict myself. I am not a fan of DA/SA guns, but I do like this pistol. I have actually used one in a 3-gun competition and have shot them quite a bit on the training range. I am a fan of the .45 ACP in a fighting handgun and this gun deals with the issues raised with this cartridge in some other handguns, such as magazine capacity. The FNX-45 is affordable, it has a large magazine capacity, and is designed so that people without mutated, giant-sized hands can shoot it well.

It offers a very good option for those looking for an affordable double-stack, high-capacity handgun in .45 ACP that, even if you have stubby fingers like me, is pretty easy to shoot.

# The Middle Ground

*Smaller pistols for concealed carry and backup.*

▲ S&W Shield in front. Back is SCCY (left) and Ruger LC9s.

A hard-core gun guy might feel good about carrying a full-size 1911 or striker fired handgun, but most people do not. In fact, I'll admit that much of the time I do not and you won't find a more hard-core gun guy than me. The truth is, a full-size handgun is heavy and hard to hide. It will pull your pants down and by the end of the day it will make your back hurt. While I carry full-size guns a lot, I find that more and more I am moving into another category of handgun for my everyday carry.

Why is a discussion on current everyday carry part of a book on prepping? Well, for now we are going about our everyday lives. Nothing of the magnitude of TEOTWAWKI has happened. We should not be just

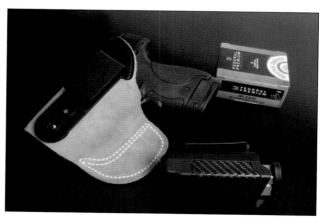
▲ S&W Shield.

buying guns for prepping and then sticking them away unused. Part of prepping is buying guns that we will also use for everyday protection and that we will enjoy training with and shooting on a regular basis.

The truth is that the odds still favor that we will not see any kind of long-term survival situation become dominant in our lives. The world has gone on for a very long time and it will probably continue to self-correct and continue on for a while longer. While I think the odds have changed considerably that bad stuff is coming and that the possibility is much stronger today than it was a decade ago, the optimistic outlook is that somehow the grownups will regain control and life, as we know it, will continue without serious interruption.

Of course, if we could predict the future we could just buy lottery tickets until we have enough money for a private island where nobody will bother us. But we can't. Or at least I can't and I assume you can't either, so the smart money is on preparing for the worst while we hope for the best.

A functioning society doesn't mean we should bury our heads in the sand. Even in today's still (relatively speaking) stable society, there is a pervading evil that is growing. Even if it never grows enough to create a serious survival situation, it's a dangerous world out there and becoming more dangerous every day. The responsibility for your personal safety is yours alone. I know you believe that or you would not be reading this book. That probably means you are carrying a gun now.

Another worn-out platitude is that "the best carry gun is the one you have with you when you need it." If you are of the build and temperament that allows carrying a full-size gun all the time, then you are ahead of the game in that department. For many other people, including myself sometimes, there is a compromise; a category of carry gun that addresses the "comforting, not comfortable" issue with handguns that are easier to carry, but still are viable fighting guns.

The idea of a carry gun is that it should be in a cartridge powerful enough to be considered a serious defensive handgun. It should also be in a handgun that you can shoot well, actually hit the target with, and it should hold a reasonable amount of ammo. Lots of handguns fit those guidelines. But if carrying the gun is "comfortable" wouldn't that also be a huge asset?

We covered the little, polymer-frame .380 ACP guns in another chapter. Assuming you have not read that one yet, they are not the guns that solve the problem. The .380 is really a bit small and underpowered to be considered a serious fight-stopping pistol cartridge. The guns themselves are difficult to shoot under stressful conditions and it's often hard to shoot them with precision beyond powder-burn distance. The guns have their place, but in my never-humble opinion that place is not as a primary carry gun, either now or after a disaster.

It used to be that the next step up were the compact guns that were simply scaled-down versions of the full-size pistols, like the mini-Glocks or others like the FNH FNS-9C, S&W M&P Compact, Ruger SR40, and many others. These are smaller guns that typically are around seven inches long and weigh twenty to twenty-five ounces empty.

They are great guns for the most part and are relatively compact, but still maintain good magazine capacity. For example, the Glock G26 holds ten rounds in the magazine and the slightly larger FNS-9C has a twelve-round magazine capacity.

▲ Ruger SR40c.

The Ruger SR40 in .40 S&W holds ten rounds. Clearly that's less ammo capacity than a full-size gun, but it's a lot more than a micro or most revolvers. At the lower end in size and weight spectrum in this class would be guns like the SCCY, double-stack 9mm. It's 5.7 inches long and weighs fifteen ounces. This inexpensive, double-action-only, polymer-frame gun

▲ FNS-9C.

is small and compact. The magazine capacity with a double-stack magazine is ten rounds of 9mm. The upper end is the FNS-9C that is 7.25 inches long and weighs 25.5 ounces.

This class of handgun is usually described as a sub-compact pistol: smaller than full-size like the Glock G17 and its CCCs (copies, clones, and competition), but not exactly small. The footprint is smaller than a full-size or even a compact, but most of these handguns still use a double-stack magazine, so they maintain the width of a full-size gun and much of the weight due to more steel in the slides.

Then in 2012, along came the S&W M&P Shield, a striker-fired, polymer-frame handgun that created a brand-new category. I am not sure what the category should be called and neither is the industry. The guns are smaller than a subcompact but larger than a micro pistol. Glock calls theirs a "subcompact slimline," Ruger calls the SR9s a "Lightweight Compact Pistol" and S&W just calls the Shield a "Compact Pistol."

Clearly these guns need a catchier name and of course, an acronym. After all, you are nothing in the gun industry today without an acronym.

Maybe super-micro, SM? Micros on steroids, MOS? Sub-Sub-Compact, SSC? Super Sub-Compact, also SSC? Double-Sub-Compact, DSC? The little handguns that could, TLHTC?

Maybe not that last one.

The Shield split the difference in size between the little .380 handguns and the larger handguns. The key is that it's a true, scaled-down handgun in every dimension. The slim, "less than an inch" width made it a very light and very comfortable gun to carry. It also made the gun feel good in a smaller hand, which is important for a lot of gun owners. While most men have little trouble with a smaller handgun grip and can adapt easily, those with small hands find a large grip difficult to deal with.

The Shield has high-quality, three-dot sights that are easy to see. The striker-fired trigger pull is about 6.5 pounds, so the gun is easy to shoot. But the best aspect of the Shield, other than its size and weight, is that it's available in true self-defense cartridges.

The 9mm Parabellum is the best seller in the Shield. It is considerably more powful than the .380, averaging about 300 foot-pounds, while some +P loads can nearly double the power of the .380 ACP.

The great thing to my way of thinking that all fighting handgun cartridges should start with a four, is that you can buy the Shield in .40 S&W. This cartridge uses a larger diameter, heavier bullet than the 9mm, and will produce nearly 480 foot-pounds of energy with some loads.

Some will say the .40 S&W is harder to shoot than the 9mm. However, in a blind, side-by-side comparison I did with several shooters and two Shields it was extremely difficult to tell the difference in recoil between .40 S&W and 9mm +P.

The M&P Shield features a black polymer frame and a coated stainless steel slide and barrel that are rust resistant, which is important in a carry gun where sweat is unavoidable. The barrel is 3.1 inches and overall length is just 6.1 inches. The empty gun weighs only nineteen ounces, which is less than two spare loaded magazines weigh for a double-stack, full-size handgun. The sight radius is 5.3 inches and trigger pull is 6.5 pounds. Unlike some other striker-fired handguns, the Shield can be disassembled without pulling the trigger.

The guns ship with two magazines, one of them with extended capacity and an insert to extend the grip. These magazines hold eight and seven rounds of 9mm. The .40 S&W magazines hold seven and six rounds. The Shield has an eighteen-degree grip angle for natural point of aim for most shooters.

The Shield can be ordered with or without a safety. As with most striker-fired handguns, no secondary safety is required. However, the option is on the table for those who wish to have the redundancy of a safety.

The M&P Shield is a very easy gun to shoot and on the range it acts more like a full-size handgun. I find that I can run drills and make hits easily. Of course, with any carry gun it's important that you be able to shoot it well and this is a gun that is fun and easy to shoot, which encourages practice.

I am a huge advocate of laser sights on any carry gun and the Shield can be ordered with the Crimson Trace Green Laserguard installed. The green laser is very bright and unlike most red lasers it can be seen in most daylight conditions.

Crossbreed makes a holster that will fit the Shield with the green laser. I also have one of my Shields fitted with a Viridian green laser with a magnetic switch. This takes a special holster so that the laser is off in the holster and comes on when you draw the gun. The laser comes with a holster, but one designed for the commoners, not we special people. Crossbreed again came to the rescue with a left-handed version.

One of my other Shields in .40 S&W is fitted with the CT green laser and with Trijicon HD Night Sights. These sights are another add-on that I highly recommend; these are some of the best night sights for a carry gun I have tried. This set up has become my go-to carry gun much of the time. I trust my life and the life of my loved ones to this gun. That's something I do not take lightly and I believe makes a strong statement about the Shield.

In fact, I liked the Shield so much I bought three of them. I got a couple of .40 S&Ws for myself and my

▲ This S&W Shield is fitted with a Viridian green laser with a magnetic switch. The crossbreed holster has a magnet that turns the laser off when the gun is holstered. The dot of the laser is pointing at the magnet.

wife to carry. I also bought a 9mm because I think this cartridge is important for prepping due to the ammo availability issue. It's a NATO cartridge and very popular with law enforcement and civilians, so even in times of shortages this is the ammo voted most likely to be available.

Don't think these SSC handguns (that's the acronym I like best) are carry guns for women, feeble old men, and wimps. I have a buddy who is six-foot-five-inches tall and weighs more than 350 pounds. He is a big, very tough guy—you would be making a huge mistake to mess with him—and he carries a Shield. I have another weightlifting buddy who is close to six feet tall, very fit, and big enough nobody messes with him. He can bench-press a Prius and he carries a Shield.

I was in a small local gun shop a few weeks ago and the guy behind the counter was showing a Shield to a customer. He knows me well and mentioned that I carry one. He asked if I minded showing it to the guy and telling him why I like it so much. Three other guys in the shop spoke up and said they were also carrying Shields. He made the sale.

▲ Ruger LC9s.

This class of guns is too good for the Shield to stand alone. If you are a Ruger fan, you will love the LC9s, which is the striker-fired version of the LC9. It can be ordered with or without a safety. Offered in 9mm, this 6-inch, 17.2-ounce handgun has a magazine capacity of seven rounds. The sights are white, three-dot. My gun has one of the nicest striker-fired triggers I have seen in this class of handgun.

Like any Ruger it's rugged and dependable. Mine runs and runs and never complains or jams.

If you are a Glock guy, the G43 is their gun in the SSC category. This little 9mm has a six-round magazine, is 6.26 long and weighs eighteen ounces. It's a small, single-stack gun, but otherwise is pretty much a Glock in every other way. Not sure what I can say that has not already been said elsewhere in this book about Glocks. The G43 is so dependable that it's boring. Any ammo I feed it is ingested and expelled without fanfare or drama. The sights are classic Glock, white-dot front, and white outline rear. It's a very "shootable" handgun, one that will no doubt become a best seller in this category. Can we dare hope that Glock will introduce it in .40 S&W?

Let's be clear on one point. I don't think that the Shield, Glock G43, Ruger LC9s, and all their CCCs, or any subcompact for that matter, should be a primary carry gun after TSHTF.

They are an acceptable compromise now. Although comfortable and easy to carry, they are serious fighting guns; but they are still a compromise. We give up magazine capacity, sight radius, and the faster follow-up shots that come with recoil dampening weight. For most of us, right now, the odds of actually using our carry gun are infinitesimal. But when you need one, you really need one. These are guns people will carry and so the compromise is acceptable. Better to have a SSC on your belt when trouble finds you than a big 1911 back home, sitting on your dresser.

If things go bad and we find ourselves in times of serious duress, then a serious prepper should be carrying a serious handgun. For most, that means a full-size handgun. It might be a double-stack or if you prefer, a 1911. If TSHTF then the odds of needing our handguns for protection go up until they blow off the chart. It there is a total social and economic breakdown those odds will crowd 100 percent. When danger becomes very real and almost a guarantee it only makes sense to carry a grownup-size fighting handgun.

If that happens, you may wonder, where does the SSC I bought fit in? Why did I talk you into buying a gun that I no longer recommend for a primary carry gun?

Simple, backup. If things really do get bad it will be smart to carry at least two handguns at all times. These SSC handguns are comfortable, can be chambered for the same cartridge as your primary handgun, and can do some serious damage in a fight for your life. They make the perfect backup handgun for preppers.

# The Little Fellas

*Backup guns for bad situations.*

▲ Ruger LCP.

The firearms industry has its share of platitudes and, like most, they can be cute and catchy the first time you hear them. But by the eleven-millionth time some dorky, bearded butthead in tactical garments repeats it to you with a smug "I-am-smarter-than-you" look on his face, you want to choke him out.

One saying that reached that level of annoyance years ago is, "two is one and one is none."

It means simply that you should always carry two guns. I suppose there is some credibility to this in our daily lives, but the philosophy has reached absurd heights with some of the tactards. Sorry, but for now I am not carrying two full-size Glocks with a dozen loaded magazines in addition to my "open carry" AR-15 carbine and battle load of eight fully loaded

thirty-round magazines, plus a backup pistol, just to go to the grocery store to buy bread and milk. My abused knees hurt enough these days without that extra weight.

However, it does make sense at times to have a backup pistol. If we enter into a survival situation where society has degraded, it would be a must. I am not talking about an extra fighting pistol here, although that would not be a bad idea in times of serious trouble too. Rather, a backup handgun that is hidden away and is in addition to whatever larger handguns you may carry.

There are a lot of scenarios in which this could prove useful. Your primary handgun could run dry or stop working. You might lose it in a fall or any of a hundred different ways. Or perhaps you are captured by bad guys and disarmed. I know that sounds pretty Hollywood, but stop and think how the world might be if there is no government, no police, and no rules. Anything is possible and we ignore that at our peril. Maybe it is tinfoil-hat stuff right now, but it could well be reality someday. A lot of smart gunfighters in the Old West kept a derringer-type handgun hidden for these kinds of scenarios. They lived in times and places with little or no law enforcement and they had to solve their own problems; maybe we should take a lesson. Even now, in your everyday life, how many times have you taken off your carry gun and then later stepped out to the driveway to retrieve something from your truck or maybe to take out the trash? What if there are people with bad intentions waiting for you? The list of possibilities is pretty long and to be honest this book is not about exploring all those, it's about the guns you may need. But when we do consider even a short list of potential problems, it all leads to a compelling argument in favor of having a deeply concealed backup gun.

The midsize guns like the S&W Shield, Ruger LC9s, Glock G43, or even the J-Frame-size revolvers are just a bit large for this category. They are fine backup guns, but what I am exploring here are the smaller guns, ones that fit easily and unnoticed in a pocket, yet are still viable in a fight. Perhaps we should call them a backup to the backup gun.

The mini-guns like the NAA rimfire revolvers are a bit too small. They are a little underpowered and tough to hit anything with past the "screw-it-up-their-nostril-and-pull-the-trigger" range. They are more of a backup to the backup of the backup. Great little guns, but one step past the concept we are exploring here.

This category is pretty much defined by the polymer-frame .380 autos that became so hugely popular a few years 'bout the time "shall-issue" concealed carry laws started sweeping the country, the little polymer frame .380 ACP guns became popular. It started with the Kel-Tec P3AT. When Ruger announced the LCP in 2008 and put the force of the Ruger name and marketing behind it, the LCP was the most popular handgun in the world for a while. That launched a revolution of micro .380 handguns and a multitude of gun companies offer them today.

The tiny guns are lightweight, inexpensive, comfortable to carry, and easy to conceal. But the .380 ACP cartridge is considered by most self-defense experts to be underpowered and inadequate. Most loads produce at best a puny 200 foot-pounds of energy with the popular 90-grain bullet.

Factory ballistics for Federal Premium Personal Defense Hydra-Shok ammo (one of the best ammo choices) lists the .380 with a lightweight 90-grain bullet at 1,000 feet per second from the muzzle. This creates 200 foot-pounds of energy which, to be honest, when trying to stop a drug-crazed, prison-hardened bad guy . . . ain't much.

It's even less in the real world where the ballistics are diminished by the short barrels used in the sub-compact pistols, often losing more than 10 percent of the published velocity. That drops the energy down to about 180 foot-pounds or lower.

A true fighting cartridge like the .45 ACP with a 230-grain Federal Hydra-Shock has 414 foot-pounds, an increase of 159 percent, or 2 ½ times the energy of the .380. There is also a 27.32-percent increase in bullet diameter and a 155-percent increase in bullet weight. All this matters.

Also, the little guns tend to have hard trigger pulls and crude sights (or in some cases no sights at all) making any sort of precision shooting difficult. As with any defensive firearm it's imperative that you practice with the guns, but even with training they are close-range-only handguns.

My point is, these are not a great choice for a primary carry gun. However, as a backup last-line-of-defense handgun, they are pretty much spot on.

You can find some micro pistols in smaller cartridges, but it's a mistake to carry one. Rimfire cartridges are not powerful enough for serious defense, nor is the .25 ACP or really even the .32 ACP. The .380 ACP is not really a fighting cartridge either, but it's getting closer. Its supporters are quick to point out that the new ammo has vastly improved the effectiveness of the .380. That's true, to a point. I bought my first .380, an AMT Backup, back in 1985. At that time .380 factory ammo was not all that refined. There were some hollow-point loads that didn't expand or FMJ bullets that also didn't expand. Today we have better options. The bullet technology that was developed following the Miami FBI shootout in 1986 trickled down to this cartridge as the ammo companies chased the boom in sales of the guns. The result has been ammo with better terminal ballistic qualities. (Terminal ballistics are what the bullet does after hitting the target.) But, putting a supercharger on a Volkswagen beetle does not make it win NASCAR races. There is only so much that bullet technology can do. Any bullet still needs horsepower driving it to be effective and there is a serious lack of power from any .380 ACP.

That said, the .380 ACP has been around since 1908. It has been used by various military and law enforcement agencies as well as for civilian self-defense by millions of people. It has seen a lot of use in Europe where their liberal guilt has edged them into using cartridges for law enforcement that don't hurt people as much.

James Bond used a Walther PPK that could have been a .380, but was probably the even less powerful .32 ACP. He always got a one shot kill, even on moving targets, often while he was shooting on the move himself. So it has to be effective, right?

Ian Fleming, the author who created Bond, admitted that he was not an expert in the field of firearms, and said, "Quite honestly, the whole question of expertise in these matters bores me." So, using Bond as example is kind of foolish.

Fantasy aside, the .380 has kept a lot of people alive and made a lot of bad guys not alive. It might not be a hard-core fighting cartridge, but it can stop a fight. It doesn't matter in this discussion, because the bottom line is the .380 ACP is the most powerful cartridge available in this class of handgun, so it's the cartridge of choice by default.

There are some 9mm handguns that are getting down to being very close in size to the .380 polymer pistols and they might merit looking at, as the 9mm has considerably more power than the .380 ACP. I must say, though, that some of the mini-sized 9mm handguns I have tested have not functioned reliably. Often a finicky gun will like one particular brand of ammo and will run well with that. If you sort through the ammo on the market you can often find something with a decent defensive bullet that will function, but for a prepper that causes problems as we are not ensured that specific ammo will be available in the future.

I might add that not all of these polymer .380 handguns are created equal, either. The reliability of those I have tested has run from very good to pretty awful.

Here is a look at some of the guns on the market that I have tried. There are plenty of .380 micro pistols on the market. Some I have tried and they are not here for a reason, but most I simply can't comment on because I have not used them. If you are looking to buy one of these guns, do your homework. There are a lot of great micro guns on the market and a few that are not so great. Make sure you spend your money on quality and reliability.

## Kel-Tec P3AT

▲ Kel-Tec P3AT.

This is the gun that started the category. I have owned one for a long time. After a few hundred rounds it broke. They replaced it and this one is running great so far. So I can't complain about the customer service. It's less expensive than a lot of the other handguns and has been around a long time, so it has a track record.

The gun weighs 8.3 ounces. It is 5.2 inches long, 3.5 inches high, and 0.77 inches thick. The magazine holds six rounds.

## Ruger LCP

The Ruger LCP I have has never hiccuped, even once. True, it's new to me and I have maybe only 150 rounds through it, but usually problems show up early and this gun is really making me like it. The LCP has a great reputation and is considered to be among the best of the polymer .380 mini guns. The gun weighs in at 9.65 ounces empty, so you hardly know it's in your

▲ Ruger LCP .380 with laser sight.

pocket. It is 5.16 inches long, 3.6 inches high and 0.86 inches thick. The magazine holds six rounds, as do all of these pistols.

## Smith & Wesson BODYGUARD

▲ Smith & Wesson BODYGUARD .380 with laser sight.

Another gun I have had for a while that has never failed is the S&W BODYGUARD .380 ACP. I trust it enough that I gave it to my wife to use as a carry gun. It's just slightly heavier than some of the others at 11.5 ounces. It is 5.25 inches long. S&W doesn't post the other dimensions on their website, but I measure it at 0.7 inches wide and 3.8 inches high. The gun's larger sights are easier to see than those of many of the other micro pistols. But they are black on black, which is not the best for defensive sights. Mine came with a laser

sight, which makes a huge difference when shooting with these little guns.

## Glock G42

▲ Glock G42.

The Glock G42 is, like all Glocks, well made and very reliable. It weighs 13.76 ounces empty, which is 4.11 ounces more than the LCP. The G42 is 5.94 inches long, which is 0.78 inch longer than the LCP. It's also 0.53 inches higher and 0.12-inch wider. Those numbers don't look like much here on the page, but in your hand the G42 is considerably bigger than the other guns. To my thinking it is a bit on the large size to be used as a deep cover, backup gun. But you may disagree. Check it out for yourself. It's a great .380, but I think Glock made a mistake making it this large. The G43 in 9mm is only a little bit bigger and makes more sense as it's chambered for a more powerful cartridge.

## Diamondback DB380

This is the Florida gunmaker's signature pistol. I have to be honest, the first one I had didn't function very well. But they replaced it and this new one runs fine. I probably have a bit more than one hundred rounds through it without any ammo-caused issues. I have mixed and matched the ammo and it seems to digest most of it pretty well, with one exception; it's just one of those incompatibility things.

The DB380 is a well-made gun that has decent sights that you can see and shoot with. The front has a large

▲ Diamondback DB380.

white dot. The windage adjustable rear sight has two smaller white dots. I can run my six-plate MGM plate rack with this gun from ten yards relatively fast. With many of the other micro 380 handguns that is impossible, as they lack useable sights. The DB380 weighs 8.8 ounces. The length is 5.26 inches, height, 3.75 inches and width, 0.750 inches.

## Kimber Micro Raptor

▲ Kimber Micro Raptor.

If you like the small size, but not the plastic, then the aluminum-frame Kimber Micro Raptor might be the gun you are looking for. This is more or less a scaled-down 1911 with a hammer, ambi safety, and single-action trigger. The trigger pull on my gun is way too high at ten pounds. It needs some work to bring

it down to make the gun viable as a shooter. It has highly visible, glow-in-the-dark, three-dot sights and is one of the most shooter-friendly micro guns when it comes to hitting a precision target. Good sights make a difference.

If you like 1911 pistols and are looking for a deep cover backup pistol, this might be your gun. The gun is 5.6 inches long and 4.0 inches high. I measure the width at 0.71 inch. The downside of all that metal construction is weight. It's still very light at 13.4 ounces, but when you compare it to the Ruger LCP at 9.65 ounces, there is a difference. Enough to matter? That's up to you. The other issue is cost. This is a custom shop gun from Kimber and their current listed MSRP is almost two and a half times the MSRP for the bare-bones Ruger.

## Lasers

▲ A laser sight is a big asset to any handgun.

I am a huge advocate of lasers on all carry guns, but can't stress enough how much they change the way we can shoot these little micro pistols.

Yes, you read that right. I am writing about lasers on prepper guns. Let's face it, if you stock up on batteries and store them properly you can get years or maybe even decades of use from a laser sight. Why would you not do that?

I had a guy on Facebook recently post that I was all wrong about survival guns. He had it all figured out and insisted that a flintlock rifle and two flintlock pistols were the way to go. He even planned to make his own black powder.

That reaches new heights of stupid when you think it through. How long will he last against a gang of bad guys armed with AR-15 rifles and pistols with laser sights? None of us will live long enough to see the world's supply of guns and ammo exhausted to the point where we are forced to return to making black powder and shooting flintlocks. It's all a great romantic notion, but not practical. Neither is avoiding any modern sighting system because it uses batteries. If you run out of batteries, where does that leave you? Right where those who say we should not have them at all want us to start. Meanwhile, we can have several years of use of the better sights. So yes, put a laser on your micro pistol and stock up on batteries. It lets you hit stuff and that's important.

## Conclusions

I think that a deep cover backup pistol is a very good idea for any prepper. The micro-size .380 ACP handguns are perhaps the best option for that use.

These micro pistols can save your life. If you carry one, train with it often. Load it with only the best ammo and put a laser sight on the gun. Learn and understand the limitations of the cartridge and act accordingly. The .380 ACP is a long way from perfect, but if it saves your life you won't care.

# Revolver Introduction: Don't Ignore the Wheel Gun

*Revolvers have a place in survival.*

▲ Revolvers are still a viable option for self-defense.

*I*n today's world of high-capacity, polymer-frame, semiauto pistols we often forget about the original repeating handgun. While the roots of the revolver go back to the revolving arquebus, produced by Hans Stopler of Nuremberg in 1597, it was 1836 before Sam Colt figured out how to make it work best. Once Colt started making revolvers, the world of defensive handguns changed forever. It wasn't so long ago that almost everybody, law enforcement and civilians alike, car-ried double-action revolvers for self-defense. A surprising number of gun-savvy people still do.

Critics argue that most revolvers only hold six shots. But for other than a Hollywood-style fantasy shoot-out or a zombie apocalypse, that has traditionally been more than enough. Don't be fooled by *The Walking Dead*; Rick's choice of a Colt Python would have resulted in his death with the first zombie horde attack. If the zombies show up, a magazine-fed semiauto is the best . . . the only . . . choice for survival. That might also be true for a mob situation such as preppers might expect to encounter, particularly in the early days of a crisis. But for most self-defense situations a revolver is enough gun if you can shoot and actually hit the target. The spray-and-pray crowd will never be fulfilled with a revolver.

Or sights, for that matter.

The same critics also argue that a revolver is slower to reload than a semiauto. They are but, surprisingly, not by much if you train. With a speedloader, or moon clips, the difference is less than you might think. Check out your local ICOR match and watch those guys run their wheel guns. They shoot them very fast and reload them with blinding speed.

How fast can they shoot? Well, Ed McGivern gave up on semiauto pistols because he said they were too slow to cycle and he didn't like waiting. He is famous for his ability to put five shots on a playing card in 2/5 of a second with a double-action S&W revolver. That 1934 record still stands and, remarkably, McGivern set it at fifty-seven years of age when arthritis was messing with his hands.

My friend Jerry Miculek is currently the fastest man alive with a revolver and he did five shots in 0.57 seconds using modern and more accurate timing equipment than McGivern had available. Jerry also fired six shots, a reload, and six more shots in 2.99 seconds. He can empty an eight-shot S&W revolver in less than one second and hit the target with every shot. So no one can argue that a wheel gun is slow to shoot, or reload for that matter. Slower than a magazine-fed semiauto? Yes. Slow? No.

One big upside of a revolver as a defensive gun is that it is almost totally reliable. A high-quality revolver that is maintained and fed a proper diet simply does not jam. In the event of a misfire, another pull of the trigger lines up a fresh cartridge with the barrel. It is versatile too, because a double-action revolver has the option of a fast, double-action trigger pull for defensive situations; or, for a precision shot, cocking the hammer results in a light, crisp single-action trigger pull.

The longer, heavier, double-action trigger pull is an advantage in some tactical situations where it can help prevent an accidental discharge. For example, while holding the gun on a bad guy and waiting for the police to arrive. If the person with the gun is stressed and nervous, it might not be a good idea to have a light trigger pull. The double-action helps prevent shooting at the wrong time. Remember, the main goal here is to protect yourself and your family. But a secondary goal should be to not shoot anyone unless you absolutely must.

At least for now, we still live in an ordered society with cops, judges, and juries. Unfortunately, even a justified self-defense shooting in today's America will alter your life dramatically. You will need a lawyer and will almost certainly be charged and brought to trial. Even if you are found not guilty it will drain you financially and emotionally. Then you can expect the victim's family to sue you in civil court, where there are much different rules and it's easier for them to win. It's not fair, it's not what America should be about, but it is the reality.

While you hope that the system works and you are exonerated, it will be hugely expensive, as in bankruptcy-inducing expensive. That's if you act within your rights and defend yourself against somebody trying to do you harm. If you shoot some douchebag because you were stressed out during that assault and accidently pulled the trigger on your gun at the wrong time, the prosecutor will hang you out to dry. Even if he needed shooting. It doesn't matter that none of it would have happened if the bad guy had just left you alone; it will be your fault in the eyes of the law and the court of public opinion.

It's a fine line that we law-abiding people must walk and it's very easy to step off. We must know and follow

▲ Modern revolvers are reliable and powerful.

the rules, while the bad guys do not. So, make sure you train hard and bring the right gear. In this case, a double-action revolver can be a good choice.

Learning the basics of how to run a revolver has a shorter learning curve than a semiauto handgun. Say you are in the middle of a firefight and need to give a gun to somebody to help. Which is better?

"Here, take this pistol and get in the fight.

"No, it's not a Glock, it's called a 1911.

"What? Yes, it kicks.

"Push down on that lever and then pull back on this thing.

"You didn't pull it far enough. Pull it until it stops. Yes, I know it's hard.

"Don't let it close slowly like that, pull it all the way back and let go so it slams shut.

"Never mind, you need to do it again.

"No, don't push that button!

"That 'thingy' that just fell out is called a magazine. Pick it up and put it in that hole in the grip it fell out of.

"Yes, the 'handle' is called a grip.

"Not that way. Turn it around so the pointy end of the bullets are facing to the front.

"Yes, I can see it fell out again. Pick it up and this time push it into the grip harder.

"Good, now, rack the slide again.

"Yes, that's the 'thingy' on top that moves back and forth.

"You already took the safety off, don't worry about it.

"Okay (sigh) yes, that cute little lever you are pointing at is the safety. Yes down is off. Yes, that means the gun can shoot, if you depress the grip safety.

"That's right; the 'little lever' on the back of the 'handle' is the grip safety. You need to hold the gun so that is depressed before it will shoot.

"I don't know why there are two safeties, just do it! In case you didn't notice, *there are people shooting at us!*

"Now, for God's sakes, point the gun at the bad guys and pull the trigger."

Or: "Here, take this revolver, point it at the bad guys and pull the trigger."

Clearly, if you have little time to train somebody, a revolver is the best handgun option. Of course, mastering one to the point where you can shoot very fast using the double-action function and can reload very quickly takes a lot of training. But anybody can take a few minutes of instruction and then operate a revolver reasonably well.

Revolvers can be chambered for much more powerful cartridges than a semiauto handgun. Cartridges like the .44 Magnum are a big advantage for foraging situations or if you are in a remote area where you may encounter big game or four-legged predators. They can also be a benefit if you must penetrate barriers when shooting at bad guys hiding behind them.

Yes, the capacity of a revolver and the slower reloading are factors if you are in a firefight with multiple opponents. Even those top shooters are only reloading six shots back into their guns. Nobody is under the illusion that a revolver is even close to a magazine-fed semiauto in firepower. But they still have a place with preppers. I do not advocate a revolver as a primary defensive carry handgun for most survival situations, but there are exceptions and there are plenty of reasons for a prepper to have one or more revolvers.

# The Middle Ground Revolvers

*The medium-size revolvers are probably the most versatile.*

This category would include the S&W K and L-Frame guns, Ruger GP100, Dan Wesson 715, a bunch of guns from Taurus, and all the triple Cs. I suppose you could also lump many of the single-action revolvers into this category, including the Ruger Blackhawk and many of the imported Colt clones, but a single-action revolver is even more limited as a defensive survival gun.

▲ This S&W .357 Magnum revolver holds seven shots.

Common cartridges would include .38 Special, .357 Magnum, .41 Magnum, .44 Special, .45 Colt, and even .44 Magnum. That last one, the .44 Magnum, would be the S&W Model 69, which is the new five-shot L-Frame handgun.

▲ The S&W M-69 .44 Magnum is a light and easy-to-carry handgun suitable for defense and foraging.

These middle-of-the-road revolvers strike a balance between ease of carry, power, and function. The Model 69 holds five shots, some of these guns hold seven or eight, but most of these guns will be six-shooters. Compared to a lot of magazine-fed pistols that's pretty low capacity. Plus as noted, a revolver is slower to reload. They simply don't make a lot of sense in an urban setting as a primary defensive handgun. The capacity is too low if you have to deal with a riot or multi-shooter attack. Yes, they can do the job, but there are better choices.

That said, these medium-frame guns make a huge amount of sense for preppers who are in a retreat, or live in a rural or wilderness setting. The odds of dealing with multiple attackers are lower, while the powerful cartridges allowed in these guns are far better for hunting, foraging, and dealing with livestock. If you have a bad guy or two show up, they hit just as hard on two-legged vermin as they do with four-legged predators.

▲ A .44 magnum is powerful enough for defense against two- or four-legged vermin.

The primary advantage of belt-carried revolvers is that they can be chambered for much more powerful cartridges than most semiauto handguns. The .357 Magnum, .41 Magnum, .44 Magnum, and the .45 Colt (if handloaded) all work for shooting hogs and deer-size game. They will put down rogue or dangerous livestock and work well for killing livestock for butchering. They are also very effective for personal defense, except for the limited ammo capacity issue.

The slightly larger S&W N-Frame guns as well as the Ruger Redhawk and Taurus Large Frame revolvers also fit the same criteria, except they are a bit heavier to carry. Of course, they are a bit tougher as well, so (at least in theory) they will hold up longer to a lot of shooting. They are often in even more powerful cartridges.

▲ This custom .44 Magnum by Ken Kelly at Mag-na-port International is a very effective carry gun for all predators, two- or four-legged.

The magnum cartridges like the .357 Magnum, .41 Magnum, or .44 Magnum balance nicely with a 5- to 7-inch barrel. This provides a long sight radius for hunting and other shots that require some precision. The longer barrels milk some velocity out of the cartridge and the added weight helps counter the recoil. My first .44 Magnum was a S&W Model 29 with a 6 ½-inch barrel. It's Dirty Harry's gun and to this day it's my all-time favorite.

But don't rule out a shorter barrel. Elmer Keith, the father of the .44 Magnum, preferred a 4-inch barrel. I thought that would be a beast, until I shot one and learned it is not. I have found that even shorter is fine.

While I have been with the same woman for nearly forty years, I am much more fickle when it comes to guns. My latest "favorite" .44 Magnum is a custom Model 629 revolver that Ken Kelly at Mag-na-port worked over for me. I find this lightweight .44 is very handy to carry both for urban and wilderness settings. I have carried it in Alaska for protection against brown bears and in the city as protection against bad guys. I never felt compromised in either setting. I have a handload that pushes a 300-grain cast bullet to just over

1,000 ft/s, which I carry in bear country. For urban predators I usually load the gun with Hornady, .44 Special 165-grain FTX, Critical Defense ammo.

The gun is designed for concealment and power. Ken Kelly reworks the grip frame to a round-butt, K-Frame design. He then cuts the barrel to 2.5 inches. The package, of course, includes Mag-na-port recoil reduction ports. Ken works his magic to fine tune the action so the double action is slick and smooth and the single-action trigger is crisp and clean.

One of the great things about a .44 Magnum revolver is that it can also fire .44 Special ammo for urban concealed carry. The recoil of this .44 Special ammo is very mild in the Mag-na-port handgun, on par with a 9mm. I shot several ten-yard drills with this ammo and my best split times, that is the time between shots, ran about 0.22 seconds. The average for splits was

▲ This custom .44 Magnum is based on a S&W M629 and was modified by Ken Kelly at Mag-na-port International.

0.24 seconds. That's four shots in less than one second. That's with my sixty-year-old arthritic hands and is about as good as I can do with a revolver, so it is representative of what the gun can do in the hands of the average shooter.

With Federal full-power .44 Magnum Personal Defense 240-grain Hydra-Shok loads my split time averages opened up to 0.28 seconds. Still not bad, considering the level of power. That means I can put six .44 magnum shots on the target in less than 1.7 seconds. Not much on Earth can walk away from that.

I carry the gun in a Galco Combat Master CM135, left-handed holster. While not heavy by .44 Magnum standards, the revolver is not a flyweight. It tips the scales at 2.5 pounds empty, which is exactly the same as my S&W 1911. But, it's more comfortable to carry all day due to the smaller footprint. It also hides well with the short barrel, bobbed hammer, and the round butt. I carry my reloads in Safariland speed loaders, in two Galco belt holders. This gives me the ability to reload quickly for twelve more shots.

This is a custom gun, but Smith & Wesson, Ruger, Taurus and perhaps others offer short barrel versions of their powerhouse revolvers in big cartridges. They are designed and marketed for carry in bear country and they make a good "carry" gun for those who prefer a revolver and need a little extra power now and then, no matter where they live.

One caution about any of these powerful revolver cartridges; they are very loud, no matter what the barrel length. That is something to be aware of before you are forced to shoot for your life. If you fire one without ear protection, particularly inside a building or a vehicle, it can be very disorienting. I always keep earplugs handy and put them in if possible, but in a survival situation you may not have time. However, if you are prepared mentally you can stay in the fight. A small loss of hearing is a fair trade for staying alive.

If you are planning to survive what's coming in a rural setting and if you plan to forage and perhaps have some livestock, then you should look at owning one or more of these revolvers.

# The J-Frame and Its Triple Cs

*Be faithful in small things because it is in them that your strength lies.*
—*Mother Teresa*

*(She probably didn't mean guns, but the message resonates here.)*

n the ride back from the Rocky Mountain 3-gun match a few years ago I shared a rack of miniature airplane seats with two very nice women. Both were grandmothers in their late fifties and both were schoolteachers, liberals, and past anti-gun advocates. When conversation came around, as it always does, to my profession I told them: "I am a writer and I write about guns and hunting."

I used to duck the question and hide my profession to avoid the hassle, but many years ago I decided I am proud of what I do and that I will never again apologize for being a gun guy.

With these two ladies, I figured that would be the end of our conversation and that they would do as good liberals on dozens of airplanes have done in the past and frostily turn their backs to me for the duration of the flight. Usually that's just fine with me, but my book sucked on this trip and I was bored so I was glad when the conversation continued.

Surprisingly, both asked me to help them choose a pistol for personal defense. I said I would be happy to do that while advising them to also get professional training not only on how to use it, but when to use it. Then I asked them to join the NRA. I doubt that they will, but you never know.

These women represent a growing demographic of gun buyers. Like they both said, "I never dreamed in my life I would own a gun, but. . . ." The bottom line is they are scared of what is happening in the world and have decided to take charge of their destinies. (One little handgun, of course, is not the answer, but it's a start.)

▲ The S&W J-Frame revolvers define this category of carry guns.

Even though it has fallen from grace with the Internet experts, I keep recommending the same handgun I have always suggested to first-time carry-gun buyers: a small double-action revolver in .38 Special or .357 Magnum, like the Smith & Wesson J-Frame.

Sorry, but I don't follow the herd or often buy into the latest groupthink with anything, including guns. I still think this is one of the best options for a first-time carry gun buyer. Particularly one who is probably going to shoot the gun a little bit and then put it away until a bad guy shows up. Gun guys like to pretend we have evolved past the little revolver, but we must remember that these people are never going to be gun guys. They will start and end with the same gun. They are not going to go shooting on the weekends and are not going to take any continuing training. A small revolver makes a lot of sense for that kind of new-gun owner.

Besides, let's face it, a lot of hard-core gun guys, including me, carry small revolvers. If that's the case, they must be effective, right?

How does that old saying go? We gun guys talk about 1911 pistols, we shoot Glocks and we carry J-Frames. A good friend of mine is a very serious and very good competitive shooter. He is a very big man and could easily conceal and carry any handgun on earth. But his carry gun of choice is a J-Frame. I joke with him all the time about that, but I have no doubt about his ability to protect himself and his family with that little revolver.

▲ A J-Frame in a Front Line holster is light and easy to hide.

For a new shooter, it's the simplicity that is attractive. Even a simple semiauto has activation and function problems that can confuse and stall a person who is unfamiliar with the gun, especially when things are happening fast. We gun guys shoot a lot, so we have the muscle and mental memory to deal with it, but for somebody who is going to buy a gun, get some initial training and then probably not shoot it again unless trouble shows up, I think a semiauto is generally a bad idea.

The revolver is about as idiot-proof as a repeating handgun can be, powerful enough with most cartridges to stop the bad guys quickly and, in this configuration, small and light enough to appeal to anybody making the decision to carry a handgun.

you can't see your sights and, of course, every bad guy on Earth knows what that red dot means. The hope is they will soil their pants and run away when they see it presented by what they assumed was an easy victim.

For the most part, the definition of the guns we are talking about here is a small-framed, double-action revolver. The J-Frame is the smallest of the S&W revolvers. It is the one that is commonly called a "snubnose" as it usually has a short barrel. While there are endless variations on the S&W J-Frame concept, there are plenty of other guns from other makers in this category too. So, this discussion will also include all of the three Cs.

▲ This category of handguns includes (clockwise from the top): S&W Model 340, Ruger SP101, Charter Arms Bulldog, and Ruger LCR.

So, in continuing the trend I have followed for more than thirty years, I recommended that these ladies buy J-Frame Smith & Wesson revolvers or one of its CCCs (clones, copycats, and competition). Which one is up to their personal choice and budget, but I recommended at minimum the .38 Special for a cartridge. Finally, I added the one thing that has changed with my advice over the years: Get it with, or quickly add, a Crimson Trace laser grip.

The laser changes the "shootability" of the pistol. The short sight radius of a 2-inch or shorter barrel revolver is not easy for anybody to shoot. But a laser sight makes this gun essentially no more difficult to shoot than any other revolver.

Beyond that are all the other reasons for a laser sight. You can shoot without exposing yourself, you can keep your eyes on the bad guy, they work in the dark when

Colt made some wonderful revolvers in this category for years and you can still find a few on the used-gun market. But they are very expensive due to collector's

▲ Ruger LCR .357 Mag.

status and are not all that relevant to a discussion on which guns to buy for prepping.

Ruger has the LCR, which is a very popular, reasonably priced handgun. This gun makes use of polymer in the frame, which keeps both weight and cost down, yet it can handle a powerful cartridge like the .357 Magnum.

▲ Ruger SP101.

The Ruger SP101 is slightly larger and heavier and is as tough a gun as you can find in this category. In fact, that's a trait with Rugers: They are always well-made, tough, and dependable.

Charter Arms has several small revolvers in a wide range of cartridges. So does Taurus. I have a lot more experience with Smith & Wesson and Ruger firearms than with Charter Arms or Taurus revolvers. I tried to get both to test and evaluate for this book, but they

▲ S&W Bodyguard in .38 Special with a laser sight.

never showed up. Those few I have used are not as refined as the Smiths or Rugers, but they seem to work okay and they are often less expensive. However, I would always caution against buying on price for any prepping guns. Your life may depend on the gun, so why compromise? Also, in a survival situation it will be difficult to replace or repair any gun that fails. The old adage of "buy once, cry once" refers to spending the money the first time to get the best. I would say that's excellent advice for these little revolvers.

I would caution against any rimfire cartridges or pistol cartridges like the .380 or 9mm. The rimfires are underpowered for defense and the .380 and 9mm are not designed for use in revolvers and work much better in semiauto handguns. A revolver works best with a rimmed cartridge and for defense a reasonable power level should be maintained. It makes much more sense to buy a .38 Special or .357 Magnum. Either of these can shoot .38 Special and ammo is plentiful and relatively inexpensive. You can use .38 Special +P ammo for defense and practice with the cheaper stuff. Or, if you buy the .357 Magnum, you have the option of using full-power .357 Magnum ammo as well as all of the .38 Special options.

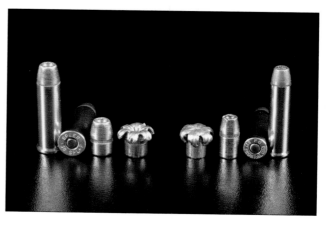

▲ Revolvers are chambered for effective cartridges. With modern bullets they are even better.

I suppose an exception could be the .327 Federal cartridge, as it will work for self-defense, but ammo is harder to find than more common cartridges. The .38 Special is as common in the shooting world as Hoppes Number 9. Not too many mom-and-pop stores have .327 Federal. My preference is to get the guns in .357

Magnum. That cartridge can be a fire-breathing beast with a lot of recoil in these little revolvers, particularly in the alloy frame guns like the S&W M&P Model 340 that I carry. But I want all the power I can handle in a fight. So I make sure to train with full power .357 Mag loads with these guns, at least on a limited basis, so I can learn to handle the recoil. Most of my practice is with .38 Special ammo, but I try to end every training session with some full-power .357 Magnum ammo.

I loaded about ten thousand .38 Special cartridges for Cowboy Action Shooting several years ago. Then I found 3-gun shooting and I quit competing in CAS, but those moderate loads with cast bullets and Trailboss powder were perfect for practice with my little revolvers. They don't beat up the guns or the shooter too much and they let me have some pretty intense shooting sessions. I am down to just a few hundred rounds of ammo now, but as a result I got pretty good with my little carry revolvers.

▲ Charter Arms Bulldog in .44 Special with Hornady ammo.

Another consideration is the Charter Arms .44 Special Bulldog. While there is no clear definition of a "small-frame revolver," this gun is a little larger than the .38 Specials, but uses a much larger cartridge. I have one and have shot it a fair amount and like the gun.

To my mind, it's still a small handgun. It's chambered for the .44 Special which can be a formidable round for defense, particularly with some of the newer ammo like Hornady's Flex-Tip loads. Factory .44 Special loads of any brand are loaded to low pressure and low velocity. That's due to the older guns on the market. If you have a modern full-size gun, the .44 Special can be handloaded hot enough to use for shooting deer, hogs, and similar game if needed. I would never recommend a steady diet of that ammo in this little gun, but in a survival situation, a 250-grain hard-cast bullet with a stout charge of powder can be deadly on deer and hogs.

The Bulldog had its fifteen minutes of fame when David Berkowitz, also known as Son of Sam and the 44 Caliber Killer, used one during his reign of terror in New York City during the summer of 1976. That story is yet another illustration that it's not the gun but the shooter who determines if a gun is used for good or

▲ I carry a Model S&W 360 when I am hunting. This is a lightweight, scandium-frame gun with an external hammer. It's so light that it's no more noticeable on my belt than a big knife or plier tool, yet it's there for defensive use or to finish off a wounded big game animal.

evil. The Bulldog is an inanimate object, incapable of action on its own. It can save lives as well as make a whack job famous. Either way, it's a big-bore, small-frame revolver that packs a lot of punch.

These little wheel guns are a very good choice for a backup gun. I carry mine in a pocket holster where it stays hidden. While I would not use it as a primary carry gun after TSHTF, for now it's often the only gun I carry. It is easy to carry, easy to hide, and is light enough that it's no burden. In hot weather it's one of the few guns that I can hide easily in a pair of shorts and still have the full power of a serious defensive cartridge.

I also carry a Model S&W 360 when I am hunting. This is the same lightweight, scandium-frame gun, but with an external hammer. It's so light that it's no more noticeable on my belt than a big knife or plier tool, yet it's there for defensive use or to finish off a wounded big game animal.

These small, easy-to-hide revolvers represent the most power you can find in so small a handgun. Every prepper should consider having one or more of them. They are an option for concealed carry now, and after TSHTF they are great for backup carry.

Oddly enough, just about every serious gun guy I know has at least one of these little revolvers and most carry them regularly. That alone should tell you something.

# The Littlest Wheel Guns

*Dynamite in a small package.*

▲ The North American Arms .22 Long Rifle Mini-Revolver on top and .22 Magnum with a laser sight on bottom.

love 3-gun competition, but I started much too late in life to ever be a top contender. I was in my fifties before I even shot a match. It's a very physical game and younger men generally do better. There are exceptions, but to a man the guys who are the top shooters and are close to my age pretty much all started when they were young, so they now have a lot of experience to help offset the aging issues.

I also have much too busy a lifestyle, so I never get to practice much. As a result, I am in no danger of winning any of the big national matches.

If you play golf, first of all let me express my sympathy; it must be painful to compete in a sport with so little noise and no guns! But let me also draw an analogy. Those big, national 3-gun matches are like playing the Masters; the best of the best are there competing. You might be a hotshot at your local club, but in the big leagues it's hard to keep up. Most of us can't beat Tiger Woods unless he has a really, really bad day. It's the same with the national 3-gun matches and at most of them my goal is to place in the top 50 percent.

The prize tables for many of the matches are filled with lots of new guns, but there have never been enough so that any are left when my name is called.

Except for the Superstition Mountain Mystery 3-Gun in Arizona a few years ago. I heard somebody say there was a gun still on the table, so I made a beeline and grabbed it.

The top shooters won high-end AR-15 rifles, fancy handguns and even a few precision rifles, but my prize was something else. I won a North American Arms .22 Long Rifle Mini-Revolver.

I flew from that match directly to a pheasant hunt in Kansas and I used the revolver to finish off a few roosters, mostly so I could brag about shooting game with this gun and so we could all have a good laugh. But since then I have found this gun to be very versatile. In fact, it's an amazing little gun, mostly because it is so small. I carry it in my pocket every day, just like a pocketknife. This tiny revolver only weighs 4.5 ounces and most of the time I forget it's even there. But that's the beauty of this gun.

It's not by any means a powerful gun and the short barrel bleeds off velocity and energy from the already low-power .22 LR cartridge. But I have finished off wounded deer with it and have little doubt that it is still a deadly tool.

It's a last-resort, hide-out gun, because it's always there. That counts for a lot. It's also better than no gun at all. This is never a primary gun, but more like a backup to the backup. It's the gun that's in your pocket when you go outside to take out the trash at night and your main handgun is on the table in the kitchen. Or it's the gun you hope they don't find if you are disarmed by the bad guys. In fact, there have been some stories of people hiding these little revolvers in some very creative places.

It's an ultra-close-range defensive gun for sure. It's a bit awkward to hold and kicks more than you would think. But it's amazing how well you can shoot it with practice and ammo the gun likes. Most ammo barely stabilizes in these short barrels and often accuracy is not guaranteed beyond in-your-face ranges. But at five yards I can put five into center mass on a USPSA target, and do it reasonably fast.

North American Arms makes a wide range of these little handguns, including a slightly larger .22 Magnum model that weighs 5.9 ounces or the 1 1/8-inch barrel version that provides a bit more power.

They offer a wide range of accessories including laser sights, holsters, and even a belt-buckle holster. There are grips that serve as a holster and fold down to become a larger grip and several more innovative accessories designed around these tiny guns. Laserlyte also has a laser for the .22 Mag gun. With a laser sight, it becomes even easier to shoot.

These little revolvers are inexpensive, with MSRP for the .22 LR base model like mine at just over $200 in 2015.

While you won't often find me advocating for any rimfire for a defensive pistol in this book, here I'll make an exception. The tiny size and ultra-lightweight make them as easy to carry as a pocket knife. The guns are very easy to hide. When it comes to fighting, these revolvers are a last resort. But it's always good to have a last resort, one that may make all the difference in the world on whether you will survive or not. Because without a "last resort," you are done and you are dead. I think of this gun as a good luck charm, one that's deadly in a pinch.

It's also handy for everyday use around your home or retreat. You can dispatch vermin caught in your traps, put down sick livestock in an emergency, and finish off wild game, while preserving your centerfire ammo and keeping the noise level down a bit. With the short barrels they are loud, but a lot quieter than an M4 carbine.

I have even used mine to punch drain holes in a new trashcan or to put a hole in a shed wall to run a wire through. The uses are almost endless.

I would recommend that every serious prepper have one of these mini-revolvers hidden away someplace on their person, *just in case*.

# The "Other" Handguns

*The misfits and leftovers are some of the more interesting handguns.*

Each of the three primary gun sections, rifle, shotgun, and handgun, are subdivided into different chapters about the various types and styles of guns. But, when it's all done, there always seems to be a few that just defy convention. They don't really fit any category, yet they may be important guns for a prepper to consider. Here are a few of those rebels in the handgun category.

## The .410 Handguns

*A new kind of revolver.*

▲ The S&W Governor (top) and the Taurus Judge represent a new type of defensive handgun.

The young lady hiker was lost in her thoughts as she sat in the summer sunshine and she didn't notice me until I said hello. As is common with just about everybody I meet on this trail, her eyes immediately went to the handgun on my backpack's hip belt.

"Are you armed?" she asked with a bit of fright in her voice.

"Of course, are you?" I replied.

She smiled and said, "You sound like my father."

That started a conversation in which she asked fair and honest questions. I explained my reasons for carrying a handgun. First and probably most important was that this section of the Appalachian Trail is frequented by a lot of bad people and some areas not very far from where we stood are a hot bed of drug activity. I also pointed out that there have been several murders over the years along the trail. Then I told her about the rabid coyote that tried to attack me near this spot just a few days earlier.

"The bottom line," I told her, "is that I carry this gun for problems I sincerely hope will never occur. I am betting you have insurance on your car and house right? Out here in the woods, you have only yourself to rely on and a gun is the insurance policy."

"Now you really sound like my dad," she laughed.

"Your dad is a smart man, you should listen to him."

"I do," she said with a smile.

That's when I realized she never answered my question on if she was armed.

Smart girl.

I carry a gun every time I enter the woods. Not just when I am hiking on a trail that is the habitat of some of society's scum, but also when I am scouting for new deer stands, shooting photography, fishing, or any other activity off the pavement. I would sooner leave my truck without pants than leave my gun behind.

Just a few days ago I was hiking on that same trail mentioned earlier when I almost stepped on a huge snake. In fact, my dog did step on it. That snake was so well camouflaged I didn't see him and Clyde didn't smell or see him, so he got nipped for his indiscretion. Luckily, we don't have poisonous snakes in this area so I just flipped the thing off the trail with my walking stick and let him go on about his business. Clyde seemed pretty happy with that decision.

The last time I was that close to a big snake was in Texas. That one was a four-foot rattlesnake and he actually struck at me. I was moving an old plastic chair that was left in a turkey blind and by pure luck he hit the chair instead of me. I have a firm policy about rattlesnakes: I leave them alone if they leave me alone, but when they try to kill me, I kill them back. That one quickly lost his head.

That is just one of the many reasons I carry a handgun, you just never know what you will run into.

There is a type of handgun I sometimes carry that has brought a new approach to the concept of wilderness protection.

▲ The S&W Governor.

"The Judge" is a revolver made by Taurus and it started the trend. Later, Smith and Wesson added the "Governor," and between the two there are a bunch of

▲ The Judge can take small game if the distance of the shot is short.

different models and designs to choose from. The guns are chambered for .45 Colt and/or .410 shotshells. In theory, they are designed to handle just about any conceivable wilderness or urban self-defense scenario.

These revolvers not only defend you from trouble, but are also designed for use in a wilderness survival situation. This is important because danger in the wilderness isn't always from attacks of four- or two-legged predators. Getting lost or stranded presents a unique set of problems, as does survival after TEOTWAWKI. One advantage is that this gun can feed as well as defend you.

▲ These .410 handguns can be very versatile.

The guns are five-shot, .45 Colt revolvers with an extra-long cylinder that will handle .410 shotshells. The versatility is that this handgun might have .45 Colt, .410 buckshot, .410 slugs, and .410 birdshot loads in it, all at the same time.

While not recommended for high-pressure handloads, the .45 Colt can be used to kill big game in a survival situation. The long jump for the bullet to contact the rifling due to the extended cylinder reduces the accuracy, but this is intended to be a short-range handgun anyway.

It's also more oriented to using the .410 ammo and, for close-range problem solving, the .410 is a good choice. In fact, these handguns inspired most of the ammo companies to make self-defense loads just for the revolvers.

Buckshot loads can deliver as many as four, 000, 36-caliber, 70.5-grain pellets to the target with each pull of the trigger. The 3-inch loads have five pellets. If you pick #4 buckshot there are nine pellets. The Hornady Critical Defense load uses a 41-caliber Flex-Tip expanding slug and two 35-caliber buckshot pellets. Or of course, you can use a .410 slug.

Finally, the guns will shoot .410 shotshells, which is what I like best. The barrel is rifled, which is why it's considered a .45 Colt handgun by the government and not a short-barrel shotgun, which would be against federal law. Spinning the shot column as it passes through the rifled barrel disperses the shot pattern rather quickly, but if the range is kept short this is a formidable gun capable of taking small game as well as protecting you from man-size predators. Large pellet sizes like #4 birdshot will work for many close-range defensive situations, but if you are hunting for the cook pot or for survival I have found that a high pellet count is the key with a .410 handgun. Shot size #7 ½ to #9 works best.

When The Judge first came out I was having an ongoing problem with red squirrels that take up residence in my shed each winter. Like vengeful ex-wives, they seemed determined to destroy everything I valued, so I declared war. When the smoke cleared, The Judge had ruled and eliminated the problem. Not one squirrel that was within range survived the wrath of The Judge and trust me, the body count was high. I have also used The Judge and The Governor pistols to shoot a wide range of small game and pests including gray squirrels, grouse, rabbits, raccoons, and even a few snakes. Pests can't take a ruling from these guns.

For self-defense, survival or just to carry in the woods, The Judge has set a new precedent and this revolver gets a favorable decision. With the S&W Governor there is no reprieve for pests of any kind.

Both are handy guns to keep around if you are in a rural setting, but they will also work for self-defense, and with .45 Colt loads, the guns can deal with livestock that needs putting down or take a deer at close range. In addition to often carrying one when in the woods, I keep two of them loaded and stashed strategically at hand to deal with any pests that show up at my house or shop.

While not priority guns for preppers, these are two that you should consider. It's much safer to use a .410 #9 shotshell to deal with pests and pestilence around your property. There is no danger of ricochet or over-penetration of whatever you are shooting. Shooting a snake or a rat with #9 shot is a lot safer for neighbors or family than using a centerfire handgun.

We live in a rural area, but do have neighbors. Recently Clyde was raising hell in the woods behind my shop. I grabbed a Judge we keep loaded with #9 birdshot for snakes and went to investigate. He was barking at a sick raccoon. We are unsure if he had distemper or rabies, but the Judge ended his misery without any danger to the neighbors.

Even inside the home, the self-protection ammo is not as prone to over-penetration through walls. That keeps anybody else in the house safer, as well as any neighbors. Any prepper might be glad to have one of these unique handguns in the toolbox.

## Bond Arms

▲ The Bond Arms Derringer in .45 Colt/.410.

Bond Arms makes a line of derringer-style handguns. Some of the most popular guns are chambered for .45/.410, just like the revolvers. The difference with the Bond guns is that they are much smaller than the revolvers and are easier to carry in a pocket. Of course, you can also get a selection of holsters for the guns.

The Bond is a double-barrel, two-shot derringer-style handgun. The barrels are hinged on top and swing open to reload. There is a safety that blocks the hammer. They make the derringers in a wide range of cartridges, ranging from .22 Long Rifle through .44–40 or .45 Colt. They have interchangeable barrels so they can be switched out to meet your current needs. The most popular, and the one I have, is chambered for .45 Colt/.410. The 3-inch barrel can fire .45 Colt or 2 ½-inch .410 shotshells. That doesn't leave much barrel left for rifling, which is a good thing in terms of birdshot or buckshot patterns. Of course, shooting the gun with .45 Colt ammo is not going to win any bull's-eye matches for accuracy, but that's not the intent of this gun. This is an "in-your-face" defensive handgun. Besides, like all derringers, it's a bit awkward to shoot and has a tough trigger.

The gun is primarily designed for the .410 function rather than the centerfire handgun cartridge. If the centerfire handgun cartridge is the goal, it would be best to buy the gun, or at least a spare barrel, chambered for the cartridge of your choice, including .45 Colt. That will give you a shorter chamber and more rifling. But to my mind the .410 is the way to go with this gun. It's going to be nasty for personal defense and it can handle close-range pest control with birdshot.

This is strictly a short-range handgun. It patterns #9 shot well enough to kill a snake or small game out to about seven yards or perhaps a little bit more. It is perfect for controlling pests around the compound and for a backup snake gun when you are out and about and don't want to use your rifle or primary handgun.

It also handles the 2 ½ defensive .410 loads well. I found that I could keep most rounds centered on the target out to seven yards. This is a great hideout gun option, a backup to your backup when you will be using it up close and as a last resort.

They are well-made, high-quality firearms and the $440 price (2015) reflects that. But remember, your life may depend on this gun; do you really want to go cheap?

## Kel-Tec PMR-30

The PMR-30 is without a doubt one of the most unique pistols on the market. I do not advocate any rimfire as a fighting cartridge, but I have shot a lot of game with a .22 Magnum, including a deer or two, and I am always amazed at the nasty holes it produces. There are some knowledgeable people in the defensive handgun world who think this is an interesting approach to a carry gun. I am not one of them, but I am not saying they

▲ Kel-Tec PMR-30.

are wrong either. Certainly the thirty-round magazine is a start. The gun is light, easy to shoot, and reliable.

It's also following the continuing theme here in this book that you should have as many guns in as many chamberings as possible so that you have something to fit whatever ammo you can find after TSHTF. The .22 Magnum is a pretty common cartridge and the odds of finding ammo are reasonably high.

This pistol is a lightweight 13.6 ounces, even though it's full sized. It's chambered for .22 Magnum. It operates with what Kel-Tec calls "a unique hybrid blowback/locked-breech system" that adjusts to pressure differences between different brands of ammo.

The double-stack magazine holds thirty cartridges and is a flush fit in the grip. The trigger on mine breaks at three pounds ten ounces. There is a manual thumb-activated, ambidextrous safety. The sights are fiber optic: green front, and red rear. The front sight is in a dovetail so you can adjust for windage. There is no elevation adjustment, which is one of the few complaints I have. Adjustable sights would be a huge improvement on this gun.

This gun has a lot of modern and innovative features. Several of these Kel-Tec guns have surprised me and this is one of them. I don't think it is of a power level or construction to consider for your primary handgun for survival, but I do think this is a gun that could have a lot of usefulness for survival. It's not horribly expensive and any prepper might do well to consider adding one to the collection.

# SHOTGUNS
## Introduction

*Is a shotgun the secret to survival? Maybe, maybe not. But, you need at least one.*

*"Buy a Shotgun. Buy a Shotgun."*
—*Vice President Joe Biden*

That was VP Joe Biden's advice while on the ABC News network in response to a question from a reader of *Parent Magazine*. If you heard the rest of the segment you should understand that taking self-defense advice from Joe may be like taking career advancement advice from Lindsay Lohan.

He went on to say that he told his wife if she heard something suspicious to walk out on their deck and fire a couple of blasts into the dark. It was probably one of the most stupid things ever said by a vice president known primarily for saying stupid things.

Some say that he at least had the part about buying a shotgun right. But did he? Is a shotgun the best gun for defense?

The answer is, "It all depends."

I don't want to sound like some sniveling politician trying to play both sides, so let me make a more definitive statement.

Is a shotgun the best defensive long gun for a prepper? No.

Should preppers buy shotguns? Yes.

Contradictory?

Not really. I'll explain. This goes back and forth, sometimes in a single paragraph, so pay attention.

The shotgun is not a good choice as a primary defensive long gun. Forget all the myths and misinformation out there. Forget Hollywood and forget the romance of racking that pump during a fight. From a tactical point of view, a shotgun is a poor choice for a prepper as a primary defensive long gun.

However, a shotgun does have a very strong position within the battery of guns that a prepper should have.

First, let's consider why they make poor primary defensive long guns. A shotgun has limited range, holds limited ammo and is very slow to reload. The ammo is heavy and bulky and it's difficult to carry a lot of it on your person.

There is nothing that a shotgun can do in a fight that a rifle can't do as well or better. Even for close-range fighting, a carbine-style rifle in trained hands is as effective as a shotgun. Remember, when you are close (like inside-your-house distances) the shotgun is throwing a pattern with buckshot or birdshot that is effectively no larger than a single bullet. If you move to more open ranges, say in your yard, then the pattern of pellets will rapidly disperse until it reaches a point where it's no longer an effective fight-stopper.

If you shoot slugs, then you have a single projectile, just like the rifle except it is effective to about 1/10 the distance of a rifle.

With a tactical shotgun, you have less than ten rounds in the gun, usually much less. The shotgun is very slow to reload, perhaps two seconds per shell or slower. A rifle will have thirty or forty or more rounds and reloading takes two or three seconds. So, with both guns empty you can have the rifle back in the fight with another thirty or forty-round magazine in about the same amount of time it takes to put one shell back in the shotgun.

I am sure some will disagree with that so, okay, take two rounds. In fact, I'll give you three new shells. Does that really make a difference?

The one exception might be a magazine-fed shotgun. You can reload a ten-round magazine relatively quickly, but all the other issues still apply. Also the reliability of magazine-fed shotguns is a bit spotty.

It's easy to carry lots of ammo for a rifle in pre-loaded magazines. Most people can manage ten magazines easily enough. A loaded thirty-round magazine for an AR-15 weighs a pound. Ten loaded thirty-round mags will weigh ten pounds. That gives you three hundred rounds of ammo. To carry three hundred rounds of shotgun ammo on your body would be all but impossible. The weight alone would be too much, as it would weigh thirty pounds. Besides, where would you put it all? You would need a backpack just for the ammo. In the end, there is absolutely no tactical advantage for a shotgun over a battle rifle, particularly in a survival TEOTWAWKI situation where we may be dealing with social unrest and mobs of desperate people.

It's true; a shotgun is an excellent fight-stopper at close range. Nine 00 buckshot pellets to the chest will knock the dickhead out of anybody's attitude. But buck is only effective at relatively close ranges, and if

▲ You can never go wrong with a Remington Model 870 in 12 gauge.

▲ A shotgun is versatile with lots of ammo and choke options.

the range extends much, it wounds more than it kills. Some loads like Federal's FliteControl buckshot can extend the effective range much beyond traditional buckshot, so how far buckshot remains effective varies. The choke can have an effect, too. Most tactical shotguns are cylinder-bore and the shot with traditional buckshot loads disperses quickly. That set up may fail to put all of the buckshot pellets on a man-sized target in as little as twenty-five yards. A little choke, like a modified choke, can extend the effective range of buckshot, as can the new generations of wad systems like FliteControl. But no buckshot load I have tested is 100 percent effective at distances past fifty yards or so. Usually it is much closer than that. The key in knowing how far is to pattern your gun and load. You might get a pellet or two into the target, but that does not ensure the fight is over. Buckshot depends on multiple hits to be effective. Single pellets are not effective fight-stoppers.

▲ Foster-style slugs are a very effective fight stopper.

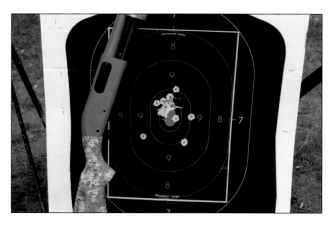

▲ Buckshot is very effective at close range.

**To recap:** At close range, buckshot can be very effective. But if that range extends, all bets are off. I have seen it used on deer, black bear, and hogs with mixed results. It can be very impressive or hugely disappointing. The reports of its use for defensive applications pretty much say the same thing. If you are close, like inside your home, it's great stuff. But outside where the distance can increase rapidly, it loses effectiveness quickly.

Slugs are very effective out to 50 or 75 yards, maybe more if you can hit the target. That last part

is tough without sights. We use Foster-style slugs in 3-gun competition, which are the same slugs that you would use for defense. I have seen them be very effective out to 75 or even 100 yards, if the shotgun has sights and the shooter is exceptionally skilled. With a bead, most guys are done at half that distance or less.

The one thing about slugs is that they hit very hard. I know a cop who had to shoot a guy with a slug and he told me that it was the fastest he has ever seen somebody stop trying to kill him. I have seen Foster slugs used on deer, hogs, and black bears. They are very effective. When you get hit with a 1-ounce, 73-caliber projectile, it's going to be effective. The slug is nearly ¾ of an inch in diameter and a full-power load will leave the barrel of the shotgun at something like 1,600 ft/s and carry in excess of 2,500 foot-pounds of energy. That's more than five times the energy of the best defensive pistol rounds. Make no mistake, a slug is a fight-stopper.

Birdshot is also very effective inside a building at close "bedroom-type" ranges that are measured in feet rather than yards. With a magnum "turkey" load you are pretty much dumping a couple of ounces of lead into the bad guy at 1,000 ft/s. Something's gotta give. Yet, birdshot is less likely to go through the walls and kill your neighbors in their house across the street while they sleep.

A shotgun is no good if you are dealing with a mob or a mass attack because it does not hold enough ammo and is too slow to reload. But it can be a very good defensive gun during most other situations. If you are dealing with single-issue problems, that is one or even a few bad guys, a shotgun is very effective in trained hands. It's safer to use around your home, compound, or in urban areas—or anyplace that has other people lurking about whom you would rather not shoot. At least in terms of the projectiles not penetrating walls and hitting people on the other side.

You must be aware of pattern dispersion and that pellets can hit a person downrange who you think is out of the line of fire. Sometimes the pellets will spread out to amazing places, so the shotgun has an increased danger of collateral damage. When you fire a rifle or handgun you need to worry about one projectile on a relatively predictable path. With a shotgun there are multiple projectiles on a path that nobody can precisely predict.

▲ The UTS shotgun works well with slugs.

A shotgun is very effective for dealing with pests and predators around the home and compound. It is the best choice for fixing problems like snakes, rats, coyotes, and varmints of all kind. A shotgun does the job without the risk of over penetration or ricochet.

If you are foraging for food and hunting for small game that scurries and flies, a shotgun is by far the best choice. It's very hard to hit a flying grouse with a rifle and I can tell you from experience that unless you make a head shot with a centerfire rifle there is nothing left to eat. A shotgun was designed for shooting birds and it's by far the best choice for that chore.

A shotgun can handle big stuff too. Slugs were developed for hunting big game and are very effective on deer. They are safer than a rifle to use in settled areas because they do not fly as far before hitting the ground and stopping, which is why so many urban areas are shotgun-only for deer hunting. You can't shoot deer very far away, but in the woods where ranges are not long, a shotgun will work. Out to 50 yards or so, a tactical shotgun with a Foster slug is a deer-killing machine.

So yes, Joe was right about one thing: "Buy a shotgun." Every prepper needs a shotgun or two. Just get the right shotgun and then learn how and when to use it.

While a lot of fools promote the shotgun as "point and shoot" and the gun for people who don't want to train, it's all BS. Running a shotgun effectively in a defensive situation requires a skillset that is probably more difficult to master than a rifle. So, get some training.

Even from a foraging point of view, you need training. Hitting moving targets with a shotgun is much more difficult than the uneducated like Biden believe. It's a much different shooting technique than with a rifle or handgun and it takes refined skills that are developed over time. If you are trying to feed your starving family, every time you miss is a tragedy. So spend some time on the sporting clays range and learn to shoot a shotgun well before it becomes life or death.

Yes, by all means follow Joe's advice and "buy a shotgun!"

But do try to get the right shotgun.

Politicians seem to love the double-barrel shotgun. Remember that other fool John Kerry when he was trying to convince hunters he was one of them?

When asked what kind of hunting he preferred he answered:

*"I'd have to say deer, I go out with my trusty 12-gauge double-barrel, crawl around on my stomach . . . that's hunting."*

Well, maybe that's hunting in his over-privileged, never-been-hunting, liberal, trying-to-fit-in mind; but every hunter on Earth knew he was full of shit.

First off, I have shot a lot of deer, but I can't remember the last time I crawled on my stomach to shoot one. It happens, but not very often. Also, nobody but a novice or a dumbass, lying politician thinks about

using a "trusty" double-barrel for deer hunting. They do not play well with slugs and it's all but impossible to hit a deer with one past powder burns on his hide distances.

Doubles are great; I love them and use them often. They epitomize the true concept for shotguns. While they are a bit outdated these days, those who love doubles use them for shooting flying objects, which is the primary reason shotguns exist.

(The exception might be Cowboy Action shooters who use doubles in competition. But those are mostly short-barrel "Coach Guns" designed for the sport. Many have external hammers, which are great fun and historically accurate, but a horrible choice for a fighting gun because they are slow to use.)

Traditional doubles are hunting or clays guns and are used mostly out of love for the design rather than any advantage they have over a modern shotgun. I have a Fox 16-gauge that is about a hundred years old. It is one of my favorite shotguns and I use it a lot hunting birds and rabbits, never deer; but if TSHTF I doubt it will see the light of day again.

No matter what Biden might think, doubles are not for defense. Sure, they will work. So will a single-shot. For that matter, so will a rock. How far do we want to take this line of thinking? Do you want something that will work, but with great compromise? Or do you want the best tool available to help you survive?

If you are serious about prepping, forget double-barrel shotguns. They are fine for foraging small game, but not much else. They are poor for defense. Why? Two shots, remember? What if there are three bad guys? They are poor for foraging for big game because they do not manage slugs well, which is also an issue for defense. Hitting a target at any distance with a double-barrel shotgun and slugs is a function of luck more than anything else.

As a prepper, you need a single-barrel, repeating pump-action or semiauto shotgun.

Which one?

Now we are opening a wide-ranging topic. There are a lot of options: tactical, hunting, and hybrids that bridge the gap; pumps; and semiautos. We have tube-fed traditional-style shotguns, bullpup shorties, and even magazine-fed guns based on the AK-47 or similar designs.

Read on, the information may make the choice easier.

To quote my least favorite president, "let me be clear," as a prepper you will need a shotgun or two. Not for an everyday-carry, first-line-of-defense, personal long gun, but for all those uncounted other things when a shotgun is the best tool for the job.

Make sure you stock up on shotgun ammo too—lots and lots of birdshot, slugs, and buckshot.

How much? Figure out the worst-case scenario you can possibly imagine and how much ammo you will need for that. Then double it . . . twice.

Why?

If this thing goes south everybody, the misinformed and the informed alike, will have a shotgun. Most will not think ahead enough to have extra ammo.

That ammo you hoarded will be worth more for barter than gold.

Just think about how those antibiotics that ammo can buy will help keep your kid alive. Or how good a fresh, juicy steak will taste after a diet of MREs.

"Buy a Shotgun. Buy a Shotgun!"

Then buy lots and lots of shotgun ammo.

▲ Buy a shotgun. Buy a shotgun.

# What's the Action with Shotguns?

*Pick your poison, pump or semiauto; they both get the job done.*

▲ Semiautos are faster, but is speed everything in a defensive shotgun?

When it comes to defensive shotguns, there are really only two options for the action type: pump action and semiauto. Double barrels are limited to just two shots and are very slow to load. I know they are favored by Joe Biden, but taking gunfighting advice from him is like having Michelle Obama cater your kid's birthday party. It's just not going to end well.

Single-shots, the other option, are, well . . . single-shots. Not the best for fighting.

It comes down to a semiauto or a pump action. While there are a tremendous number of variations in semiauto or pump guns, we will address those in another chapter. For now let's look at these two actions and explore the pros and cons of each.

Currently the pump-action shotgun is almost universally used for tactical and defensive situations. While I am a huge fan of pump shotguns and they work very well for that use, I can't help but wonder why that is still the case. We have embraced semiauto handguns and rifles for defensive use, but when it comes to shotguns we continue with an antiquated, manually operated system.

Don't misunderstand this to mean a pump shotgun is a bad idea. It's not. I shoot them often and have several for defense of my home, family, and life.

They do have some advantages. One is that they are far less expensive than a semiauto. That brings up a good point. If you are on a budget, an inexpensive pump-action shotgun will usually function pretty well, but a cheap semiauto is often a mistake. Unless you can afford a high-quality, top-of-the-line semiauto shotgun, stick with the pump.

If you are considering a new defensive shotgun and can afford a good one, it might be time to look harder at the semiauto option.

A couple of years ago I was asked by NRA's *Shooting Illustrated* magazine to take the semiauto side in a "Pump vs. Semiauto" argument. I was very happy with the position, as I sincerely believe that a high-quality semiauto is the best option for a defensive shotgun. They are faster than a pump action to cycle and operate. But more importantly, machines do not have emotions and because a semiauto is not depending on a panic-stricken human to operate it in a stressful fight situation, they are more reliable for most shooters.

The tendency with most people under stress is to try to go faster and that will often result in short stroking a pump action and jamming the gun. The semiauto can't panic and it will usually keep running no matter how stressed out you become. Of course training and experience can overcome much of this, but it can't eliminate human error.

My friend Sheriff Jim Wilson from Texas, another writer for NRA publications, took the pump side. Jim has a wealth of experience in law enforcement and has been in a few shootouts, so he speaks from experience. He favors the pump and took very willingly to defending that style shotgun.

We talked it over and decided to have some fun with a made up "feud" between gun writers. Jim focused on my competition background (while ignoring all the training for defense I have done over the years) while I poked fun at his age, even though he is only a decade older than me.

(Of course I might point out that an old guy, who spent his life in a dangerous profession, probably has a reason he got old. It's certainly not because he lost any of those gun fights.)

I could not resist adding to my section a little bit for the book. Magazines work on very strict word counts, so I had to cut a lot from my article. I added most of it back in here for the book, plus a little more, as it's important information to a prepper. That's the reason my section is so much longer than Jim's, which remains pretty much as he submitted it to the magazine.

▲ Jim Wilson with a borrowed repeating rifle, trying to prove he is hip and happening. Photo courtesy of Jim Wilson.

I include the articles here, not because I dislike pump shotguns, but because I felt both of our arguments were valid. The goal here is to provide all the information available to help you decide which guns are best for you. If you are buying a shotgun for prepping, you need to look at all the options. Here are two old shooters' opinions about some of them.

## Make Mine a Pump

### By Jim Wilson

▲ Pump-action shotguns dominate with tactical shooters.

Folks, you are just going to have to overlook my friend Bryce Towsley and his argument supporting the autoloading shotgun. I suspect that those long winters in Vermont have finally gotten to Ol' Bryce and begun to affect his judgment. Nice fellow, though, he's just a bit misguided.

The biggest mistake that Towsley makes is basing his opinion on his experiences in competition shooting. The defensive shooter needs guns that are as reliable as it is humanly possible to manufacture and guns that are easy to understand and easy to operate. That is the reason that the venerable pump is still the defensive shotgun to choose.

The first consideration of the defensive shotgun should always be reliability. A fighting gun simply must function and the pump shotgun will do this under the most adverse conditions. The pump shotgun will continue to function in spite of dirt, burned powder, and lack of lubrication. The pump gun will still be running long after the autoloading shotgun has gone belly up from lack of attention.

Bryce fails to realize that competition shooters have plenty of time between stages to add a little lubrication to their shotgun, clean the gas ports, and replace broken parts. In the middle of an engagement, the defensive shooter simply does not have this luxury. Bryce also makes a big deal about the large number of rounds of light birdshot loads that he has run through his favorite auto. I would simply suggest that he run that same number of high-velocity buckshot and slug loads through an autoloader and see if it can remain problem free.

Another reliability value of the pump shotgun is that it will handle ammunition that would have an auto hiccupping in no time at all. A couple of years ago I was invited to test a new autoloading shotgun on a bird hunt in South America. This was a very nice

shotgun and it had functioned extremely reliably with American ammunition. However, the designers had not taken into account the poor quality of some South American shotgun shells. There were about eight of us on this hunt and every one of us had numerous malfunctions due to the sorry ammunition. However, these same shotgun shells fed reliably in pump shotguns. In times of trouble, one may not have much choice as to what quality of ammunition he is able to get his hands on. It is comforting to use a gun that will handle virtually all of it.

*(Note: Jim has a very valid point here, particularly if you select a conventional gas-operated semiauto. In a survival situation we may need to use the ammo we can find, not the ammo we want. While it's unlikely that we will be forced to use that ratty stuff he found in South America, there are some pretty poor shotshells being sold in the states as well. For the most part they are imported ammo and if you stick with brand-name, American-made fuel for your shotgun you should be fine. But, as a prepper, you must plan for all scenarios. The newer semiautos like the inertia driven Benelli or the Remington VERSA MAX with its unique gas system are very tolerant of fouling. But, any semiauto is more susceptible to failure from crappy ammo than a pump.)*

In all fairness, I have to say that auto shotgun manufacturers have made and continue to make, great improvements in the reliability of their products. In fact, these new guns are almost as reliable as pump shotguns have been for years. But I'm sorry folks, in a gunfight "almost" just isn't good enough to suit me.

A second factor that supports pump shotguns for personal defense is ease of function. While gun handling is a subjective thing, most shooters will find the pump shotgun easier to understand and easier to manage.

*(Another valid point.)*

Much is often made about the tendency of a shooter to short-stroke a pump gun when the shooter is under stress. However, failing to properly function the pump is not a design flaw, it is a training flaw. It is amazing, when properly trained, how few shotgunners will short-stroke a pump.

Because shotguns don't have a very large magazine capacity, it is important for the defensive shooter to know how to quickly reload the shotgun. Again, the

▲ Jessica Stevens from Barnes Bullets finishes a pump shotgun drill.

pump shotgun shines. It is dead simple to learn to palm a shell into the shotgun's open ejection port, run the support hand forward to the pump, and get back into the fight.

The competition shooter will probably never be required to transition from buckshot to slugs in the middle of an engagement. (Not true, it happens all the time in 3-gun and tactical shotgun matches.) Yet this is a very possible situation for the defensive shooter to deal with, and the ability to do this is one of the things that makes the shotgun such a great defensive tool. With an autoloader, the shooter is faced with using fine motor skills as he tries to find the little action-release button and one should avoid having to use fine motor skills in any sort of deadly confrontation. On the other hand, the Select-Slug drill is accomplished with a pump shotgun using gross motor skills, as the whole support hand uses the pump to function the action and facilitate the transition.

A third factor that favors the pump shotgun as a defensive tool is cost. Suitable defensive pump shotguns can be purchased for a good deal less cash than a comparable autoloader. And, most importantly, the money that one saves can be properly spent on practice ammunition and defensive training tuition.

*(Again, Jim has a good point here. The cost of a decent pump-action shotgun is far lower than the price of a good semiauto. Also, as noted earlier and probably again later, if you do select a semiauto shotgun for your defensive shotgun, you should only buy the best. Cheap semiauto shotguns are often unreliable. If money is a big issue, buy a brand-name pump shotgun and odds are it will give you little trouble. Jim is right about training as well. As my competition-shooting buddy Pat Kelley likes to say, "the best accessory you can buy for your gun is ammo. The way you get better at shooting is by shooting." It's always best to get some formal training to help build a strong foundation for that shooting.)*

Better yet, one has only to visit any gun show or gun shop to see the large number of perfectly serviceable used pump shotguns that are available. And let me share a little secret with you, your shotgun does not have to have synthetic stocks to make it suitable for personal defense. The wooden ones will work just fine. Any competent gunsmith can easily and quickly shorten the barrel of this used shotgun to a manageable

18 to 20 inches, thread the muzzle for choke tubes, and add ghost-ring sights, should that be desired.

*(Replacement barrels for most pump shotguns are inexpensive, probably even cheaper than paying a gunsmith. That leaves the first, longer barrel to use for foraging and hunting.)*

So there you have three arguments that favor the pump shotgun for personal defense. It is more reliable, it is easier for most people to learn to handle efficiently, and it costs a good deal less than an autoloader.

Soldiers, lawmen, and gunfighters first recognized the value of the pump shotgun as early as 1900. It is still being used by most soldiers, lawmen, and gunfighters because it is reliable, dependable, and meets their needs. In short, it does its job and it does that job well.

Poor Brother Towsley, on the other hand, has made the mistake of comparing competition to personal defense. Competition shooting is great fun and it is a great way to test and improve one's shooting skills. Unfortunately, it does not teach one how to fight, nor does it test one's ability to fight. The disciplines are different and therefore the tools are often different.

So when you see Bryce and me sitting in a dark bar during the NRA annual meeting or at the SHOT Show, please know that we are not goofing off and avoiding our responsibilities. You should just know that I am doing my best to straighten him out on fighting shotguns.

## Smart Choices about Fighting Shotguns

### By Bryce M. Towsley

▲ Two empty hulls in the air and a third in the gun ready to go—most can't do that with a pump. The author favors semiauto shotguns for competition and, under some circumstances, for defense.

*"Don't get stuck on stupid!"*
—General Russel L. Honoré to a reporter after
Hurricane Katrina

As shooters we do indeed tend to get "stuck on stupid" sometimes. Case in point, the continued reliance on the pump-action tactical shotgun.

That's not to say that my buddy Jim Wilson is stupid, quite the contrary, but what you need to understand about Jim and his love affair with antiquated gun designs is that he is an old man with old ideas.

In fact, Jim is one of those guys who was born an old man. He thinks single-action revolvers are the "cat's meow" and he hunts with a single-shot rifle, presumably because he believes that repeaters are still unproven technology. The word around the industry is that he writes his articles on parchment with a quill pen. Heck, based on all this, I'll bet Jim's truck still has a hand-crank starter.

Jim's writing in other articles about competition shooting is filled with confusion. For example, much of it is focused on PPC, a sport that was popular for training back when dinosaurs were still roaming the earth and one that has nothing to do with modern action shooting.

He beats me up for using competition as a proving ground for defensive guns, but neglects that many of the elite fighting men in law enforcement and the military are right there beside me shooting in the same matches. In fact, every branch of the military now has a 3-gun team to help develop tactics and test equipment. There are techniques that were developed in 3-gun competition that were taught to military operators and used in Iraq and Afghanistan. Those techniques were credited with saving lives because they were so much more effective than the "old" way of doing things.

The matches are full of SWAT operators and elite military guys including Special Forces, Delta, and the SEALs. Why? Because they know that 3-gun and Tactical Shotgun Matches are proving grounds for fighting guns and techniques and are great training.

We left the revolver behind decades ago as a fighting handgun and now semiauto handguns predominate. When is the last time you saw a SWAT team member kicking in a door while holding a bolt-action rifle?

Again, semiauto rifles are the overwhelming top choice for anybody expecting trouble. But when it comes to our shotguns, we remain stuck on stupid while we stubbornly cling to nineteenth century technology.

Why?

Because the bad guy will hear you rack the action and it will scare him so much he will wet his pants, curl into the fetal position and placidly suck his thumb while he waits for the police to rescue him from the badass homeowner? Have you ever considered that perhaps you are watching too much television? Or that you spend way too much time on the Internet?

Speaking for myself, I would rather the bad guys didn't know where I am during a fight. Sorry, call me foolish, but I prefer not to gamble my life on a "sound" tactic.

Sure, the good guy in every TV show or movie will rack his pump in every scene, just to make that cool noise. But do you seriously think it's effective? Or intelligent for that matter? It's a myth perpetuated by Hollywood and lazy gun guys who keep repeating it without actually thinking it through.

First off, let's say that this guy has entered an occupied dwelling in the night and has advanced, looking for prey. Do you really think he will give up because he hears a shotgun pumping? This is not some wimpy NPR fund-raiser you are dealing with; it's probably a hardened, dangerous, and aggressive criminal. One who is likely armed. I don't want to give away my position by "racking" my pump.

The best way to survive this thing is to use stealth and surprise. Don't rack the action, yell out, "I have a gun" or even think about a warning shot. The first time he realizes you are there, your gun should be pointed at his center of mass and your finger should be on the trigger.

Racking the shotgun gives them an audible location and just might invite a swarm of hot, angry bullets to a party at your place. Racking a pump shotgun alerts the bad guys that you are armed, which I suspect might make them more cautious and faster on their own triggers when you encounter them. It also tells me that you didn't have a round in the chamber before your problems started. Bad tactics all the way around.

Forget the "sound" of the pump shotgun as a tactic. That's stuck on stupid.

Reliability? That's the same argument that the wheel gun guys used against semiauto handguns back in the day. Today there is not a bit of doubt that a semi-auto handgun in the hands of a competent operator is superior in every way to the revolver. Heck, even Jim carries a 1911 now and then, just to prove he is hip and happening.

But let's take a look at the 1911. When I started shooting Bulls-Eye with handguns competitively back in the Pleistocene Epoch I watched with horror as Gold Cup after Gold Cup jammed on the shooting line. I was well aware of the fact that there are no alibi runs in real life and it turned me off to the defensive use of semiauto pistols for decades. Today I understand that a properly made 1911 with good ammo is one of the most reliable handguns you can buy.

If you don't trust a 1911, buy a Glock; nobody argues against the reliability of that gun. The point is, technology has progressed. Today's semiauto handguns have become incredibly reliable. There is not one bit of doubt in most modern shooter's minds that a semiauto handgun in the hands of a competent operator is superior in every way to the revolver as a defensive handgun.

So why do you think a semiauto shotgun is unsuited for fighting? Technology has moved way past the old "Jam-O-Matics" of your daddy's era. We now have options on the operating systems that are far superior to some of the stoppage-prone early semiauto shotguns.

Of course, not every semiauto on the market is reliable, some suck. But the same might be said about rifles and handguns as well. For example, my son-in-law bought a new carry pistol from a well-known company a few years ago. Despite our best efforts, it simply would not run. So he sold it and bought a Glock G23, which runs 100 percent. Does that mean we should condemn all semiauto pistols because that one sucked? Of course not. Anybody not stuck on stupid knows that not every semiauto on the market is reliable. Jim clearly used one of the "sucky" guns on his hunt in Argentina. Then again, given his age, they were likely shooting black powder, which does tend to foul up the gas ports of any shotgun.

It's the same with semiauto shotguns as any other firearm; some work, some don't. One good clue is to look at the guns being used for 3-gun competition and

Tactical Shotgun matches. If a shotgun stands up to serious action shooting competition, you can be sure it's tough enough for defensive use too. No sport in the history of the world stresses a shotgun more and those with inferior capabilities are very quickly left behind, shattered, broken and sobbing with shame along the muddy road of progress.

Just as with the handguns and rifles, a modern semi-auto, tactical shotgun is extremely reliable. In fact, they are more reliable than a pump-action shotgun, which relies on human interaction to operate.

▲ A competition shooter puts a lot of ammo through a shotgun.

I might also point out that few 3-gun shooters use "light birdshot" loads as Jim suggested. A great many targets are steel and must be knocked over or off a stand and light loads do not work well. Yes, it's true that a lot of the shooting is with birdshot loads, the most popular load is 1 1/8 ounce of shot at 1,200 ft/s, which is not a wimpy shotshell. We also shoot a lot of slugs and a few buckshot loads. In 3-gun competition it is very common to switch from buckshot to slugs and back to birdshot, all in one stage and all on the timer. It's fair to say that at some matches a 3-gun shotgun will see more action, including slugs and buckshot, in one stage than it would in a dozen gunfights, all without time out for maintenance.

Three-gun competition simulates battle and if pumps were better, the pump-action shotguns wouldn't need their own division to be competitive. Jim's contention that the sport allows time to work on the guns just shows he is not a 3-gun shooter. I think he is confusing

3-gun with skeet, or perhaps trap, probably from back when they still used round, glass balls for targets.

There is no time to clean guns at most matches. I run my guns from start to finish without cleaning, sometimes even multiple matches without cleaning or maintenance. One exception might be the finely tuned Open Class guns, particularly the magazine-fed shotguns. They do require a lot of maintenance. Many of the Saiga shotgun shooters have to make the time to clean between stages to keep the gun running. What that proves through competition is that not all shotguns are suitable for defensive use. I have never seen a Saiga that has been tuned for competition that was reliable enough that I would consider using it for defense.

That said, 3-gun shooters can't leave well enough alone. It's not uncommon for them to "tune" reliable shotgun designs until they won't run.

At the 2011 Superstition Mountain Mystery 3-gun match I listened to one competitor as he explained to another an elaborate and complicated process of milling parts and pieces on the operating system for the guy's Benelli shotgun. "If you do all that it will run without a hitch," he smugly finished. The other guy looked at him like he had two heads and said, "It runs without a hitch right now, why on Earth would I want to mess with that?" I'm with that guy! I have seen too many modified shotguns go on strike in the middle of a stage, including several at that match.

My point is, I can't comment on how well the Saigas will run without anybody trying to "improve them" by tinkering and tuning. While I was the first American to ever fire that shotgun when I was at the factory in Russia, years before they started importing them, I have never owned one. By the time I started writing this book, Obama had used his pen and his phone to ensure they are no longer imported, so I was unable to secure a gun to test.

I can, however, comment on the guns I know. I used my first semiauto Benelli competition shotgun for several seasons of serious shooting. I would guess conservatively that I have somewhere in the neighborhood of twenty-five thousand payloads down the barrel. Most have been birdshot target loads, the kind that are prone to malfunction in a semiauto. But I have also fired several thousand slugs and buckshot rounds as well. The gun has gone hundreds of rounds between cleaning,

and I have used it in grueling matches like the MGM Iron Man when high winds and blowing sand filled every crack and crevice with grit and grime. I have also used semiautos in rain, mud, snow, ice and just about every other conceivable condition while hunting. Conditions that would make a Spartan sob in frustration, but the guns keep working. That competition gun has digested birdshot, buckshot, and slugs and never had a single jam with factory-loaded ammo. I am still using it today and have put about three thousand rounds through it in the past few months. It should be worn out, but it just keeps working. I have never even replaced a part other than the magazine spring. I don't know how much more proof we need that technology has improved the reliability of semiauto shotguns to the point where it should no longer be an issue.

Jim's statement that "the competition shooter will probably never be required to transition from buckshot to slugs in the middle of an engagement" is further proof that he is confused about what we do in modern action shooting. Confusion is something that happens to older people and I don't hold it against him. Switching from one load to another in the "heat of battle" is something we do all the time. He also mentions loading a single round in an empty gun. The semiauto is much faster because the action is already open, so there is no need to pull back on the operating handle and then close it again by hand after you load the shell. Just toss in the shell, hit the release, and shoot. Much faster. Those of us who practice this technique with a Match Saver, or a hand-held shell, can reload and shoot in less than a second, including reacting to the buzzer, so actual loading time is about half a second. Try matching that speed that with a pump. If you are worried about manipulating a small release button, just install a larger one as most 3-gun shooters do on their guns.

The human is the weak link in an operator-dependent, pump shotgun. When things are happening fast it's very common for a shooter to short stroke the gun and jam it up. Time and time again I have witnessed shooters, even highly trained shooters, who are trying to go fast, short stroke a pump-action shotgun. I have done it myself and I love pump shotguns and train with them often. (I never said they were a bad idea, just that there are better options.) A semiauto is not dependent on the operator working the action correctly and so is not as subject to operator errors.

Speed? Semiautos again have the advantage here. Many of the big 3-gun and tactical shotgun matches will run a side match in which everybody competes head to head and winner takes all. Usually the side match uses multiple targets, which are all shot from one position. Nobody has to run or jump or reload the shotgun on the clock. So, it's not about physical fitness or hand coordination or loading technique, it comes down to shotgun shooting speed only. The fastest gun to shoot all the targets wins the match and the semiautos always win. Pumps can come close, but they don't win . . . ever.

Price? Well, I concede that the pump action will win that one. If you can't afford a good semiauto, buy a pump. In my opinion you will not have the best fighting shotgun available, but you will have the best fighting shotgun you can afford.

But I would refer back to my days racing motorcycles and the catch phrase we had regarding helmets. (Remember, it was many inflation-filled years ago.)

"If you have a ten dollar head, then buy a ten dollar helmet."

The implied message was that if you value your head and its contents, you must buy the best helmet you can find, not the cheapest. I would offer that the same applies to fighting shotguns. If you value your life, doesn't it make sense to buy the best fighting shotgun you can find regardless of the price?

Trust me, once you perform an intelligent analysis of all the variables, that gun will be a semiauto.

So when you spot Jim and me in a bar at SHOT or NRA you can be sure of two things. That I will be sipping good bourbon and Jim will be talking while I am pretending to listen. I found that with old men going on about the "good old days" usually it's best to just let them ramble.

## A Brief History of the Remington Pump-Action Shotgun

### *How the most popular shotgun got started.*

The first American slide-action or "pump" shotgun was made by Spencer Arms in 1882. Winchester picked

▲ The Winchester 1897 is an early pump-action shotgun and it paved the way for today's tactical shotguns.

up on the concept with the Winchester Model 1893. That gun proved problematic and was soon replaced with the Model 1897, which became a million seller. Marlin had the 1898 model and it was clear that the pump-action shotgun was here to stay.

Remington was undergoing some hard times back then. In 1886 the company had been placed in receivership and remained there for two years. In 1888, Hartley & Graham, owners of Union Metallic Cartridge Company (UMC) and Winchester Repeating Arms joined forces and acquired joint ownership of E. Remington and Sons. They renamed it Remington Repeating Arms Company.

Now Winchester, their main rival, owned half of Remington Arms Company, which explains why Remington never entered the lucrative lever-action rifle market. In fact, in 1892, Remington let a guy named Arthur Savage use their facilities to develop his lever-action rifle. It could be assumed that they wanted to produce the gun, yet they never introduced it. Instead, Savage formed his own company and the Model 99 Savage rifle is one of the most historically important and successful lever-action rifles ever made.

Winchester also was preventing Remington from entering the emerging pump-action shotgun market and not allowing them to produce a slide-action shotgun to compete with Winchester. Their association ended in 1896 and that freed Remington to start development of a gun in preparation of entering the pump-action shotgun market.

A few years later a Denver-based gun designer named John D. Pedersen was issued patents for a unique pump-action shotgun. Remington soon joined with him, launching one of the more historic partnerships in gun history. As with Browning and Winchester, Pedersen became synonymous with many Remington gun designs.

Remington announced its first pump-action shotgun under Pedersen leadership in 1908. They named it the Remington Model 1908 Repeating Shotgun and announced it would be ready for delivery in the early part of . . . you guessed it, 1908!

In 1909 the Remington Catalog listed the gun as a Pump Action Repeating Shotgun, with no mention of a model number 1908. In 1911 the name was changed to the Model 10. That gun had a good run in spite of the fact it had some strength and design issues.

In 1921 Remington announced the John Browning–designed Model 17 in 20 gauge. (That design was later adapted by Ithaca into the Ithaca Model 37.)

The Model 10 was replaced by the Model 29 in 1929. But that shotgun had a short run. When Dupont took over Remington in 1933 they dropped the Model 29.

The Model 31 came out in 1931, during the Depression. It was a fine shotgun, but struggled to compete with the Winchester Model 12. The Model 31 was Remington's first side-ejecting repeating shotgun. It was made in 35 variations and was used by the military during World War II for aerial gunnery training.

The war interrupted everybody and when it ended the new generation of hunters was champing at the bit to find a shotgun that would define them. Remington was ready to launch that gun.

# America's Number One Pump-Action Shotgun

*The Remington 870 has been kicking ass for sixty-five years.*

▲ Remington 870 Tactical.

The year was 1950. President Truman sent our first troops into North Korea, North Korea invaded South Korea, and Americans were watching the *Texaco Star Theater* on television. Movie theaters were showing *King Solomon's Mines* and radios were playing "Mona Lisa" by Nat King Cole. The first credit cards were introduced and Remington brought out a pump-action shotgun that would make history.

As we are constantly reminded in the media, it was a simpler time. World War II was over and we won, the Depression was fading from memory, and the average annual salary was a whopping $3,210. People were feeling good about the country and the future. Gas was eighteen cents a gallon, inflation was 1 percent, a new car cost $1,500, and this new shotgun would set you back $80. Shooters recognized the value and with anticipation of nothing but better times ahead, the Remington Model 870 sold well.

With the idea to use parts from the Remington Model 11–40 autoloader, the design team of L. Ray Crittendon, Phillip Haskell, Ellis Hailston, and G. E. Pinckney developed a new pump-action shotgun. Introduced in 1950, this shotgun was called the Model 870 Wingmaster. It became the single bestselling firearm ever produced by Remington and the best-selling pump-action shotgun in firearms history.

The Model 870 breechblock locked into the hardened barrel extension for a strong lock-up. The dual slide bars made for a smooth, bind-free operation.

This five-shot gun was easy to take down for cleaning and was offered with replaceable barrels, so it was extremely versatile.

It would be all but impossible to list every variation that has been offered in the Model 870 over the years, but it has been configured for every use possible with a shotgun and just about every finish. Stocks have been wood, very good wood, synthetic and even folding wires. The finish has run from deep, high-polish blue to camouflage. Hunting, self-defense, military, law enforcement, and every single form of competition that uses shotguns has seen an 870. Hunters even have a rifled-barrel Model 870 shotgun for shooting sabot slugs.

The Remington Model 870 was the first pump-action shotgun ever to be offered in all five popular shotgun chamberings. Starting with the .410 (not actually a "gauge") through the 28, 20, 16, and 12 gauge. It's even offered in 3 ½-inch 12-gauge magnum. (I have one; it's my "go-to" turkey gun.)

Sales of the Remington Model 870 reached a million guns in 1966 and two million guns by 1973 (ten times the number of Model 31 shotguns it replaced). In 1978 it passed three million. In 1984, four million, five million was in 1990. By 1993 it reached six million. Seven million were sold by 1999. On April 13, 2009, the ten millionth Model 870 was produced. Today Remington has sold more than eleven million Model 870 Pump Action Shotguns.

The 870 has dominated every single shotgun shooting sport or discipline at some time. Trap, skeet, sporting clays, action shotgun, or 3-gun, it doesn't matter. If a competitor is shooting a pump shotgun then odds are high that it's a Remington Model 870.

In 1950, Remington field rep Rudy Etchen took one of the first twelve production Model 870 shotguns to the Grand American Trap Championships. He became the first shooter to ever break a registered one hundred straight targets with a pump-action shotgun. The 870 became his gun of choice after that and he competed with it so much his nickname became "Mr. 870."

Rudy made it into the Trapshooting Hall of Fame while shooting an 870. In 1982 he pulled that original thirty-two-year-old 870 out of storage for a "little practice" and shot another one hundred straight. In fact, Rudy shot so many one hundred straights over the years with an 870 that he lost count.

The Model 870 is still one of the favorite shotguns of hunters for upland, turkeys, waterfowl, and even deer, as this gun is a no-compromise choice for those who love pump-action shotguns.

The pump-action shotgun remains the top shotgun for defensive use, both with law enforcement and civilians. The low price, rugged dependability, and the ability to shoot just about any type of ammo from less-than-lethal to full-blown, magnum buckshot make it the top choice. Of the pump-action shotguns that are used by gun-savvy people putting their lives on the line, the Remington Model 870 is by far the front-runner. More shooters trust this gun to protect their lives and the lives of others than any other shotgun on the market.

That alone is a testament to the trust this American classic shotgun has earned over the past sixty-five years.

The Remington Model 870 is the gun to which all other pump-action shotguns are compared. While there are a lot of good pump-action defensive shotguns on the market, no prepper can go wrong with an 870.

While the vast majority of these shotguns have been sold to wing shooters and the guns used for blasting flying targets, both feathered and clay, the 870 has always had a fighting side. Even back in the simpler times of that first year of production in 1950 there was a Model 870R Riot Grade with a 20-inch barrel. Actually, what we now call a "tactical shotgun" went by "riot gun" until the Rodney King mess. That's when it was realized that we no longer try to stop riots for fear of offending somebody, so the name had to be changed. No matter, the design is pretty much the same: a short-barrel, full-length extended magazine and a color scheme designed to make it look menacing.

For decades this style of shotgun was sold primarily to law enforcement and military. It was assumed that the civilian market either wasn't interested or couldn't be trusted. But then, simpler times are long past and times now are complicated, uncertain, and a bit scary. The concept of a civilian fighting shotgun, while maybe still not completely embraced by some manufacturers, has definitely taken hold with the gun-owning masses. The Model 870 Remington has emerged as the premiere shotgun for this use.

Right or wrong, many believe that pump-action shotguns are more dependable than semiautos. Many have also been convinced that the sound of a slide-action being worked will release the bowels of anybody intending to do us harm and send them squirming away, never to darken our doors again. But perhaps the most important reason is that the 870 is tough, dependable, and very affordable.

An entire industry has sprung up around converting these shotguns into fighting tools. Magazine extenders, pistol grips, tactical stocks, and forends, along with sighting systems, oversized safeties, and attached ammo carriers ensure the Model 870 does not suffer from a lack of bolt-on accessories designed to make it a better fighting shotgun.

Remington offers a wide range of configurations suitable for survival situations, but for a do-it-yourself kind of shooter the door is wide open with aftermarket accessories for the Model 870. There is no other shotgun with as many options for bolt-on changes. You can easily configure the gun to exactly what you want in a defensive shotgun.

Any prepper should have a shotgun or two and dollar for dollar, it's pretty hard to find one better than the Remington Model 870.

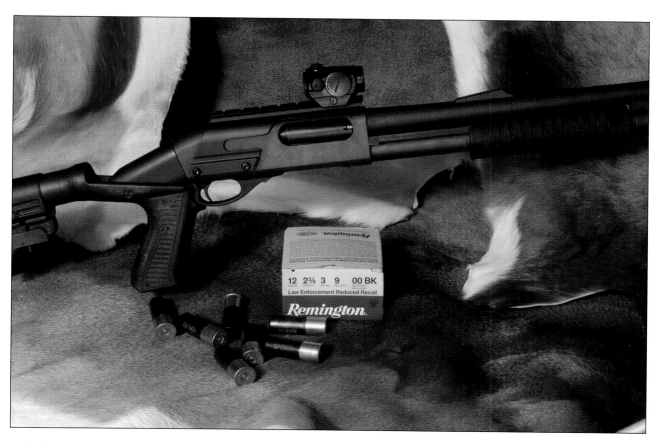

▲ The Remington Model 870 is a great defensive shotgun.

# Semiauto Options

*Got problems with your semiauto shotgun? It's probably because it has gas.*

▲ The author shooting a Benelli M2 shotgun in 3-gun competition.

rom a tactical application, the biggest problems with a semiauto shotgun come from heat and dirt. It's one thing if your shotgun goes on strike in the middle of the duck blind. You can take the time to fix the problem and at most you will need to put some money in the swear jar when you get home, but a prepper who is depending on his gun to stay alive doesn't have that luxury. If the gun stops working in the middle of a fight for your life, the least of your worries will be your language.

Usually when I am writing about tactical shotguns and advocating for a semiauto it is with the issues of a civilized world in mind: a home invasion, robbery, or the similar issues we may face in normal times. A prepper is preparing for more drastic situations. We

▲ This Benelli M2 has been modified for 3-gun but can be used for defense as well.

might not be defending our homes against a couple of home invaders; it might be a big, angry horde of people. While the issues of the past could be settled with a relatively small amount of ammo, a rioting crowd bent on killing you and taking your food is another situation. You may need a gun that will keep running even after it's been shot so much that the heat of the barrel is charring the forend. You may need a gun that can shoot not dozens, but hundreds of rounds without stopping. I am not entirely sure that shotgun exists, pump or semiauto. There is little question, however, that some have a better chance than others of surviving the abuse.

Most semiauto shotguns were designed for hunters and hunters simply don't shoot as much or as fast as you may need to in a tactical situation.

▲ Dove hunting stresses a shotgun.

The possible exception might be dove hunters in South America. Those guys pound shotguns and only a very few can stand up to use there, particularly the rental guns that see almost constant shooting day in and day out.

Only one really stands out—Benelli. There are a few others that seem to hold their own; Beretta is one, but the top choice is the Benelli. It's also the top gun for 3-gun and tactical shotgun shooting as well. If anybody puts more ammo through a shotgun in a shorter period of time than a competition shooter, they have escaped my notice.

The problem with most shotguns is that they use a gas system to operate the shotgun's action. Usually there is a port in the barrel that will bleed off some of the propellant gas and direct it into the operating system. Rifles use this same concept, but have far fewer problems. One reason is that a rifle operates at much higher pressure, so the ports are smaller and don't let the volume of fouling crud pass into the guts of the gun.

Another difference is that shotgun shells have much different internal ballistics. They have a lot of "stuff" going down the barrel with wad material, shot buffer, etc. These shed particles and combined with the unburned powder and fouling from the burned powder can result in a lot of debris traveling down the barrel. Also, because shotshells are low-pressure rounds, they tend to not burn the propellant powder as cleanly, which creates more fouling. As a result, these gas systems tend to choke up with crud. When that happens, the gun stops running.

▲ This Benelli M2 is a good choice for defensive use.

## Benelli

The Benelli system works off the inertia and there is no port in the barrel to bleed off gas filled with debris. The inertia of the bolt trying to stay in place when the gun fires and recoils, loads a spring with energy and, through a series of events, that energy operates the shotgun.

Everything that leaves the shell leaves the barrel and no gas is used to operate the gun. That means that all the operating parts are protected from dirt and fouling. So they keep running because they don't get clogged up. That and they are very well made, so they don't break down as often as some other designs.

I have used the Benelli M2 inertia-driven gun for 3-gun shooting for several years. My first gun has maybe twenty-five thousand rounds through it and it's still running fine. But that is nothing compared to what my buddy James Darst has put through his M2. "Pallets and pallets," he said when I asked how many rounds he had through that gun.

The Benelli problem is that, with the import laws and the politically correct European executives in charge, you can't buy an M2 configured for tactical use. But if you are willing do some modifications, this is a gun that will run and can do a good job as a survival shotgun.

The Benelli M4 tactical shotgun uses a different operating system. I have less experience with this gun, but it has a good reputation with law enforcement and military. The same Benelli problem applies; they won't sell a gun that's configured correctly for tactical use.

They just pretend it's a tactical gun. The M4 I have on loan has enough magazine tube length for at least seven rounds, but they block it so it only holds five, because five is a safe number that is common to hunting guns and management is much more comfortable with selling guns for hunting than fighting. It's convoluted and foolish thinking, but that's the way it is. In their defense, they also have to operate under some foolish American laws about how shotguns must be configured if they are to be imported.

Any Benelli you buy will require that you spend some money to bring it up to its potential. As they are already very expensive shotguns, this can be an issue with some preppers.

## Remington VERSA MAX

The Remington VERSA MAX shotgun uses a different gas system than their other shotguns, one that has similarities in concept with the Benelli M4.

The VERSA MAX has seven ports that are strategically placed in the chamber. These ports are located, sized and shaped to act as an "adjustment valve" for the shotgun's gas system. The simple genius is that the "valve" is controlled by the shotshell itself. When firing a 2 ¾-inch shell all seven ports are exposed. This allows the maximum amount of gas to bleed off and cycle the action. The longer 3-inch magnum shell blocks three of the ports, leaving four to bleed off gas and cycle the gun. With a 3 ½-inch shell, which is not only longer, but operates at a higher pressure, only one port is left exposed.

The gas is bled into a yoke attached to the bottom of the barrel under the chamber. This yoke contains

▲ The Benelli M4 Tactical Shotgun with a Zeiss red-dot sight.

two parallel tubes and in each tube is a rod that is machined so it has six rings or disks of steel along it to capture the pressure of the gas and push the rod. When the action is closed, the bolt pushes the rods forward. When the gun fires the gas bleeds into the yoke, pushes against the rings, and the rods are violently pushed back four-tenths of an inch to cycle the action. Once the last ring passes a port on the yokes, the gas is bled into the forearm of the shotgun and out a couple of ports on top, just ahead of the action.

There are no rubber O-rings on the rods to wear out, blow out, or add friction, just the steel rings. They are self-cleaning, as they scrape off the carbon and other debris with each pass and the shavings are blown out of the ports in the side of the yoke by the escaping gasses. However, they can also be disassembled for cleaning. This gun will keep running when dirty and hot and will last a long time with normal use.

There may be other semiauto shotguns on the market that can handle the abuse and stand up to sustained fire over a long period of time, but these are the guns I have used and abused and know I can trust.

If any prepper wants to go the semiauto route with a shotgun, these are guns they can trust.

# The Other Shotguns

*The mutts and misfits of tactical shotguns.*

▲ Ted Hatfield with a UTS-15 shotgun.

*M*ost of our shotguns are conformists. That is to say they pretty much look alike and it's easy to tell they are of a single species, with a few notable exceptions. The full-auto AA-12 comes to mind. Terry Crews ran one in *The Expendables* and it has to be the loudest shotgun on Earth. But forget it; the government doesn't trust you to have one.

Here is a look at some of the other shotguns, those that don't fit the traditional pump-action or semiauto mold.

## Pistol-Grip Shotgun

▲ Brendan Burns shooting a pistol-grip shotgun.

This gun looks cool. Who can forget Sarah Connor in *Terminator 2: Judgment Day* pumping her pistol-grip shotgun one handed? Pretty badass, right? (Actually that Remington 870 had a folding stock, which was folded up to run as a pistol grip.)

But the trouble with a pistol-grip shotgun is it's almost impossible to hit anything with it. It's true that with a lot of practice you can develop some skill, but you will never as good as with a gun fired off the shoulder.

▲ Pistol-grip shotguns look cool in the movies, but are a poor choice for self-defense.

I bought a pistol-grip shotgun in the '80s and have shot hundreds and hundreds of rounds through it so I do speak with some experience. It's fun to shoot, but as a fighting gun it's not a strong option. It's okay for close range, but that's about it. It's not the gun I would pick to bring to any fight. As far as foraging with it? I have used it a bunch to shoot clay targets and would never consider it a serious wing-shooting shotgun. Mine mostly gets used to shoot snakes in my yard. It's overkill, but a fun way to take them out. I know that cops and elite military units use them to blow out door locks, which might be the only tactical situation when they are useful.

▲ A pistol-grip shotgun looks cool in the movies, but it is a poor choice when fighting for your life.

The truth is a pistol-grip shotgun serves okay for defensive encounters across small rooms and to look cool for Hollywood. For serious work where your life is on the line, get a shotgun with a stock.

## Bullpup Shotguns

The bullpup design has the action behind the trigger, which makes for a shorter gun. There are lots of advantages to a shorter overall length: easier to carry, easier to enter and exit a vehicle, easier to manage in a confined space. The designs covered here hold a lot of ammo, at least when compared to other tube-fed shotguns.

Most of all, though, they look cool as hell. Hollywood loves this one too. The SUB is in *Jurassic World* as well as several other movies and television shows. Keanu Reeves puts the Kel-Tec KSG to serious use in the movie *John Wick*. That gun shows up in a lot of other movies and television shows as well and is a director's favorite. It's right up there with the pistol grip in "cool"

factor, but one big difference between the bullpup and the pistol-grip shotguns is the bullpup is actually an effective fighting shotgun.

## UTS-15

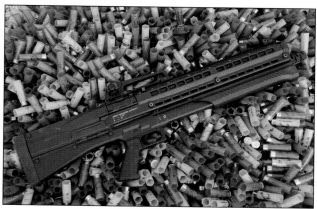

I feel some kinship to this pump-action shotgun. I first saw it at the IDEX arms show in Abu Dhabi, UAE in February of 2011. I was wandering around when I unexpectedly ran into my friend, Ted Hatfield. Ted was there introducing the gun and had a few prototypes with him. I had no idea he was there or that he was working on a new shotgun. The last time we talked he was making hunting shotguns in Turkey for import to the United States under several names like Smith & Wesson and Kimber.

That fall, NRA asked me to travel to Turkey to visit the factory and see what this gun was all about. We had a lot of fun during that trip, traveling around Turkey. (Ted is the kind of guy who knows the secret, back-alley doors to knock on to find a drink in a strict, Muslim-controlled Turkish city. He also knows the codes to use so they will let you through the door to get the drink. One night, we wound up in some guy's dark kitchen with a bunch of lapsed Muslims and drinking Raki. It was an underground bar right out of an adventure movie and I can also tell you that Raki is powerful stuff!)

There were a few growing pains with the shotgun, mostly due to our government and the Obama administration's anti-gun policies. They made Ted jump through a lot of hoops before he could import the gun and I think he finally gave up and started making it here in America. Ted is as tenacious as a bulldog and despite our government's efforts to stop him, he is now selling a serious defensive shotgun, one preppers would do well to take a look at owning. The fifteen-round magazine addresses one of the major deficiencies in a fighting shotgun—magazine capacity.

This rather unique, bullpup-style shotgun uses a two-tube magazine system. Each tube holds seven shells, plus one in the chamber for a total of fifteen shots. The magazine tubes can be used together, or separately. That means you can feed from both, with the gun automatically alternating side to side for a total of fifteen shots, or you can pick which tube to use. For example, you could have buckshot in one and slugs in the other and selectively decide which to use, depending on the situation. Changing magazines is as simple as moving the lever on top of the gun, which takes a fraction of a second. Or you can run all fifteen shots in a row with the gun alternating tubes with each shot until they are empty.

The bullpup design ensures that the gun is short and easy to maneuver in close quarters. It has a pistol grip (not to be confused with the pistol-grip-only shotguns covered above. This shotgun has a pistol grip in addition to a buttstock, similar to an AR-15 or AK-47 rifle). This allows holding the gun in one hand, ready to fire, while the other hand is free to open doors, turn on light switches, or throw a punch. The pistol grip also gives more control and a tighter hold on the gun if a bad guy tries to grab it from you.

The 18.5-inch smoothbore barrel is threaded for screw-in chokes with Beretta-style threads. Included with my gun was a cylinder bore, ported tactical "breeching" choke.

The gun's comb is straight and in line with the top rail, which means that the shooter's eye is positioned well above the line of the barrel. The UTS-15 is designed to be used with sights. Any sighting system that is designed for an AR-style rifle should work fine, as the rail and the offset are similar.

The gun has optional adjustable rear and front sights that mount on the top rail. The UTS-15 also has an optional, integral light and laser system to illuminate the target or help aim in poor light. This mounts below the barrel and the laser is nonadjustable.

▲ The UTS-15 shotgun in action.

The gun's construction makes use of fiber reinforced, injection-molded polymer to keep its weight down. It is only 28.3 inches long with a flush mount choke and it weighs 6.9 pounds. It is chambered for 2.5-, 2.75-, and 3-inch ammo.

The length of pull is just a foot, the idea being that it can be used while wearing body armor. The buttpad is held in with just a couple of easy-to-remove pins and the plans are to offer more options for a longer length of pull.

The rear "stock" is on a hinge so that it can be opened to access the simple feeding mechanism to clean, service, or to clear a jam.

This gun is a lot of fun to shoot and with its radical looks it is sure to gather a crowd anytime you break it out at the shooting range.

Then, of course, there is the "cool factor," which I think this shotgun wins over any other, hands down. It looks like what it is, a badass shotgun! No matter if it's hunting, target shooting, protecting your family, or fighting the zombie apocalypse, the UTS-15 does it with style.

## Kel-Tec KSG

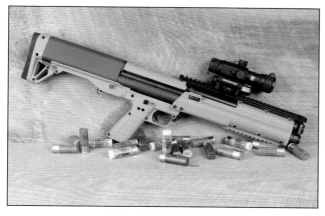

▲ Kel-Tec KSG shotgun.

The KSG (Kel-Tec Shotgun) is similar to their RFB rifle and is this Florida-based gunmaker's first shotgun.

It's a pump-action, bullpup shotgun with dual-magazine tubes that hold six rounds each. It weighs 6.9 pounds and is 26.1 inches long with an 18.5-inch cylinder bore barrel, so it's all government approved for civilians to be trusted to own. It's a compact and lightweight shotgun, which makes it a good choice for preppers on the go.

The gun feeds from either the left or right tube. The feed side is manually selected by a lever located behind the trigger guard. This allows the use of different loads in each tube.

There is a Picatinny rail on top as this gun is designed for use with optics. Also, the grip has a rail for mounting a light or laser, although it would be right in the way of your hand. Forward and rear sling loops are included and a simple sling comes with the gun.

So far I have been pleasantly surprised with this gun. While it's still relatively new, it has run everything I put in it with no issues or problems. That includes everything from light birdshot target loads, through full-power slugs and buckshot.

It's probably the most compact, high-capacity tactical shotgun you can buy.

## SRM Model 1216

▲ SRM Model 1216.

This is a semiauto version of the bullpup. Some argue it's not a true bullpup because the ejection port is above the trigger, not behind it, but that's splitting hairs. It's a short, compact, semiauto shotgun that holds sixteen shots in a removable magazine with four tubes of four shells each. You can have pre-loaded spare magazines, which can be swapped out quickly. The only downside is that after firing four shots you must manually index the magazine to the next tube.

On the other hand, in a tactical application you can select the tube loaded with the ammo you need, slugs, buckshot, or even less lethal. Once the magazine is

▲ Eric Reynolds shooting the SRM Model 1216 shotgun.

empty, pressing the release switch to drop the magazine allows it to be replaced with a full one in a few seconds.

The manual safety, charging handle, and ejection port can all be removed and relocated to either the left or right sides of the receiver to accommodate lefties. This gun is designed to run with sights and there are three Picatinny rails to allow mounting sights, lights, and lasers.

The action is a delayed blowback design. Mine is a little fussy about ammo and likes stout loads. Target loads or low recoil ammo will not always operate the action. But this is a very early gun and I am told that the current Gen II models have eliminated that issue and will run with just about any ammo.

The gun is 32 ½ inches long with a "government approved" 18-inch barrel and weighs 7.25 pounds. It is short, compact, easy to carry, and with a lot of firepower. They even make a full-auto version, but we citizens are not allowed by the government to buy one. The government can have them, but not us peons.

## Box Magazine-Fed Shotguns

▲ Shooting the Century Arms Catamount Fury shotgun.

In the world of fighting shotguns, this concept makes the most sense. You have a magazine-fed shotgun that can be re-fueled quickly by swapping magazines, just as with a battle rifle. The only trouble is that most of these guns can be a bit tricky about reliability. If they ever achieve the reliability of a pump or even a Benelli semiauto, they will rule the tactical world. But in my experience they are not there yet. They can run pretty well, but usually only with select ammo. That can present a problem for a prepper who may have to use the ammo available, rather than the ammo the gun demands. That said, when they run, these are badass fighting shotguns.

Perhaps the best known of these is the Saiga shotgun, manufactured by the arms division of Izhmash, in Russia. Think of it as an AK-shotgun.

In fact, I believe that I am the first American to shoot this gun. I visited the factory in Izhevsk, Russia in the late '90s and shot an early version of the Saiga shotgun. In typical Russian fashion it was loaded with very hot, magnum rounds and the recoil was unpleasant. I didn't think the gun would amount to much at the time, but that was before the boom in tactical guns in the United States and before most of us ever heard about 3-gun competition.

Most of my experience with the gun after that has been in 3-gun shooting, and it's a very rare Saiga that is reliable in that sport. That's the one thing that has kept it from dominating open class.

Of course most of the guns are heavily modified, so I don't know if it's the basic design, the modifications, or a combination of the two that is the source of the problems. It no longer matters, as Obama specifically targeted this gun with his pen and his phone and he stopped it from being imported. Executive Order 13662 issued on July 16, 2014, blocks the importation of all Izhmash products, including Saiga shotguns and rifles.

There is activity to manufacture the guns in the United States, but a phone call to the factory was met with a lot of suspicion and no information forthcoming about when or if the guns will be available. In fact, they were very uncooperative. I guess you can take the factory out of Russia, but you can't take Russia out of the factory.

There are other magazine-fed shotguns and the concept makes sense from a tactical standpoint, but so far the execution has not panned out. If these were the best fighting shotguns, they would dominate 3-gun and I am seeing a move back to tube-fed shotguns in Open Class. Of course, there are a lot of reasons that magazine-fed shotguns have not completely taken over 3-gun Open Class or defensive shotguns in general, but the main issue, at least with the Saiga, is reliability and quality. I know from talking with those who worked on the Saiga shotguns that tolerances were all over the map.

Another problem is that shotgun shells were never meant to feed from a box magazine. The rimmed shell creates problems. But never rule out anything when it comes to the ingenuity of the human mind. I fully expect to see magazine-fed shotguns reach a point of total acceptance and reliability one day.

Here are a couple of guns that I have been messing with. They are the same basic "AR" design, with a few changes here and there. The big thing is that, unlike the Saiga, they are currently available for sale in the United States.

I must admit I started out a skeptic, as the Saiga experience soured me on the design. While these shotguns do not run as well as I would like, they do run much better than I expected. Like any semiauto, they are a little bit fussy about ammo, but if you feed them what they like the guns run surprisingly well. It might simply be asking too much for any semiauto shotgun to run any and all ammo. Still, these came closer than I expected they would. They run full-power, defensive-type slugs and buckshot well, but balk a bit with light target loads. I will note, too, that the Catamount Fury is not broken in and that is important. The more I shot it, the better it ran.

I do need to qualify that by telling you I do not have huge amounts of trigger time with either of these guns— maybe one hundred rounds each. So my experience may not be indicative of their performance capabilities.

If a prepper is looking for a tactical shotgun to run any and all ammo available, then a pump is the only sensible option. Shotgun ammo varies a great deal in power levels and anytime you have a gun dependent on the ammo to operate the action you will have trouble making one size gun fit all ammo.

If you are looking for high performance and the highest sustained volume of fire from a shotgun, then using one of these magazine-fed shotguns makes sense. Just make sure they play nice with your ammo.

Any prepper looking for a magazine-fed shotgun might do well to check these guns out.

## The Century Arms Catamount Fury

The Catamount Fury is a Chinese-made tactical shotgun, based more or less on the AK design. It is imported and sold by Century International Arms.

▲ Eric Reynolds with the Century Arms Catamount Fury 12 gauge, magazine-fed shotgun.

It's a gas operated, piston-driven, semiauto 12-gauge that has an adjustable gas system so that the shooter can adjust for a wider range of ammo options. It handles 2 ¾-inch and 3-inch shells. It comes threaded for choke tubes and is supplied with cylinder, full, and modified tubes.

The gun comes with two five-round mags and one ten-round mag, while extra magazines are available. The magazines are rocked in as with an AK-47 rifle. That is, tilt the front in first and then rock the bottom back to click into place.

The gun has a 20.125-inch barrel, is 42.5 inches long, and weighs 8.7 pounds. My sample has a hunting-style stock, but the Fury II has a more tactical-looking, skeletonized stock with a pistol grip. It has

▲ Eric Reynolds with the Century Arms Catamount Fury 12-gauge, magazine-fed shotgun. Note the Mepro M21 self-powered sight. This type of shotgun benefits greatly with the addition of an optical sighting system. This sight does not need batteries and is a good choice for preppers.

crude open sights and a rail on top to mount sights or an optic. With the barrel well below the line of sight due to the gas system on top, these guns are best suited with sights or an optic anyway.

This is a very affordable gun and MSRP in 2015 is just under $600.

## VEPR-12

The Vepr-12 is an AK-style tactical shotgun made by Molot-Oruzhie Ltd in Russia. It's a mystery to me why this Russian gun is still available when the Saiga is not, but it is.

This gun has a magazine well and the magazines are pushed in straight, more like an AR design than the AK style that must be rocked into place. This will work out

better if you are an AR shooter and are used to this motion to switch magazines.

The gun has a rail on top and is equipped with adjustable sights. The rear sight is adjustable for long-range shooting, which is a bit odd on a shotgun. Clearly these are rifle sights installed on the shotgun, but it might be interesting to mess with slugs and the sight at long range to see how far you can hit with them. Like any of the AK-style shotguns, the best option will be with an optic like a red dot mounted on the rail. I have seen some of the top shooters in the world, including some Russian shooters, do amazing things with these guns and a red dot.

▲ Wolf Buckshot, also from Russia, proved to be a good match for this shotgun.

The barrel is threaded for choke tubes. The gun comes with one five-round magazine, but additional magazines holding eight, ten, or twelve rounds are available.

This is a more expensive gun than the Catamount Fury, costing about a grand in 2015. Its advocates tell me it's worth it and I have little reason to doubt them. The shooting I have done with the gun has proven to me that if you run ammo that gets along with this gun it will run great.

## Not a 12?

There is no question that the 12 gauge is the king of the tactical shotguns. It dominates the class almost completely, but with the prepper concept of trying to predict all scenarios, it might make sense to have shotguns chambered for other gauges.

▲ Savage Stevens Model 320 Security shotgun in 20 gauge.

The 20 gauge is the next most popular. There are a reasonable amount of different buckshot and slug loads on the market. It's a very popular hunting round and I see 20-gauge guns show up in 3-gun and tactical shotgun matches now and then, so the ammo is out there and may show up on the market in lean times. It makes sense to have at least one shotgun chambered for 20 gauge, just in case.

One that I have been using and like is the Savage Stevens Model 320 Security. This is an inexpensive tactical shotgun that thinks it is high dollar. It comes with a pistol grip, adjustable ghost ring rear sight, and a protected fiber-optic front sight. The 18.5-inch barrel is cylinder-bore and the magazine holds five rounds.

For a prepper who wants to try to cover all the bases and have a tactical 20-gauge gun on hand, this one works great and it won't break the bank.

# OTHER STUFF
## Body Armor

*For most body armor makers, your life is not important.*

▲ Eric Reynolds in a BulletSafe Ballistic Vest.

*I* don't claim to be an expert on this topic, but I figured that anytime we are in danger of being shot, body armor makes sense. Right? The cops have it, the military has it, and it makes sense as civilians that we should protect ourselves too. That's what freedom is all about, right?

After all, this is a defensive thing. It's for protection and in no way can it hurt anybody else if a law-abiding citizen has body armor. So, I was shocked at how many people think we should be prevented from buying something that can save our lives.

I spent a good bit of my time at the 2015 SHOT Show researching body armor, or at least trying to research body armor. Almost without fail, the people manning the booths I approached were standoffish and condescending right out of the gate. I assume that's because I had a press badge. As soon as I told them I was researching a book and wanted to talk about body armor options for civilians, their heads started spinning and they began to spew pea soup out of their mouths. You would have thought I told them I was selling Ebola samples and giving away memberships to ISIS.

Almost to a man (and a few women) they wanted nothing to do with civilians. Most would not even talk to me once I told them who I was and what I was doing. I suppose in their little minds they believed that selling to civilians would put their other contracts in jeopardy. Who knows, maybe it would. There is a very clear "them-against-us" mentality with a lot of law enforcement today and it was never more clear to me than at the SHOT Show.

One honest guy did talk with me off the record and told me I was right and that he agreed with me, but he added that his management did not and he would probably be fired for even suggesting that civilians should be able to buy body armor.

There is even a bill in Congress to ban body armor for civilians, H. R. 378. It wants to charge anyone with body armor with a felony and put them in prison for ten years, Seriously? For protecting yourself with a product that in no way hurts others?

I am not sure how much traction it's getting or what the current status is with this, but it makes a clear statement about what the government thinks about the value of civilian lives. I suppose a more extreme view is that they don't want civilians to be able to protect themselves from the government. Or maybe that's not so extreme; what other explanation is there?

The lesson from all this is that as a prepper you probably very much do need body armor. If this many people don't want you to have it, it's sending a message.

I know that there are companies on the Internet that sell body armor and it's not that hard to find. I know some of that is from third-party vendors who are selling it without the blessing or knowledge of the manufacturer, because I see it from at least two of the companies who told me their policy is no sales of their products to civilians. I think that maybe we need to think long and hard about the kind of people we are giving money to and support those who support us and American freedom.

After I got home I found a company that is very happy to sell to civilians and supports the concept that our lives are important, too. There may be others, but this one made it clear to me they want to help protect American citizens.

BulletSafe offers a vest with class IIIA protection. That means it protects up to a .44 Magnum and is the highest level available from soft armor. The vest has pockets front and back for plates that will protect against cartridges up to a 308-caliber rifle. Best of all, it's affordable.

It's a very good idea to also include plates for protection against rifle fire. BulletSafe sells ceramic plates, which is the standard with the military and law enforcement. Also, there are a few companies selling plates made from AR500 steel that will stop a .308 rifle round. These steel plates are less expensive than ceramic. I have a lot of AR500 targets and have seen how they hold up to rifle bullet strikes and that gives me some confidence.

I tried repeatedly to contact one of the biggest names in supplying AR500 plates and they would not return calls or emails. I know some other writer friends with the same experience, so again it comes down to spending money with companies who appreciate their customers.

▲ Installing the Spartan Armor Systems AR500 ballistic plates in a BulletSafe vest.

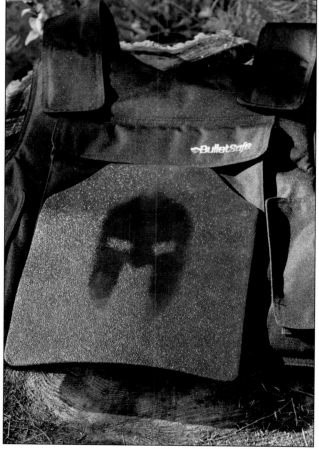

▲ Spartan Armor Systems AR500 ballistic plates.

I know that MGM targets is working on plates. I know the owners well and they are good people and strong supporters of the Second Amendment.

My plates were a Father's Day gift from my daughter and son-in-law. They are from Spartan Armor Systems. I have spoken with the owner and they are strong supporters of a civilian's right to buy body armor.

As I said, I am hardly an expert on this topic, but this is the gear I trust my life to. I am sure there are other good companies that make armor. I strongly suggest you find one that will work with you and that you buy some armor before the government decides you are not worth protecting.

It's going to seem like a waste of money if nothing happens and in hindsight it probably will be. At least you'd better hope it turns out to be wasted money. Nothing good can come from needing body armor. But a lot of bad can come if you don't have it and do need it.

Body armor is like truck insurance or fire extinguishers: When you need it, you will need it badly and by then it's too late to go find some.

# Guns for Bugging Out

*When the shit hits the fan nobody can predict the splatter pattern.*

▲ This bag weighs ninety pounds and has food, water, medical supplies, shelter, and fire-making gear. The guns that you bring ensure you get to keep that gear.

*I*n the world of understatement it might be a classic to say we live in uncertain times. Floods, fires, severe weather, social or economic collapse, and terrorism all hang over our heads like the sword of Damocles.

It's been proven time and again that in the real world, it's the self-sufficient, problem-solving person who survives, not the "victims" who beg for the government to save them and whine and complain when it does not.

It would appear more and more that it's not so much if disaster will find you, but when. There are times when it's best to hunker down, arm yourself,

and wait it out. But there are other times when you need to move and move fast. This chapter is about those times.

It doesn't really matter what—tornado, wildfire, hostile troops, or a raging mob—but something very bad is headed your way. You need to evacuate now, in fact now is almost too late. You have ninety seconds to get yourself and your family out the door, into your vehicle, and down the road.

(Let's be honest, it's not going to work for me. I can never find my damn truck keys!)

You could well be in for an extended stay away from home and you will probably be on your own. You can't count on "the social safety net" to protect you and feed you. Survival for you and your family in the next few days or even weeks depends on what is in the vehicle when you pull out of your driveway. But you have only seconds to load up.

You may not be able to find food, water, shelter, or safety unless you provide it yourself. You will probably encounter desperate people who may be armed. Law enforcement may not be around of if they are they may not be helpful. In fact, the opposite, it's far more likely that they will try to disarm you. Your family's only first responder is you, so be ready.

The first thing to remember is firearms; partly because this is a firearms book, but even more importantly because without them you have no way to protect the rest of your survival gear.

Back when Y2K was the next looming crisis, there was an exchange at a neighborhood Christmas party. One participant was a gun owner and an NRA member (me). The other was a social worker who is anti-gun (my neighbor). The social worker was talking about all the food, seeds, and water she had stored in preparation to the possible social collapse. The other guy, who may have consumed a few adult beverages in the spirit of the season, interrupted her and asked if she had any guns. She spat back at him with the predictable venom of a committed anti-gunner that she most certainly did not. Then she condescendingly asked him what he had done to prepare for the coming social collapse.

"Nothing," came the reply.

"You are a fool," she said.

"Maybe, but I am a fool with guns, so I'll just come to your house and take your stuff."

I was just yanking her chain and having some fun. I got a wifely elbow poke in the ribs for my trouble, but the message was clear. The social worker, in predictable liberal fashion, asked me to *"give"* her a gun a few minutes later.

Enlightenment is always a wonderful thing to witness.

For the record I turned her down. I did offer to help her buy a gun, but only if she would let me give her and her family some training and if she joined the NRA. That was the last I heard on the matter. Y2K passed with a whimper and she stuck her head back in the sand where it firmly remains today.

Now that we are facing a much more real possibility of social and economic collapse, she refuses to believe it. Like all true progressives, her faith is firmly behind the government and the system. Oh, yeah, she still hates guns.

I really don't expect people like her will do well after the collapse. It's like the Duke said, "Life is hard. But it's harder if you're stupid."

I know we all think that we will never leave our homes or retreats. We have prepared for disaster and plan to ride out any crisis there. But it can all change in a heartbeat, no matter who you are or how well you planned.

Don't think for a minute you are immune to a disaster that can force you from your home. I would use one of my close family members as an example. His house came under an evacuation order during the California wildfires some years back. He packed up his wife and young daughters and sent them to safety in a hotel several miles away. He, his adult son, and a few employees stayed and used the heavy equipment he owned to clear the trees and brush back away from the house, preventing the fire from reaching his home. Then they gathered the heavy equipment, the life's blood of his business, into a nearby open field and kept an armed watch over it to prevent looting. All the while they kept a 4x4 truck pointing out of the driveway, fully gassed up and ready to go at a moment's notice.

In the end they did have to deal with looters and managed to scare them off without shots fired, but if he had evacuated he would have lost thousands of dollars' worth of equipment. The police were no help. They couldn't have cared less about the looters. Instead they tried to intimidate the guys fighting to save the house. Every day they would come by and threaten them with arrest. They would also get on the loudhailer and shout things like, "We need a headcount so we know how many body bags to bring." But, looters? They didn't even want to talk about them.

In the end they saved the house and the business because my relative was resourceful and self-dependent. Some neighbors who simply trusted in the government returned to find everything they owned stolen or in ashes.

Those who believe in the nanny state will no doubt say they were fools to defy the evacuation order and to take things into their own hands. But this is a guy who runs a successful, multimillion dollar construction business. He takes risks every day that most of us would never consider. He is also smart enough to evaluate the risks and make the correct choices. Had he simply done what he was told by the government, his family might be living in a FEMA trailer right now.

Self-sufficient people with brains enough to make decisions built this nation. If you are going to survive a disaster you must be one of them. If you are going to act like a sheep, meekly follow every order, and expect the government to take care of you, life after TSHTF is not going to be pretty.

So for those of you in charge of your own lives, let's take a look at bugging out.

Full disclosure: I am a gear nut and a bit of a hoarder. In spite of decades of international travel and backcountry hunting trips I have never mastered the art of packing light. I am constantly fighting with airline clerks about the weight of my bags and there are packhorses and bush pilots reported to have put a contract on my head.

My bug-out bag is stuffed with a lot of gear and it continues to grow and evolve as I discover more things that I see as helpful. Right now, you almost need a crane to move it!

I am a big, strong guy and my plan is to get it to my truck, which is only about twenty feet away. If that fails, I can carry it long enough to get out of the immediate area (after all, I have carried a lot more weight when packing out moose quarters or backpacking to hunt sheep). Once I am in a safe area there are a lot of things that can be jettisoned to get the weight down.

I am tempted to go into a long and wordy dissertation on what should be in your bug-out bag, but I must remind myself that this is a gun book. So the focus will remain on the guns. Regardless of what is in your bug-out bag, you need to be able to protect yourself and your gear.

The quick version is that my bag has the food and gear I would take for an extended camping trip. Plus firearms.

▲ My bug-out bag has food and gear as well as guns.

It's important to remember, you cannot add anything you need once you bug out. You can always get rid of things, but it's all but impossible to add to the kit once you are out the door, so mine is stuffed full and heavy. That includes a pistol that stays in the bag at all times.

I have a full-size, 1911 .45 ACP handgun dedicated to this bag. This is a spare in addition to my normal carry gun. If I don't have the time or opportunity to bring my normal carry gun, this one is in the bag. If I do have my carry gun, this 1911 is a spare, which is never a bad thing. I keep it in the open center pocket section of the backpack, inside another small bag, where I can access it quickly. This bag can be removed and worn on its shoulder strap. That gives me easy access to the handgun, while adding a level of "diversion" camouflage. The bag is "tactical" looking, but doesn't scream "gun." The gun is a Smith & Wesson 1911 .45 ACP pistol, with four spare magazines (five total) and one hundred rounds of Federal 230-grain Hydra-Shok ammo. I also pack a holster and a couple of mag holders so I can transfer the pistol to my belt. There is a SOG SEAL Pup fixed-blade knife attached to the bag, which also can transfer to my belt. Guns are great, but at times I believe that a knife is the best survival tool you can have.

I also keep a Leatherman and a smaller fixed-blade Swedish FireKnife, which has a fire starter in the handle. As with firearms, redundancy is important in knives. One is never enough.

If you bug out, every adult in the party should have access to a long gun, rifle or shotgun, as well as their primary handgun. It's easiest if all the long guns are the same, so that ammo and magazines are interchangeable. The Brownells 3-Gun Competition Case is perfect for storing them. This soft bag has compartments to hold two long guns as well as the pistol, all the magazines, and some ammo. It also handles well, as it has backpack straps.

I don't believe you can have too much ammo, particularly if you are in a vehicle where weight is not a major issue. With my truck hauling the weight, I would pack a minimum of two hundred rounds for each gun, but more is better. One reason is that if this problem goes on longer than expected, ammo will be very good currency for barter. You will probably be able to trade it at a premium for food or medical supplies.

If you decided to bring a shotgun, it should be 12 gauge, as it will be much easier to find ammo if the crisis drags on for longer than expected. Any rifle should be a NATO chambering for the same reason. Civilians are not restrained on bullet selection as is the military, so

▲ Remington Model 870 modified for tactical use.

with good bullets, the .223 Remington should serve well for most of your survival needs. If this goes bad enough that you must forage for food, the .223 Remington will work even on big game, if you use selective bullet placement. It makes sense to pack a few boxes of ammo with hunting bullets like the Barnes TSX, Hornady GMX, or Federal Trophy Bonded Tip to use for foraging.

Every adult member of the group should carry at least one handgun on them at all times. One good option is to use your current carry gun, as that's what you know best. I suspect that most of us don't carry our handguns on our person while at home. You need to store them someplace, so why not get in the habit of storing your carry gun with your bug-out gear. It's right by the door anyway, so it makes sense. You come in that door when you arrive home so you can drop off your gun. You leave by that door when you exit, so you can gun up before heading out. If security is an issue, a small, tasteful safe will complement the decor of the room.

Make sure you have extra ammo and some extra magazines for the carry gun in the bag. Again, the more common cartridges make more sense. It's going to be easier to find 9mm, .40 S&W, or .45 ACP ammo than .38 Super or .45 GAP.

You have three goals here. Short term is to survive the day and perhaps the next few days. The second is, after the immediate crises have been dealt with, to survive until you can go home. That might be a few hours, a few days, or even a few months. Finally, you should also have a long-term plan just in case things are permanently FUBAR.

Did I mention I am a gear junky? If possible, I want to make sure I have lots of guns with me if I have to leave. My plans are to bug out by truck and my truck

can handle lots of weight. If I have time to get them out of the vault I have two other 3-gun competition bags full of guns. Each has an AR-15 M4-style carbine in 5.56 NATO with ten thirty-round magazines, a 12-gauge, short-barrel shotgun with an extended magazine, and a handgun with ten extra magazines. I also have another rifle case with an AR-10-style carbine in .308 and ten extra twenty-round magazines.

I have three hundred rounds of ammo for each gun ready to go. The shotgun ammo is split with 150 buckshot, one hundred slugs, and fifty rounds of birdshot for foraging.

This is a lot of guns and ammo and a lot of weight, but we are a large extended family group and I have a plan to meet at another location with several other family members in the case of a serious national emergency. We cannot be absolutely certain they will arrive with their guns and what I bring may be all the entire group has to survive with. I would much rather have the problem of too many guns and too much ammo, than not enough of either. Once again, guns and ammo will be worth a lot for barter.

There is overlap in any survival situation and the guns you use here will also serve to protect you at home. But you must remember that in a "bug-out" situation things are different and you must pick your guns accordingly. You will only have what is with you and if for some reason that's not working there is no option to switch. If you need another gun you can't go to the safe and get it like you can at your home or retreat. You can't grab some extra magazines or another box of ammo. If the shotgun isn't working, you can't just pick up a rifle. If your gun breaks you can't replace it. So it's best to select the best. Don't skimp on the guns; buy high quality. Also pick the model and cartridge carefully.

In many bug-out situations you will need to travel light, often with the guns you can easily carry. While I plan to load up my truck, there may not be time. Plus that approach puts a lot of guns at risk.

If there is a fast-breaking emergency and you have seconds to evacuate, your bare bones, "hit the door running" guns may be all there is to protect you and your family. In that light, the options must be weighed carefully when setting up your bug-out gear.

If you must bug out on foot and/or try to keep a low profile and fly under the radar of local law enforcement or nosy neighbors, you may be forced into bringing only your handgun, as it is easiest to conceal. Still, a rifle is far better to have for fighting and foraging. It's far easier to shoot a deer or even a rabbit with a rifle than a handgun. So even if you must keep a low profile, consider that you can take an AR-15 rifle and break it down so that it will fit out of sight in a backpack. Every situation is different and you must plan for what works best for you.

If you are on foot, every pound that you carry is important. That means fewer guns and a lot less ammo. So it is even more crucial that you choose carefully when preparing your bug-out guns.

## Long Guns

▲ When bugging out, you will be best served with an AR carbine and a high-capacity handgun.

This is your primary firearm for defense and for foraging, so a lot of thought must go into your choice.

If you are bugging out with one long gun, I think we can eliminate the shotgun rather quickly. It has a very limited range, even with slugs. While a specialty shotgun with a scope and rifled barrel using sabot slugs is capable of accuracy to 150 yards or farther, a smoothbore "tactical" shotgun with Foster-style slugs is reliable to about seventy-five yards at best. (Yeah, yeah; I know you can hit targets farther than that. But not with the precision needed and not under a wide range of stressful situations, and not every time.)

▲ Slugs weigh more and take up more room than rifle cartridges.

The ammo capacity of a shotgun is very low, five to eight shells for most tactical models, and they are extremely slow to reload. Finally, the ammo is heavy, bulky, and difficult to transport. Twenty Federal TruBall slugs weigh two pounds, while twenty Federal 55-grain Ballistic Tip .223 Remington rifle cartridges check in at half a pound. The volume of space that the ammo takes up is hugely different, with the shotgun ammo requiring many times more cubic inches than the rifle ammo.

There is a lot of misinformation out there about defensive shotguns. The common belief that you can't miss with a shotgun and that it takes little or no skill to operate is a Joe Biden myth. Running a fighting shotgun effectively takes a skillset that is close to the level of difficulty to that of running a rifle effectively. If you are in a fight where you must reload, the needed skills for a shotgun are beyond what it takes to be effective with any tactical rifle. The most common AR-15 rifle magazine holds thirty shots and can be swapped for another fully loaded magazine easily in two seconds. The shotgun holds five shots and it takes most people two seconds *per shell* to reload in a stress situation. So that's ten seconds just to reload five shots.

While a shotgun is a very good tool for foraging, especially if you are trying to shoot little critters that scurry and fly, there is not much else it can do that a rifle can't do as well or better. If weight is not a huge issue, I would encourage at least one shotgun in any survival group that is bugging out, but only as a backup and never as a primary long gun.

A magazine-fed, semiauto rifle is by far the best choice for a bug-out long gun. It can do anything a shotgun can do and a lot more. In the hands of a trained shooter it is very effective for close-quarter battle (CQB), yet it can reach out hundreds of yards with precision. A magazine-fed rifle is much faster to reload, has a much larger magazine capacity, and uses ammo that is lighter and smaller than any shot-

gun. A battle rifle is just as effective as a shotgun at close range and exponentially more effective at longer distances.

The rifle you choose should be powerful enough to fight with and it should have a ready supply of ammo. That means it should be a popular cartridge, one that is also used by law enforcement and the military. That probably eliminates the AK-47, AK-74, and other such rifles. It also eliminates cartridges like the .300 AAC Blackout or the 6.8 SPC. They might be good cartridges, but how easy is it going to be to resupply ammo? It is much smarter to pick a cartridge that is popular with civilians, LE, and the military. That means the .308 Winchester or the .223 Remington are your best options.

Of the two, the .223 is probably the most common, particularly if there are military forces in the area. It's a smaller cartridge that is easier to transport in quantity than the .308. The magazines and the rifles are also smaller and lighter. While I generally tend to gravitate to larger cartridges, in this case, when you weigh all the factors, the .223/5.56 emerges as the best choice, particularly when using civilian ammunition and expanding bullets. We are not bound by foolish nineteenth-century rules made by dopey politicians, and unlike the military, we can use the most effective bullets.

With high-quality bullets, the .223 is a viable defensive round. It will also serve for foraging. While I don't like it for sport hunting big game, the rules are different when survival is the goal. The .308 would be better for

▲ The logical choice is between the .308 Winchester and the .223 Remington for a bug-out rifle. The nod goes to the .223.

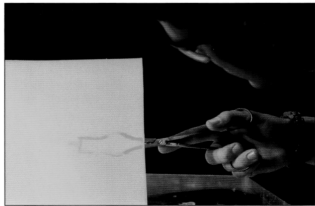

▲ Civilians can use expanding bullets in their rifle ammo, which are a lot more effective than military ammo.

foraging, but the .223 will suffice and when weighing all the other options, the .223 is still in first place as the best choice for your bug-out rifle.

Depending on availability, I keep my rifle magazines loaded with Federal Premium 55-grain Nosler Ballistic Tip or Hornady Tap 55-grain V-Max ammo. Both are good choices for defensive use and they shoot to the same point of impact from my gun. I also load at least one magazine with Barnes Vor-Tx ammo with 55-grain TSX bullets. This is a better bullet for foraging big game and will still work well in a fight. In fact, I understand the TSX bullet has been tried and tested and it will work extremely well for shooting bad guys.

There are a lot of magazine-fed, semiauto .223 rifles and carbines on the market and we look at most of them in other chapters. Many of them are good guns, but I think the clear choice for bugging out is one of the AR-style rifles.

It's important that the rifle be able to use both .223 and 5.56 ammo, so it must have a 5.56 chamber. It must also use AR-15 magazines, as these are very common and easier to find than other styles. That reason alone is enough to make the AR-15 the top choice. A light, easy-to-transport carbine is probably best. I am a strong believer in optical sights, but the gun should have a backup set of iron sights as well.

I am a gun guy who makes his living shooting and testing guns. (Well, not really. I get paid to write. But I write about guns and so I must test them to write about them. It's a great way to make a living.) While I am in love with every gun I meet, I am not married to any of them. I play the field enough that my "favorite" gun changes often.

My current bug-out rifle is an M4-style carbine that I built from parts I ordered from Brownells. It is basically the same gun that most AR makers sell as the M4 model or some variation on that. It is a semiauto, civilian version of the select-fire M4 carbine used by the military. Mine might have a different forend, buttstock, or trigger than yours, but they are all the same basic configuration with a 16-inch barrel and an adjustable buttstock. This short, carbine-style AR-15 is probably the best choice for a bug-out long gun. It is short enough to wear on a sling comfortably, it's easy to shoot, fast in a close quarters fight, and accurate

enough to reach out several hundred yards if necessary.

My gun has a 3X Trijicon ACOG as the primary sight. I also have a red-dot reflex sight on an offset mount for close work. I carry a set of pre-zeroed iron sights in my bag. The gun is equipped with a Crimson Trace CMR-204 Rail Master Pro Universal Green Laser Sight & Tactical Light. This gives me a laser that is visible in daylight as well as in the dark and a bright weapon-mounted flashlight.

I am a strong believer in laser sights on all defensive rifles and handguns. They allow you to focus on the target, they work well in poor light, and add a "compliance" factor that will often eliminate the need to shoot. Make no mistake; not shooting is always the better option.

Lights, lasers, and red-dot sights? No doubt somebody will criticize me for suggesting anything that needs a battery for use in a survival situation. Don't bother. I have heard all the arguments, and they only work if you don't think too hard about things. The best tool you have for survival is your brain. Don't limit it with foolish thinking or romantic notions about survival. Think everything through to the end and consider every aspect. This is about staying alive by the best means possible, not living some fantasy life.

I get it that a lot of survivalists have some romantic notion that it's all going to be Mad Max and they get to

▲ This Mepro MOR Tri-Powered Reflex Sight with Red Laser combines a red-dot sight with a visible and an IR laser. This is one of the finest fighting sighting systems available. Why not take advantage of it as long as the batteries last? The reticle illumination uses a fiber-optic collector system during the day, a miniature self-powered tritium light source at night, and a three-position LED enhancer for different ambient light conditions. This allows the sight to work without batteries in any lighting condition.

be a badass with a crossbow. Or they think that they can go live off the land like the mountain men, using a flintlock rifle and a tomahawk. Well guess what, the mountain men updated their gear every chance they got. John "Liver Eating" Johnson, the guy that *Jeremiah Johnson* was based on, might have started his mountain man career with a 30-caliber Hawken, but he upgraded constantly. As soon as they proved reliable, he got a repeating Spencer cartridge rifle. He also upgraded to repeating revolvers and upgraded those to cartridge revolvers as soon as he could. He survived a lot of fights and died of old age. Part of the reason he lived so long is that he used the best fighting gear he could find. He didn't get stuck on stupid and stay with his muzzle-loading flintlock because of some romantic notion. Those notions simply do not have any place in survival.

Think about it; why not use the best you can find for as long as it lasts? I see no point in handicapping yourself, particularly with guns you are using to defend your life. Especially when that handicap can mean the difference between winning and losing. Yes, lights and lasers need batteries. Yes, batteries will deplete and will be hard to replace. So what are you suggesting? Don't bother with them? Take a rifle with iron sights and be done with it? That's foolish, don't you think?

I keep fresh batteries in the sights and lights and spares with the gun. That allows me the use of the light, red-dot sight, and laser, which in their given circumstances of use are the best options available. If all the batteries become depleted and I can't find replacements, I'll take the light, red-dot, and laser off the gun.

Where does that leave me? Right exactly where the knuckleheads wanted me to start out. Well no, actually I'll still have the ACOG. But then again I have even seen survival "experts" argue against optical sights because they can break. Anything can break, that's why you should have redundancy. If the batteries fail and the ACOG breaks, I'll use the iron sights. In the meanwhile, before any of my gear is broken, depleted, or whatever else is supposed to happen to it, I'll have a few months or perhaps even a few years of using a rifle that is far better equipped to win a fight.

That subtle point may save somebody's life, maybe mine, maybe even the short-sighted guy who didn't think I needed a laser. If all of the electronics and

optics crash and burn, which is unlikely, I will still have my iron sights. The upside is I can fight better with the other sights while they work, so I might be alive at that point when the batteries are gone. Without the best gear possible, the chances of surviving are reduced. We are all going to die someday, but it would be damned embarrassing to die because of foolishness.

## Handgun

I recently made some changes here. While I own and shoot just about all types of handguns, I am a hardcore 1911 disciple. There is a reason it's the handgun the protagonist in my novel *The 14th Reinstated* used to survive a scenario much like what we may be facing. For a long time that is the gun that resided in my bug-out gear and as mentioned, there is still one in my bug-out bag. But for my primary bug-out handgun, the one I keep ready to go and expect to have as my carry gun, I switched to another.

Why?

Simple: magazine capacity. You can only carry so many magazines when you bug out and the 1911 magazines I use hold eight cartridges. So I decided to look at double-stack handguns. Considering pricing and availability, that more or less meant exploring the world of striker-fired polymer handguns. There is a wide range of handguns in this category and I have experience with most of them. That said, I don't think you can go wrong with any name-brand handgun.

Cartridge selection, though, is another consideration. My stubby fingers don't play well with most striker-fired, double-stack .45 ACP handguns, as the grip is too big and the trigger too far forward for me to use properly. I don't care what some on the Internet are saying, I don't trust the 9mm. Unlike most of those "experts" I have actual experience shooting things with handgun rounds. I have seen a lot of human-size game shot with various pistol cartridges and have watched the 9mm fail horribly time and again on hogs, deer, and black bears. The true warriors I know who have used pistols in battle during multiple engagements universally tell me the 9mm fails on two-legged critters as well. While there is a strong argument for the 9mm because of ammo availability, in this circumstance, I'll pass. Call me old fashioned, but I want a cartridge that starts with a four.

I have seen the .40 S&W perform well on hogs and even deer. While I think it's too light for sport hunting, seeing this has instilled more confidence in that cartridge than I have in the 9mm. I also know of a lot of shootouts where it stopped the bad guy very effectively. In the end, though, it's just math. The .40 S&W has a bigger bullet and carries more energy than the 9mm. How can that be a bad thing?

While most of the better, high-capacity handguns will work well here, I swapped out the 1911 in my bug-out vest for an S&W M&P40 VTAC handgun in .40 S&W.

There are a lot of excellent handguns in this category and I had to make a choice when deciding which gun will go in my bug-out gear. Most guns didn't make the first cut simply because of popularity, or the lack of it. The two most popular striker-fired, double-stack handguns are the Glock and the S&W M&P. That means that it will be easier to find magazines and parts for these guns. Some of the more obscure guns might be well made and dependable, but if you lose the magazines, finding replacements will be difficult.

I looked long and hard at the Glocks and even had a G22 in my vest for a while, but in the end I decided I like the M&P better. Much of that is the ergonomics; the M&P just fits my hand better and I like the grip angle.

I also like the metal magazines for the M&P in a bug-out bag situation. They are tougher and usually drop free from the gun more reliably than plastic mags. While the Glock mags still seem to work fine, they often will not drop free from the gun when empty and must be pulled out.

Durability? Glocks are hard to beat and they set the standard. But the new generation of M&Ps is pretty good too. I see them all the time in competition with thousands and thousands of rounds through them with no problems.

I can put a Crimson Trace laser on the M&P easily, where on the Glocks the laser will add bulk to the already big-for-my-hands grips. Of course, the LaserMax guide rod laser works fine in the Glock and doesn't change the grip. I have the green model in my G23 and it works great, so there are always options.

All that said, I own a bunch of Glocks and will buy more. I am not a fan of the grip angle, but they are simple, tough, and reliable.

▲ Today's prepper has lots of options for guns and cartridges, options that were not available a generation ago.

Of course, I own a bunch of M&P handguns too. My favorite carry gun right now is a .40 S&W M&P Shield. Bottom line, I don't think you can go wrong with either gun, but I had to make a choice and I picked the M&P.

Another reason is that this VTAC model has a sighting system designed by Kyle Lamb of Viking Tactics (Kyle is a true warrior with real life experience—look him up). The sight combines fiber-optic and tritium night sights so that it works well in any lighting scenario. Of course, I also installed a Crimson Trace Lasergrip sighting system.

The biggest reason for changing to this pistol is that the magazine capacity is fifteen cartridges. I have almost doubled the ammo in any given magazine over the 1911, while still using an effective cartridge. I'll give up two rounds of magazine capacity (over most 9mm handguns) for terminal performance that means I probably won't need them. The .40 S&W is a very common law enforcement cartridge, so ammo should be available.

Any good defensive ammo will work, but always make sure it runs well in your gun. I load my magazines with Federal 180-grain HST JHP. It is affordable, is excellent defensive ammo, and has a good track record with civilians and with law-enforcement use. My son-in-law is a federal agent and this is the same ammo they are issued. He tells me it has a good record in the field and that he trusts it, even off duty, to defend his life and the life of my daughter.

## Carrying It All

How to keep it all ready to go is another issue. The key is to have it all in a package that you can grab and go. After experimenting with several systems, I finally settled on a load-bearing vest. It's a BLACKHAWK! Omega Vest, Cross Draw/Pistol Mag model. One big attraction is that they offer this vest with a holster set up for lefties.

In the vest, I have the loaded M&P and four extra loaded magazines in the pistol mag pouches. I also have two more magazines in the radio pouch along with a high-quality flashlight and spare batteries for the lights and lasers.

The three rifle-mag pouches have room for two magazines each, so I have six loaded Brownells thirty-round AR-15 magazines in addition to the two with the rifle. Finally, I have a SOG SEAL Pup knife attached to the vest with a Benchmade folding knife also in the dual pouch. A knife is second only to your firearms for a survival tool and having two gives me some redundancy. The knives are not for fighting—if it comes to that, you messed up—but for a million other chores from processing game to peeling potatoes.

I have a belt holster and a couple of magazine pouches along with a spare box of ammo in a bag that is attached to the vest. This lets me move the S&W to a concealed carry position. That allows me to be armed without calling attention to myself in situations when wearing the vest would not be a good idea.

This vest hangs by a door ready to go, so all I need is to grab it, the rifle bag, and my bug-out bag on the run. If there is time I'll get the other guns and gear, but if seconds count, this is what is going with me.

While the vest can attract unwanted attention if it's worn in an urban area, it has everything I need in one place. I can toss it on the back seat, or hide it inside a backpack, trunk, or tool box. If the circumstances are right, I can wear it.

The rifle, two magazines, and backup sights are in a diversion bag that looks like a case for a musical instrument. That helps to keep it out of sight unless it's needed. Remember, you are probably going to hit some check points and keeping your guns hidden is the key to keeping your guns.

If I can wear it without attracting unwanted attention, I have a two-point Vero Vellini tactical sling on the rifle.

I have never liked single-point slings, but when I was writing *The 14th Reinstated* I got lazy and gave one to the protagonist. I had a longtime Delta Force operator read the manuscript to make sure the fight scenes were accurate. The only change he suggested was a two-point sling. His reasons were many and all made tactical sense, but he made the point best when he said, "None of my guys would ever use a single-point sling in combat."

Good advice from a guy who has been there, got the T-shirt, and then wore it out.

## Backup

It's important that you never give up your guns. But at some point that choice might be made for you. Remember during Hurricane Katrina, when law

▲ My backup gun is a S&W M&P Shield in .40 S&W. The sights are Trijicon HD night sights and I have a Crimson Trace LaserGuard mounted on the gun.

enforcement took the guns away from law-abiding citizens and left them defenseless? I think it's a good idea to have a backup gun of some sort—one that hides easily on your person, in your vehicle, or in your gear. While I love my S&W J-Frame .357 for its "hideability" and its power, a gun that uses the ammo you already are carrying makes sense. My hideout gun is a S&W M&P Shield in .40 S&W. The sights are Trijicon HD night sights and I have a Crimson Trace LaserGuard mounted on the gun. (Are you seeing a pattern here yet?)

It's my personal carry gun much of the time, but when I am not carrying it, I keep it with the bug-out gear, along with the holster and spare mags. Of course that's so that it goes with me; once we are bugging out, I'll hide it in a place I have no intention of mentioning in print.

## Keeping Your Guns

This is controversial, but the police and military are not necessarily your friends in an emergency, bug-out scenario. They are trying to deal with an out-of-control situation just as you are. They will be scared, confused, and will react in a way they think is best for them. Remember, many law enforcement personnel, particularly the political bosses, do not like or trust armed citizens. The police on the street will not know who you are and won't have time to explore the issue. Chances are high that if you have an encounter, they will disarm you and take your guns. This will leave you defenseless in a time when the system is failing and you are on your own.

Sure, there are a lot of good people in law enforcement or the military who believe in the Second Amendment, but they don't wear signs to identify themselves. There are plenty more who will use this emergency as an excuse to take your guns. You can't know which way anybody is leaning, so the best approach in my opinion is to avoid contact with them, if at all possible.

If you are in areas with people who may go to the police and report you, or where the police may see you, keep your guns hidden. It's important to have a defensive firearm with fast access, so practice concealed carry with your handgun. That means you should have a carry holster somewhere in your bug-out gear.

Keep your rifle out of sight and in a diversion bag that does not look like a gun case. Keep your vest or bag full of ammo and magazines out of sight. Lock them in the trunk or put them in a large backpack or hidden under camping gear. Expect to be searched, as the Constitution will be ignored, so hide all this gear as well as you can until you are out of the urban areas and away from the multitudes of "authority figures." If you just look like another helpless *sheepeople* to the guy doing the search, he might not make a big effort. If you look "tactical," act defiant or have pro-gun stickers all over your vehicle, he probably will be more diligent about finding your guns. A lot of survival is going to be flying under the radar.

The most important thing is to keep possession of your firearms, even if you have to give up access temporarily while in transit. That might be an acceptable risk in exchange for having them with you later.

# Hiding Your Guns in Plain Sight

*Sometimes staying below the radar is important.*

Anybody paying attention understands that our country is changing and some of the changes are dangerously contradictory.

We recognize that it's becoming a dangerous place with mass shootings, bombings, and terrorist attacks. The government can't, or won't, protect us so the responsibility falls on our shoulders to make sure we and our families remain safe.

But it is also becoming a country filled with scared and foolish people. Nobody seems to embrace the concepts of self-reliance or minding your own business anymore. A large number of people have lost perspective on reality and they see everything they don't understand as a threat. They have also been indoctrinated to turn to the government to solve every single problem, even those they imagine.

When a guy shows up at a tourist site during turkey hunting season, dressed in camo, it used to be that we understood he was taking a break from hunting and was checking out the local sights. Now they call a SWAT team, send everything into lockdown, and arrest the guy at gunpoint for the crime of mottled clothing. (It happened in Pennsylvania in 2013.) Recently, a Texas man out for a ten-mile hike to help his son get a merit badge for his Eagle Scout program was worried about cougars, wild boars, and other predators, so he brought his rifle. In the past we considered that smart thinking. This guy got arrested. He was perfectly legal, but the cops arrested him anyway and took his gun. The reason? He made somebody *uncomfortable.*

Yes, it's a dangerous world out there, but the nanny state is making it much harder to protect yourself and your family. People freak out and call the cops over things that never would have even raised an eyebrow a generation ago. If they call because you have a firearm in public, even if it's perfectly legal, you may be in big trouble. Death by cop, even with innocent victims, is on the rise.

Then there is after TSHTF to consider. As a prepper on the move in a time of crisis, it may be even more important to hide the fact that you have guns. You do not want to call attention to yourself with busybody people who will call the cops. Nor do you want any law enforcement you do encounter to know you have guns. You can't possibly know how they will react and many will try to disarm you, or even shoot you. Both are death sentences in time of trouble.

A diversion bag is a good answer to the problem of moving guns unnoticed, now as well as after TEOTWAWKI.

It's easy to conceal a handgun, but a rifle is much more difficult. Yet, where legal, it's a very good idea to keep a rifle handy in a lot of situations. The trouble is that even a cased rifle looks like a cased rifle, unless you choose a bag designed specifically to not look like a rifle case.

With the right diversion bag, you can carry your guns out of your apartment without your silly Obama-voting neighbor freaking out and calling 911.

If you choose to keep a rifle in your vehicle, as many people do, it can become an issue. Some busybody looking in the windows will ensure that a cop is waiting when you finish your shopping. With roadblocks and random stops becoming increasingly more common, even the safest most law-abiding driver can expect to be stopped by the police at some point, and if you are bugging out, it's all but a sure thing that you will encounter a road block.

If the police see a rifle in your vehicle, chances are good that even if the gun is legal, they will question you and maybe take your rifle, perhaps at gunpoint. But if they see a case for a tennis racket or a musical instrument they probably won't give it a second thought.

Diversion bags make a lot of sense for today's gun owners. Here are a few I have used and can comment about.

BLACKHAWK! has a rather extensive line of diversion products. There are also a few others I have used and highly recommend.

## BLACKHAWK! Diversion Carry Racquet Bag

Nothing about this bag looks "tactical." In fact, it looks like something my social worker neighbor might take to her tennis lessons. But then, that's the point isn't it?

▲ The BLACKHAWK! Diversion Carry Racquet Bag lets me hide an AR-15 pistol in plain sight.

## BLACKHAWK! Diversion Wax Canvas Messenger Bag

▲ The BLACKHAWK! Diversion Wax Canvas Messenger Bag carries a folded Kel-Tec SUB-2000 carbine and a handgun, hidden and out of sight.

The twenty-nine-inch case has padded walls with an internal divider for carrying up to two handguns or an AR-15 with upper and lower receivers (up to twenty-nine inches long) separated. It's also a great fit for a fully assembled and ready-to-rock AR pistol.

I can slip an AR pistol in one side and another handgun in the other with the padded divider separating them. Or I can break down an M4 carbine and slip the upper in one side and the lower in the other. Reassembly only takes a few seconds.

It comes in non-tactical colors like red/white or blue/gray for when you absolutely, positively have to convince them that you don't have a gun.

Finish out your ensemble with Capri pants, Birkenstock sandals, and a Che T-shirt and you won't be bothered.

This is a very stylish messenger bag that you would be proud to carry anywhere. It has a pocket in the back for a handgun and I've found that the Kel-Tec SUB-2000 carbine will fold up and fit nicely inside this bag as well. I can go out in public and nobody will ever suspect I have a handgun, much less a carbine, with me.

### Vanquest

This company has some excellent diversion bags. Their Envoy 2.0 messenger bag will hold several handguns. It also will fit the Kel-Tec SUB-2000 carbine when it's folded up.

### Vanquest RACKIT-36 Covert rifle pack

▲ Vanquest RACKIT-36 Covert rifle pack.

This is a bag that somebody who understands guns designed. It is large enough for a carbine, but looks like a sports equipment bag. The shoulder strap is fully adjustable for right or left shoulder carry. The "FASTab" zipper system gives you fast access to the gun.

The padded main compartment is 36x12x2 inches and has fastening points for the gun. Note the "36-inch" part. Too many so-called "diversion" bags are too short for an assembled M4 carbine.

Other bag makers say they keep them short because they want to keep the size small enough to hide that there is a gun inside. I get that and taking the gun apart is fine for transporting it, but if you are in a situation where you may need to get the gun into action fast,

having it ready to rock is a huge advantage. The longer bag may or may not be a giveaway, but I'll chance it to have my carbine in one piece and ready for action.

The large front pocket is lined with Velcro so you can attach carriers for magazines or a handgun holster. The padding significantly reduces the "print" of your rifle and magazines.

It's available in several color options. This is the bag I grab most to carry my carbines. It's well thought out and designed and well made. Best of all, I can carry the gun in a ready condition if I choose.

### ThugCase M4

▲ The ThugCase M4. Although the gun must be broken down, this case hides what it truly is and may allow you to keep your rifle in times of trouble.

Inspired by Al Capone and the probation era thugs who favored violin cases for their Tommy Guns, the ThugCase is a modern-day incarnation of the concept.

The outer hard-shell is made from heavy thermoplastic with protective molded lining inside. Velcro straps are installed to secure the contents. Each case includes a lockable latch. The case I have has three latches, the center one has a lock and comes with two keys.

I have the M4-size case. It's designed to take a 16-inch-barrel M4-style carbine that is broken down. It will fit the upper and lower receivers, with an area to stash a couple of thirty-round magazines. This case will accept upper assemblies up to 25.5 inches long. It will handle most tactical style optics installed on the upper. The lower must have a collapsible stock to fit.

This is a very small case, so small that most people would never believe it has a rifle inside, which is a very good thing when you are trying to keep a low profile. But it's also a very snug fit. My lower has an aftermarket grip that is slightly longer than the standard A2 grip. As a result I had to crush some of the protective lining and wedge it in the case to make the lower fit. I tried an upper with an aftermarket muzzle brake and it would not fit, but one with a birdcage flash hider fit well. For a standard M4-style gun with a 16-inch barrel fitted with a flash hider and a collapsible stock, this is the best option. However, if you deviate much from that, you may need a larger case. The M16 size will take uppers to twenty-nine inches. It can handle larger optics and will take a full-sized fixed stock. If I had it to do over, I would order this model as it gives me more options with my multiple AR rifles.

There are several other models for pistol-grip shotguns, AK-47 rifles, M14 rifles, and many more. Of course, there is one for a Thompson submachine gun. Plus, there are some generic foam-lined cases to fit most guns not specifically listed, or you can simply custom order a case to fit your needs.

The ThugCase is designed and produced in the USA by veterans. A percentage of each sale is donated to the Wounded Warrior Project.

This hard-shell case provides a high level of protection and diversion. The M4 model looks like it is designed for a mandolin. When asked, I just tell them I am Vince Gill's long-lost brother.

# The Sounds of Silence

*Sometimes quiet is the best option.*

▲ These guns have silencers, or suppressors, or "cans." No matter what you call them, they do two things: dampen noise and register with the government.

It's a good idea to stay below the radar and be quiet around your home or even in some hunting situations. There is no point in calling unneeded attention to where you are. If you must deal with pests or if the opportunity presents itself to shoot a squirrel or rabbit for food, it would be better to do it quietly.

Also, there are plenty of tactical situations where being quiet, or at least reducing noise to levels that are not dangerous, is a very good idea.

Here is a look at a few options.

## Silencers

*Call them what you will, they muffle the noise.*

If you want to stir something up, go on one of the tactical forums on the Internet and open a discussion about whether they are called "silencers" or "suppressors." Then sit back and watch the sparks fly.

They probably should be called mufflers. That's all they are, a muffler for your gun. They quiet the noise. How much depends on a lot of factors. If the bullet is supersonic, and is flying faster than the speed of sound, it will still make a sonic crack. If it's flying slower than the speed of sound it will be quiet. The silencer will muffle small muzzle blasts almost entirely and with big loud blasts they sometimes suppress rather than silence the noise. But no matter what, they always reduce the noise level when used on a firearm.

The rest of the world thinks that silencers are a good idea and in some locations it's considered bad form not to have one on your gun when hunting. I have hunted in Europe and in Africa where they were very common on rifles. They not only protect the hunter's hearing, they do not spook the game as much as guns without mufflers.

For a prepper, a silencer is a very handy tool. It will let you hunt or deal with pests on your property without calling attention to your location. Staying alive means staying under the radar and being quiet is important.

In a fight, particularly inside a building, a silencer can control the disorienting and hearing-destroying muzzle blasts from a carbine or handgun.

The downside is they are expensive and a bit clumsy to use because they extend off the barrel and add length and weight. The gun (particularly handguns) may require special sights to clear the large diameter of the silencer.

The biggest downside is our government requires that you register the silencer and pay a $200 tax. This puts you on a list with the government and tells them you have guns and that they are not just for duck hunting. The waiting list to be approved is very long right now and that's an indication that a lot of people want to own a silencer. But you must decide how much you trust the government in a time of crisis. Do you want to draw attention to yourself? Do you want to be on a list confirming that you own guns if things go south for any reason?

If you decide the risk is worth it, a silencer or two can be very useful tools.

There are a lot of companies making silencers and the list is growing longer every day.

My home state of Vermont would not allow its citizens to own or possess a silencer until just a few weeks ago. Even now we are very restricted as to where we can use them. While I have fired hundreds, maybe even thousands of rounds through guns with silencers, I have never owned one. Now that I can, I am struggling with if I should.

My situation is a bit different as I have held an FFL to sell guns since the 1970s, so I am already on the government's radar. Plus, I write for the NRA magazines and other publications, so it's not like I am "low profile." I think it is time to get a "can," as they are called, on one of my AR-15 carbines and I doubt it raises my profile much. But Joe Average, the guy who just wants to protect his family and who has not been out there in the public eye, should ask if the benefit of getting a silencer and registering with the government is worth the risk. It's a personal decision. But every prepper should at least consider it and investigate silencers. They can be very useful tools.

## A Couple of Other Silent Options for Pest Control

### Pellet Guns

▲ This Remington 17-caliber air rifle is powerful enough to shoot pests or hunt small game.

*They aren't just for kids.*

Air rifles have come a long way and some of them are pretty potent today. There are several on the market that are accurate and powerful enough for hunting small game and varmints. They are quiet so you can stay unnoticed. A prepper might do well to check out a high-end pellet gun.

### CCI Quiet-22 LR 40-grain Segmented Hollow-Point

*Every prepper should have a .22 rifle on hand.*
*Here is an option that is hush-hush.*

CCI addressed the noise problem with their Quiet-22 .22 LR ammo. This features a 40-grain bullet at subsonic, 710 feet per second. The Quiet-22 uses a standard Long Rifle case and bullet size, but at reduced velocity and with a powder charge engineered to produce very low noise. CCI says it's a 75 percent reduction in noise over conventional ammo.

Sound is measured in units called decibels. Normal conversation is approximately sixty decibels; heavy city traffic is about eighty-five decibels. A gunshot might be as loud as 170 decibels. Hearing loss occurs when your ears are exposed to continuous noise above eighty-five decibels or impulse noise (like a gunshot) above 140 decibels. The louder the sound, the more damage it causes.

The CCI Quiet-22 ammo creates sixty-eight decibels at the shooter's ear, well below the threshold for hearing damage. It's also low enough that the neighbors probably won't even notice you are shooting.

One version of it has a "Segmented HP" bullet. This is a hollow-point bullet that is designed to expand slightly and then separate into three segments on impact, even at these very low velocities. The idea is that three projectiles will do more damage than a single, round-nose bullet.

This is not new technology, as CCI used it in their Quick-Shock ammo a few years back. That ammo developed a reputation as a good game stopper.

I lack the equipment to measure sound with anything other than my ears, but I shot the ammo out of several rifles and handguns, alternating with CCI .22 Long Rifle ammo, and the difference in sound volume was staggering. The sound of Quiet-22 was so much softer that it made the .22 LR sound like a rocket launcher by comparison. When fired from a rifle, the Quiet-22 is no louder than a pellet gun but is more effective.

No ear protection is needed. In fact, the first time I fired with ear protection I could not tell for sure if the gun went off. The ammo is slightly louder from a handgun barrel, but still quite mild. When comparing the Quiet-22 ammo against the full power .22 LR, the difference was again very pronounced. There is no question whatsoever that this ammo produces a much lower noise level than any other .22 LR ammo I have tested.

The Quiet-22 ammo will not cycle the action in semiauto rifles. However, the guns could be cycled by hand to feed from the magazines.

Quiet-22 reduces noise and allows discrete pest control. It's a good idea to have a brick or two of this ammo so that you can hunt small game and deal with vermin without calling attention to your location.

# Night Vision

*If you don't own the night, the night will own you.*

▲ FLIR Scout TS thermal night vision scope. This is the tool I used to watch for lions attacking at night in Africa.

This is another area where I don't claim to be an expert, but I have used night vision and thermal vision gear for hunting and during nighttime shooting competitions just enough to know that it's a very good idea for a prepper to have some on hand.

I once used thermal to stand guard from the top of a termite mound in Zimbabwe. The area was infested with lions and we were trying to cut up and load a Cape buffalo that had been shot right at dark. I watched for lions while the PH and trackers took care of the buffalo. It was an exciting time.

I have also hunted coyotes and hogs several times using both night vision and thermal vision. I have used night vision in competition a few times, usually with IR laser sight on a handgun or carbine. A couple of times

we ran stages with full-auto, short-barrel M4 carbines. It is both awesome and an eye opener that to protect your home and family you really need to have some night vision.

As this is a gun book, I won't explore the topic too deeply. Besides, there is a lot of information out there, so use the time now to educate yourself and decide what's best for your unique situation.

Without going into a lot of technical detail, there are two basic types in common use. What we call night vision uses ambient light to allow you to see. This is the ghostly green screen that most people have seen with the night vision cameras used on some television shows. The other is thermal, which works off heat. Everything has a different heat signature and with thermal vision that is shown in black, white, and shades of gray.

▲ The Bushnell Equinox Z Digital Night Vision with Zoom is relatively inexpensive, but let's you view your property at night, undetected.

Both have their pros and cons, including cost. But it's a good idea to have some night vision to help protect your home or compound when there is no light.

It's a good idea that you have something with the ability to aim and shoot a rifle using night vision for one or more people in your party.

# FINAL THOUGHTS
## The End?

*Is this the end?*
*Of the book? Yes.*
*Of the world? Who knows?*

This is a gun book much more than it's a book on prepping. I trust that if you have read this far you know a lot more about guns than when you started. That's useful information for survival, with or without TEOTWAWKI.

The truth is, we are probably going to be okay. I have no doubt that some very bad stuff is in our future, but the world has been through bad stuff before and survived.

However, if you want to be there at the end, you need to be ready to deal with anything that comes your way. That's the true spirit of prepping. You can store all the beans, Band-Aids, and bullets on Earth; if you are not smart, flexible, and able to deal with what comes, it won't matter. The best survivalists are also the best problem solvers.

The thing about prepping, from a gun standpoint at least, is that while you are collecting and shooting all those guns, you can have a lot of fun and what good is life without fun? Shooting is a great hobby. No matter what level you end up at—training at the top schools, shooting competitions at a national or local level, or just practicing with friends and family on the weekends—shooting is big fun! I have introduced a lot of people to shooting over the years, and they all end the day with huge smiles, asking when we can do it again.

I recognize that this is a lot of information, and we covered a lot of guns. Clearly you can't buy them all. Well, at least most of us can't. If you made a billion on the dot-com market, that's something else, I suppose. Call me; you need a good consultant.

For the rest of the world, start small and think about your protection now as well after TSHTF. Survival means living through today as well as surviving any future problems. You can't predict when or where disaster will strike.

I just finished reading a series of novels on survival. It follows several people through months of problems after the world falls apart. In the first book, the guy was two hundred miles from his home when an EMP struck and shut down everything.

No biggie, right?

Think again! He had to walk the two hundred miles through chaos to get home. All he had was what was in his truck when the event happened. Two hundred miles is nothing by car—three or four hours of driving. But think about what would happen to you if you were two hundred miles away and had to walk home. Could you do it? Sure, good shoes, water, and some food are important, but how would you survive after the wheels came off society and all the stuff you stored up in preparation was at home?

What if you are just out shopping and you get caught up in a terrorist attack? What if you are carjacked? Robbed as you leave a movie theater? You can't schedule these events and you can't just carry a gun when you are sure you will need it. So when you buy your guns for survival, start with those you need now, today. Build from there.

I think your first priority is a good carry handgun. Then carry it every day. You will feel foolish at first, and most of your friends and family will give you crap about it. But you need to stay focused and all that will pass. How do I know? Because most people who decide to carry, including me, experienced the same thing.

Carrying a gun will seem awkward to start and you will feel sure that everybody you meet will know you have a gun, but they don't. Most never notice anything if you conceal carry. I can't tell you how many times I have taken my gun out to show somebody and they have said, "I had no idea you had a gun." My response is always, "Yeah, that's the point." This has happened a bunch of times even with experienced, "switched-on" gun guys. If they don't notice, that woman at the table next to you in the restaurant, the one with her nose stuck in her phone, won't have a clue either. Don't worry about her.

At first, the gun will always be on your mind. You will worry about getting into trouble for having it, even though it's legal. You will find yourself apologizing to your friends and family for it and trying to explain your reasoning. Then you will be mad at yourself for doing that, because you know you should not have to. It's a process and a lot of people have experienced it.

Before long you will realize that the awkwardness and uneasiness you were experiencing has passed. Carrying will be comfortable, natural, and at times you will forget it's even with you. Then one day you will discover that you don't have your gun and that will make you uneasy. Suddenly, not having a gun feels unnatural and uncomfortable. That's when you are starting to get it. Having a gun is not the total solution to surviving, but it's a good first step. So start with the handgun, learn how to use it and when to use it. Then ABC, Always Be Carrying.

The next gun should be a personal defense rifle. Pick some kind of semiauto, magazine-fed carbine. Equip it with good sights and maybe a few other extras; a quality trigger is one. Avoid the rookie mistake of loading the rails up with goodies. It makes the gun heavy and the other gun guys will mock you. Besides, the best accessory you can buy is ammo. Practice is how you learn to shoot any gun well and there is no substitute. Take some classes and shoot your guns a lot. Don't worry about all the latest gadgets; just shoot that gun. You won't wear it out, but you will become a better shot.

Those two guns alone will provide the foundation of what you need, even from a prepping standpoint. From there you can start building your personal collection of guns based on your specific and unique situation.

Or just buy guns based on what you want. No gun is ever a mistake. If you see something that catches your eye, buy it! Sure, there are some guns that will be better for prepping than others, but so what if you buy the gun you "want" today and leave the one you "need" for later? Isn't it better to have a gun you want to take out and shoot, rather than one you will mostly leave at home waiting for when the world ends?

Notice I didn't go right to the shotgun. I think you should have one or more shotguns, but I do not think they are as necessary or as useful as the handgun and rifle. As explained in the shotgun section, I do not share the belief of some other preppers that a shotgun is the best "do-all" gun for a prepper.

Shotguns can be a good defensive tool and in some circumstances they can have a tactical advantage. I think shotguns are important to a prepper, but not as a primary defensive gun. That statement alone is going to raise some hackles but I don't care; the truth sometimes hurts.

That said, I think that shooting a tactical shotgun is edging close to first place as the most fun you can have with a firearm. (It's hard to beat shooting machine guns!) Shooting in a tactical shotgun match or a 3-gun match with a shotgun is great training for gun handling and shooting ability, but it's also a pretty exciting way to spend your day.

Don't rule out any gun. Whatever floats your boat, buy it if you can and shoot it all you can. Just don't get stuck on stupid. I met a guy the other day who had just joined our club. He asked if we shot IDPA pistol competition and we told him we did not, but that we shot USPSA Pistol competition and that we would welcome him at the next match. He got mad, waved us off, and walked away, mumbling that he *only* shoots IDPA. His loss. We had fun and we worked on our pistol skills. I can only assume he spent the day mowing his lawn and grumbling about not having IDPA at the club.

We also set up some tactical shotgun stages to shoot after the match. I even offered to let anybody who wanted to shoot to use my gun. Several people left because they "only shoot pistols." The rest of us had a blast (pun intended) shooting the shotguns.

Don't ever limit yourself. You will meet friends at the shooting range, gun shows, and gun shops that will take you in directions you never expected, if you let them. Not only will you open new horizons in the shooting world and perhaps discover your next great love, you will also be learning valuable skills for survival. That IDPA shooter might be in deep doo-doo if he is trying to survive with a tactical shotgun and no skills in how it works.

Keep it fun and keep it interesting. If you go at this like it's a job, or it's something you *must* do, it will burn you out. We see them every Spring, right? They're the slightly overweight people with the hand weights and determined scowls on their faces? They are staring straight ahead as they execute a forced power walk while swinging their arms with precise gusto.

You know they won't last. A month later they are nowhere to be seen. Why? Because they attack it like it's a job they have to do. It pisses them off and burns them out. The people who just walk and enjoy it? They are still there every day. The "power walkers" will bitch that the other guys "aren't doing it right," but my point is they are still doing it. Who cares if it's right or wrong, at least it's getting done.

Look at the gun side of prepping the same way. Do what's fun, what interests you—whatever makes you excited about the prospect of "going shooting!"

Don't "specialize." Instead, try to learn it all. Don't get caught up in the trap of thinking that sticking to one "platform" or one shooting style is the way to excel. That is foolish on too many levels to list. The best shooters in the world, guys like Jerry Miculek and Danny Horner, can pick up any gun and shoot it well. They can enter any style of competition and win. Jerry is a buddy of mine and he is a hard-core gun guy. He shoots anything and everything and yet he wins just about every major competition he enters. (Danny and Jerry shoot in different classes so they rarely go head to head.) It doesn't matter: rifle, shotgun, revolver, or pistol, he wins them all. It's the same with Danny, who is the best shooter alive. I doubt there is a gun out there he can't run, and run well. Those guys who think they will excel if they stick to a single gun or shooting style lose to these two every time and they also don't have half the fun or build a fraction of the skills. It's a big world of shooting out there; explore all you can of it.

One day you will wake up and realize that you are now a gun guy. It may even surprise you to discover that you have a lot of guns and you can shoot all of them pretty well.

How can that be a bad thing?

I guess my point is that the key to *Prepper Guns* is building a lifestyle around the guns that will make them part of your life. If you are in the "gun culture," as the left loves to label it, your collection just seems to grow. If you shoot, your skills will grow too and in the end you are well prepared to defend your family and yourself if it becomes necessary.

The best defense against the potential problems that may force us to use these skills, though, is not found in the bullet box. It's found in the ballot box.

Our best defense is to become active and aware of what is happening in the world. Learn the issues and vote. The best survival tactic is to avoid getting into a survival situation. We have some people in leadership positions in our country and around the world that do not have our interests at heart. Here in the United States they gain power by depending on an uninformed and greedy voting population. The best way we can prepare is by getting rid of those people and putting true leaders in charge, leaders who follow the Constitution and who will always have America's back.

But remember, in case that fails, always have a backup plan!

▲ Nathan Towsley shooting a custom-built 6.5 Creedmoor rifle. It has a Stryker Ridge action, Bartlein barrel, and an Accuracy International chassis with an X-Treme Shooting Products trigger and Leupold scope.